AF412044

ISLANDICA

A SERIES RELATING TO ICELAND AND THE

FISKE ICELANDIC COLLECTION

CORNELL UNIVERSITY LIBRARY

EDITED BY P. M. MITCHELL

VOLUME XLVIII

Manuscript Material, Correspondence, and Graphic Material
in the Fiske Icelandic Collection
A Descriptive Catalogue
Compiled by Þórunn Sigurðardóttir

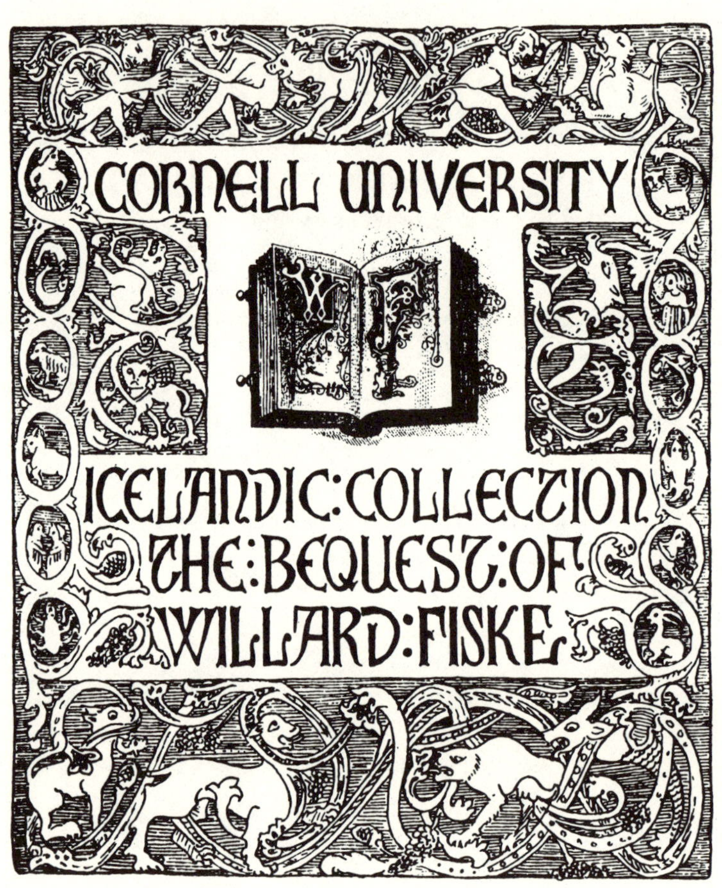

CORNELL UNIVERSITY
ICELANDIC:COLLECTION
THE:BEQUEST:OF
WILLARD:FISKE

Manuscript Material, Correspondence, and Graphic Material in the Fiske Icelandic Collection

A DESCRIPTIVE CATALOGUE

COMPILED BY

Þórunn Sigurðardóttir

ISLANDICA XLVIII

Cornell University Press

ITHACA AND LONDON

1994

First published 1994 by Cornell University Press.

Printed in the United States of America.

Library of Congress Cataloging-in-Publication Data

Fiske Icelandic Collection.
   Manuscript material, correspondence, and graphic material in the Fiske Icelandic Collection : a descriptive catalogue / compiled by Þórunn Sigurðardóttir.
      p. cm. — (Islandica ; 48)
   Includes index.
   ISBN 0-8014-2993-5
   1. Iceland—Manuscripts—Catalogs. 2. Iceland—History—Sources—Bibliography—Catalogs. 3. Manuscripts, Icelandic—United States—Catalogs. 4. Cornell University—Catalogs. 5. Fiske Icelandic Collection—Catalogs. I. Þórunn Sigurðardóttir. II. Title. III. Series.
Z6621.C8363I254 1994
[DL305]
016.94912—dc20   93-29520

This book was set by SKERPLA, Reykjavík, Iceland.

CONTENTS

Preface

The diverse material listed and described in this volume is a testimony to the career and interests of the two prominent men who founded and developed the Fiske Icelandic Collection at Cornell University. On the one hand, it portrays the dedication of the American librarian Daniel Willard Fiske to Iceland and Icelandic culture. On the other hand, it is a source of information on the work and research of the Icelandic scholar Halldór Hermannsson, who served as the first curator of the Fiske Icelandic Collection from 1905 to 1948.

Daniel Willard Fiske was an avid collector of Icelandic books in the latter half of the nineteenth century. As can be seen from the correspondence preserved in his collection, he had a number of agents both in Copenhagen and in Iceland who searched for specific titles and notified him about available books, new publications, and the latest scholarly activities in the fields of Old Norse and Icelandic studies. Fiske did not, as a rule, purchase Icelandic manuscripts, most likely because he thought they should remain in the country of origin. After Fiske's death in 1904, Halldór Hermannsson continued the same policy in his acquisitions for the collection. All the same, the Fiske Icelandic Collection owns a few Icelandic manuscripts, most of which seem to have been bought outside of Iceland. Among these are the sixteenth-century vellum of the Icelandic law code *Jónsbók* which Fiske purchased in Spain, an eighteenth-century Icelandic translation of *Itinerarium sacrae Scripturae* by Heinrich Bünting bought in New York, and some other manuscripts acquired in London and in Stockholm. Additional manuscripts were given to Fiske or to the collection by the authors, such as Jón Borgfirðingur's *Fáeinar athugasemdir við prentsmiðjusögu Íslands*, Ólafur Davíðsson's bibliography of Icelandic subjects in Scandinavian periodicals, and a transcript of Professor C. C. Rafn's correspondence made by his daughters Caroline and Dagmar.

This catalogue lists all Icelandic manuscripts in the possession of the Fiske Icelandic Collection, rotographs of Icelandic manuscripts made for the collection, manuscripts written by others than Icelanders on Icelandic or Nordic subjects, handwritten marginal notations and glossaries in printed works, interleaved books with manuscript material, and, finally, Fiske's and Halldór Hermannsson's personal manuscripts. The most significant of Fiske's material are bibliographies, catalogues, his diaries written in Copenhagen and Stockholm during the mid-nineteenth century, material for dictionaries, manuscripts for his publications on chess and one unpublished book on that subject, and 49 notebooks, including his notes written in Iceland during the summer of 1879. The manuscripts of Halldór Hermannsson constitute the most voluminous part of the manuscript collection, or 71 entries in all, which include his 36 notebooks. These manuscripts contain the bulk of Halldór's scholarly work after he became the curator of the Fiske Icelandic Collection, as well as drafts of his publications, manuscripts of unpublished material, notes on different subjects, and comments on the works of other authors.

The catalogue of the letters preserved in the Fiske Collection is divided into three parts. The first lists the letters to Fiske from Icelanders, from Icelandic emigrants to America (*Vestur-Íslendingar*), and from others who wrote on Icelandic subjects. The correspondents make a diverse group. The clear majority of them comprise scholars and students (many from *Lærði skólinn,* or the Junior College in Reykjavík), but among them we find people ranging from farmers to book dealers and publishers. The most common topics in these letters are various subjects concerning Old Norse and Fiske's book collection, but they also manifest his great interest in the general welfare of Iceland and its inhabitants. Thus, issues such as education in Iceland, the economic situation of the country, the question of a telegraphic cable connecting Iceland with other parts of Europe, the conditions of the National Library of Iceland, chess in Iceland, and the state of book publishing in Iceland are all mentioned in the correspondence. The letters from Bjarni Jónsson, Björn M. Ólsen, Bogi Th. Melsteð, Jón Þorkelsson (the archivist), Ólafur Davíðsson, Sigfús Blöndal, and not least the letters between Halldór Hermannsson and Fiske are an invaluable source on the services these men rendered for Fiske in his efforts to collect as great variety of Icelandic books and publications as possible.

The second part catalogues letters to Halldór Hermannsson which begin at the time when he became Fiske's assistant in Italy at the end of the nineteenth century, and they span the whole period he served as the curator of the Fiske Icelandic Collection and as professor of Scandinavian languages and literature at Cornell University. Among them are only a few personal letters, however, and then primarily from old schoolmates and close friends such as Bogi Th. Melsteð, Matthías Þórðarson, and Sigfús Blöndal. During his long career, Halldór corresponded with all the most prominent scholars in the field of Old Norse studies, and also with a number of Icelandic politicians, officials, writers, and poets. The main emphasis in the letters is on Old Norse and on matters concerning Icelandic scholarship, but there we find also frequent comments on Icelandic politics, on Icelandic publications, on Icelandic-American relations, on the affairs of the various Icelandic societies and institutions, and on the history of Iceland and its literature. Finally, in Halldór's collection there are many letters from the arctic explorer Vilhjalmur Stefansson, mostly on the Vinland question, and from two of Halldór's countrymen and colleagues in America, Stefán Einarsson, professor at The Johns Hopkins University, and Richard Beck, professor at the University of North Dakota, regarding their common interests and Icelandic literary matters in general.

The final sections in the list of correspondence are of miscellaneous letters, several of which are from Fiske's time, including Fiske's letters to the Reverend Jón Bjarnason in Winnipeg. Here also are letters that either Fiske or the collection has purchased, such as two letters written by the brothers Grimm and a letter by the Icelandic poet Grímur Thomsen. Furthermore, in this section are listed Halldór Hermannsson's letter books and some letters to Halldór's successors at the Fiske Collection. Diplomas and honors comprise a special section in the catalogue.

The most interesting parts of the graphic material are two collections of photographs, the one from Frederic W. W. Howell and the other from Eiríkur Þorbergsson. Howell's collection is a compilation of photographs taken on his travels in Iceland during the last decade of the nineteenth century. The pictures are of Icelandic landscapes, of people, and of houses. Eiríkur Þorbergsson's collection is a testimony to Fiske's fascination with and devotion to the people of Grímsey, the small island north of Iceland proper. Fiske corresponded with several of its inhabitants, sent them presents, established a library on the island, and, at his death, bequeathed a considerable sum of money to the people of Grímsey for construction of a school. In memory of Fiske, the people of Grímsey still celebrate his birthday every year. In 1902 Fiske hired the Icelandic photographer Eiríkur Þorbergsson to take pictures of the inhabitants of Grímsey and their abodes, and these pictures are now in the possession of the Icelandic Collection.

In addition to these two collections of photographs, the Fiske Icelandic Collection owns a considerable number of pictures of Icelanders from various periods. Among them are two albums of photographs from Fiske; one contains various portraits, most of which were probably sent to him by people he corresponded with through the years and by his friends, and the other is a collection of photographs that students in the Junior College in Reykjavík compiled and sent to Fiske in gratitude for his donations to the school. Finally, the collection has a great number of pictures of Halldór Hermannsson from different periods of his life.

The manuscripts in this catalogue are classified by centuries, according to the time when they were written or transcribed. Each group is arranged alphabetically by author, or by title if the manuscript has no author or the author is unknown. Some discrepancies occur, as in the compilation of Icelandic catalogues of books and manuscripts (No. 62), which is arranged with the nineteenth-century material, although some of the lists are from the beginning of the twentieth century. In each entry, the years of birth and death of the respective authors are given, and the titles of the manuscripts are reproduced diplomatically. If the title is not written on the manuscript, it is put into brackets— and the same is done where untitled items are given descriptive titles. In the entries, following the title, the dates of writing or transcription of the manuscripts are recorded. Then follows a description of the manuscript's content and of its physical features. Finally, its provenance is recorded when possible. Where personal letters were included with the manuscripts, they were retained at their original place, but a cross-reference is given in the correspondence section of the catalogue.

The catalogue lists the letters by the names of the correspondents in alphabetical order, and the years of birth and death are noted where they are known. Persons are identified by profession whenever there was easy access to the information, for example in the letters themselves or in standard collective biographies. Where there are five letters or fewer from the same correspondent, full dates are given for each letter, but only the month and year of the first and last letter where the letters are more than five. The entry lists the number of items from each correspondent and the language used for the correspondence. A brief description of the contents of the letters concludes each entry to give an idea of the topics of discussion in the correspondence. In the list of Halldór Hermannsson's letter books, I give only a few examples of the letters he wrote. The letters in the section of Miscellaneous Correspondents are arranged by the name of the correspondents or the subject where they are more than one (see for example the Islandica-correspondence, *Mímir,* etc.). Finally, Diplomas and Honors are divided into three categories; first, formal letters addressed to Cornell University; second, formal letters and diplomas to Daniel Willard Fiske; third, the same presented to Halldór Hermannsson.

Some of the graphic material was classified prior to the compilation of the present catalogue. Thus, Halldór Hermannsson arranged Howell's photographs into albums, Fiske collected the pictures in album 1 in box 9, and the Students' Society of the Junior College in Reykjavík compiled the photographs in album 2 in box 10. The stereoscopes and lantern slides were also placed together in boxes. Other items, such as the pictures in box 6, were found scattered among the various unclassified materials. In box 5 were placed pictures that have been treated by the conservation department of the Cornell Libraries. In box 8, I grouped together loose portrait photographs, cartes-de-visite, and cabinet cards; other portraits in box 7; pictures of Fiske and his wife, Jennie McGraw, in box 11; and portraits and snapshots of Halldór Hermannsson in box 12.

The graphic material is grouped by artists, topics, or types, depending on which method best applies. The material within each group is placed first by artists and then by subjects (titles). Titles are reproduced diplomatically, if they are recorded, but where titles are missing the subjects are identified and names put within brackets. Dates of birth and death of artists are given where possible, and also dates of production or publication. Physical descriptions and explanatory notes are given when needed.

Finally, it must be noted that throughout the catalogue, Icelandic names are in alphabetical order under the given name and not the patronymic. That holds true also for Icelandic emigrants to America, whether they had become American citizens or not. When Icelanders have obviously changed their names according to English rules, they are usually placed under the surname with a cross-reference under the given Icelandic name. No distinction is made between the Icelandic characters *á, é, í, ó, ú, ý,* and *a, e, i, o, u,* and *y* respectively in the alphabetical arrangements. The Scandinavian characters *ø, ä,* and *å* are arranged with *o* and *a*. The Icelandic character *ö* is arranged with *o, ð* with *d, æ* with *ae,* but *þ* is put at the end of the alphabet.

I started this project when I served as a visiting curator in the Fiske Icelandic Collection in the spring of 1990, and it was completed with the help of two generous grants from Vísindaráð Íslands in 1991 and 1992. I am particularly grateful to Professor P. M. Mitchell, former curator of the Fiske Icelandic Collection and the editor of Islandica, for his support and invaluable help in completing this volume. Stefán Karlsson at Árnastofnun in Reykjavík provided much help during the time he served as a visiting curator in the fall of 1991. He examined and gave information on manuscripts 1, 4, 10, 11, 13, 15, and 23. Furthermore, I thank Ólafur Pálmason and Ögmundur Helgason for recommending this project to Vísindaráð Íslands; the staff of the History of Science Collection and of the Fiske Icelandic Collection for their support; and finally Cornell University Library for permission to use its facilities.

Þórunn Sigurðardóttir

Reykjavík

Manuscript Material, Correspondence, and Graphic Material in the Fiske Icelandic Collection

A DESCRIPTIVE CATALOGUE

I. MANUSCRIPT MATERIAL

1. Sixteenth Century

1   [*Jónsbók*]. Vellum manuscript from the middle of the sixteenth century. Halldór Hermannsson and Ólafur Halldórsson dated this manuscript from the fifteenth century. That date was corrected by Stefán Karlsson at the Arnamagnæan Institute in Reykjavík. In the last chapter, following words are omitted: "ok árnaðarorð frú sancte Márie ok hins heilaga Óláfs konungs", which might indicate that the book was written after the Reformation. Same hand may be on manuscripts AM 84, 8vo (Arnamagnæan Institute, Reykjavík), Perg. 8vo nr. 8 (Royal Library, Stockholm), GKS 3273, 4to (Royal Library, Copenhagen), and a charter No. 1549, written at Eiðar around the middle of sixteenth century (*Diplomatarium Islandicum* X, Reykjavík 1911-1921, No. 437).

The book is complete, 153 leaves, numbered in pencil; 18 x 14.2 cm. Written by one hand, which is, according to additional clause on the last leaf, one Jón Oddsson. Label on front cover, with gilded letters: JÓNSBÓK: LÖGBÓK MAGNÚS NOI.EGS KONUNGS. Chapters numbered in margin; section headings at head of page, added by later scribes from seventeenth and eighteenth century, the older ones erased in some places; chapter headings in red, initials occasionally in blue; additional words and phrases frequently in margin, but much of that has been erased. Marginal additions and corrections mainly on: 3r, 11r-v, 12r, 18r, 26r, 27v, 46r, 52r, 66v, 67r, 70r, 78r-v, 84v, 85v, 94r, 96v,

101v, 102r, 103v, 105v, 107r, 117v, 118r, 121v, 127r, 128v, 134v, 135r, 137v, 151r-v, and 153v.

Contents: [Bréf Magnús konungs] 1r-3r; [Þingfararbálkur] 3r-11r; [Kristindómsbálkur] 11r-17v; [Hirðsiðir] 17v-19v; [Konungs þegnskylda] 20r-22r; [Mannhelgi] 22r-44r; [Kvennagiftingar] 44r-71v; [— Um skrúðklæðaburð] 63r-v; [— Framfærslubálkur] 63v-71v; [Landsbrigðabálkur] 71v-77r; [Landsleigubálkur] 77r-119r; ([Réttarbót] 78v-79v); [— Rekaþáttur] 111-119r; [Kaupabálkur] 119r-132r; [Farmannalög] 132v-145r; [Þjófabálkur] 145r-153v.

On leaf 66v is written "eyulfvr arna son med eiin he[ndi]", at head of leaf 85v "Sueirn ogmund(son)", on leaf 94r "mijnum liuffum uin *og* brod*ur* J christo Sr Rognalldi", on 101v "olafur .....s son" (the same name appears also on 151r), at bottom of leaf 105v "ein*ar* einar son e*r* þ*ad* mitt naf*n*, gvd g*e*fi mi*er* af bokin*n*e gagn", on 137v is a stanza with the name Arne Andresson beneath, and at bottom of the last leaf, 153v "Ind*r*ide þoru*a*rds son ä boke*n*a. En*n* Jo*n* oddzson hef*ir* kl[or]*ad*." A note in Spanish is pasted inside front cover "<u>Magnus Noregs Konongs Laugbok</u>. Este famoso código de leyes fué promulgado por Magnus Hakonarson, Rey de Noruega (1263-1280) es conocido generalmente por el nombre de <u>Jónsbok</u> y es aún hoy dia, la ley fundamental de ese pais. London hoy (1886) Quaritch (£5)." [i.e. Bernard Quaritch, bookseller in London].

Willard Fiske mentions a manuscript of *Jónsbók* in a letter to the Rev. Jón Bjarnason in Winnipeg, dated Florence, July 19 [189?]: "The other day I bought in Madrid a very good fifteenth-century vellum MS of Jónsbók (Lögbók Íslendinga)." Ólafur Halldórsson mentions this manuscript in his edition of this law-code, p. xlvi, No. 11. The MS was catalogued by Halldór Hermannsson in *Catalogue of the Icelandic Collection Bequeathed by Willard Fiske* (Ithaca: Cornell University Library, 1914).

2   **Magnús Jónsson** (ca. 1525)-1591. [*Spegill þeirrar sönnu Rhetorica*]. Written 1587. (Cf. Kr. Kålund comp., *Katalog over den Arnamagnæanske håndskriftsamling.* Copenhagen: Kommissionen for det Arnamagnæanske legat, 1894.) Specimens of Magnús Jónsson's translation of Fridrich Riedrer's *Rhetorica.*

3 photostats from AM 702, 4to (Arnamagnæan Institute, Copenhagen), leaves 60r, 38r, and 22v-23r.

2. Seventeenth Century

3   **Guðbrandur Þorláksson, Bishop** (ca. 1541)-1627. [*Tungubréf*] 1608.

Fragment of a document headed: "Eign *og* maldagi Jardaren*n*ar tungu j fliotu*m* 1608", signed by the Bishop at Tunga on "föstudaginn fyrir Þorláksmessu 1608." A second heading with a different hand is on the document: "Tungu Brief Gunnars Orms Sonar."

4   **Jón Þorsteinsson** píslarvottur (ca.1570)-1627. [*Davíðssálmar og Genesissálmar*]. Transcribed between 1622-1634 and 1627-1682.

106 leaves, recently numbered, besides two fly-leaves in front with an additional double sheet pasted on the first one (with a description of the MS in Danish, written by an Icelander around the middle of the nineteenth century; also "George Stephens, Copenhagen, 1853", and "O.N.10"), no title-page; 17.1 x 13.8 cm. This is actually two manuscripts bound together, leaves 1-76 and 77-106. The first part is richly ornamented with colors and gold; ornaments are used to fill lines at the end of stanzas; colored initials at beginning of each stanza; large ornamented initials at the beginning of each psalm. 40r-v: sketch drawings of hands, pointing fingers at the text. 73r-v: red lines intended for musical notes. The latter part has headings and sometimes the beginning of stanzas and names in blue or red ink. Initials of hymns are large and ornamented. Bound in wooden boards dressed in leather, spine is damaged; the initials H S D on the front cover, and "ANNO 1682" on the back.

Contents: The author's foreword to "Dauijds Psalltara" with the heading "Til Lesarans" and the initials "S.J.Þ.S." beneath. Leaves 2-74 contain Davíðssálmar, heading: "Sa I. Psalmur D[avids]. Med lag: Halltt oss Gudi." Leaf 20 is blank; missing are: two leaves between 41 and 42 (the most part of psalm 74 through the beginning of 78); 2 leaves between 67 and 68 (the last part of psalm 119 through the beginning of 127); two leaves between 69 and 70 (last part of psalm 132 through the first lines of 137); one leaf between 72 and 73 (most of psalm 144 and 145); one leaf between 74 and 75 (the last part of psalm 149 and through 150). Following (ll 75v-76r) is a stanza with musical notes for the first line: "EN LIRE. Vtsett a Islendsku. Tenor." 76v is blank. Several marginal notes, mostly corrections of scribal errors, but also changes to the text. Leaves 77r-104r contain Genesissálmar, which are incomplete. They bear the heading: "GENISIS BOK Snuin*n* J Psalma Aff Syra Jöne S:

Þorsteinssyne ä Westm*annae*yi*um* I Psalmur. Tön: Jesus Gudzson Eing*etinn*.", in green ink. 104v-106 are blank. Two leaves are missing from between 92 and 93 (most part of hymn 37 and first verse of 38); also two leaves between 94 and 95 (the most part of hymn 41). 2 end leaves.

Davíðssálmar is written by one hand. On leaf 75r, following Davíðs-sálmar, in red ink: "Skrif*at og* Endat af Bir*ne* Grims." Björn Grímsson was known for his artistic abilities. Cf. Halldór Hermannsson *Illuminated Manuscripts of the Jónsbók* (Islandica XXVIII, 1940), pp. 18-21. This part of the book was then written sometime between 1622 when Jón Þorsteinsson finished working on the psalms. (Cf. Páll Eggert Ólason, *Menn og menntir siðskiptaaldarinnar á Íslandi* IV (Reykjavík, 1926), p. 645) and 1634 the death year of Björn Grímsson. On leaf 75r is also stamped "T. Gudmundsson. 1791", possibly a former owner. Genesissálmar were written by two different hands, the first leaves 77-90 and the second 91-104. Genesissálmar were written after 1627, for the author is listed as deceased in title (i.e., S[áluga]), and before 1682 when the manuscript was bound. Bought by Fiske from H.H.J. Lynge & Son, Copenhagen. (Cf. Willard Fiske, *Bibliographical notices* VI., 19). Formerly in the library of Prof. George Stephens.

Catalogued by Halldór Hermannsson in *Catalogue of the Icelandic Collection Bequeathed by Willard Fiske* (Ithaca: Cornell University Library, 1914).

5   [*Jónsbók*]. *Logbok Jslendinga. Utgiefin*n *af kong Magnusi Hakonarsyne med odrum* kon*glegum Riettarbötum — Mandatum: oc alþijngiz Sampyktum er almen*nil*ega snerta landit.*

454 pages with pagination, unnumbered title-page, three blank leaves in front of the book, and two at the end. Beneath the title is written the abbreviation: "d.m.m.s.", with a different kind of script. Illuminated title-page. 15 large initials and 16 head or tail pieces; marginal notes and additions occasionally in red, yellow or green ink; section initials are large and ornamented with drawings of animals or people; section headings and first lines in large script and various types; chapter initials colored and ornamented; reference to different chapters occasionally in margin; sketch drawing of a man on p. 5. Blank space in various places for initials or paragraphs to be added. In other places paragraphs have been added, with smaller script, but apparently by same hand. The manuscript seems to be written by at least two different hands, probably

from around the middle of the century. The manuscript was cut in binding so some marginal notes are incomplete. Otherwise it is clean and well preserved. Bound in leather, somewhat impaired; gold decorations on covers and spine, "ISLANSKE LOWBOG" written in gilded letters on spine, a tag is pasted above with "51." in ink, "51-", "£ 480", and "gss" inside front cover in pencil; 19.5 x 15.4 cm.

The book is complete. Contents: Title-page; Kong Magnusar Brief Og Formale (pp. 1-5); Hier Heffur Up þann fyrsta hlut lógböcar er heiter þijngfararbälkur (pp. 6-31); Hier Byriar þan Fyrsta Bälk logbocarennar er heiter Christendömzbälkur (pp. 32-81); Kongs Þegnskyllda (pp. 82-88); Hier Biriar Hinn þridia balk logbokar. Þath er fyrst j Mannhelge... (pp. 89-149); Hier hefur vpp 4a hlut lógbokar er heiter kuennagiptingar (pp. 150-202); Hier Byriar Frammfærslubälk (pp. 203-227); Hier Byriar fimta hlut logbokar er heiter landabrygde (pp. 228-247); Hier hefur upp hinn Fimta hlut lógbökarennar. er Heiter Bunadarbalkur (pp. 248-344); Hier Byriar Siótta hlut lógbökar er Heiter Reka Bälkur (pp. 345-366); Hier hefur vpp Sióunda hlut lógbokarinar. er heiter kaupabalkur (pp. 367-398); Hier Hefur vpp attunda Hlut lógbokar Er heiter Farmanna lóg (pp. 399-427); Hier Hefur vpp Nijunda Hlut lógbokar. er heiter thiöva Balkur (pp. 429-454).

The manuscript was offered to the Fiske Icelandic Collection in 1972. Cf. a letter from Vilhjálmur Bjarnar to Jónas Kristjánsson, director of the Arnamagnæan Institute in Reykjavík, 25 September 1972, and his reply from 28 February 1973 with a description by Stefán Karlsson based on a photocopy of a few pages from the MS.

6 **Ólafur Jónsson,** 1560-1627. [*Vísnabók*]. *Ein lijtil summa edur vijsna Samdrättur þeirra kvædis erenda sem aa tuttugu aara tijma hafa til andlegrar skiemttunar og skammdægurz vid og vid af munne fallid. Nu upp teijknud þeim til gagns og göda sem þaug vilia þiggia og fijrer munne sier kveda. Af si*ij*ra Olaafe Jonssijne ortt og samsett aad Søndum j Dijra firde Skrifad ä nij anno 1686 af Jone Biarna sijne aa Høfda vid D f."* Poems by the Reverend Ólafur Jónsson from Sandar in Dýrafjörður, transcribed in 1686.

Title-page (text starts verso), 133 numbered leaves (text 128, index and provenance 5); cover is red leather with gold decorations; on spine in gilded letters: "Ólafur Jónsson. Vísnabók. MS 1686"; fore-edge gilded; 17.4 x 14.5 cm. Bound and repaired by Zaehnsdorf, late nineteenth century.

Contents: Title-page; foreword by the author, partly illegible; 150 poems, mostly hymns, but also epistles, nursery rhymes, etc.; a poem of ten lines about the poet by the Reverend Stefán Ólafsson from Vallanes, a contemporary of his; a nineteenth-century index of 4 leaves by first line, on verso of the fourth "Síra Ólafur Jónsson á Söndum í Dýrafirði, fæddur 1560, prestur að Sauðlauksda[l] 1590; til Sanda í Dýrafirði 1596 [d] 1627. Var talinn skáld mikið." The last leaf (same as main text's) has some information on previous owners of the manuscript, written in a different hand. "Þorbiorg Eiulfs Dotter", and "Sueirn Gudna Son a Stad vid Hruta Fiord", are apparently previous owners. Furthermore are the names "Eijúlfur" and "Hólmfrijdur" written there and "Monsr Gudm. Stad."; at bottom of 128v: "JBorgfirðingur á kvæðin." Jón Borgfirðingur Jónsson (1826-1912), was probably the last owner prior to acquisition by the Fiske Icelandic Collection.

Transcribed 1686 by Jón Bjarnason from Höfði in Dýrafjörður. Cf. title-page. Portions of the MS are, however, of a later date (leaves must have been lost and been replaced later): leaves 60r-71v, 73r-77v, and 104r-128v by an unidentified hand and leaf 103 as well as the index apparently by Páll (stúdent) Pálsson (1806-1877).

Catalogued by Halldór Hermannsson in *Catalogue of the Icelandic Collection Bequeathed by Willard Fiske* (Ithaca: Cornell University Library, 1914).

Virgils saga. See **Þórður Jónsson.**

7   **Worm, Ole,** 1588-1654. *Spicilegium eorum, quae perfectissimus nostri seculi antiquarius Wormius in Monumentis editis se forte nescire aut simulavit, aut dissimulavit.* Undated.

10 leaves in a green brownish patterned hardcover, paginated 1-18, but with pages 13-14 lacking. Some runic inscriptions and illustrations; 16.1 x 10.4 cm. Probably transcribed by someone named Helwerskov. Cf. preliminary page.

Catalogued by Halldór Hermannsson in *Catalogue of Runic Literature. Forming a Part of the Icelandic Collection Bequeathed by Willard Fiske* (London: Oxford University Press, 1918).

8   **Þórður Jónsson** (ca. 1609)-1670. Rotograph copy of *Lijfsaga Markölfs og Samtal þeirra Salomöns köngs Ens Wijsa*, from British Museum

Add. MS 4857. The rotograph contains also *Hier byriast Lijfs saga Þess Nafn fræga Virgelij. Vtløgd vr hollendsku Maale.*

15 and 20 numbered sheets; 25.3 x 20.2 cm. At the end of former: "Skrifað og endädt ä Skarde aff Þörde Jönssyne Anno 1670 þan*n* 17. dag Jänüarij." At the end of latter: "Endar Hier Historiu Virgilij Anno 1694." One hand. Enclosed are also Halldór Hermannsson's transcripts of: "Virgils saga"; 27 light blue unlined sheets, written on recto, numbered. One sheet of notes. Also "Markólfs saga"; (1), 38 unnumbered leaves in a maroon paper cover notebook with black spine, the rest is blank; white label on front cover with title and MS number; 21.2 x 16.2 cm. One additional single sheet. Both transcribed from the same manuscript at an unknown date.

3. Eighteenth Century

9   **Árni Magnússon,** 1663-1730. [*Notes*]. [1702-12].

2 sheets and 1 envelope (addressed to Árni Magnússon and Páll Vídalín at the Alþing) of notes, mainly names, in the hand of Árni Magnússon. 1) "Þord*ar* Gudlaugs sonar i Eyrarsveit." 2) "Ragneidar Jónsdottur *og* barna hennar." 3) "Sr Halldors Palssonar", "nock*ur* i bland af elldra slage" [crossed out], "Hier i bland 2. bref mediæ ætatis." [crossed out]. The sheets were probably placed with letters and/or MSS he borrowed from these people.

10   [*Barnaspurningar*]. *Þær Einföldustu Barna Spurningar Ut af siälfum CATECHISM[O] og Pontoppidan[s] Utskíringu. dregnar og Samann skr[ifadar] 1764.* Lutheran catechism based upon Erik Pontoppidan's *Sandhed til Gudfrygtighed*, first published in 1737. Probably copied late eighteenth century from a book dated 1764.

32 unnumbered leaves, including title-page; fragile, missing a great deal at the end, possibly ca. half of the original; written by one hand; 16.7 x 10.5 cm. Wrapped in a front cover torn from a Reville Writing Tablet on which is written title and where obtained, placed in an envelope pasted inside gray cardboard with "Barnaspurningar MSS. 1764" in Halldór Hermannsson's handwriting on front cover. This was replaced by blue hardcover bindings, encapsulated in mylar and boxed by Cornell University's conservation dept. in 1991. Bought 9 August 1915 from Reginald Atkinson, London.

Catalogued by Halldór Hermannsson in *Catalogue of the Icelandic Collection Bequeathed by Willard Fiske. Additions 1913-26* (Ithaca: Cornell University Press, 1927).

11 **Bünting, Heinrich,** 1545-1606. An Icelandic translation of Heinrich Bünting's *Itinerarium Sacrae Scripturae*, a description of the towns and places to which the Holy Patriarches travelled. Included in this manuscript are three different works. Transcribed in 1720.

Contents: *Itinerarium Sacræ Scripturæ. Þad er ein reisu book ifer þa h: skrift sundurdeild ÿ tvær bækur. — Firri Parturinn innehelldur allar Reisur þeirra H: Patriarcha, Konga, Fursta, og Propheta, med Wtskÿrÿngu þeirra landa, Stada, Vatnsfalla, Fialla, og Dala, sem H: Ritnÿng umm Gietur, efter frekustu uppgrundan kostgiæfelega saman- skrifad med wtleggÿngu þeirra Hebræsku og grisku nafna, samt þar medfilgiande efterlÿkÿnga, og þeirra andlegre wtþydÿng. Annar part- urenn — Hliodar um þad nya Testa mentum, og sÿner ferdalag Iomfru Mariu, Iosephs, Austurvegs vitrÿnganna, herrans Jesu Christi og hans H: Postula af þeim merkilegustu bökum utdreiged, Geometrice nidur- reiknad, iferlesid og endur bætt med stærstu aastundan af M: Henrico Bunting, Predikara til Grimaw, i Brunschwiglande af þÿsku maale i danskt üt løgd, og Prentud i Kaupenhafn, Anno 1615. — AA ÿslendsku af dønsku utløgd af heidurlegum* Sira *Nichulase Gudmundssine saluga anno MDCLXX — AA Svefneium a Breidafirde skrifud af Olafe Gunnlaugssine ar*um *efter Guds burd Anno MDCCXX.*" With foreword by the author, a list of contents (pp. 597-609), and an index of place-names (pp. 609-622).

On pp. 41-55, and on 12 unnumbered pages inserted between pp. 54 and 55, is an insertion into Bünting's work titled: *Nv Efterfilgir vm Foreidslu og nidurbrot Borgarinnar Jerusalem Huøria Eideleggÿng saa Romverske herzhøfdÿnge Titus Vespatianj son, Framm kvæmde. Lesaren*n *vite Ad Author þessarar Bökar, hefur ej þessa Frædslu histo- riu samantekid, nie hier med filgia lätid, Helldur Er hün af bökum Josephi sagnameistara vt dreiginn og hier jnn færð, Firerfarande Og Effterfilgiande mäle til uppfillijng*ar *Ordriett effter þeirre sem prentud var ä Hölumm J hiallta dal Anno 1617.* This part of the MS is by a dif- ferent hand, except the title, and another title on p. 54: *Vidbæter þess- arar Historiu, sem er frekare fraaskÿrÿng margra þeirra hluta sem skiedu j þuÿ Romverska Strÿde þegar jerusalem varun*in, which seem to be by Ólafur Gunnlaugsson. This part is transcribed from a book printed at Hólar in the year 1617. Described in Halldór Hermannsson, *Icelandic Books of the Seventeenth Century* (Islandica XIV, 1922), p. 36.

Also included are: *Æfesaga Paals postula af hans sjaalfs pistlum, postulanna giørnijngu*m *og* kirkiu*historium, wt dreigid. — Samanskrifad ÿ Latinu maale af Georgio Maiore til Vittenberg Anno 1555. Utlagt a nÿ anno 1666*, i.e., by Georgio Maiore (1502-1574), pp. 623-650, and *Um*m *gull mynt, silfur mÿnt, vict og mæler hebreskra og huørnin*n *þetta saman*n *ber vid griska latinska og vora danska mint vict og mæler. Item nockur exempla saman*n*tekid af Heilagre Ritnÿngu, wtdreigid af mørgum autores og trwverdugum skrifurum*m, by anonymous, pp. 651-679.

708 pages, with pagination and signatures both somewhat irregular. The three title-pages are unnumbered. Bound in eighteenth-century blind tooled sheepskin with a crown stamped in centers of both covers. Richly ornamented in colors and gold with 25 full-page decorations, about 180 large initials, 40 head or tail pieces and 5 borders; 18.8 x 15 cm. According to title-pages this translation is from the Danish version, published in Copenhagen 1615. The Reverend Nikulás Guðmundsson (ca.1630-1710) translated it in 1670, but this manuscript was transcribed in 1720 by Ólafur Gunnlaugsson (1688-1784) in Svefneyjar in Breiðafjörður. The Life of Paul the Apostle was translated from Latin in 1666 by an unknown translator.

The manuscript was examined by Halldór Hermannsson, February 1923, and then purchased. Cf. letters from Wilfrid M. Voynich of 33 West 42nd Street, New York, dated 6 and 10 February 1923. With the letters came a description of the manuscript, 2 sheets. Enclosed with the letters are bits extracted from the manuscript with the following clause: "Allar blaðsíður í rauðum bekk, margir upphafsstafir litaðir og misjafnir að stærð, ýmislegt annað skraut, sérstaklega fuglamyndir." A few biographical details about the Reverend Nikulás Guðmundsson, compiled by Halldór Hermannsson; 12 sheets and 2 slips of paper.

12   **Eggert Ólafsson,** 1726-1768. *Stutt Aagrip ur Rettrita-Bók Islendinga hvors Titill er Nockrar Oreglulegar Reglur, I Spurningum framsettar epter A B C um þad Hvørn veg Rett eiga ad tala, bókstafa oc skrifa þaa nú Lifande Islendska Tungu. Fyrsta Aavarp I flýte samanteked Aar MDCCLvij.* A treatise on Icelandic orthography.

Rotograph copy of MS. British Museum Add. 11200. 85 leaves, bound in green hardcover at Cornell University. On spine in gilded letters: "Eggert Ólafsson. Nockrar óreglulegr reglur."

Catalogued by Halldór Hermannsson in *Catalogue of the Icelandic Collection Bequeathed by Willard Fiske. Additions 1927-42* (Ithaca: Cornell University Press, 1943).

Einar Einarsson yngri. See **Páll Jónsson Vídalín.**

13   [*Fornbréf*] i.e., charters. 6 Photoprints, on both sides of 3 sheets, of three letters, written on vellum, concerning Reykir in Tungusveit in Skagafjörður. The oldest letter is written 1311 and the next in 1520. On the back of the latter is a forged border list said to be from 1521 but written in the eighteenth century as is the third letter, said from 1621, containing a forged decree on the borders of Reykir.

The photographs were sent to Fiske to Florence from the Embassy of the United States of America in Berlin. The original letters were bought in Iceland in 1898 by Albert Parker Hanson, engineer in Berlin, but presented to the National Archives of Iceland by his son, Prof. E. Parker Hanson, University of Delaware, in 1951. (Cf. *Diplomatarium Islandicum* II (Copenhagen, 1893), pp. 372-3, *Diplomatarium Islandicum* VIII (Reykjavík, 1906-13), pp. 754-58, and *Islandske originaldiplomer indtil 1450*. Edited by Stefán Karlsson (*Ed. arnam.* A7, Copenhagen, 1963), pp. 7-8.) These charters are mentioned in letters from Halldór Hermannsson to dr. Jón Þorkelsson. Cf. Halldór Hermannsson's letter-book, 1917 - 1927, ll. 160 and 165.

14   **Gracian y Morales, Baltasar,** 1601-1658. *Nockrar Hnyttelegar heimsspeke Greiner, Og Lijttkunnar forsialnis og Lifnadar Reglur üt-dregnar af Þesz Spanska herra Balthasar Gracians Hofmanne enn Ur Frónsku aa Islendsku ütlagdar Anno 1753.* Preliminary title: "Balthazari Graciani, Hispani, Sententiae philosophicae et regulae ethicae a cl. Eggerhardo Olavio in lingvam Islandicam elegantissime translata 1753."

Rotograph copy of Bodleian Library MS. Boreale 97. 40 leaves, including title-page; written in two columns; bound in red hardcover at Cornell University; on front cover, vertically along spine, in gilded letters: Gracian — Heimspekigreinar — 1753. Chapter headings usually written in the margin; 21.8 x 17.3 cm.

An Icelandic translation by Eggert Ólafsson (1726-1768), of selections from *Oraculo manual* by Gracian. The translator used Amelot de la Houssaie's French version, *L'homme du cour* (Paris, 1684). The French translator's footnotes have frequently been incorporated without any indication that they did not belong to the original text. Also a paraphrase by the translator. For further analysis of this translation see: Halldór Hermannsson, *Eggert Ólafsson. A Biographical Sketch* (Islandica XVI, 1925).

Catalogued by Halldór Hermannsson in *Catalogue of the Icelandic Collection Bequeathed by Willard Fiske. Additions 1927-42* (Ithaca: Cornell University Press, 1943).

15   [*Gull-Þóris saga or Þorskfirðinga saga*], "Her hefz Saga Gull-Þoris", and [*Huldar saga*], "Sagann af Hulld Trøllkonu enni Ríku."

66 leaves (*Gull-Þóris saga* 33 leaves, numbered in pencil; *Huldar saga* 34 leaves, pages numbered in ink; two blank leaves, unnumbered, between the sagas). No title-page; bound in brown marbled hardcover, red fore-edge, titles engraved in golden letters on spine; in various places words and sentences in the latter text are underlined in pencil, and lines are drawn down the margin on several pages; 19.9 x 15.8 cm. Written by one hand, which probably is Magnús Ketilsson's (1732-1803).

The text of the first saga is probably transcribed directly or indirectly from AM 495, 4to (Arnamagnæan Institute, Reykjavík). The second saga ends in chapter 25 with the words "enn hér skaltu gisting hafa i Nótt, og skemt þier vid gódan fagnad." The same sentence is towards the end of ch. 25 of the longer version of this saga (162 chapters in all). The Danish translation by W. H. F. Abrahamson (In *Extr. fra Skand. Lit. Selsk. Skrift.* 1805. 1. Bind, pp. 263-334) may have used this manuscript because it ends at the same place.

Catalogued by Halldór Hermannsson in *Catalogue of the Icelandic Collection Bequeathed by Willard Fiske* (Ithaca: Cornell University Library, 1914).

Huldar saga. See *Gull-Þóris saga.*

16   **Knopf, Thomas Hans Henrich.** *Minning efter ett samtal med inge-nieur capitainen Hans Henric Christopher Knoff, om Island, sedan han tillika med sin broder, på kongl. daansk befalling afmått samma land-*

skap och ö, åhren... A rotograph copy of a MS in the Royal library in Stockholm. The date 14. Aug. 1741 at end of text.

7 leaves, numbered in red ink, bound in grey cardboard. Inserted at end a letter to Halldór Hermannsson from O. Wieselgren, the Royal library, Stockholm, dated 30 June 1931, presenting him with the rotograph; in English.

Catalogued by Halldór Hermannsson in the *Catalogue of the Icelandic Collection Bequeathed by Willard Fiske. Additions 1927-42* (Ithaca: Cornell University Press, 1943).

17   ***Kort underrättelse om Runstafwar. Anno 1737.***

13 unnumbered leaves, bound together without cover, including one sheet of 31.4 x 38.7 cm, that shows an illustration of a runic calendar used in Scandinavia; title-page, with text starting on verso; at bottom of title-page: "Apus primum"; illustrated chart; main text is 20.2 x 16 cm.

Catalogued by Halldór Hermannsson in *Catalogue of Runic Literature. Forming a Part of the Icelandic Collection Bequeathed by Willard Fiske* (London: Oxford University Press, 1918).

Maiore, Georgio. See **Bünting, Heinrich.**

18   *Mitt mun hiartad so med sier ...* A poem of two stanzas. Eighteenth century?

1 sheet, written lengthwise, one side only; 18.9 x 16.3 cm. Possibly a fly-leaf torn from a book. Some names are scrawled on the sheet, i.e. "Ragnhildur" in large script right above the stanzas, "Thorsteirn", "Jon Briniol…", "J. Gud.", and "Halla Johns Dotter."

Nv Efterfilgir vm Foreidslu og nidurbrot Borgarinnar Jerusalem… See **Bünting, Heinrich.**

19   **Páll Björnsson,** 1621-1706. *Speculum Patientiæ. Edur Þolinnmædin-nar Speigill. Samanntekinn af Hälærdum Kennemanne Sira Paale Biørn Syne. Fordum Profaste i Bardastrandar Syslu, og Preste ad Selaardal.*

66 recently numbered leaves, including a flyleaf at both ends; fragile, bound in leather, which was replaced by blue hardcover bindings, en-

capsulated in mylar and boxed by Cornell University's conservation dept. in 1991; on 1r: "3/6", "2/3MS"; 16 x 9.8 cm. The manuscript was transcribed in the eighteenth century. Parts of letters pasted on the inside of cover. Letter on front cover has the name Þórður Sveinsson hreppstjórnarmaður, and the letter on back cover is signed by Magnús Teitsson and dated: "Watnsfirde d. 30. Januarii 1750". The thesis is dedicated to the brothers Sigurður Björnsson, Chief Justice of the south and east, and the Reverend Hannes Björnsson from Saurbær on Hvalfjarðarströnd, dated 12 February 1687. On page preceding title-page is written the place-name, "Stad vid Hruta Fiørd", probably home of a previous owner. Contents: Title-page 2r; "Dedicatio" 2v-3v; text 4r-65v; 66r blank, on 66v is scribbled "þolin*n*mædde*n*ar spegell", "spegell þolin*n*mæden*n*aar" several times, and more.

Catalogued by Halldór Hermannsson in *Catalogue of the Icelandic Collection Bequeathed by Willard Fiske* (Ithaca: Cornell University Library, 1914).

20 **Páll Jónsson Vídalín,** 1667-1727. [*Autographs*].

Wrappings twice used, partly by Einar Einarsson yngri (1682-1737), in 1704, and partly by Páll J. Vídalín. Cf. an unidentified twentieth-century statement.

21 [*Rúnakver*]. A manuscript in Icelandic, with runic inscriptions, containing various runic alphabets, crypt-runes, etc.

231 pages, portions numbered, fragile, fore-edge tattered. Bound in hardcover; 8.3 x 9.8 cm. Halldór Hermannsson dates this manuscript from the eighteenth or the beginning of the nineteenth century. Written by one hand.

Catalogued by Halldór Hermannsson in *Catalogue of Runic Literature. Forming a Part of the Icelandic Collection Bequeathed by Willard Fiske* (London: Oxford University Press, 1918).

22 [*Signatures*]. A slip of paper with 13 Danish and German names, dated Copenhagen, 20 May 1767; 3.9 x 14.3 cm.

Umm gull mynt, silfur mÿnt... See **Bünting, Heinrich.**

23 *Vm Tyund ä Jarda gotze.* [Icelandic laws].

3 leaves and a fragment of the fourth. Apparently an eighteenth-century hand. 1r-3r contains the so called "Bergþórs-statúta", printed (after a different manuscript) in Halldór Einarsson, *Om Værdie-Beregning paa Landsviis og Tiende-Ydelsen i Island* (Copenhagen: S. L. Møllers Bogtrykkeri, 1833), pp. 165-175. Cf. also Jón Sigurðsson's introduction to *Diplomatarium Islandicum* I, p. 73, and "Bergþór Hrafnsson" and "Daði Halldórsson" in *Íslenzkar æviskrár* I. The remainder of the text which starts on 3r "Forn Alþingis Catastasis" is incomplete. It is printed (after a different manuscript) in Matthías Þórðarson *Þingvöllur. Alþingisstaðurinn forni. Saga Alþingis* II (1956).

Enclosed is another MS of 4 leaves (4v is blank). It begins thus: "Best mun vera ad Gissurar tiundar statuta gylde fyrer Grundvallar Reglu Tiundar vorrar i Jslande ..." The text refers to the deceased, "Sal. Biskup", Dr. Finnur Jónsson [Bishop], (d. 1789), and to sources from 1777 and 1778. This MS is written by a different hand, probably around 1800.

Þorskfirðinga saga. See ***Gull-Þóris saga.***

Þær Einföldustu Barna Spurningar. See ***Barnaspurningar.***

4. Nineteenth Century

24   ***Almanacs.*** The Fiske Icelandic Collection owns five volumes of printed and handwritten almanacs from the years 1790-1838.

358 leaves, unnumbered; 10.8 x 8.5 cm. Some are of various different sizes, and a few are written on strips of paper. Volumes i-iv are bound in marbled hardcover with dark brown spine, v is unbound (with the almanacs of 1830 and 1838 in heavy paper wrapper). Illustrations in vol. ii, 1810-1812, and vol. v, 1831.

Contents: Vol. i includes printed almanacs from the years 1790-1805; vol. ii: printed almanacs from 1806-1808, 1816-1818, and 1820, MS almanacs 1809-1815 and 1819 for Reykjavík, Trondhjem, København, Christiania, and Eyjafjörður; vol. iii: printed almanacs 1816-1834; vol. iv: printed 1821-1827, 1830-1831 and 1837-1838, MS almanacs 1828-1829, 1832-1836 for Eyjafjörður; vol. v: printed almanac 1835, MS almanacs 1808-1812, 1815, 1818, 1821, 1823, 1828-1831, 1833, 1835, and 1838 for Trondhjem, Eyjafjörður, København, and Christiania.

The MS almanacs were composed by B. Jóh., Thomas Bugge, Hans von Frisak, Hans Jacob von Scheel, H. Chr. Schumacher, E. G. F. Thune, and G. F. Ursin. Copied by various unknown hands.

Names and phrases indicating possible owners: volume v, 1808: "Ólafar Magnús Son[ar], Biarne Flovents Son "; 1812: "Til Þordar"; 1821: "Jóhann Halldórsson a þessa bók med Riettu"; 1830: a stanza naming Sigurður from Krínastaðir; 1831: "Þetta almanak hefur skrifad kararinn sem var i Saurbæ í Eyafirde"; 1833: "Biórn Biörnsson"; 1835: "Magnus Asgri[msson]." Stamped in blue on first page of volumes i, ii, and iv: Br. Oddsson.

Catalogued by Halldór Hermannsson in *Catalogue of the Icelandic Collection Bequeathed by Willard Fiske* (Ithaca: Cornell University Library, 1914).

Ambales saga kongs. See ***Ymsar sögur.***

Arbman, O. E. See **Richert, Mårten Birger.**

Árna skjal. See *Ymsar sögur.*

25 **Banks, Sir Joseph,** 1743-1820. [*Untitled*]. A message from Sir Joseph Banks to someone by the name of Percy (about returning a book), written by a third person; undated; with red seal. The document was acquired April 1927. Cf. invoice from Goodspeed's Book Shop, Boston, Massachusetts.

One sheet, folded.

26 **Barclay, John,** 1582-1621. *Sagann af Argenide dottur Meleander Kongs I Sikiley.*

Translated into Icelandic from the Latin by Jón Einarsson ((ca. 1674)-1707), Sub-rector of the school at Hólar. The original translation is from the year 1696. This manuscript is copied by an eighty-year-old man, the Reverend S. S., in 1808, according to title-page.

233 numbered pages, bound in leather; 19.8 x 15.2 cm. On spine in gilded letters: "Barclay Argenis", and below: "Jón Einarsson". Contents: Title-page, 5 sections, each divided into 14 to 21 chapters, and a register.

On last two pages are names of numerous borrowers of the book, with expressions of thanks — one in stanza form. Names of owners include Jón Helgason, G. S. Dottir, and Jón Þóraren Son from Skriðu-Klaustur.

Catalogued by Halldór Hermannsson in *Catalogue of the Icelandic Collection Bequeathed by Willard Fiske* (Ithaca: Cornell University Library, 1914).

27 **Bertel (Stefánsson) Gunnlaugsson,** 1839-1918. *A retrospective glance at the historical vicissitude of the Icelandic Commonwealth from the first Althing in 929 to the union with Norway 1262.* About the Icelandic Commonwealth. In two parts, the first part deals mainly with the age of the Sturlungs, and the second part with the history of the Icelandic Commonwealth.

Title-page, 1-32, 35 and 1-35 (two leaves 19) numbered leaves in a fragment of a notebook in a grey cardboard; "Gunlögsen, B. H. S.: Icelandic Commonwealth." handwritten on spine. Written on recto, except for occasional notes on verso; the second part is defective at the end; undated; 18 x 11.5 cm.

The author published articles on this subject in *The Open Court* Nos. 146-147 (vol. IV, 16-17) (Chicago, 1890).

Catalogued by Halldór Hermannsson in *Catalogue of the Icelandic Collection Bequeathed by Willard Fiske* (Ithaca: Cornell University Library, 1914).

28 [*Bibliographical Notations*]. On Old Norse and Scandinavian literature and history. By an unknown hand. The latest title is dated 1899.

5 sheets, folded, unnumbered; 21 x 13.5 cm.

29 **Björn Gunnlaugsson,** 1788-1876. *Vasa-Blød til gamans þeim er skák-Spil læra vilia. Úr þijdsku útlagt af.* A collection of chess games translated from German into Icelandic by Björn Gunnlaugsson in the early nineteenth century. This is a holograph copy.

(1), 36 leaves, unnumbered. Bound in brown and blue patterned hardcover, dark brown spine and corners; 13.1 x 8 cm.

The manuscript belonged to Matthías Eggertsson in 1904. It was given

to him by Þórður Jensson, the grandson of Björn Gunnlaugsson. Cf. preliminary page.

Catalogued by Halldór Hermannsson in *Catalogue of the Icelandic
Collection Bequeathed by Willard Fiske* (Ithaca: Cornell University
Library, 1914).

30   **Cuir.** *The Discovery of America by the North men. Written by Cuir.*
Undated.

10 sheets, torn from an exercise book; written in ink; numbered 1-10;
33 x 18.5 cm. Last sheet verso: "Prof. Fiske. America by North men.
Cuir."

31   **[*Eddas, the*]**. Three MS-leaves containing quotation on the *Eddas* from
Nicholson's *English historical library.* Lond. 1736, fol. 52.

The first leaf recto has the name Francis Place and the date 1806, on
verso is written: "Edda Islandorum, the meaning of which appellation
they that published the book, hardly pretend to understand." The text is
on 2r-3r, 3v is blank. The MS is inserted before the title-page of
Icelandic Poetry, or The Edda of Saemund. Translated into English
verse, by A. S. Cottle (Bristol: Joseph Cottle, 1797).

32   **[*Egils saga*]**. Glossary of *Egils saga.* 4 leaves inserted at the end of
*Egils-saga, sive Egilli Skallagrimii vita. Ex Manuscriptis Legati Arna-
Magnæani cum interpretatione Latina Notis Chronologia et Tribus
Tabb. Æneis* (Hafniæ: Sumptibus Legati Arna-Magnæani, MDCCCIX).

Written in ink on both sides; in three columns with headings: "Ord og
Talemåder", "m[ed] H[ensyn] til Sproglæren", and "Andre Mærke-
ligheder." In Danish.

33   ***Eitt lijtid Bæna Kver...*** A handwritten title-page copied from a book
printed in Skálholt by Henrick Krusi in 1687.

1 leaf, 7.4 x 4.7 cm. Also a printed page from the same book, headed:
"Olearii bænir", and a letter to Fiske from Jón Þorkelsson, dated 9
November 1899. In an envelope marked: "titill á Olearii bænir 1687."

34   **Finnur Magnússon,** 1781-1847. *Adversaria excerptoria, &c. Tom. VI-
II.* Undated.

107 leaves, including 12 from *Forordning om Tolden og Kiøbstæd-Consumtionen i Danmark og Norge* (Copenhagen, 1797), inserted and used for notes; portions numbered; 2 blank leaves between 6 and 7. 8 single sheets of notes. Bound in leather, but fragile with loose leaves; 19.2 x 15.2 cm.

Contents: Paleographic extracts, annotations, deciphering of runic inscriptions, etc. Extracts from i.a. A. Brohm, "Geschichte von Polen und Lithauen", Leipzig 1810; Ole Worm, "Wormii Antiqvett. Dan. Litt. Run: 1651"; "Formáli Bárðar Gíslasonar fyrir hans utskíring vandskilinna lagagreina. dat. Vatnsdal i Fljótshlíd 20 jan. 1665"; "Vedkommende Nordisk Tidskrift for Oldkyndighed. 1832"; F. G. Osann, "Midas oder Erklärungs Versuch der erweislich ältesten Griechischen Inschrift etc. von Fr. Osann", Leipzig 1830; "Staats und Gelehrte Zeitung des Hamb. Correspondenten, 28 April 1836 No. 100"; H. E. Thunmann "Om den ældste Preussiske skrift Thunmann Untersuchungen uber die Geschichte einiger Nordische Völker. Berlin 1772"; F. H. W. Gesenius, "Ny Sammenligning mellem Phoenicisk Skrift etc og Runerne, efter Gesenius 1837"; Owen, Druidernes eller Bardernes Brittiske Alphabet efter Owen; E. Ledwich, "Antiqvities of Ireland. Dublin 1796, and more."

The manuscript was bought at the auction of Finnur Magnússon's books (Cat. No. 8) in March 1857, by George Stephens.

Catalogued by Halldór Hermannsson in *Catalogue of Runic Literature. Forming a Part of the Icelandic Collection Bequeathed by Willard Fiske* (London: Oxford University Press, 1918).

35   ____, *Literære Smaa Optegnelser. 1823.* Literary notations in Danish.

62 pages, numbered 23-84, in a brown marbled hardcover notebook; 21.4 x 17.3 cm. Inside front cover in pencil: "Adversaria 16, 1823-1824." White label pasted on front cover with title in brown ink.

The manuscript was bought at the auction of Finnur Magnússon's books (Cat. No. 16) in March 1857, by George Stephens. Cf. inside cover.

Catalogued by Halldór Hermannsson in *Catalogue of the Icelandic Collection Bequeathed by Willard Fiske* (Ithaca: Cornell University Library, 1914).

36   _____, [*Notes and Commentaries in Danish on Interleaved Copy of Herman Wahn's Teutsche Orthographia und Orthotonia*]. Undated.

33 MS leaves, including a preliminary page with information about provenance, unnumbered, bound in leather; 15.1 x 9.3 cm. On preliminary leaf, verso: "Sigurður Þórðarson cand. jur. gaf mér 11/8 85", and signed by Jón Þorkelsson. Furthermore: "NB Allar uppfyllingar á innskotnu blöðunum eru meðh Finns Magnússonar."

The manuscript was bought at the auction of Finnur Magnússon's books (Cat. No. 5) in March 1857, by George Stephens. Cf. preliminary leaf, recto.

Catalogued by Halldór Hermannsson in *Catalogue of the Icelandic Collection Bequeathed by Willard Fiske* (Ithaca: Cornell University Library, 1914).

37   _____, *Over det Aar 1639 fundne danske Guldhorn.* Undated.

3 1/2 folio sheets, partly numbered, marginal notes; 33.7 x 21.3 cm.

Catalogued by Halldór Hermannsson in *Catalogue of Runic Literature. Forming a Part of the Icelandic Collection Bequeathed by Willard Fiske* (London: Oxford University Press, 1918).

38   _____, *Store og gode Handlinger af islandske Republicanere.* 1802.

Separate sheet with title and table of contents; a second title-page: "Store og Gode Handlinger af Danske Norske og Islændere. Förste Hæfte 1802. Crossed out: "Et sidestykke til Etatsraad Mallings Værk."; text pp. 2 (t-p verso)-175, additional folio sheet, written on 3 pages, placed between pp. 116 and 117, apparently replacing pp. 117-118, which are partly crossed out; additional 14 unnumbered pages, 2 single sheets and 2 folded, mainly concerning Greenland. The main text is in seven parts: "Förste Hæfte" p. 2, "Andet Hæfte" p. 21, "Tredie Hæfte" p. 49, "Fierde Hæfte" p. 73, "Femte Hæfte" p. 101, "Siette Hæfte" p. 125, "Syvende Hæfte" p. 149. Unbound; 33 x 21 cm.

Catalogued by Halldór Hermannsson in *Catalogue of the Icelandic Collection Bequeathed by Willard Fiske. Additions 1913-26* (Ithaca: Cornell University Press, 1927).

39   **Fiske, Daniel Willard,** 1831-1904. [*Bibliographical Notations and Desiderata Notes in Icelandic*]. Made sometime between 1885 and 1904.

43 sheets, portions numbered; mainly 22 x 17.2 cm.

40   _____, [*A Bibliography of Icelandic, Scandinavian, French, and German Publications about Iceland and Icelandic Literature*]. 189?

31 sheets of various sizes, mainly 18 x 11 cm sheets, folded. Enclosed are biographical sketches about Hallgrímur Pétursson (ca. 1614-1674), and Jón Þorláksson (1744-1819). Besides Fiske's there are at least two other hands.

41   _____, *Books printed in Iceland 1601-1844 not in the British Museum nor in my collection.*

One sheet, folded, with black borders; 16 x 12.9 cm. Additional single sheet with same title, partly a duplicate of the first 1 1/2 pages of the former.

42   _____, [*Books to be Bound in 1899*]. An index of books sent by Fiske from Copenhagen to London to be bound in the summer and autumn of 1899. Cf. Halldór Hermannsson's note on first pages of each book. The list is in alphabetical order.

2 black hardcover register books, a red label on front covers with "REGISTER" in gold; 35.3 x 21 cm.

43   _____, [*Chess in Scandinavia. A Bibliography*]. Includes biographical sketches of authors. Enclosed: 1 postcard to Halldór Hermannsson from Fiske; a pencil drawing of three men playing chess; a typewritten letter from John G. White (a lawyer from Cleveland, Ohio) dated 10 April 1902, concerning the Alphonsine Treatise; a typewritten copy in Spanish relating to Albuquerque.

219 sheets (mainly unlined sheets, folded); some pagination; 22.6 x 17.7 cm. Enclosed: a list of books from Hallgrímur Melsteð, National Library of Iceland, dated 8 April 1900; one sheet. Fiske's and Halldór Hermannsson's handwriting, ca. 1899-1904. This was intended as a second volume of *Chess in Iceland*, but was never published.

44   _____, [*Diary I*]. Written by Fiske in 1850 in Copenhagen. On preliminary page: "Bought in Syracuse. Brought to Copenhagen."

(1), 14 leaves, unnumbered, some leaves excised; in a variously colored
marbled folio notebook with brown spine; 30.8 x 19.2 cm.

Contents: Diary from November 1850; glossary of Icelandic words;
copy of an introductory letter from J[ames] J[ohn] G[arth] Wilkinson to
Thomas Carlyle, on behalf of Fiske, dated 7 August 1850.

45   ____, [*Diary II*]. Written in English and Swedish by Fiske in August
and September 1851, during his stay in Stockholm and Uppsala,
Sweden. Includes a list of Icelandic publications, and 4 sheets of Latin
exercises.

       14 unnumbered leaves in a purple hardcover notebook (and 27
blank); 20.4 x 16.7 cm. 4 additional single sheets.

46   ____, [*English-Icelandic Dictionary*]. Materials for an English-
Icelandic dictionary based upon F. W. Thieme's "Pocket-dictionary of
the English and German languages, 7th edition, Berlin, 1844," which is
inserted between the MS.-leaves. The fly-leaf has the signature and
date: "Daniel W. Fisk [sic] Stockholm, September 1st, 1851."

184 leaves, folio.

Catalogued by Halldór Hermannsson in *Catalogue of the Icelandic
Collection Bequeathed by Willard Fiske* (Ithaca: Cornell University
Library, 1914).

47   ____, *Icelandic Bibliography. Exclusive of the authorities cited in the
British Museum Catalogue.* A list of bibliographies and catalogues that
deal with books on Icelandic and Old Norse literature, manuscripts, and
authors. 1885-1904.

37 sheets of various different sizes, chiefly 22.2 x 17.8 cm. Only a small
portion is numbered. Includes another manuscript of 11 numbered
leaves, written on recto, but with occasional additions and comments on
verso. The second manuscript bears the title *Rit þess íslenzka
Lærdómslista fjelags.* A list of books and periodicals owned by the
Society.

The former manuscript is in Fiske's handwriting. The latter has the
name Stefán Stefánsson on the last page, and the address, Regensen 4-
12, Köbenhavn.

48   ____, [*The Icelandic Catalogue*]. Notes by Fiske on his Icelandic Catalogue. [189?]

2 different sheets, one of which has the heading "Notes."

49   ____, *Ein Isländisches Schachbuch.* Fiske's manuscript for his article in *Deutsche Schachzeitung* 35 Jahrgang. (Leipzig, 1880), pp. 129-134. The book referred to is Jósef Grímsson's *Spilabók* (Akureyri, 1858). The manuscript is dated at the end: "Berlin, am 4. December 1879."

23 sheets, a strip of paper pasted on the last one. Written in ink on one side only, a pencil remark on 1st page, sheets numbered 1-16 (and 1a-b, 7a-c, 10a, 12a); 22.2 x 17.1 cm.

50   ____, [*Miscellaneous Notes in English and Swedish*].

One sheet, 2 cards, and an envelope used for notes; probably written in 1899. Cf. Halldór Hermannsson's comment on the envelope.

51   ____, *Mr. D. W. Fiske's Collection.* An article about Fiske's collection of Icelandic books and books on chess. The article was published in *New York Evening Post*, April 27, 1857, under the heading *Private Libraries of New York. No. XXII.*

8 typewritten carbon copy sheets, numbered; 28 x 21.6 cm. In grey cardboard with brown spine, white label on front cover with title written in ink. Inserted: a letter from H. S. White to Halldór Hermannsson concerning the article, dated 23 June 1918. White suggests in the letter that the article was written by Fiske himself.

52   ____, [*Natural History of Iceland*]. Bibliographical notes about the natural history of Iceland. Undated, but the last publication year noted is 1894.

7 sheets; 17.3 x 10.3 cm.

53   ____, [*Notebooks*].

48 different notebooks in English and Icelandic, ranging from 13 x 7.8 cm to 20.8 x 13 cm in size; written in both ink and pencil; also 63 sheets of various sizes and 34 index cards.

1-18) Bibliographical notations of Icelandic books. Notebooks numbered I-XVIII on labels pasted on front covers. I) purple hardcover. II-IV, VI-VIII, X-XI, XV-XVIII) black soft cover. V) green soft cover. IX) maroon soft cover. XII) red soft cover. XIII) black hardcover. XIV) purple hardcover. Index to the first 15 notebooks on the 34 index cards. 15 pieces of paper enclosed in books II, VI, XII, and XIII.

19-21) 3 yellow marbled hardcover notebooks, blue fore-edges, two with brown spine and corners, and one with green. Marked A, B, and C on white labels pasted on upper left side of front covers. A contains 17 numbered leaves of bibliographical notations and an index of titles on 2 preliminary sheets, which are inserted. B and C give records of books belonging to different farms in the north-eastern part of Iceland, occasionally with detailed descriptions of title-pages. At the top of B's first page: "from B. H. of Laufás", and C's: "Laufás book by Björn Halldórsson continued." The Reverend Björn Halldórsson from Laufás (1823-1882) may have met Fiske in the summer 1879. Fiske must have copied the records from his documents. Enclosed in C is a title-page of the tenth edition of Hallgrímur Pétursson's "Pijslar-Psal[mar]." The page is fragile and edges tattered.

22) Blue and pink marbled hardcover notebook with red fore-edge, unpaginated, some blank. The largest part deals with Petrarch material, but also with Icelandic bibliography and "Books printed in Iceland 1601-1844 not in the British Mus*eum* nor in my collection". The notebook is from about 1889.

23) Black soft cover address book with marbled fore-edge, "ADRESS-ES" printed on front cover in gold, unpaginated, some blank. Fiske started here a subject index to books in Icelandic and about Iceland.

24) A list of Icelandic addressees to whom Fiske sent chess material, listed in alphabetical order. A black soft cover indexed book with gilded fore-edge, "Where is it!" printed in gold on front cover. Unpaginated, some blank.

25) A list of Icelandic authors with dates of birth and death, and a number following each name, possibly cataloguing numbers from Fiske's collection; alphabetically listed. Black soft cover indexed book, fore-edge marbled, "Where is it!" in gold on front cover. Unpaginated.

26) A list of Norwegian publications on Old Norse, Norwegian history, literature, and language; also some memoranda. Black soft cover notebook, fore-edge marbled. Unpaginated, a few blank pages.

27-28) The first is a black soft cover notebook with red fore-edge, only few pages used, and the second a reddish marbled paper cover notebook; both unpaginated. A list of publications dealing with runic material. No. 28 includes addresses of Sigfús Blöndal and J. C. Poestion inside front cover.

29-30) Black soft cover notebooks, red fore-edges, both unpaginated. Bibliographical queries, not in Fiske's handwriting. No. 30 gives also a list of names, pseudonyms, Latin forms of Icelandic names, etc.

31) References to articles in newspapers and periodicals, mostly Danish, but also Icelandic and Norwegian in a black soft cover indexed book with red fore-edge, unpaginated, only partly used.

32-38) Bibliographical notations and desiderata lists of books in Icelandic and about Iceland. The publications mentioned are mostly from the 1890s and around 1900. No. 33 has cover title: "Works wanted. Parts of works lacking." One sheet, folded, pasted to the back cover of 33. No. 38 has written on endpaper: "W. F. Hovedvagtsgade 2/I juli 1899", and on back endpaper is a list of few names and addresses in Copenhagen. Black soft cover notebooks, some indexed, except No. 36 which is a green paper cover notebook and 38 which is a red soft cover book.

39-41) Lists of names, addresses, authors, and titles in three variously colored marbled paper cover notebooks, indexed; red labels on front covers with "Rubrica" in gilded letters.

42) List of names and addresses, and bibliographical notations in a black and white cross-hatched soft cover notebook with red fore-edge. In pencil, unpaginated.

43) Notes on books in one of Fiske's collections after his death. Black soft cover notebook, red fore-edge, white label on front cover: "List of Professo[r] Fiske's Books." Only partly used, unpaginated.

44) "Catalogue rules" in a thin dark-blue soft cover notebook; title on white label on front cover; only partly used, unpaginated.

45-49) 5 volumes of Icelandic words alphabetically listed (a — fyndni), apparently as a bases for a dictionary. Dark hardcover books, marbled fore-edge, leaves blue; unpaginated.

50) 46 loose sheets of various sizes, including 8 postcards; with bibliographical notations and desiderata lists.

Most of the notebooks are in Fiske's hand, but a few in Halldór Hermannsson's hand and possibly Bjarni Jónsson's.

54   ____, *Origin of Chess.* Fiske's manuscript of his *Chess in Iceland and in Icelandic Literature with Historical Notes on Other Table-games* (Florence, 1905). Various other material regarding chess and the publication, both handwritten (various hands), and typewritten; in English, Italian, and Swedish.

343 sheets of various sizes, mainly 21.9 x 17.5 and 22.2 x 17.6 cm; some pagination. Most of the text is written on recto, with additions and remarks on verso. Also a red soft cover notebook with marbled fore-edge and a white label on front cover with the title handwritten. 6 sheets enclosed.

Contents: About origin of chess; the preface to Chess in Iceland (12 sheets, handwritten by Fiske, Horace White, and typewritten); "Tables and Hnefatafl"; "Riddles and Proverbs" about chess; "Back-gammon" (26 sheets, handwritten and typed); "Hand-Bibliothek för Sällskapsnöjen eller Systematiskt ordnade spel, lekar och konster. Andra delen. Figurspel. Stockholm, hos L. J. Hjerta. 1839" (a duplicated copy of 34 sheets, 26.5 x 21.2 cm, with handwritten remarks); "From: "Sveriges medeltid, kulturhistorisk skildring af Hans Hildebrand. II. Delen. Stockholm 1884-98." pag. 501-510 (10 sheets, handwritten with notes by Fiske, and various other material about chess and the publication of *Chess in Iceland*. A letter to Halldór Hermannsson from A. J. W. Mollerup (1846-1917), at the National Museum in Copenhagen, dated 12 Febr. 1902, enclosed is a transcript of "National Museets Protokoller", i.e., a description of medieval chess-pieces in the museum, 34.3 x 21.1 cm; two letters to Fiske from Halldór Hermannsson, regarding chess and the publication of *Chess in Iceland*, dated 12 Febr. 1902 and 21 Sept. 1904; extracts from letters of Fiske to J. G. White about chess-matters; one stamped envelope.

55   ____, Review of *"Viking Tales of the North. The Sagas of Thorstein Viking's Son, and Fridthjof the Bold. Translated from the Icelandic by Rasmus B. Anderson, and Jón Bjarnason. Also Tegnérs Fridthjof's Saga, translated into English by George Stephens. Chicago. S. C. Griggs + Co. 1877. 8°. pp. xvi, 370. 2. Fridthjof's Saga, a Norse Romance, by Esaias Tegnér, Bishop of Wexiö. Translated from the Swedish by Thomas A. E. Holcomb and Martha A. Lyon Holcomb. Chicago: S. C. Griggs + Co. 1877. 8°. pp. vi, 213."*

9 numbered sheets; 20 x 12.5 cm.

56   ____, [*Travels through Iceland*]. Notes from Fiske's travels in Iceland in the summer of 1879, bibliographical information about Icelandic books, obituary inscriptions from gravestones (Skagafjörður district), etc.

57 unnumbered leaves in a dark-blue soft cover notebook, red fore-

edge; a pocket inside back cover; in pencil; 14.8 x 8.9 cm. Written on insides of front and back cover. 2 additional sheets.

Based on this notebook is *Willard Fiske in Iceland,* edited by P. M. Mitchell (Ithaca: Cornell University Library, 1989).

57   ***Genealogy.*** Fragment of a genealogy in Latin from the early nineteenth century. One sheet only.

Gibbons saga og Greka. See ***Ýmsar sögur.***

58   **Guðmundur Jónsson,** 1763-1836. *Safn af ÍSLENZKUM ORÐSKVIÐUM. FORNMÆLUM, HEILRÆÐUM, SNILLIYRÐUM, SANNMÆLUM og MÁLS-GREINUM, Samanlesið og í stafrofsröð sett af Guðmundi Jónssyni. (= Gudmund Jónsson) Prófasti i Snæfellsness-sýslu og Presti í Stáðarstaðar sókn. Útgefið að tilhlutan Hins íslenzka Bókmennta-Félags. Kaupmannahöfn, 1830. Prentað hjá S. L. Møller.* MS copy of the edition of 1830 with translation or equivalent of the proverbs in Swedish. [Around 1869].

421 leaves, paginated from page 21, where main text starts; 26 x 21 cm. "Fortale" in Danish by B. Thorsteinsson, Stappen i Island 1823, "Formáli" by the author, dated Staðastað þann 10 Júlíí 1823, and the title-page are on 16 unpaginated pages, preceding main text; 21 x 17.3 cm. Bound in blue marbled hardcover, with brown spine; on spine is written in gilded letters: "G. Johnsson. Isländska Ordspråk"; the book is written in two columns, on left in Icelandic and on right in Swedish translation; inside front cover: K. Strömbäck 1869, and same name is written on flyleaf recto; on flyleaf verso: "Isländska Uttalet", and a phonological list of Icelandic characters. According to Halldór Hermannsson many corrections and additions in the MS are by Kasper Strömbäck.

Catalogued by Halldór Hermannsson in *Catalogue of the Icelandic Collection Bequeathed by Willard Fiske* (Ithaca: Cornell University Library, 1914).

59   ***Guli snepillinn.*** A reproduction of a note quoted below, signed by the initials V. G. The note was sent to members of the Icelandic parliament with a letter written 8 April 1896 by Valtýr Guðmundsson. See "Guli snepillinn", *Dagskrá* 31 July and 1 August 1897.

The note goes as follows: "Þess skal getið, að jeg þori að fullyrða, að landshöfðingi Magnús Stephensen yrði <u>ekki</u> skipaður ráðgjafi þó til kæmi, og óvíst hvort hann yrði einu sinni spurður til ráða um það, hvern ætti að setja yfir hann. V. G."

The note is pasted on stiff board 10.2 x 8.3 cm; title written on verso. With an envelope addressed to Mr. Fiske, stamped 1901 in Sout[…].

Gunlögsen, B. H. S. See **Bertel (Stefánsson) Gunnlaugsson.**

60   **Hallgrímur Jónsson,** 1780-1836. *Uppteiknunar Tilraun Islendskra Skálda og Rithöfunda. Med stuttu Ágripi af Æfi nockurra þeirra, 1824. samin af Hallgrími Jónssyni Djákna til Þingeyra klausturs.* 1824.

A holograph manuscript with many notes and additions in the margin. The work contains a biographical sketch of every author and a list of his works published and unpublished. The introduction is dated "Sveinsst. þan*n* 18da Maii 1824", and signed by the author.

384 pages, and 16 additional slips with notes by the author and others; 2 leaves from a printed book in Latin tipped in before title-page and other 2 at the very end, with notes handwritten by the author; fore-edge tattered; bound in leather; 21.7 x 16.7 cm.

Contents: Title-page; "Skammstafanir", p. 2; "Formali", pp. 2-4; "Fyrir sidaskiptin", pp. 1-31; "Skald og ritsmidir eptir sidaskiptin", pp. 31-244; "addenda", pp. 245-384. Pagination starts after Formali.

Catalogued by Halldór Hermannsson in *Catalogue of the Icelandic Collection Bequeathed by Willard Fiske* (Ithaca: Cornell University Library, 1914).

An extract from this work was made by Halldór Hermannsson, with comments and notes. See Halldór Hermannsson, *Útdráttur úr Rithöfundatali Hallgríms Jónssonar.*

61   **Hart, James Morgan,** 1839-1916. [*Glossary Notes in English on Old Icelandic Language and Literature, Mainly the Eddic Poems*]. Undated.

91 sheets of miscellaneous sizes, some of which are colored.

Hermóðs saga og Háðvarar. See ***Ýmsar sögur.***

62   [*Iceland*]. Notes made apparently by a traveller; about Iceland, Icelanders, nature, literature, etc. One sheet only, written on both sides; undated; in English.

63   [*Icelandic Catalogues of Books and Manuscripts*].

63 sheets, mostly folio sheets, folded.

1) A list of a manuscript collection (73 titles) owned by Valdimar Ásmundsson (1852-1902), teacher and editor of the journal *Fjallkonan*. 10 paginated sheets of a duplicated typewritten copy, with additional information handwritten; 33.7 x 20.9 cm. Enclosed is a letter from Sæmundur Bjarnhéðinsson, his brother-in-law, dated 19 November 1910. The letter is written on behalf of Ásmundsson's widow, Bríet Bjarnhéðinsdóttir, offering Halldór Hermannsson the manuscripts for sale.

2) "Bækur mjer sendar tilh. dánarbúi Jónas*ar* Hallgrímssonar prófasts:" A handwritten list of 22 rare books and 7 manuscripts, dated: "Rvík 27/10 '15", and signed by Björn M. Ólsen. One sheet, folded; 16.8 x 12.9 cm. The owner of the collection was the Reverend Jónas (Pétur) Hallgrímsson (1846-1914) from Kolfreyjustaður in Suður-Múlasýsla. Halldór Hermannsson wrote 31 December 1915 asking for 9 books from the list. Cf. pencil remarks on the list. Enclosed: invoice of same to Cornell University Library, 16 March 1916.

3) "Skrá yfir bækur sendar Rosenthal." A handwritten list of 35 books, undated and unsigned. 1 folio sheet, folded; 33.4 x 21.2 cm. At end is written in pencil: "NB. Líklega koma bækurnar ekki hjéðanaf en/ef það verður þá skal jeg strax gera yður aðvart."

4) "Commissionær: B. M. Ólsen"; added in pencil: "Bækur Síra J. K. Briem í Hruna?", i.e., the Reverend Jóhann (Kristján) Briem (Gunnlaugsson) from Hruni (1818-1894). A list of 77 books and 5 manuscripts, handwritten in ink, additions in pencil. 1 folio sheet, folded; 32.9 x 20.2 cm.

5) "CATALOGUE of books from the library of the deceased scholar Arnljótur Ólafsson [1823-1904]. The books will be sold by public auction at Reykjavík. Sept. 28th 1912." 11 folio sheets of a duplicated copy (a list of 284 titles), occasional check-marks in pencil (possibly titles of interest to Halldór Hermannsson); 36.2 x 22.4 cm.

6) "Lítilfjörleg upptalning a handritum mínum", dated: "Bægisá 3/1 1890." A handwritten list of 45 books and 14 manuscripts. 3 numbered sheets, folded; 21 x 17 cm.

7) "Yfirlit yfir þær íslenzkar bækur og aðrar, er að Íslandi lúta, sem Jón Árnason [1819-1888] í Reykjavík vill láta falar." On top is written in pencil: "c. 1879." 11 handwritten sheets, folded; 34.2 x 20.5 cm. The list is divided into sections: "Guðfræðibækur, Bibliusaga, Trúarfræði, Siðafræði, Sálmabækur og andleg kvæði, Prédikanir, Lögfræði og stjórnfræði, Læknisfræði, Náttúruvísindi, Stærðafræði, Skáldskaparrit, Heimsspeki, Sagnfræði, Lifes and epitaphs of distinct eminent men in Iceland. In 7 volumes, Old sagas (histories) on Norway, Historical works on other countries, Búnaðarrit, Málfræði, Menningarrit, rit ýmislegs efnis, Tímarit, Skýrslur, bókaregistur o.fl."

8) "Skrá yfir ýmsar gamlar bækur." A list of 28 titles, undated and unsigned. 1 folio sheet, folded; 35.2 x 23.4 cm.

9) "Bókaskrá. (Dánarbú H[alldórs] Kr[istjáns] Friðrikssonar, yfirkennara)" (1819-1902). A handwritten list of 414 titles; occasional checkmarks in blue or red pencil, additions in pencil; 10 folio sheets, 8 numbered I-XXXII, and two unnumbered; 36 x 23.1 cm.

10) An undated handwritten list of 166 titles. 2 sheets; 35.4 x 23.1 cm.

11) "List of Icelandic Books." An undated handwritten list of 35 titles, with prices. One sheet.

12) List of publications, one dated: 11 February 1900; a desiderata list. 8 sheets of various sizes.

13) "Bækur sendar Professor W. Fiske frá Stiptsbókasafni Íslands." A handwritten list of 14 titles, undated. One sheet, folded.

See additional catalogues with letters from Björn M. Ólsen.

64   [*Icelandic Colony in Alaska*]. A copy of a letter to President Grant regarding immigration of Icelanders to Alaska and a possible establishment of an Icelandic colony there. The letter was originally written in Icelandic but translated into English. It is dated 2 August 1874 and signed by 43 Icelanders.

4 sheets, unnumbered; 31.6 x 20.2 cm.

Sent to Halldór Hermannsson by J. Christian Bay, Librarian of the John Crerar Library in Chicago. Included is a typewritten letter from Bay, dated 31 August 1939.

Jarlmanns saga. See *Ýmsar sögur.*

65   **Jón Borgfirðingur [Jónsson],** 1826-1912. *Fáeinar athugasemdir við*

prentsmiðju sögu Íslands. Notes and additions to his *Söguágrip um prentsmiðjur og prentara á Íslandi* (Reykjavík, 1867). Dated at end: Reykjavík 30 September 1879, and signed by the author.

7 leaves, unnumbered (title-page 1r, text starts 1v); blue leaves before and at the end of MS., on the first is written: Hr. Prófessor W. Fiske; 17.8 x 11 cm. Bound with the publication. Given to Fiske by the author.

Catalogued by Halldór Hermannsson in *Catalogue of the Icelandic Collection Bequeathed by Willard Fiske* (Ithaca: Cornell University Library, 1914).

66   ____, *Íslenzk bókmennta saga frá 1400-1878. í stuttu máli ritin, af Jóni Borgfirðing*. Contains Jón Borgfirðing's first draft of *Stutt rithöfundatal á Íslandi 1400-1882*, published in Reykjavík in 1884. On preliminary leaf, inserted: "Uppkast í fáeinum púntum til bókmenntasögu Íslands. Jón Borgfirðingur." At end: "Óleiðrjett uppkast. Endað 8. april 1878."

(1), title-page, 66 pages, and 5 inserted leaves with notes; marginal notes; bound in variously colored marbled hardcover, with red spine and corners; 33 x 20 cm. On spine in gilded letters: Jón Borgfirðingur. — Uppkast til Bókmenntasögu. — Author's MS.

Catalogued by Halldór Hermannsson in *Catalogue of the Icelandic Collection Bequeathed by Willard Fiske* (Ithaca: Cornell University Library, 1914).

67   ____, *Nýir rithöfundar*. A list of Icelandic authors. [Not before 1881].

3 blue sheets.

68   **Jón A[ndrésson] Hjaltalín,** 1840-1908. *The Saga of Iceland. An account of Iceland's golden age by a native scholar. True story of the island's discovery and colonization. The ancient republic, its heroes, its skalds and its sagamen. How the Icelanders themselves look at the millenial and the new Constitution.*

62 numbered sheets, written on recto only; 20.2 x 12.5 cm. An envelope with information about the work written on the front side by Halldór Hermannsson: "(This is a Ms. of the pamphlet: The thousandth Anniversary of the Norwegian settlement in Iceland. Reykjavík, 1874. It is in the handwriting of Mr. Geo. Wm. Harris, except the heading and

the signature, which is written by Mr. Fiske. This Ms. differs slightly
from the printed work, and presumably the changes are due to Mr.
Fiske). H. H."

69   _____, *The Thousandth anniversary of the Norwegian Settlement in
      Iceland.* Written between 1871 and 1879.

34 pages, mainly on folded sheets; written in ink, on recto only; unbound; 20.7 x 13.2 cm. Written while the author was an Assistant
Librarian at the Advocates Library in Edinburgh (1871-1879). This is a
holograph of a work published in Reykjavík in 1874.

Catalogued by Halldór Hermannsson in *Catalogue of the Icelandic
Collection Bequeathed by Willard Fiske* (Ithaca: Cornell University
Library, 1914).

70   **Jón [Jónsson] Norðmann,** 1820-1877. *Grímseyjar lýsing.* A transcript
      from ÍB 21, fol. in the National Library of Iceland. Included is another
      transcript from the same manuscript: **Magnús Jónsson,** 1809-1889.
      Grímsey. Both essays describe the island Grímsey. The former includes
      an index. Transcribed 1901.

28, and 18 paginated pages (the rest is blank); title-pages are blank verso; 22.2 x 17.7 cm. Grey paper cover notebook bound in grey cardboard
with green spine. On white label on front cover: "Jón Jónsson: lýsing
Grímseyjar."

The Reverend Jón Norðmann served Grímsey district in the years 1846-
1849, and the Reverend Magnús Jónsson in the years 1838-1841. The
manuscripts were transcribed in Copenhagen 1901 by Bjarni Jónsson,
an assistant to Fiske.

Catalogued by Halldór Hermannsson in *Catalogue of the Icelandic
Collection Bequeathed by Willard Fiske. Additions 1913-26* (Ithaca:
Cornell University Press, 1927).

71   **Jørgensen, Jørgen,** 1780-1841. *Enghien and Adelaide a Tragedy in 5
      Acts by Jorgen Jorgensen a Dane.* [Before 1841]

56 leaves, unnumbered; 3 blank leaves preceding title-page; 4 blank
leaves at end of text; bound in red leather with gilded borders on both
front and back cover besides inside the covers; on front cover in gilded

letters: "E.L. XVIII", and on spine "Enghien and Adelaide"; flyleaves dressed in green cloth with gilded borders; a dedication on page following the title-page: "To His most Christian Majesty Louis XVIII King of France and Navarre"; undated; 21.3 x 16.2 cm.

Contents: Title-page 1r; Dedication 2r; Advertisement, signed at end by the author, 3r-7r; Dramatis Personæ 7v; text: Act.1. - Act.5 8r-56r.

Catalogued by Halldór Hermannsson in *Catalogue of the Icelandic Collection Bequeathed by Willard Fiske* (Ithaca: Cornell University Library, 1914).

Konráðs saga keisarasonar. See **Ýmsar sögur.**

72   ***Kveðjusending frá Grímseyingum til herra V. Fiske's í Flórenz.***
A poem in Icelandic from the inhabitants of Grímsey to honor Fiske. A few lines are missing. Dated 24 December 1900. Copied by Fiske. The name A. Þorkelsson is stamped on the sheet in blue, possibly Árni Þorkelsson, Overseer of Grímsey (ca. 1827-1901). One sheet only. Björn M. Ólsen mentions a poem by Árni Þorkelsson in a letter to Fiske, dated 31 March 1901.

Luckunnar knattleikur. See **Ýmsar sögur.**

Magnús Jónsson. See **Jón Norðmann.**

73   **Magnús Stephensen,** 1762-1833. *Nogle Anmærkninger samt de vigtig-ste Varianter til den Islandske Lovbogs, Jonsbogens Text samt Forklaringer af mörke Ord og Perioder ï samme ved Dr. M. Stephensen. Efter de fortrinligste Afskrivters paa Pergamen[t] og paa Papïr nöie Sammenhold med trykte Udgaven af denne Lovbog samlede og nedskrevne ved Dr. J. Magnus Stephensen conferense-raad og Justitiarius ï den kgle isl. Land... Medlem af adskillige lærde Selskaber.* Commentaries and annotations in Danish and Icelandic of the Icelandic law-book, *Jónsbók.*

130 leaves, unnumbered and unbound, fore-edge tattered, undated; 21 x 16 cm. A holograph. A note by Halldór Hermannsson concerning provenance, one sheet: "Þetta eiginhandarrit Magnúsar konferensráðs Stephensens af athugasemdum og skýringum við Jónsbók var í eign föður míns, sýslumanns Herm. E. Johnson's og gef ég það hérmeð Landsbókasafninu. 24. ágúst 1921" signed by Halldór Hermannsson.

[Underlined is crossed out]. This manuscript belonged to Hermann E. Johnsson (1825-1894), Halldór Hermannsson's father.

74   **Matthías Jochumsson, the Rev.,** 1835-1920. [*Beitilyng*]. Ca. 1880. A piece of paper, made into a pocket, holding a dried "beitilyng" (ling or Calluna vulgaris). Addressed to Mrs. Fiske from Matthías Jochumsson with an inscription in ink: "Ást fylgir aums giøfum." Inserted in his book *Víg Snorra Sturlusonar. Kvæði eptir Matthías Jochumsson.* 2nd ed. (Eskifjörður: á kostnað Jóns Ólafssonar, 1879).

75   [*Maurer, Konrad von. Frederick I — Ueber ein Islandisches Lied auf Kaiser Friedrich den Rothbart*]. Some marginal notes to the poem in pencil, and 1 leaf pasted inside back cover with glossary notes in Icelandic and German, dated 4 March 1868.

The book belonged to the Zarncke Library.

76   **Munch, P[eter] A[ndreas],** 1810-1863. *Runic Inscriptions in the Isle of Man and the Hebrides, communicated by P. A. Munch.* Adapted from P. A. Munch's *Runic inscriptions in Sodor and Man.* In *Mém. Soc. Roy. Ant. du Nord.* III. 1845-49, pp. 192-208.

8 leaves marked 1-4, last page blank; written in ink by an unknown hand.

5 leaves of same kind of paper, in same hand. 1r: *Royal Society of Northern Antiquaries at Copenhagen.* Listing new members in 1847-50. 1v-5r: *The Ante-Columbian History of America.* On Rafn's work *Antiquitates Americanæ,* published by the Society in 1837.

77   **Münter, Friedrich.** [*Notes on "Die Odinische Religion. Aus D. Stäudlins und D. Tzschirners Archiv für alte und neue Kirchengeschichte 5n Bdes 1s St. besonders abgedruckt" [Leipzig], 1821*].

Interleaved copy, with 24 manuscript notes by the author. On interleaves: 5, 23, 26-7, 29, 32, 40-44, 47, 57, 61, 68, 70, 79, 100, 108, and 112. Corrections in margin and between lines: 8, 16-17, 21, 23, 44, 46, 51, 56, 63, 79, 80, 81-2, 103, 107-8, and 110.

Catalogued by Halldór Hermannsson *Catalogue of the Icelandic Collection Bequeathed by Willard Fiske* (Ithaca: Cornell University Library, 1914).

Nikiða saga frægu. See *Ýmsar sögur.*

78   **Ólafur Davíðsson,** 1862-1903. [*A list of Scandinavian periodicals
     through ca. 1890, with a subject index of Old Norse and Icelandic mate-
     rial they published*].

     255 sheets and strips of paper, portions numbered, unbound.

     Sent to Fiske by the author. Cf. his letters of 15 March 1892 and 16
     May 1892. See also with letters from Ólafur Davíðsson to Daniel
     Willard Fiske: "Áætlun um hvernig haga ætti íslenzku rithöfundatali,
     ritatali og skrá yfir útlend rit, sem snerta Ísland."

79   ____, [*Skagfirðingavísur*]. A handwritten note on the title of *Skagfirð-
     ingavísur* by Gísli Brynjúlfsson.

     One sheet inserted in Gísli Brynjúlfsson's *Miscellanea,* compiled by
     Halldór Hermannsson and catalogued in *Catalogue of the Icelandic
     Collection Bequeathed by Willard Fiske* (Ithaca: Cornell University
     Library, 1914).

80   [*Old Norse Mythology*]. A list of Old Norse mythological names with
     explanations in Danish.

     3 leaves, written on both sides, paginated, fastened with a thread.
     Enclosed in a pocket pasted on the back cover of N. M. Petersen,
     Nordisk Mythologi (Copenhagen, 1849).

81   **Rafn, Carl Christian,** 1795-1864. [*Correspondence*]. Copies of unpub-
     lished letters from and to C. C. Rafn together with other documents re-
     lating to him. Correspondents are i.a. O. M. Schiötz, Ove Höegh
     Guldberg, R. Nyerup, Bjarni Thorlacius, Finnur Magnússon, Rasmus
     Rask, Sveinbjörn Egilsson, John Russell Bartlett, and D. Willard Fiske.
     The MS contains also Rafn's genealogy, sections from his diary, his last
     wishes, a printed obituary poem by Benedikt Gröndal, photographs
     mounted on stiff paper preceding text: of Rafn's birthplace, Brahesborg,
     Funen; of a portrait of Rafn as a boy, painted by his father; of a portrait
     of Rafn; of his study in Kronprindsensgade, Copenhagen.

     152 leaves (2), unnumbered; 23.6 x 18.5 cm. 4 photographs. Bound in
     leather with gilt border ornamentation on cover and spine; "C. C. Rafn"
     in gilt script on red plate on spine. Compiled by Rafn's daughters,

Caroline and Dagmar, and presented to Fiske. Cf. a letter from Dagmar Rafn, 21 November 1894.

Catalogued by Halldór Hermannsson in *Catalogue of the Icelandic Collection Bequeathed by Willard Fiske* (Ithaca: Cornell University Library, 1914).

Rémundar saga og Melusine. See ***Ýmsar sögur.***

82   **Richert, Mårten Birger,** 1837-1886. *Anteckningar vid Doc. Richerts Föreläsningar öfver Eddan. Höstterminen 1869. O. E. Arbman.* Notes on Mårten Birger Richert's lectures on the Eddic poems: *Grípisspá, Reginsmál,* and *Fáfnismál.*

Title-page, 10 unlined paginated pages in a brown and black patterned hardcover notebook with blue spine; some blank at the end. White label on front cover with title in ink; 16.7 x 10.5 cm.

The manuscript was bought 3 April 1920 from the booksellers Björck och Börjeson, Stockholm, Sweden.

Catalogued by Halldór Hermannsson in *Catalogue of the Icelandic Collection Bequeathed by Willard Fiske. Additions 1913-26* (Ithaca: Cornell University Press 1927).

Rit þess íslenzka Lærdómslista fjelags. See **Fiske, Daniel Willard.** *Icelandic Bibliography.*

83   **[*Scandinavian Mythology*].** A list of some work dealing with Scandinavian mythology published between 1808-1864.

A sheet inserted in front of the title-page of *Nordische Mythologie nach den Quellen bearbeitet und systematisch zusammengestellt* by Carl Ernst Hachmeister (Hannover: in Commission der Hahnschen Hofbuchhandlung, 1832). On recto is written "Hinrichs? 1832", possibly the owner of the book.

Sigurðar saga fóts og Ásmundar Húnakongs. See ***Ýmsar sögur.***

Sigurðar saga gangandi. See ***Ýmsar sögur.***

Sigurðar saga turnara. See ***Ýmsar sögur.***

Sigurgarðs saga frækna. See *Ýmsar sögur.*

84   [*Skúli Þórðarson Thorlacius. Antiqvitatum Borealium observationes miscellaneæ*]. Comments, translations, and notes to this work of Skúli Thorlacius, in English, Swedish, Icelandic, and Latin, by an unidentified hand. [18—].

3 pages of handwritten notes tipped in before the title-page of vol. v. In same volume notes in margin and between lines: pp. 14, 16, 18, 26-28, 32-34, 40, 42-44, and 46-47. 2 pages before title-page of vol. vi, and in margin: pp. v-vi, 10, 16, 43, 45, 51, and 59. In vol. vii: pp. xi-xii, xv, 2, 6, 36, 38, 54, and 138.

85   [*Thunmann, Johann Erich*]. Nineteenth-century notes in German; illegible hand. Written in ink on the inside of the back cover of M. Johann Thunmann's *Untersuchungen über die alte Geschichte einiger Nordischen Völker* (Berlin: Im Verlag der Buchhandlung der Realschule, 1772).

86   [*Uhland, Ludwig, Der Mythus von Thór*]. After 1836. Handwritten table of contents by an unidentified hand, tipped in before title-page of Ludwig Uhland, *Der Mythus von Thór* (Stuttgart und Augsburg, 1836). At the top of the leaf is written the name Ludwig Frauer. Also marginal notes in red ink to pp. 65-68.

Valdimars saga kóngssonar. See *Ýmsar sögur.*

87   **Verner, Karl [Adolf]**, 1846-1896. [*Notations*]. Notations in the several Germanic languages inserted in *Oldnordisk Ordbog ved det kongelige nordiske Oldskrift-Selskab af Erik Jonsson* (Copenhagen, 1860). 1863.

The Old Norse dictionary is bound in 2 volumes with 207 and 196 interleaved notes by Professor Karl Verner, and his autograph on the flyleaf of volume 1, dated 1863; 22.2 x 14 cm.

Catalogued by Halldór Hermannsson in *Catalogue of the Icelandic Collection Bequeathed by Willard Fiske* (Ithaca: Cornell University Library, 1914).

Vilmundar saga viðutans. See *Ýmsar sögur.*

88   [*Völuspá*]. *Analysis of the Völuspá. I.* Ca. 1875. A glossary on words of

Völuspá, with English translations. Possibly by a student of Fiske. The edition used is *Norræn fornkvæði. Almindelig kaldet Sæmundar Edda hins fróða* Ed. Sophus Bugge (Christiania, 1867).

(1), 47 unnumbered leaves in a green and brownish marbled hardcover notebook with black spine; white label on front cover with title in brown ink; 20.1 x 16 cm. The text is written in English and Icelandic on recto, with occasional additions and comments on verso. The leaf preceding text has some notes verso.

Catalogued by Halldór Hermannsson in *Catalogue of the Icelandic Collection Bequeathed by Willard Fiske* (Ithaca: Cornell University Library, 1914).

89 **Weitberg, C. F.** *Florens.* 1882. A poem of four stanzas in Swedish. One sheet, folded.

90 [*Ýmsar sögur*]. 1824. Various Icelandic Romances: *Jarlmanns saga; Konráðs saga keisarasonar; Ambales saga kongs; Vilmundar saga viðutans,* incomplete (only 8 lines existing); *Sigurgarðs saga frækna; Þorsteins saga bæjarmagns; Hermóðs saga og Háðvarar; Sigurðar saga gangandi; Sigurðar saga fóts og Ásmundar Húnakongs; Nikiða saga frægu,* ch. 4-6 are missing; *Valdimars saga kóngssonar,* only last page; *Gibbons saga og Greka; Árna skjal (Árni Hjal.); Sigurðar saga turnara,* last part missing; *Luckunnar knattleikur; Rémundar saga og Melusine.*

169 leaves, dark paper, tattered, and the manuscript is defective in places, encapsulated in mylar, bound in blue hardcover, and placed in three boxes by Cornell University's conservation dept. in 1991; 15 x 9.5 cm. Transcribed by one unidentified hand. Some of the transcripts are dated at the end: *Nikiða saga frægu* and *Valdimars saga kóngssonar,* January 1824; *Gibbons saga og Greka,* February 1824; *Árna skjal,* August 1824. The manuscript was bought in 1915 from Reginald Atkinson, second-hand bookseller, London.

Catalogued by Halldór Hermannsson in *Catalogue of the Icelandic Collection Bequeathed by Willard Fiske. Additions 1913-26* (Ithaca: Cornell University Press 1927).

Þorsteins saga bæjarmagns. See **Ýmsar sögur.**

5. Twentieth Century

91 **Árni Þorvaldsson,** 1874-1946. *Æfiatriði og umhverfi.* A biography based on the author's diaries from the years 1874-1927. The author was a teacher in Akureyri.

299 and 409 leaves, numbered. A typewritten carbon copy with portions handwritten; bound in 2 hardcover volumes, one green, blue, and black marbled with black spine and corners, the other all black. Author's name and title in gilded letters on spine of both volumes; 27.7 x 21.5 cm.

92 ____, *Ætterni og æskuár.* The author's genealogy and biography, written in the years 1939-1941.

A typewritten carbon copy of 110 leaves, numbered in pencil, including a handwritten title-page. Bound in two paper cover volumes (one yellow with brown spine, the other blue with red spine); 28.5 x 23 cm. Enclosed is the author's letter to Halldór Hermannsson of 2 October 1939 and a card of 24 September 1941.

93 ____, *Dagbók.* The author's diaries from 1891-1897.

A typewritten carbon copy of 312 numbered leaves, bound in variously colored marbled hardcover with black spine and corners. Author's name and title in gilded letters on spine; 27.7 x 21.5 cm. Author's letters to Halldór Hermannsson of 3 August 1939 and 30 November 1942 are inserted. Also a letter from 11 September 1943, including two poems in Danish: *Min Søsters Veninde* by Árni Þorvaldsson and *Til Frida Frida's Datter* by his brother, the Reverend Jón Þorvaldsson (1876-1938).

According to the letters only four copies were made of the three manuscripts sent to Halldór Hermannsson.

Catalogued by Halldór Hermannsson in *Catalogue of the Icelandic Collection Bequeathed by Willard Fiske. Additions 1927-42* (Ithaca: Cornell University Press, 1943).

94 *Aurora.* A periodical published by the *Icelandic Student Assembly* in Winnipeg. It contains mostly stories and poetry. The editors were: Johann G. Johannsson, Salome Halldorsson, Jonas Jonasson, Magnea Bergmann, and Hallgrimur Johnsson. The Fiske Icelandic Collection

owns 5th-7th issue from 1911, which was the 2nd year of publication, and one copy lacking the first page, thus undated.

36 leaves of typewritten duplicated copies, blurred; 35.3 x 21.7 cm.

On an envelope in Halldór Hermannsson's hand: "These leaves were sent to me by Halldór Daníelsson, Wild Oak, Man. Canada, who writes March 26, 1918: "Blöð þessi hef jeg fengið frá námsfólki, sem verið hefur í Stúdentafjelaginu í Winnipeg. Blöð þessi eru að öllu leyti að skoða sem handrit þó alt þetta sje óraunsætt er það að mínu áliti betur geymt enn glatað. Blöðin frá Stúdentafjelaginu álít jeg rjettast að senda þjer svo þau geymdust. Þau geta máskje á sínum tíma gefið upplýsingar um stúdentafjelagsskapinn, hvað hann hefur þrátt fyrir alla örðugleika, reynt að viðhalda íslenzkunni."

95   **Benedikt Gröndal,** b. 1924. *The Meaning of the Fiske Icelandic Collection to the Icelandic Nation.* A speech given at a Library Visitation at Cornell University, March 1990.

7 sheets of typescript, numbered.

96   **Bjarni Thorarensen,** 1786-1841. [*Poems Translated into Italian by Eomo*]. The poems are transcribed by Halldór Hermannsson from *Corriere del mattino* (Anno II. No. 37-38; Palermo, 6.-7. febbrajo 1893).

One sheet, folded.

97   **Boak, Jeffrey**. *Ford's Revenge.* A parody of *Hrafnkels saga* in English. Undated.

17 numbered sheets of a typewritten duplicated copy; 27.9 x 21.5 cm.

98   **Brix, Hans.** [*Untitled*]. Holograph of an article and notes by Hans Brix concerning the inscriptions on the Gylling, Haerning and Grensten stones. Inserted in pocket pasted to the cover of Erik Moltke, *Nytolkning af Gylling-stenen* (Aarhus, 1930), which has an inscription on t-p "Hr professor Dr. phil Hans Brix. Venligst, E. Moltke."

11 sheets, written on one side only, and notes on the back of an envelope addressed to Brix. In Danish.

Erasmus Rotterodamus. See **Halldór Hermannsson**. *Hrós heimsk-unnar eptir Erasmus Rotterodamus, þýtt af Hjörleifi Þórðarsyni, 1730.*

Finnur Magnússon. See **Halldór Hermannsson**. [*Finnur Magnússon*].

99   [*Grímsey*]. Miscellaneous items relating to Grímsey. 1903.
1) A typewritten duplicated list of 38 questions concerning living conditions in the island Grímsey, additions in ink. The questionnaire was apparently sent from Fiske to Þorvaldur Thoroddsen. The answers are handwritten on a folio sheet, headed "Grímsey."
2) "Svör uppá Spurningar Prof. W. Fiske's í Florence í brjefi dags 21/1 - 1903", in two parts marked I and II. The first part contains 18 paginated pages and a title-page, the second part 8 partly paginated pages; dated at end: "Miðgörðum í maímán. 1903" and "Miðgörðum 7. dag júlímán. 1903." Signed by Matthías Eggertsson. On living conditions in Grímsey.
3) "Saga frá Grímsey tekin úr Grímseyjarlýsing eptir Sr. Jón Norðmann." One single sheet, signed "P. Z." (i.e. Pétur Zophoníasarson).
4) "Stutt lýsing á Grímsey og íbúum hennar, bjargræðisvegum o.fl." 19 paginated pages fastened with a thread. Dated "Miðg. 6. dag júlímánaðar 1901" and signed by Matthías Eggertsson.
5) "Fólkstal í Grímsey um miðjan maímánuð 1903." A list of farmsteads and inhabitants, with age, place of birth, and other occasional notes. Title-page, 3 p. folio. Dated "Miðgörðum 13. mai 1903", by same.
6) "Manntal í Grímsey árið 1901." One sheet folded (3 pages and a title-page). "Miðgörðum 6. júlí 1901", by same.
7) "Yfirlit yfir veðurlag í Grímsey, árið 1900. Útdráttur úr *Meteorologisk Aarbog for 1900*." One sheet, unsigned, but in Matthías Eggertsson's hand. Another weather report for Grímsey in March 1903 on form sheet from *Det danske meteorologiske Institut*. Dated 26 April 1903, by same.
8) Description of Grímsey in Danish, extracted from "Reise igiennem Island... by Eggert Ólafsson. II, Sorøe 1772. pp. 624-626." Unidentified hand. 7 sheets, numbered, written on one side only.
9) "Grímsey, Saga hennar í fornöld." By Bogi Th. Melsteð. 11 pages, undated.
10) Bibliographical data concerning Grímsey; extracts from records, letters, descriptions, etc. Also "Grímseyjarvísur ortar af Síra Guðmundi Erlendssyni", and a description by Jón Jónsson Norðmann from Lbs. 124, 4to (National Library, Reykjavík). All transcribed by Jón Þorkels-

son, archivist. Furthermore some biographical accounts of clergymen on Grímsey, and a transcript of "Grímseyjarvísur" by Árni Jónsson.

100 [*Grímsey. Eyjarbókasafn*]. 1) 5 lists of books arriving in Eyjarbókasafn (the library of Grímsey) in 1901-1903; the lists are numbered 1-5; 13 pages; all made by Matthías Eggertsson. 2) A typed "list of books sent to Grímsey by Putnam"; one sheet, dated 23/10 1901. 3) A statement from St. Guðjohnsen, postman in Húsavík, 18/5 1903, confirming that the books sent by Fiske between 24/9 and 26/11 1902 had been destroyed in the fire in Húsavík on 26/11 1902.

Grímur Thorkelín. See **Jón Eiríksson.**

Guðmundur Andrésson. See **Halldór Hermannsson.** [*Guðmundur Andrésson*].

101 **Guðm[undur] Finnbogason,** 1873-1944. *Ein isländischer Vorschlag zur Abschaffung des Krieges.* 193? [An unpublished paper].

9 numbered sheets of a typed duplicated copy; some corrections in ink.

102 **Gunnar Pálsson,** 1714-1791. <u>*Gunnar Pálsson*</u>: *Typographia Islandica.* Transcribed by Halldór Hermannsson, probably from Lbs. 75, fol. (National Library, Reykjavík) at an unknown date.

62 paginated pages, some blank at end, in a black marbled hardcover notebook; 21.5 x 18.1 cm. White label on front cover with title. Also: *Ex Gunnari Pauli fil.* <u>*Typographæ Islandicæ*</u> *Lbs. 75, fol.* 2 sheets, folded, numbered 1-6.

103 *Gunnlaugs saga.* An anonymous translation into English of portions of Gunnlaugs saga ormstungu. Undated.

8 sheets, numbered 4-7 and 10-13, unbound; 31.1 x 19.4 cm. Written in pencil, only on recto. The translation starts in chapter 3 (*Íslensk fornrit,* p. 56), "Thorvarth did, as she said. He rode west to Hjartharholt with the child and placed it in Thorgerth's hand..." The first part of the translation ends with the first stanza "To a man of no might / a mark I offered..." (*Íslensk fornrit,* p. 63). The second part starts with "disposition, I should not hesitate long" (*Íslensk fornrit,* p. 67) and ends with stanza 7 "I praise in his prime / the prince of Kvaran..." (*Íslensk fornrit,* p. 75).

104 **Halldór Hermannsson,** 1878-1958. [*The Ancient Laws of Norway and Iceland*]. An interleaved copy of Islandica IV, 1911. 37 leaves with additional bibligrapical data; 4 slips of paper. Marginal notes and corrections on pp. 5, 19, 25, 48-49, 60, 67, 73, 77, and inside back cover. Also notations and bibliographical data concerning the writing of Old Norse law in the Middle Ages. One sheet only, torn from an exercise book.

105 _____, [*The Arnamagnæan Institute*]. Notes and comments on 21 interleaved sheets of various sizes in *Skýrsla um skjöl og handrit í safni Árna Magnússonar, sem komin eru úr opinberum skjalasöfnum á Íslandi* (Reykjavík, 1908); also marginal notes on pages of the report.

106 _____, [*The Arnamagnæan Commission*]. Papers relating to The Arnamagnæan Commission, chiefly from 1936-1939. Typewritten and duplicated copies of: calls for meetings, minutes, resolutions, regulations, invoices, flyers, reports on *The Icelandic Dictionary Project,* and newspaper clippings. Also included are: a letter from Prof. Erik Arup (24 July 1937), and a copy of a letter to Prof. Jón Helgason from Prof. Stefán Einarsson (14 August 1941); notations handwritten by Halldór Hermannsson, and extracts from "Betænkningen af Nov. 11, 1924", and "Kålunds Redegørelse af 28/VIII 1908 til Kommissionen for det AMiske Legat."

107 _____, [*Árni Magnússon*]. Notes in Danish, English, Icelandic, and Latin, concerning Árni Magnússon (1663-1730), and Icelandic manuscripts. Some bibliographical information.

Handwritten on 8 Cornell University Library sheets and one Hotel Westminster, Boston.

108 _____, [*Autobiographical Sketch*]. 1924.

6 sheets in Icelandic, and a note dated 11. Feb. 1924, giving the information that the sketch was written for Jón Sveinbjörnsson. Also enclosed: a biographical sketch in English of Halldór Hermannsson by Jóhann S. Hannesson, dated 23. Oct. 1958, and sent to Morris Bishop; 4 sheets.

109 _____, *Bibliographia Runica.* Bibliography of runic material in a large hardcover indexed book, dark-blue, with "Runica" in gold on spine. Enclosed: 6 sheets, 13 slips of paper, 2 sheets with printed runic characters, a photograph of runes on carved pieces of wood, taken for "Nordiska Museet 1910", numerous flyers and newspaper clippings.

Probably material for *Catalogue of Runic Literature. Forming a part of the Icelandic Collection Bequeathed by Willard Fiske* (London: Oxford University Press, 1918).

110   ____, *Biographical Notices. Non-Icelandic Authors.* A bibliography of articles in Icelandic books, journals, and newspapers, relating to the authors or their works [-1940].

Big black soft cover indexed book, only partly used; 25.6 x 20 cm. Authors listed alphabetically, with dates of birth and death, and bibliographical information. Also included: newspaper clippings, pamphlets, flyers, 35 sheets and 21 slips with notes and drafts of letters, bibliography of "Some Works of Gudmund Schütte" (9 typewritten sheets), 12 pages (2 of which are blank) bound with a string, containing bibliography of works by W. P. Ker, and a printed portrait of Xavier Marmier from a French periodical.

111   ____, *[Bibliographies of Guðmundur Kamban's, Gunnar Gunnarsson's, Jóhann Sigurjónsson's, and Kristmann Guðmundsson's Works and Reviews]*. Compiled about 1933.

16 unnumbered leaves in four parts; 26.7 x 20.4 cm. Chiefly handwritten, but also clippings from the first two printed catalogues of the Fiske Icelandic Collection.

112   ____, *[Bibliography of Material Translated into Icelandic]*. [-194?].

64 sheets, slips, and index cards; 22 leaves torn from notebooks (some numbered). In ink and pencil.

113   ____, *[Bibliography of the Mythical-Heroic Sagas]*. An interleaved copy of Islandica V, 1912. 48 leaves and slips of paper, some are blank; 3 loose sheets; a flyer; corrections in margin on pp. 7, 12, 23, 45, 71, and 73.

114   ____, *Books for the National Library, Reykjavík, Iceland from Cornell University Library (the estate of W. Fiske)*. 1909.

3 numbered sheets, written on recto only. On top of sheet 1: "Sent 12/7 '09."

115   ____, *[The Cartography of Iceland]*. Before 1931.

434 sheets of which the largest part is 26.7 x 20.3 cm; 16 order slips from the British Museum, dated August 1927; 5 paper cover note-books, 17.5 x 11.1, 19.6 x 15.6, 20.9 x 16.3, and 22.2 x 17.7 cm; an insert of numerous leaves in four of the notebooks. The notebooks have the following cover-titles: "Danm. + Norges Traktater I-VIII. 1523-1682. Reinecke's Article 1800"; "I-II Icelandic Cartography"; "III Catalogue of Names on the earliest maps"; "Cartographica." Enclosed in the fifth notebook is a photograph of a map. Also enclosed: Correspondence concerning the cartography of Iceland and the publishing of Islandica XXI. The correspondents are: F. C. Wieder (19 July 1927); Fabio Jacometti (22 April 1931) (with 2 photographs of a sixteenth-century map from Ditta Lambardi, received 1 May 1931, 19.8 x 25.8 cm); Donald Macbeth (17 August 1931); J. R. Gilbert, Lancaster Press (12 June 1931). Copies of letters from Halldór Hermannsson to Jacometti and Giovanni Galbiati (both dated 2 March 1931). 1 negative and 32 photographs of maps, mainly ca. 15 x 23 cm. 2 stamped envelopes.

116   ____, [*Catalogue of the Icelandic Collection*]. The manuscript for the Catalogue of 1914.

14 soft cover notebooks (7 dark purple, 3 black, 3 red, and one blue, fore-edges marbled); numbered 1-14 on spine; alphabetization on front covers; pages unnumbered; written mostly on recto; 22.7 x 18.2 cm. Three sheets tipped in the first book, between 9 and 10, with additional cataloguing records.

117   ____, *Classification of the <u>Fiske Icelandic Collection</u> Cornell University Library.*

Variously colored patterned hardcover notebook with red spine and corners; unpaginated, some blank pages. Also a typed carbon copy of same, 23 sheets.

Enclosed: *Harvard University Library Classification of Scandinavian Literature and History.* 7 sheets of a duplicated copy on Library of Harvard University sheets.

118   ____, [*Codex Frisianus*]. Notes in Danish, English, and Icelandic for the introduction to the edition of *Codex Frisianus* in *Corpus codicum Islandicorum medii aevi* (Copenhagen, 1932).

70 sheets of miscellaneous sizes and types, some torn from exercise books; some pagination; in ink and pencil.

119 ____, [*Early Icelandic Libraries*]. Notations on the early Icelandic libraries. Some information copied from letters in the Royal Library in Copenhagen.

24 different sheets, unnumbered; in Danish, English, and Icelandic.

120 ____, [*Eggert Ólafsson*]. Notes and bibliographical notations for *Eggert Ólafsson. A Biographical Sketch* (Islandica XVI, 1925).

77 different sheets (6 of which are sheets torn in half lengthwise); some pagination; in Danish, English, Icelandic, and Latin; mainly 27.9 x 21.6 cm. Also 12 slips of paper, and an unlined maroon paper cover pocketbook ("Pocket Notes" printed on cover), numbered in blue stamp, a slip pasted inside front cover and a pocket inside back cover, "Eggert Ólafsson" handwritten on cover; 10.4 x 17 cm. A letter from The University Press, Oxford, dated February 5, 1920.

121 ____, *Eiríks saga. (Hauksbók)*. A transcript from the Icelandic manuscript, *Hauksbók,* with variants from other manuscripts, and some comments and notes by Halldór Hermannsson. The saga was published in *The Vinland Sagas* (Islandica XXX, 1944).

95 numbered leaves in 3 maroon paper cover notebooks with black spine; on front covers is written: "Eiríks saga. (Hauksbók) I. - III"; 25.3 x 19.6 cm. The text is on recto, comments and notes on verso. Preliminary leaves in all notebooks with notes. Leaves 89 and 94 are blank as is the last part of notebook III. Inserted are 31 sheets and slips, some pasted to the notebooks' pages.

122 ____, [*Examination Reports from Old Norse Classes, with Names of Students and Grades*].

6 handwritten sheets and one slip of paper, some dated: 1907/1908, 1908, 1914, 1915/1916, others undated.

123 ____, [*Finnur Magnússon*]. Extracts from the correspondence of Finnur Magnússon (1781-1847), and documents relating to him, with comments by Halldór Hermannsson; biographical anecdotes about Finnur

Magnússon and bibliographical notations that have to do with him and his work. Extracted from manuscripts in the National Archives in Copenhagen in 1910. The bibliographical notations are of a later date.

21 single sheets and 14 folded; in Icelandic, Danish, and Swedish; 26.6 x 20.3 and 26.7 x 21.2 cm.

124   ____, [*Fiske*]. 1) Bibliography of articles about Fiske; one sheet. 2) Obituaries about Fiske, translated into English in 1905 by Halldór Hermannsson, from the Danish newspapers *Dannebrog* and *Illustreret Tidende*; 13 numbered pages, and 5 unnumbered on folded sheets, a few blank at end; 22.2 x 17.5 cm.

125   ____, [*Frithjofs saga*]. Bibliography of translations and scholarly work on Tégner's *Frithjofs saga*. [Ca. 1939].

240 index cards and slips; 2 sheets (Hotel McAlpin, N.Y.); 1 order sheet from Björck & Börjesson, Stockholm, dated March 1939; 5 order slips from Cornell University Library; 3 unidentified order slips; maroon paper cover notebook with black spine; 14.9 x 10.2 cm. On front cover: "Tegnér's Fritiofssaga." Unpaginated, some slips pasted on pages, clippings from the printed catalogues pasted on pages and slips.

126   ____, [*Guðmundur Andrésson*]. The works of Guðmundur Andrésson (d. 1654), and documents relating to him, transcribed by Halldór Hermannsson from Icelandic manuscripts in 1923, with notes and comments.

96 and 48 pages in 2 paper cover notebooks, one green, the other blue; pagination. 51 additional sheets, some with pagination.

Contents: 1) The verdict on Guðmundur Andrésson's case; from AM 381, fol. (Arnamagnæan Institute). 1 sheet torn from a notebook, written on both sides. 2) "Discvrsvs Oppositivus edur Gagnstæd Yfferferd Lögriettun*n* ar Dom Titils, sem geingid heffur a Alþingi Anno 1564"; from Ny kgl. Saml. 1942, 4to (Royal Library, Copenhagen), comparisons with the Latin translation of Runólfur Jónsson (from the same MS) and with the eighteenth-century transcript in Ny kgl. Saml. 1941, 4to; (5-73). Halldór Hermannsson's comments and marginal notes. Also transcripts of a letter to the Reverend Arngrímur Jónsson (lærði) (3-4); fragment of a letter to King Fredrick III (75-77); Runólfur Jónsson's

Latin version of the poem on the Discursus (79), all of Ny kgl. Saml. 1942, 4to; A letter from Guðmundur Andrésson to the Icelandic authorities 1650, from MS 21.3.4. in the National Library of Scotland, and a fragmentary translation of the letter (from Latin into Icelandic), from Ny kgl. Saml. 1891, 4to. Translations of the Latin paragraphs in Ny kgl. Saml. 1941, 4to. 96 pages (first 73 are numbered, page 78 and 80-83 are blank); paper cover notebook; information about content on both front and back cover, besides inside the front cover. The last two documents (p. 84-96) start at the end; 22.1 x 17.2 cm. Also 9 loose leaves of various sizes. 3) "Gnóþi seauton. Nosce te ipsum. Dictum Chilonis sapientis Attici" (1-22), from AM 209 d, 4to; "Deprecatio & Apologia" (23-44, numbered 1-22), from Ny kgl. Saml. 1942, 4to. Notebook, 44 pages, 2 loose sheets; paper cover with content notes on front cover; 22.3 x 18.2 cm. Copied November 1923. 4) "Per Summum Jehovam et Jehsum Immanuelem Noztrum Salutem dico Humillimus." 23 numbered sheets, written on one side only; 27.6 x 21.6 cm. 5) Transcript of a letter in JS 98, fol. (National Library, Reykjavík), written by Jón Ólafsson from Grunnavík, where he mentions Guðmundur Andrésson and his thesis on *Stóridómur*. The letter is dated: 26 Maji 1767, addressed to Monsieur John Jacobsen. 2 sheets. 6) Introduction to Snorra Edda by Guðmundur Andrésson, from ÍB 2, 8vo (National Library, Reykjavík), retold by Halldór Hermannsson, 2 sheets (3 pages). 7) "Vita Gudmundi Andreae succinté conscripta per Jonem Olavium. Hafniæ 1740". From JS 152, 4to (National Library, Reykjavík), pp. 33-47. 3 sheets (5 numbered pages). 8) About Guðmundur Andrésson's case. From Lbs. 77, 4to (National Library, Reykjavík) (pp. 378-382), "Norske Tegnelser ab Anno 1648 ad Annum 1652, No. VIII." 3 sheets written on one side only. 9) "Um Rók og uppruna Stóradóms." A transcript from MS 21.3.9. 4to ff. 9a-10a, in the National Library of Scotland, Edinburgh. 5 numbered sheets, written on one side only. Transcribed 15 June 1923. 10) A transcript from "Jón Thorkellii: Specimen Islandiæ non barbaræ. (Eptir afskript í Jón Sig. Hdritas. 333, 4to.) Gísli biskup Oddsson, pp. 228-229; Guðmundur Andrésson, pp. 76-79; Þorleifur Halldórsson, pp. 183-185." 1 folio sheet, folded, and written on all four pages.

127 _____, [*The Hólar Cato*]. Notes for the edition of *The Hólar Cato. An Icelandic Schoolbook of the Seventeenth Century* (Islandica XXXIX, 1958). Includes a letter from James Hutton, Cornell University, Dept. of Classics, dated 20 March 1958, one sheet; Rotographs of the holograph manuscript of Bjarni Gizurarson's translation of the first two books of Cato, in Thott 473, 4to (Royal Library, Copenhagen); of Johannes

Sulpicius' *De moribus puerorum in mensa praecipue servandis carmen elegiacum*; of the title-page and the first page of the Hólar edition of Cato.

53 sheets of various sizes in Danish, English, German, Icelandic, Latin, and Swedish; 12 slips of paper, some pasted on larger sheets; rotographs, 12 sheets.

128   ____, *Hrós heimskunnar eptir Erasmus Rotterodamus, þýtt af Hjörleifi Þórðarsyni, 1730.* Title-page: "Desiderii Erasmi Roterodami ΜΩΡΙΑΣΕ KOMION Þad er Heimskunnar Hrosan Hvör ed vegna Snildarlegs Mälfæris Listelegs Innehalds og þess hättar Bookafæde var nu ad nyu Maklega á þrikk ut gänga latin I Leipzig Uppa kost Christians Emmerich Anno MDCCII. Utlögd ad Þvottaa i Alftafyrde Anno 1730." This is a translation made by Hjörleifur Þórðarson in 1730, and transcribed by Halldór Hermannsson from the translator's copy in ÍB 245, 8vo (National Library, Reykjavík). At the end: information on the work, provenance of the manuscript, and comments on the translation. This is dated: 23 July 1923. There is some biographical information about the translator, written by Halldór Hermannsson much later. On a loose sheet is pasted a newspaper clipping about Walter J. Black's edition of *The Praise of Folly* from the New York Times, 30 August 1942, and on another sheet a list of Icelandic manuscripts that deal with works by Erasmus.

204 pages (note on the transcription and the translator by Halldór Hermannsson on the last 3 pages), and 2 loose sheets in 2 grey paper cover notebooks, black spine; title on front covers; 21.7 x 17.2 cm. A printed photocopy in colors of a painting of Erasmus pasted to inner cover of notebook I. Furthermore, 1 Webster Student's Notebook, light brown, pockets inside covers, with a list of manuscripts containing works by Hjörleifur Þórðarson; 9 leaves and 1 loose sheet. On front cover is written: "list of Hjörleifur Þórðarson mss & Erasmus mss."

129   ____, [*Icelandic Authors of To-day.*] Questionnaires that give biographical information about Icelandic authors and list their publications. Personal letters to Halldór Hermannsson came with some of the questionnaires. The correspondents are: Adam Þorgrímsson, Bjarni Sæmundsson, Bjarni Þorsteinsson, Björn M. Ólsen, Eggert Jóhannsson, Einar Helgason, Geir T(ómasson) Zoëga, Gestur Jóhannsson, Guðmundur G. Bárðarson, Guðmundur Finnbogason, Hannes Hafstein, Helgi Valtýsson, Jóhann Magnús Bjarnason, Jóhann Kristjánsson (2 letters), Jón Bjarnason (2 letters), Jón Borgfirðingur, Jón Friðfinnsson, Jón

Jakobsson, Jón Jónsson, Jón Ólafsson, Jón Runólfsson, Jón Stefánsson, Mrs. Jón Sveinsson, Jón Sveinsson, Jón Þórarinsson, Magnús Markússon, Magnús J. Skaptason, Matthías Jochumsson, Matthías Þórðarson, Níels Steingrímur Thorláksson, Oddur Björnsson (2 letters), Sighvatur Grímsson Borgfirðingur, Sigurbjörn Sveinsson (to Oddur Björnsson), Sigurður Júlíus Jóhannesson, Sigurður Sigurðsson, Stefán Jóhann Stefánsson, Sveinbjörn Sveinbjörnsson, Thorsteinn Jóhannesson, Torfhildur Hólm, Tryggvi Gunnarsson, Þorsteinn Erlingsson, Þorsteinn Gíslason, Þorsteinn Þorsteinsson. Enclosed is also a speech, "Á upprisuhátíð heilsuhælisins 13. nov. 1909", by Guðmundur Björnsson, head-physician of Iceland, 5 sheets. Furthermore, a flyer, *Handlækningar* by Oddur V. Gíslason, and 2 sheets of musical notes by Helgi Helgason, tónfræðingur.

211 sheets, folded, mainly questionnaires from ca. 1912; 1 postcard; 2 cards; 1 portrait photograph of Helgi Helgason (13.7 x 9.5 cm). The information was used for *Icelandic Authors of To-day* (Islandica VI, 1913).

130   _____, *Icelandic Authors*. Manuscript to a supplement to *Icelandic Authors of To-Day*. 1913-1948. Never published.

Numerous index cards in 3 black cardboard boxes, 35.4 x 14.4 cm; label pasted on each box with "Icelandic Authors A-G, J-Q [and] R-Þ" written in ink. Bibliographical information on Icelandic authors.

131   _____, [*Icelandic Books of the Seventeenth Century*]. Corrections and notes on Islandica XIV, 1922.

4 sheets and 2 slips enclosed in a copy of *Icelandic Books of the Seventeenth Century*; one postcard with a correction to page v, un-signed; 1 bibliographical clipping; page from a catalogue pasted on p. 77; sheets and slips pasted on pp. 29, 59, and 97; a letter from Jón Þorkelsson, archivist in Iceland, dated 5 November 1922, pasted on p. 121; notes in pencil inside back cover. A second copy of same, inter-leaved with 46 sheets, some are blank; corrections in margin on pp. 3, 31, 56, 57, and 113. Mainly proof-corrections.

132   _____, [*Icelandic Books of the Sixteenth Century*]. Corrections and notes on Islandica IX, 1916. 3 interleaved sheets and one loose with bibliog-raphy; list of reviews on back flyleaf; corrections in margin on pp. ii, 2, 6, 10, 17, 27, and 34.

133   ____, [*Icelandic Catalogue, The*]. An interleaved copy of the *Catalogue of the Icelandic Collection bequeathed by Willard Fiske* (Ithaca: Cornell University Library, 1914). The catalogue is bound in two parts, I and II. Additional bibliographical information and listing of reviews of material in the catalogue. A few letters and postcards are also inserted in the books. A letter from Nils W. Olsson, University of Chicago, 11 February 1941, with a reference question on *Vilmundar saga viðutan*. A letter from Pjetur Sigurðsson, Reykjavík, 10 December 1928; in Icelandic, giving bibliographical information. A letter written by Evelyn Baird on behalf of Vilhjalmur Stefansson, New York, 20 January 1940, with information about a book for sale at Maggs Brothers in London. A postcard from Arvid Uggla, Uppsala, 22 November 1930; in English, with bibliographical information. A letter from Sigurður Kristjánsson to [Fiske?], s.d.; in Danish. Containing "Fortegnelse over Tabeller (Figurer) i Lærdómslista-fjel. Rit." A postcard to the Icelandic Collection, unsigned, stamped in Boston, 4 January 1949, with bibliographical information. A letter to Otto Kinkeldey from Williams Book Store, Boston, Mass., 1 May 1942; signed by H. E. Williams; in English. Offering a 1763 edition of *Jónsbók* for sale.

134   ____, [*Icelandic Folklore*]. Bibliographical notations of Icelandic, Scandinavian, and German publications on Icelandic Folklore.

   50 blue sheets, folded, some fastened with a thread; 27.7 x 21.5 cm. 54 slips of paper and index cards. Mainly in Icelandic, English, and German. Some clippings from the printed catalogues of the Icelandic Collection pasted onto the sheets.

135   ____, [*Icelandic Manuscripts*]. Notations, lists of manuscripts, photographs from Icelandic manuscripts, and bibliographical information for the publication of *Icelandic Manuscripts* (Islandica XIX, 1929); *Illuminated Manuscripts of the Jónsbók* (Islandica XXVIII, 1940); *Icelandic Illuminated Manuscripts of the Middle Ages* (*Corpus codicum Islandicorum medii ævi,* vol. VII, Copenhagen, 1935).

   7 paper cover notebooks (2 grey, 4 brown, and 1 dark brown), 1 red soft cover; some pagination; portions from two additional notebooks without covers; the notebooks range in size from 21 x 14.8 to 22.8 x 18.2 cm. Some of the notebooks have cover titles: "Varia msorum"; "Chronological list of the Manuscripts"; "Principal MSS (Chronological)"; "Illuminated MSS. in the Arna-Magnæan Collection"; "MSS Miniatures etc"; "I. MSS Codicis legis Jónsbók il-

luminatia"; "Arnamagnæan MSS. Icelandic MSS. I." Included also are 269 loose sheets; 16 slips of paper; 437 photographs in 55 envelopes, with various information written on the envelopes; numerous extra sheets and slips pasted on pages in the notebooks and on the envelopes; 3 order slips from the British Museum; 6 invoices and receipts. Also enclosed: two letters from Matthías Þórðarson, dated 28 November 1929, and 9 January 1930, with a list of photographs; typewritten review of *Illuminated MSS of the Middle Ages*, which appeared in *Burlington Magazine* in January 1937; paper clipping of a review of same in *Gazette des Beaux-Arts*, May-June 1937; also a list of reviews of same in different newspapers and journals; an extract from a letter of Brynjólfur Sveinsson to Prof. Villum Lange, dated 10 July 1656, transcribed from Ny kgl. Saml. 1392, fol. (Royal Library, Copenhagen).

136   ____, [*Icelandic Periodicals*]. Ca. 1918-1940. Material for *The Periodical Literature of Iceland down to the Year 1874: An Historical Sketch* (Islandica XI, 1918) and additions to that. The last date recorded is 1940.

An orange cardboard box (originally containing cataloguing cards), half full of index cards with bibliography of Icelandic Periodicals, Icelandic-American periodicals, and translations from foreign languages into Icelandic, published in Icelandic periodicals.

137   ____, *The Icelandic Physiologus*. Notes and other material for the facsimile edition of *The Icelandic Physiologus* (Islandica XXVII, 1938).

88 pages in a grey unlined paper cover notebook with dark green spine, "Physiologus" on front cover, pagination in pencil, some blank pages in between; 17.8 x 10.9 cm. 79 sheets of various sizes, and 3 slips of paper. In Danish, English, French, German, and Icelandic. 3 rotographs of the *Latin Bestiaries* in MS Kk. 4.25 at the University Library, Cambridge; 18 photographs of the two Icelandic fragments of the *Physiologus* in AM 673, 4to (Arnamagnæan Institute).

138   ____, [*An Icelandic Satire*]. Notes for the edition of *Lof lýginnar* by Þorleifur Halldórsson, published in Islandica VIII, 1915, and for the introduction by Halldór Hermannsson. The notes are in two parts, marked: "Notes in Encomium Mendacii", and "Notes to Introduction I. (prior to Þ. H.)" Also a copy of same with corrections in margin on pp. iii, xi, xv, 4, 7, 11, 38, 47, 52, 53, and on back flyleaf.

86 different sheets; 11 index cards and slips of paper, most of which are pasted onto the sheets; unbound and unnumbered; mainly 26.6 x 20.3 and 26.6 x 21.3 cm. The notes are in English, Danish, Icelandic, and Latin.

139   ____, *Ink from Icelandic plants*. Notes in English and Icelandic about how ink was made from various different Icelandic plants. Undated.

6 sheets torn from a notebook; 20.9 x 17.5 cm.

140   ____, *Islandica. (Mailing-list)*.

Variously colored marbled hardcover notebook with red spine; white label on front cover with title in ink; pages numbered with stamp; some blank in between and at end; 20.8 x 17 cm. 3 slips of paper and one card. Table of content by first letter. Title-page: "Islandica. Mailing - List. The Icelandic Catalogue has been sent to those marked in red before the name!" Enclosed: letters and orders from: Prof. Paul Herrmann; Maude E. Wisherd, University Libraries, Lincoln; Kr. Kålund; Prof. A. Schepotieff, Minsk University; Joh. Brøndum-Nielsen; a copy of a letter to M. le Docteur Y. M. Goblet from Otto Kinkeldey, Librarian at Cornell. On last page is pasted a list of recipients of copies of the Icelandic Catalogue sent by H. S. White. Also numerous index cards headed *Mailing lists. Islandica.* Caption headings "Libraries and other institutions", and "Individuals. To whom a complimentary copy of Islandica is to be sent."

141   ____, *Íslenskar rímbækur og almanök*. Notes for the article in *De libris: Bibliofile Breve til Einar Munksgaard paa 50-Aarsdagen 28 Februar* (Copenhagen, 1940), pp. 45-55.

14 sheets in Danish, English, Icelandic, and Swedish; mainly 26.8 x 20.6 cm; portions numbered; 4 slips of note paper.

142   ____, *[Jón Eiríksson]*. Transcripts from manuscripts in the Royal Library, Copenhagen; a bibliography of Jón Eiríksson's works; comments and notes by Halldór Hermannsson. [Ca. 1925].

3 grey paper cover notebooks (Regensbogen Arnold Busk, København) in Danish, English, and Icelandic, two of which are paginated; several leaves excised from the first book; 19.6 x 16.7, 20.6 x 16.2, and 19.6 x 16.2 cm. Cover titles: "Bedømmelsen af Jón Ólafsson's Om Nordens

gamle Digtekonst, ved Jón Eiríksson, og andre...”; “Jón Eiríksson: Autobiographia. skr. ca. 1770. (Ny kgl. Saml. 739^ah fol.)”; “Rit, prentuð eptir Jón Eiríksson, og athugasemdir þar um.” Enclosed: letters to Halldór Hermannsson from: Hannes Þorsteinsson, dated 15 September 1925; Matthías Þórðarson, 10 September 1925, with 2 photographs of a death-mask of Jón Eiríksson; 2 stamped envelopes pasted onto the last page and a cover of a notebook.

143 ____, *Jón Guðmundsson and His Natural History*. Transcription of Jón Guðmundsson’s works from Icelandic manuscripts with comments by Halldór Hermannsson. The works are: “Tijdfordrijf”, “Lækningakver”, “Um huldupláss og heimuglega dali á Íslandi”, “Nockur undirvísun um þá fugla sem mönnum eru kunnuger í Íslandi”, and also “Dómur yfir Jóni Guðmundssyni.” Notes and bibliographical information for the edition of *Jón Guðmundsson and His Natural History of Iceland* (Islandica XV, 1923).

5 notebooks, marked a-e; a) 70 pages, and 5 sheets enclosed, pagination, some blank at end; blue paper cover. b) 46 numbered leaves (2 blank at end), and one sheet enclosed; blue paper cover. Both 22.1 x 17.6 cm. c) (4), 22 pages (1 blank at end), pagination; green paper cover; 22.6 x 17.6 cm. d) 4 unnumbered leaves with rest of book blank; grey paper cover with black spine; 22.5 x 17.9 cm. e) 19 numbered leaves, then blank; maroon paper cover with black spine; written on recto only, comment in pencil on 18v; 20.9 x 16.8 cm. Also 146 sheets of various sizes, unbound; 3 slips of paper; 22 photographs reproduced from Jón Guðmundsson’s original. Enclosed are letters from: Lancaster Press, 27 March 1924; Jón Jakobsson, 8 September 1923; Jón Þorkelsson, 14 September 1923; Matthías Þórðarson, 13 December 1923; a stamped envelope.

144 ____, [*Jón Sigurðsson*]. An address to Icelanders given on the one-hundredth anniversary of Jón Sigurðsson. [1943].

An untitled and undated typescript of 9 yellow sheets, with corrections in pencil; 10 numbered, handwritten sheets of same; 27.9 x 21.6 cm. Addressed to: “Háttvirtu áheyrendur, kæru landar.” This was a Radio broadcast on behalf of *Office of War Information*, 17 June 1943. With 7 letters from the Office, February — May 1943. Signed by E. J. Thorlakson, Kathleen Goldsmith, and Edith Silberman; 2 copies of letters from Halldór Hermannsson.

145   _____, [*Sir Joseph Banks and Iceland*]. Transcripts of letters to Sir
      Joseph Banks, mainly from manuscripts at the British Museum. Made
      ca. 1927. Comments and notes concerning the publication of Islandica
      XVIII in 1928.

      77 sheets, some pagination, chiefly 25.9 x 20.1 cm. Light-green paper
      cover notebook, only 7 leaves used, rest is blank. Also 2 letters from
      Librarians at the University of Edinburgh, dated 19 August and 2
      September 1927.

146   _____, *Lecture at Providence (Germanic Soc. of R.I.) April 17, 1931.*

      18 handwritten sheets in English, numbered, written on one side only;
      unbound; 27.7 x 21.4 cm.

147   _____, *List of Duplicates included in the Printed Catalogues.* An undated
      list of duplicates in the Icelandic Collection; 3 copies of the list which
      include the value of each item; a list of duplicates of interest to Kr.
      Kristjánsson, a second-hand book dealer in Reykjavík.

      76 handwritten and typewritten sheets; about 27.6 x 21.4 cm.

148   _____, *List of Icelandic manuscripts in the Maurer Collection, Harvard
      University Library.* Dated 26-30 June 1924. Title-page; descriptions of
      43 Icelandic manuscripts.

      83 yellow sheets. Written on recto, except for occasional remarks on
      verso; 21.5 x 13.9 cm.

149   _____, *Miscellanea.* Papers and documents relating to Iceland's com-
      merce, economy, and population, transcribed from manuscripts at the
      National Archives and the Royal Library in Copenhagen.

      46 pages in a blue paper cover notebook, unpaginated; 36 yellow sheets,
      folded, paginated; 2 single sheets; 21.9 x 17.8 cm. On front cover:
      "Skrifað 1899. Miscellanea ang. Islands Handel og Tilstand i det 18.
      Aarhundrede", and in pencil: "Property of H. Hermannsson."

      Contents: "Miscellanea ang. Islands Handel og Tilstand i det 18.
      Aarhundrede"; a letter from P[áll] Þorsteinsson to Magnús Stephensen
      (1797-1866) in Vatnsdalur, dated "Vindási þann 11 December: 1856";
      "Provst. Vigfús Jónsson í Hítardal: Om Folkemængden og Handelen i

Island"; "Frá Birni lögmanni Markússyni: (Yfirlit yfir eignir, tekjur og gjöld bænda)"; "Amtmands O. Stephensens Betænkninger om Island. Indgivne til den Kongl. Landkommission den 20 Martii Anno 1771"; "Islandske originale Lavthings-Akter 1687"; "Stríðshjálpin frá Íslandi 1681", with a title-page; a letter to Landkommissionen from the Reverend Eiríkur Guðmundsson, dated 20 December 1770; "Sveinn Sölvason: Penge udi Island."

150   ____, [*Miscellaneous items*]. 1) Income of the Fiske Salary Fund 1908-1919; 2 sheets. 2) A list of Latin and Greek books Halldór Hermannsson read in school, and "Ex Bibliotheca. Smágreinir um bækur og bókmenntir"; one sheet each. 3) A list of possible successors at the Fiske Icelandic Collection; one sheet. 4) Poems by George Herbert, Young, Sir John Denham, and Christian Molbech, transcribed by Halldór Hermannsson; 3 sheets in Danish and English.

151   ____, [*Modern Icelandic*]. Marginal notes in Icelandic and English on proof sheets of *Modern Icelandic* (Islandica XII, 1919), including additional bibliography. The notes were made ca. 1935.

68 proof sheets, and 25 additional sheets, some with strips of paper pasted on the pages; unbound; 27.9 x 20.5 cm.

152   ____, *Myndin af Brynjólfi biskupi*. A paper in Icelandic about a portrait, which is supposed to be of Bishop Brynjólfur Sveinsson. At an unknown date, but corrected much later. Enclosed is also a duplicate of the first page of the paper, written in the handwriting of Halldór Hermannsson's last years.

9 sheets, written on both sides; 26.7 x 20.3 cm, and 27.9 x 21.6 cm.

153   ____, [*The Northmen in America*]. An interleaved copy of Islandica II, 1909. 71 leaves; 99 slips of paper pasted on the leaves; several newspaper clippings; 9 loose sheets and slips; 2 flyers; marginal notes and between lines on pp. 3, 13, 29, 44, 48, 51, 73-5, 77, 79, and 82. Halldór Hermannsson's autograph on flyleaf. The greatest part of the notes are additional bibliography. A second interleaved copy of same: 6 leaves; 13 loose sheets; a few newspaper clippings; marginal notes on pp. 7, 11-13, 18-19, 31, 34, 38, 40, 45, 59, 61, 63-67, 70, 73, 75-76, 79, 83, 86, 89, and 92. Enclosed: letters from Vilhjalmur Stefansson from 28 November 1936 and 11 October 1941, with bibliographical information. A scrapbook, clippings from various American and European newspa-

pers concerning the "Discovery of Vinland" by the Icelanders. Clippings concerning "Vinland the Good" — various reviews from newspapers, e.g. Vilhjalmur Stefansson's books, Hjalmar Holand. Clippings, 3 scrapbooks concerning the same subject-matter.

154   _____, [*Notebooks*]. 36 notebooks of various types and sizes, ranging from 9.5 x 15.2 to 21.2 x 17.2 cm. Written in Danish, English, and Icelandic. Enclosed are numerous loose sheets, paper slips and index cards, order slips, letters, and newspaper clippings.

1-2) Black marbled hardcover notebooks; paginated in pencil; white labels pasted on front covers with titles: "Bibliographia II. Eddic poems I. The mythological poems", and "Bibliographia III. Eddic poems II. The heroic poems"; labels on spine: "Edda I", and "Edda II"; table of contents on first page of each book; some blank pages; clippings from the printed catalogues pasted on pages, also a few slips with notes.
3) "Cartographic notes." Brown and yellow marbled hardcover notebook with black spine; title on white label on cover; stamped pagination; some leaves excised; 2 loose sheets enclosed, torn from a smaller notebook; an order slip from British Museum and another from the New York Public Library.
4-5) "Icelandic Books of the sixteenth Century I-II." 2 different brown and yellowish marbled hardcover notebooks with black spine, numbered; loose sheets, slips, and index cards, some pasted on pages in books. Titles written on labels on front covers of both books. Also order slips from the University Library and the Royal Library in Copenhagen; sheets from Fiske's *Icelandic books of the XVIth century*, inserted with notes; a letter from Sigfús Blöndal, 25 March 1916, and a postcard from same, 30 June 1916; a letter from Páll Eggert Ólason, 24 November [1915].
6) "17th century books." A bibliography of Icelandic books. Maroon paper cover notebook; unpaginated; mostly written on recto. Enclosed: 4 sheets and slips of paper.
7-10) Bibliography of Icelandic books from the eighteenth century. 4 maroon paper cover notebooks marked: "I. 1701-1748"; "II. 1749-1796"; "III. 1797-1844"; "18th century books." Unpaginated except for No. 10. Also 47 sheets and slips of paper, some pasted on pages in books; newspaper clippings; a postcard from Ludwig Rosenthal, 20 January 1907.
11) Etymological notes, alphabetically ordered. Brown marbled hardcover indexed book with black spine; stamped pagination; mainly on

recto; only partly used. 11 slips and index cards, some pasted on pages of book.

12) "Books + Periodicals sent to the Landsbókasafn." Thin brownish marbled hardcover notebook with black spine; unpaginated; 5 leaves used, on recto only; title written on label pasted on front cover.

13-15) Notes on the illumination of manuscripts. 3 different sized paper cover notebooks (yellow with brown spine, maroon with black spine, brown with black spine), leaves of 13 and 15 numbered, 14 paginated and used from both ends. 15 has title written on cover: "MSS Illuminations. Miniatures. Initials." 45 slips, some pasted on pages of books; 2 order slips from the British Museum; a flyer announcing *The Grammar of Ornament* by Owen Jones.

16) "Memoranda." Brown paper cover notebook with black spine, unpaginated. Title written on cover. Heading: "Record of the printing of the Icelandic Catalogue 1913 + the Runic Catalogue 1915."

17) List of recipients of the Islandica series and other works by Halldór Hermannsson. Yellow paper cover notebook with green spine (Webster Note Book); unpaginated; some blank; 5 slips of paper enclosed.

18) "Alþingi." A list of articles about the Alþing and various local things. Yellow paper cover notebook (Webster Student's Note Book); unpaginated; only 3 leaves used; "<u>Alþingi</u>" written on white label on cover.

19) Bibliographical notes, chiefly on translations from the Icelandic. Brown paper cover notebook with black spine, unpaginated; 7 sheets and slips of paper enclosed, and 2 newspaper clippings.

20) "Bibliographical notes. Íslensk bókasöfn o.fl." 3 leaves in a yellow paper cover notebook (Webster Student's Note Book); rest of book is excised; fragile. Title on front cover. 5 loose slips.

21) "Bibliographical Memoranda." A cardboard cover notebook with spiral binding, unpaginated; 9 slips of paper and 6 newspaper clippings, mostly pasted on pages of book. Title written on white label on front cover.

22) Bibliographical notations about publication regarding Old Norse mythology and runes. Yellow and brown marbled hardcover notebook with black spine, paginated in pencil, pages excised. 3 slips of paper, and 2 sheets of bibliography in a different hand. Halldór Hermannsson's autograph on first page.

23) "Miscellanea." Notes on titles of books, manuscripts, letters, people, etc. Black soft cover indexed book, "ADDRESSES" printed in gilded letters on front cover, and title written in white on left upper corner; 5 sheets and slips; a newspaper clipping; an order slip from the Royal Library in Copenhagen.

24) Bibliographical notations. Black soft cover notebook, unpaginated.
25) "Runologi." Bibliography on runic material. 9 pages in a black soft cover notebook, unpaginated; red fore-edge; white label on front cover with title.
26-30) Notebooks pertaining to Finnur Magnússon, Grímur Thorkelín, and Jón Eiríksson. Extracts from letters by Olavsen á Kongsbergi, L. A. A. Thodal, Bogi Benediktsson, Sveinbjörn Egilsson, Árni Helgason, and others. A transcript of "Gríms J. Thorkelins Stambog", dated September 1925. The notebooks are brown paper cover, cross-hatched with red fore-edge, black soft cover, light-blue paper cover, and brown paper cover with green spine and "POCKET NOTES" printed on front cover. No. 27, 29, and 30 are paginated. Four have titles on front cover: "Finnur Magnússon", "Copies of letters from Finnur Magnússon", "G. Thorkelín - Finnur Magnússon", "Jón Eiríksson. Thorkelín." 22 loose sheets and slips, and 5 order slips from the Royal Library in Copenhagen.
31) "Corresponding woodcuts in the <u>Danish Bible of 1550</u> + the <u>Icel. Bible of 1584</u>." 6 leaves without a cover; 2 sheets, and 1 index card, unpaginated; 2 sheets with bibliographical notations.
32) Notes regarding Gibbon's *Decline and Fall of the Roman Empire*. Brown and yellow marbled hardcover notebook with black spine; some pages have been excised and some are blank; unpaginated; 2 slips of paper pasted on pages of book; a newspaper clipping.
33) Bibliography of James Thomson. Red soft cover indexed book with gilded fore-edge; unnumbered; some blank pages; 3 strips of paper; 4 newspaper clippings and flyers.
34) "Horatiana" on white label pasted on upper left corner of cover. Bibliography and notes. Black soft cover indexed book with marbled fore-edge; numbered; 3 slips of paper.
35) "Bibliogr. Not. VI. Copies sent out." List of names of recipients of *Bibliographical Notices* IV., alphabetically ordered in a brown soft cover indexed book with "Memorandum Book" printed on cover in black. Title is written on front cover.
36) Bibliography about Thorvaldsen. Black soft cover indexed book, gilded fore-edge, "Where is it!" printed in gold on cover, and "Thorvaldsen" written in white. Unpaginated, some pages excised.
37) Bibliographical data on Old Norse literature. 24 leaves, fully used, inside back cover, one strip of paper; paper cover maroon, with <u>Notes</u> printed on front cover in black and "Axel E. Aamodt" in gilt on bottom of front cover.

155   ____, [*Notes on Different Translations of Scandinavian Runes*]. After 1951.

5 pages in a grey paper cover notebook, front cover and first part excised, blank pages at end.

156   ____, [*The Periodical Literature of Iceland*]. Notes in English and Icelandic for Islandica XI, 1918.

167 different sheets, portions numbered; 3 slips of paper pasted to a sheet.

157   ____, [*Printing Presses in Iceland*]. A card file that gives place names and dates. The last printing press recorded is dated 1910.

22 index cards, 10.1 x 15.1 cm.

158   ____, *Record of books of the Fiske Icelandic Collection taken for home use by H. H.*

2 pink and blue marbled hardcover notebooks, unpaginated; 20.8 x 17.1 cm. The records are dated 1905-1933 and 1933-1947 (1956). Title is written on first page of each book.

159   ____, *Ritfregn. Þorv. Thoroddsen: Ferðabók. Skýrslur um rannsóknir á Íslandi 1882-1898. I.-IV. bindi. Kaupmannahöfn, Hið íslenzka fræðafélag, 1913-15.* On top of the first page is written in red ink: "Prentað með nokkrum breytingum í Lögbergi 7/10 1915 HH. No. 41, p. 4."

5 sheets, numbered 1-5, only written on recto; 26.6 x 20.2 cm.

160   ____, [*Sæmundiana*]. Notes, transcriptions, and bibliographical notations for *Sæmund and the Oddaverjar* (Islandica XXII, 1932), and "Goðorð í Rangárþingi", *Skírnir* CXVII (1943), pp. 21-31.

Contents: "Sæmundiana. Folktales", and an outline map of Rangárþing; "School — Literary Works — Edda"; "Oddaverjar, the Family History"; other notes about related material. Enclosed are letters from Stefán Einarsson, 30 July 1932, and Jón Stefánsson, undated. Both refer to Sæmundur fróði.

316 sheets of various sizes in Danish, English, German, and Icelandic; portions numbered; 32 slips of paper and index cards, some pasted on the sheets.

161 _____, *Sæmundur fróði.* A draft of an article about Sæmundur the learned, written 1933.

8 sheets, numbered; 27.9 x 21.5 cm.

162 _____, *Saga Íslands.* A bibliography on the history of Iceland and related matters. In alphabetical order by subject. Last reference dated 1948.

Green marbled hardcover indexed book, yellow spine, red fore-edge; only partly used; 26.8 x 18.7 cm. 8 slips of paper, some pasted on pages of the book.

163 _____, *A Short Biographical Dictionary of Icelandic Literature 900-1900 by Halldór Hermannsson. Illustrated. Cornell University Library, Ithaca, New York 1928.*

33 leaves of a dummy in a blue paper wrapper, and 5 leaves inserted, including title-page, which is pasted inside front cover; 6 blank leaves before index; 20.3 x 13.4 cm. On front cover in red: "Biogr. Dict. of Icel. Lit." The text is on recto with additional information on verso, written in blue and red ink besides pencil. Also photographs of the title-page from the first printed Icelandic almanac of 1684, and a Headpiece of Olavius' *Drauma diktur* (1769).

Authors' names are arranged in alphabetical order by last name; the list includes bibliographical information on each author; an index by first letter.

164 _____, *Skalds.* A list of Old Norse-Icelandic poets and poems. Undated.

23 Cornell University Library sheets, unnumbered; 26.1 x 20.2 cm.

165 _____, [*Skúli fógeti*]. A comment on Jón Jónsson Aðils' *Skúli landfógeti Magnússon og Ísland um hans daga* (Copenhagen: Hið íslenzka bókmenntafélag, 1896). Undated.

One sheet only, written on both sides.

166 _____, *Snorri Sturluson.* A bibliography. [After 1920].

25 leaves and cuttings from *Bibliography of the Sagas of the Kings of Norway and Related Sagas and Tales* (Islandica III, 1910), and *The*

Bibliography of the Eddas (Islandica XIII, 1920). The leaves are inserted in a maroon paper cover notebook with green spine; numbered in
red. Title written on front cover. With handwritten additions and remarks; 21.2 x 16.9 cm. 11 additional slips.

167 ____, *Stjórnarskrármálið 1886.* A list of articles in newspapers and
journals, by various authors, about the Constitutional question in 1886.
Undated.

One sheet, written on one side only; 28.6 x 22.2 cm.

168 ____, *The Story of Griselda in Iceland.* Notes, a list of manuscripts, and
letters regarding *Sagan af Gríshildi góðu* and the edition of same in
Islandica VII in 1914. The notes are in three folders marked "Notæ us-
atæ"; "Æfintýrið af Valtara"; "Eggert Jónsson, excerpta." The correspondents are: Sigfús Blöndal, 9 October and 22 December 1913; Jón
Þorkelsson, 27 September 1912 and 30 January 1914; Jón Jakobsson, 13
February 1914. Also enclosed are letters to Willard Fiske from Jón
Þorkelsson, regarding *Gríshildar saga;* dated 2 July and 22 October
1886; 2 lists of manuscripts by Jón Þorkelsson, and a stamped envelope.

64 sheets and 7 slips of paper and index cards, some pasted to larger
sheets. Also a copy of the edition with bibliographical information on
back flyleaf and one loose sheet.

169 ____, *Tileinkun bóka.* A draft of an article including notes about the
custom and nature of dedicating books, with examples from Icelandic
dedications. Undated.

24 sheets, mainly from a notebook of 21.3 x 17.2 cm, but few of various
different sizes.

170 ____, *Torfæana* or *Þormodi Torfæi vitam pertinentia.* Documents relat-
ing to the Icelandic historian, Þormóður Torfason, with comments by
Halldór Hermannsson. Copied from AM 219, 8ᵛᵒ (Arnamagnæan
Institute) in the autumn of 1904.

Blue paper cover notebook, a single sheet enclosed; 21.9 x 17.7 cm. On
front cover: "Halld. Herm. Þetta var skrifað um haustið 1904 áður eg fór
til Flórenz. AM 219, 8ᵛᵒ Torfæana."

171 ____, *Útdráttur úr Rithöfundatali Hallgríms Jónssonar.* An extract

from *Uppteiknunar Tilraun íslendskra Skálda og Rithöfunda* by Hallgrímur Jónsson. Made by Halldór Hermannsson in 1924.

187 alternately numbered pages, stamped pagination; in a grey ledger book with red corners, black patterned frame, and "RECORD" printed on front cover; on spine in ink: "H. J. Rithöf. tal." Written on recto, but verso occasionally used for comments. One sheet, folded, pasted on page 187, another sheet pasted inside back cover; 23.8 x 19 cm. Halldór Hermannsson's autograph on flyleaf.

172 ____, [*Vinlandica*]. Notes and bibliographical notations for his publications on the Norse discovery of Vínland. Some of the notes are titled: "Pining and Pothorst, Scolvus"; "Furðustrandir — Straumfjörður (Gulf of St. Lawrence)"; "Material for the article in Tímarit Þjóðræknisfél. The Norse discovery of America. (Greenland — Vínland)"; "Various Works on the Voyages. Storm — Nansen, Babcock — Steensby — Fossum, Gathorne — Hardy, etc."; "The Kensington Stone." Also drafts of articles on the Vinland problem, i.a., "Vinlands Beliggenhed", and "Endnu en Gang Vinlands Beliggenhed", in *Det nye Nord*, 1920; the reviews of H. P. Steensby's *The Norsemen's Route from Greenland to Wineland,* and Andrew Fossum, *The Norse Discovery of America* published in *American Historical Review* XXV, 1919/20. Also included is a typescript from "Forschungen und Fortschritte" 11. Jahrg. Nr. 14, 10 Mai 1935. Translated by: Miss McCaskill 5/29/35. Regarding the question of a German — Portuguese — Danish prediscovery of America, by Prof. Egmont Zechlin."

205 sheets of different sizes, handwritten and typed; portions numbered; part of a notebook, 4 leaves; 16 slips of paper and index cards; a sketch map with the route to Greenland and Vínland.

173 ____, [*Þorfinnur karlsefni*]. Dedication Ceremonies of Thorfinn Karlsefni Statue, Fairmount Park, Philadelphia, November 20, 1920. Addresses given by Halldór Hermannsson, J. Bunford Samuel, Charles J. Cohen, and Henry Goddard Leach.

14 sheets (11 sheets of a typewritten copy and 3 sheets of Halldór Hermannsson's draft); 27.6 x 21.3 cm. Enclosed: A photograph of the statue, 23.5 x 17.1 cm, and a note by J. Bunford Samuel, dated 19 August 1920. See also letters from Bunford to Halldór Hermannsson. The speech by Halldór Hermannsson was published in *Lögrjetta,* 19 Jan. 1921.

174 ____, [*Þorsteinn Illugason Hjaltalín*]. Biographical information about Þorsteinn Hjaltalín (1771-1817), taken from German collective biographies. Cf. Halldór Hermannsson's article in *Óðinn* IX (Reykjavík, 1913).

5 sheets, folded. Enclosed: 2 identical photographs of a portrait engraving of Þorsteinn Hjaltalín, in *Meusel's Archiv für Kunstler und Kunstliebhaber* I (Dresden, 1803); 9.8 x 7.4 cm.

Hallgrímur Jónsson. See **Halldór Hermannsson**. *Útdráttur úr Rithöfundatali Hallgríms Jónssonar.*

175 **Jóhann S. Hannesson,** 1919-1983. [*Witch-hunting in Scandinavia*]. A loose draft written while he was Curator of the Fiske Icelandic Collection, 1952-1959.

22 leaves in four Cornell University Official Examination Books; leaves unnumbered, but books marked I-IV; 21.2 x 17.5 cm.

____ See **Halldór Hermannsson**. [*Autobiographical Sketch*].

176 **Jóhann Kristjánsson,** 1884-1918. *Personalia.* A list of biographical literature in the library of Jóhann Kristjánsson, the genealogist, in Reykjavík.

6 leaves, unnumbered; in a paper wrapper; 17 x 10.4 cm.

Given to Halldór Hermannsson in September 1914. Cf. note on the paper wrapper.

177 **Jón Eiríksson,** 1728-1787 and **Sæmundur Hólm Magnússon,** 1749-1821. [*Untitled*]. A transcript of letters in Danish and Icelandic to Grímur Thorkelín Jónsson (1752-1829), the Royal Archivist in Copenhagen. Copied from manuscripts in the National Archives in Copenhagen, 15 July 1910.

4 sheets, folded, written on both sides.

Jón Guðmundsson. See **Halldór Hermannsson**. *Jón Guðmundsson and His Natural History.*

178 **Jón Þorkelsson,** 1859-1924. *Catalogue of MSS. collected by Dr. Jón*

Þorkelsson archivist now in the National-Library (Landsbókasafn), Reykjavík. The catalogue is divided into three sections: "Í folio", "Í qvarto", and "Í 8vo og 12mo." Inserted at end is a copy of an assessment of the value of the collection, dated 30 November 1902, signed by Pálmi Pálsson from the National Library's Board of Directors, witnessed by Halldór Daníelsson. Another list of manuscripts is also inserted, and a letter from Jón Þorkelsson, dated December 1902, offering the collection for sale. It was afterwards bought by the National Library.

52 and 6 leaves in a paper cover notebook, bound in grey cardboard with red spine, on which is written: "Jón <u>Þorkelsson</u>: Skrá yfir handritasafn. 1902", including one sheet pasted on the verso of leaf 51, and another one inserted at the very end; 23 x 18.7 cm.

Catalogued by Halldór Hermannsson in *Catalogue of the Icelandic Collection Bequeathed by Willard Fiske* (Ithaca: Cornell University Library, 1914).

Jón Þorvaldsson. See **Árni Þorvaldsson.**

179   **Kristmann Guðmundsson,** 1901-1983. *The Bridal Gown. An abridged version from the Norwegian by Richard Beck.* 1928-31. This is a typewritten original copy.

Title-page, 160 typewritten sheets, numbered; blank verso; pagination partly in ink; corrections to the text in ink. A note by the translator on verso of t-p: "This translation was done at intervals between Jan. 1st 1928 and Sept. 1st 1931. It is based on the Norwegian original, undertaken at the request of the author, and abridged according to his suggestions. When he sold the American rights to the book he recommended the undersigned as translator, but the publisher insisted on having their own translator and the translation in question never was submitted for publication." Signed by Richard Beck and dated 18 August 1932.

Catalogued by Halldór Hermannsson in *Catalogue of the Icelandic Collection Bequeathed by Willard Fiske. Additions 1927-42* (Ithaca: Cornell University Press, 1943).

180   **[*Leif Eriksson, Discoverer of America, A.D. 1003. By Edward F. Gray. London, Oxford University Press, 1930*]** A review by an unidentified critic. Undated.

Title-page; 4 sheets of typewritten carbon copy.

[**Letter-Books of the Fiske Icelandic Collection**]. See Halldór Hermannsson in Miscellaneous Correspondents and Recipients of Letters.

181 [**Miscellaneous authors**]. Poems in English and Icelandic by various Icelandic authors, many of whom had emigrated from Iceland. Collected and transcribed from newspapers and journals by Halldór Hermannsson. The authors are, i.a. Baldvin Halldórsson, Benedikt Gröndal, Bertel E. O. Þorleifsson, Björn Halldórsson, Guðmundur Kamban, Hannes Hafstein, Jón S. Bergman, Káinn, Páll Árdal, S. Eyjólfsson, Stephan G. Stephansson, Þjóðólfur, and Þorsteinn skelkur.

16 sheets, 5 slips of paper, and 7 clippings.

182 **Prowse, G. R. F.** *Cartological Material* [pertaining to Vinland voyages]. *Vol. I. Maps. G. R. F. Prowse, 135 Hargrove St., Winnipeg, 1936.*

(1), 35 numbered leaves of a duplicated copy, stapled in blue paper cover; cover title; marginal notes; sketches of maps; 35.5 x 21.6 cm.

183 _____, *Leif, Scolvus, Labrador and Cabot.*

(1), 19 numbered leaves of a duplicated copy in two parts, A and B, each stapled without covers; 35.5 x 21.6 cm. 2 strips of paper from a notebook, containing additions to the main text, are inserted between pp. 5 and 6 of B. At end of B: "<u>Alternative titles</u> Scolvus and Cabot, The Northwest Passage 1000-1576, The Northwest Passage 1476-1576." Sketches of maps. The typing is somewhat blurred. Enclosed is a letter from the author, dated 1 July 1937, and a second copy of A.

On preliminary page of A: "With the author's compliments. Copy of a paper submitted to the Geographical Journal. Rejected by the G. J." On preliminary page of B: "I have some remembrance that this was offered to the Geographical Review and then to ISIS, rejected by both."

184 _____, *Maps.* About old maps and expeditions to Vinland and Greenland.

6 numbered leaves of a duplicated copy; fore-edge tattered; the typing is somewhat blurred; 35.5 x 21.6 cm.

All three manuscripts are wrapped in brown paper wrapper, with Canadian stamps, addressed to Halldór Hermannsson, from G. R. F. Prowse.

185 **Runólfur Jónsson,** d. 1654. A poem in Latin transcribed by Halldór Hermannsson from Wilhelm Oleson Worm's disputatio *De Lapidis et gemmis* (Hafn, 1651). Also a note about Runólfur Jónsson's suggestion on how to use the word "norrænn."

2 different sheets.

Sæmundur Hólm Magnússon. See **Jón Eiríksson.**

186 **Sighvatur Grímsson Borgfirðingur,** 1840-1930. *Jón Oddsson Hjaltalín eptir Sighv. Gr. Borgfirðing.* The biography and bibliography of Jón Oddsson Hjaltalín, transcribed by Sighvatur Borgfirðingur from his *Prestaæfir* (a manuscript in the National Library of Iceland). [Ca. 1920].

13 leaves in a dark paper cover, unnumbered and undated; cover title; 20.4 x 16.4 cm. A letter is pasted to the inside of back cover, from the author to Halldór Hermannsson, dated Höfði in Dýraf[jörður] 18 January 1920 (1 sheet, folded). Also a manuscript of 6 sheets, torn from a notebook, cut in half; 17.8 x 22.9 cm; an index card. The second manuscript bears the title: *Æfiágrip Séra Jóns Oddssonar Hjaltalíns, skrifað af honum sjálfum, og sent Hallgrími djákna Jónssyni, 1822.* Transcribed by Halldór Hermannsson.

187 **Sigurður Nordal,** 1886-1974. *(Athugasemd við 117. bls., grein merkta f.)* A comment on "Goðorð í Rangárþingi", an article by Halldór Hermannsson in *Skírnir* 1943.

3 sheets, numbered I-III, written on recto only.

188 **Stefán Einarsson,** 1897-1972. *Bibliography 1924-1953.* A bibliography of his publications, with reviews of same listed.

23 leaves of typescript on typing paper and yellow paper from a writing tablet, pasted in brown cardboard; pagination in ink; 34 x 23.5 cm. Cover title; a head of title in ink: "Sumpart samrit, sumpart eftirrit af vélriti Stefáns, 1953." The typescript has handwritten additions and comments.

189 **Thorson, Joseph T.** [*Untitled*]. 1939. A speech given "on the occasion of the ceremonies held July 17 [1939], at the Icelandic Pavilion." Ref.: cover letter by Vilhjálmur Thor to Stefán Einarsson, dated 13 July 1939.

The Honorable Joseph T. Thorson, member of the Canadian House of Commons, spoke on behalf of the National League of Icelanders in America.

2 typewritten sheets. Included: *Press Release*. 3 typewritten sheets by the Icelandic Commission to the New York World's Fair, 1939.

190 **Vilhjálmur Bjarnar,** 1920-1983. [*Glossary notes for Sonatorrek and Arinbjarnarkviða*]. Undated.

16 sheets, unnumbered and only written on recto. The notes are written in pencil in Vilhjálmur Bjarnar's hand. In Icelandic and English.

191 _____, [*Íslenzk menning*]. Marginal annotations on a photocopy of Sigurður Nordal's *Íslenzk menning* I (Reykjavík, 1942). Undated.

192 **Þorvaldur [Valgeir Hólm] Þórarinsson,** b. 1909. *On Civil Liberties in Iceland.* The author was a student of constitutional law at Cornell University in 1942-1943. This is a copy of a paper written in January 1943.

32 leaves of a typewritten carbon copy, in a soft brown folder; author's name and title in white ink on front cover; 28.4 x 23.5 cm. A title-page and a table of contents included.

II. CORRESPONDENCE

1. Letters to Daniel Willard Fiske

Albany Institute. Office of the Recording Secretary and Librarian, Albany, N.Y. 1 letter, 15 May 1874; signed by D. J. Pratt; in English. — Plans for Americans to attend the Millennial Celebration in Iceland in 1874. Enclosed: a letter from the President of the Institute, John V. L. Pruyn, 11 May 1874, regarding the same subject. Another letter from Pruyn, 27 June 1874, with letters from Howard M. Rice.

American Geographical Society, New York City. 1 letter, 19 November 1874; signed by Francis A. Stout; in English. — Donating books to Iceland.

Anderson, Aksel, 1851-1923, Uppsala University Library. 19 letters and 9 postcards, Uppsala, Sweden, November 1886 - August 1904; in Swedish. — The arrangements for Fiske's housekeeper; the procuring of publications by Fiske; on acquiring books for Fiske in Sweden; mentions Rolf Arpi; on Uppsala Library's holdings of Icelandic books; on Anderson's work at the library; his plans to visit libraries in the United States.

Anderson, R[asmus] B[jörn], 1846-1936, University of Wisconsin and the Legation of the United States in Copenhagen. 12 letters and one postcard, May 1874 - October 1886; in English. — On his studies and research in Old Norse; his and Ole Bull's plans for a monument of Leifur

Eiríksson; Scandinavian library in Wisconsin; on the Leifur Eiríksson Observatory; requesting comments on some of his work; his trip to Boston and Cambridge to visit scholars; asking permission to dedicate his and Bjarnason's translation of Old Norse sagas to Fiske; with a message from Caroline and Dagmar Rafn.

Annerstedt, Claes, 1839-1927, Uppsala University Library. 8 letters, November 1886 - May 1890; in Swedish and English. — Bibliographical information; on the reconstruction and enlarging of the library building; presenting the library publications to Fiske; acknowledging books sent by Fiske; promising to keep an eye out for "Rugman's book." Bibliographical data included with the letters on separate sheets.

Appelton's American Cyclopædia, New York City. 2 letters, 30 March and 21 December 1874; signed by G. A. F. Van Rhyn; in English. — Returning articles by Fiske, on Icelandic and Norwegian language and literature, for revision.

Árni Friðriksson. 1 postcard, Winnipeg, 12 August, 1882; in Icelandic. — On obtaining the periodical *Framfari* for Fiske.

Árni Jónsson, the Rev., frá Skútustöðum, 1849-1916 (the letters were written when he was a student at the Junior College in Reykjavík, and later a pastor in Akureyri). 6 letters, Reykjavík and Akureyri, November 1879 - June 1901; in English and Icelandic. — Expressing thanks for books sent to him by Fiske; remarking on the backwardness of Icelanders and the need for improvements in the country; on the new parliamentary building; sending *Skin og skuggi* by Páll Jónsson as a present to Fiske; regretting inability to go to certain places in Iceland during the summer in order to describe them for Fiske; acknowledging books, chess boards, and books on chess to the school library in Reykjavík.

Árni Riis. 4 letters, Ísafjörður and Copenhagen, 27 September 1879; 2 March 1882; 10 January 1883; 23 May 1887; in Icelandic. — On his studies; requesting a photograph of Mrs. Fiske; mentions people in Ísafjörður; his intention to attend a Commercial College in Copenhagen; contemplating emigration from Iceland. Enclosed: a letter of appreciation to Fiske from Hans Christján Riis; table of the temperature at Ísafjörður in 1881-82.

Árni Thorsteinsson, 1828-1907, Bailiff of Iceland. 2 letters, Reykjavík, 10 February 1880; 10 December 1881; postcard, undated, but postmarked

13 December 1879; in Icelandic. — On the affairs of Fornleifafélagið (the Antiquarian Society). Enclosed: a speech, "Griðasetning við þorrablót í Reykjavík 21 janúar 1880", one sheet; contribution to Hið íslenzka bókmenntafélag in Reykjavík acknowledged, 26 November 1883.

Arnljótur Ólafsson, the Rev., 1823-1904. 3 letters, Bægisá, Eyjafjörður, 2 March, 21 April, and 3 July 1880; in Icelandic. — Remarking on Icelandic commerce; education in Iceland; farming and progress; export of wool to the United States.

Arnór Þorláksson, 1859-1913 (the letters were written when he was a student at the Junior College in Reykjavík). 2 letters, Reykjavík, 28 November 1879; 23 March 1880; in Icelandic. — Expressing gratitude for Fiske's goodwill towards him and the Junior College in Reykjavík.

Arpi, Rolf. 8 letters and one postcard, Uppsala, July 1889 - June 1904; in Icelandic and Swedish. — Primarily providing bibliographical data, but also expressing thanks for Fiske's publication *Bibliographical Notices* IV, and other presents; sending two lectures he wrote on Iceland to Fiske; about his children's activities.

Askdal, S. M. S. See **Sigurður M. S. Askdal.**

Baird, Henry Carey, industrial publisher. 1 letter, Philadelphia, 10 April 1874; in English. — Donating books to Iceland.

Baird, Steven. 1 letter, Washington, D.C., 16 March 1874; in English. — Donating the [Smithsonian] Institution's publications to Iceland as a reply to Fiske's appeal.

Bardal, H. S. 2 letters, Winnipeg, 7 August 1899; 4 March 1903; in Icelandic. — Business matters. [Bardal acted as an agent for Icelandic publications in Canada on behalf of Fiske, and later the Fiske Icelandic Collection].

Baumgartner, Alexander, 1841-1910. 1 letter and a postcard, Exaeten bei Roermond, Holland, 24 and 28 January 1890; in German and English. — Mainly answering bibliographical inquiries from Fiske; presenting a list of his publications on Icelandic matters, sending some, and providing information on how best to procure the ones he does not have at hand.

Beck, Richard. See **Richard Beck.**

Ben[edikt] [Sveinbjarnarson] Gröndal, 1826-1907, naturalist and author. 2
letters, Reykjavík, 8 February 1880; 8 September 1881; in Icelandic. —
About the late Jón Sigurðsson; prices of microscopes, receipt of same
acknowledged.

B[enedikt] Sveinsson, 1827-1899, county justice. 1 letter, Héðinshöfði,
Suður-Þingeyjasýsla, 23 August 1890; in Icelandic. — His financial difficulties, asking for a loan.

Bertel Gunlögsen [Bertel Högni Gunnlaugsson Stefánsson], 1839-1918. 7
letters, London; New York; Chicago, December 1878 - November
1890; in English. — Primarily on his scholarly work and lectures on
Old Norse and Icelandic language and literature; his activities in
London and the United States.

Bjarni Benediktsson, tradesman. 1 letter, Húsavík, 25 May 1902; in
Icelandic. — Reference question about manufacturers of chessboards.

Bjarni Jónsson, 1872-1948. 28 letters and 14 postcards, Regensen [student
housing in Copenhagen]; Florence; Berlin; Unnarholt, Árnessýsla,
November 1899 - June 1904; in Danish. — Bjarni Jónsson was Fiske's
assistant for a while. The letters deal chiefly with errands and research
he did for Fiske in Copenhagen, for example, procuring material and
looking for data, mainly on chess. Also on Icelandic politics; the arrangements for his going to Florence; his voyage in Germany and Italy;
on Matthías Þórðarson's discovery of a runic inscription; chess meeting
at Garður; plans to go back to Iceland. Enclosed is a desiderata list from
Fiske on a postcard, addressed to Christian Kaiser, Munich.

Björg [Karítas] Þ[orláksson] Blöndal, 1874-1934, author. 1 letter,
Copenhagen, November 1903; in Icelandic. — Acknowledging Fiske's
present; sending a photograph of herself and her husband, Sigfús
Blöndal. See Graphic Material 8.39.

Björn M[agnússon] Ólsen, 1850-1919, teacher and Rector of the Junior
College in Reykjavík. 81 letters and 11 postcards, Reykjavík, November
1879 - June 1904; in Icelandic. — Expressing thanks for material sent
to him personally, to the school library, and the students; the establishment of Lestrarfélag Íþöku (the Reading Society of Ithaca); on the "lögberg" question; Carpenter and his grammar book; pointing out a mistake

in "The Living Authors of Iceland"; on his work at the College, research and publications; bibliographical information; Icelandic politics;
mentions Fiske's and Maurer's comments on the Constitutional change
in 1886; his opinion about Icelandic orthography; presenting publications to Fiske; death notices; mentions an album of photographs compiled by students at the Junior College. (See Graphic Material, Box 10);
information on Þorsteinn Hjaltalín málari; mentions some of Fiske's
writings about Iceland; his suggestion about Fiske receiving the Order
of Dannebrog; recommending Hannes Þorsteinsson as Fiske's assistant
and later Sigfús Blöndal; acknowledging receipt of donation to
Eyrarbakki Church; on Arthur Middleton Reeves' gravestone; a list of
copies of Oddur Gottskálksson's *New Testament* existing in Iceland; offering *Biblia Laicorum* for sale on behalf of Valdimar and Steindór
Briem; chess in Iceland and the Chess Society of Reykjavík; postal service in Iceland; distributing gifts from Fiske; about the parliament's
contributing to the National Library yearly; the library building; the visit of the novelist Hall Caine from the Isle of Man; the library in
Grímsey; the largest part of the letters, however, deal with the procuring
of books for Fiske. Enclosed: four receipts, including one from Sigurður
Sigurðarson, treasurer of Lestrarfélagið Íþaka; two bibliographical
datas; an invoice of Icelandic books bought by Fiske and sent to
Grímsey; one bibliography from Jón Borgfjörð, and another from Pálmi
Pálsson; "Skýrsla Sr. Friðriks Eggertz í Akureyjum" (about Þorsteinn
Hjaltalín); "Skrá ifir nokkrar bækur úr Hruna-safninu með verði, settu
af aðjunkt Pálma Pálssini."

Björn Pálsson, 1862-1916, photographer. 2 letters, Ísafjörður, 15 November
1903; 28 February 1904; in Icelandic. — Expressing thanks for books
on chess sent by Fiske to the library in Ísafjörður; asking for books on
other matters if possible; mentions his meeting with Fiske as a boy in
Akureyri in 1879; sending photographs from Iceland with a suggestion
to Fiske to reproduce them in the next issue of *Mímir*. Possibly the photographs in Graphic Material, 4.3.

Boesen, J. E. 1 postcard, Sorø, Denmark, 13 June 1900; in Danish. —
Bibliographical information. Inserted in his *Nordisk Gudelære*
(Copenhagen: V. Thaning & Appel's Forlag, 1888).

Bogi Th[orarensen] Melsteð, 1860-1929 (the letters were written when he
was a student at the Junior College in Reykjavík, and later a scholar in
Copenhagen), 21 letters and 16 postcards, November 1879 - February

1904; in Icelandic. — Listing recent publications in Reykjavík; translating articles by Fiske for Icelandic periodicals; research on chess in Iceland; briefly relating tidings from Iceland; praising Jónas Jónasson's article "Yfirlit yfir bókmenntir Íslands á 19 öldinni"; commenting on "The Living Authors of Iceland"; acknowledging books sent by Fiske; listing his own holdings of *Alþingisbækur Íslands;* bibliographical information; coming for a visit; his voyage in Europe in 1900; running errands concerning the publishing of *Chess in Iceland;* on his research and publications. Icelanders in Copenhagen are briefly mentioned in some of the letters.

Braem, Henrik, the Danish Consulate in New York. 2 letters, 7 and 31 March 1874; in English. — About shipping cases of books Fiske and other Americans presented to the National Library in Reykjavík on the occasion of the Millennial Celebration in 1874. First letter in a folder with Baird, the second pasted with a letter from Francis J. Child.

Brenner, Oscar, 1854-1920. 2 letters, Munich, 20 February 1880; 20 July 1889; in German. — On his interest in Old Icelandic; expressing thanks for *Bibliographical Notices* IV and asking for preceding issues.

Bricka, Carl Frederik, 1845-1903, 1 postcard, Copenhagen, 7 March 1900; in Danish; inserted in his *Dansk Biografisk Lexikon* I. Bind (Copenhagen: Gyldendalske Boghandels Forlag, 1887). — Bibliographical information.

British and Foreign Bible Society. 1 letter, London, 16 January 1900; signed by R[obert] B[aker] Girdlestone 1836-1923; in English. — Description and provenance of their copy of the Icelandic *New Testament* of 1540.

Brown, Marie A. 1 letter, London, 12 January 1887; in English. — About the arrangements for an exhibit in commemoration of the Norse discovery of America; asking for Fiske's support.

Browne, A. G., Jr., *The Evening Post.* 1 letter, New York City, 22 June 1874; in English. — Accepting Fiske's article on Iceland.

Brynjólfur Kúld, 1864-1901 (the letter was written when he was a student at the Junior College in Reykjavík). 1 letter, 29 November 1879; in Icelandic. — Acknowledging receipt of books sent by Fiske; the teaching of the modern languages at the Junior College in Reykjavík; asking for a photograph of Fiske. The letter is bound with letters from John H. Dey.

Brynjúlfsson, Marie. 1 letter, Copenhagen, 21 June 1886. With postscript by Gísli Brynjúlfsson; in English. — An appeal for financial assistance to enable her husband, Gísli Brynjúlfsson, to seek proper health care and to publish his book of poems.

Bugge, Sophus, 1883-1907, Professor. 1 letter, Christiania, 5 January 1880; in Danish. — Referring to his work on Old Norse mythology; Scandinavian publications on Old Norse; sending some of his publications to Fiske.

Bull, Sara [Chapman Thorp] (Mrs. Ole Bull), 1850-1911. 2 letters, Cambridge, Mass. and Bordighera, Italy, 18 June 1887; 19 April s.a.; in English. — On the proposed statue of Leifur Eiríksson; letter of introduction on behalf of Mr. and Mrs. Francis H. Liggett. Enclosed: a list of "evidence cited by Rafn relating to the discovery of Vinland by the Northmen", 6 typewritten sheets. See also letter by Edwin F. Waters.

Bürgel, Henry C. H. 3 letters, Copenhagen and Munich, 16 September 1901; s.d.; 3 February 1904; in English. — Announcing his engagement to an acquaintance of Fiske; accepting an invitation; Bürgel's work on Old Norse and Icelandic language and literature; his wish to edit a republication of Jón Árnason's *Þjóðsögur;* suggesting a German edition of *Mímir;* proposing to compile an Icelandic dictionary.

Cady, David, First National Bank of Amsterdam. 1 note, 13 September 1882; in English. — Contributing to the disaster fund of Iceland. Two additional notes concerning the same affair are pasted together with Cady's. One anonymous, 9 September, and the other signed by M, Newport, Rhode Island.

Cahnheim, O., Dr. Med. 1 postcard, Dresden-A, 16 January 1900; in German. — Bibliographical information. Inserted in his "Zwei Sommerreisen in Island", extr. fr. *Verhandlungen der Gesellschaft für Erdkunde zu Berlin,* 1894, No. 5.

Carpenter, W[illia]m H[enry], 1853-1936, Columbia University. 1 letter, New York City, 9 February 1901; in Icelandic. — Acceptance of chess-material.

Cassino, S. E. 1 postcard, Boston, 21 June 1882; in English. — Requesting names of Icelandic naturalists.

Cederschiöld, Gustaf, 1849-1928. 2 letters, Lund, 22 December 1879; 3 March 1880; in Swedish. — An invitation to visit his home in Lund; bibliographical information on Icelandic publications in Sweden.

Child, Francis J[ames],1825-1896. 3 letters, Cambridge, Mass., 4 and 20 February, 18 June, s.a.; in English. — Requesting a translation of "grátur Jakobs yfir Rakel" from *Norðurfari, or Rambles in Iceland* by Pliny Miles (N.Y. 1854); donating books to the National Library of Iceland.

Ch[ristian] V[aldimar] Blöndal, d. 1885. 1 letter, Akureyri, 9 November 1880; in Icelandic. — Job inquiry.

Cohn, Albert, 1827-1905, Verlagsbuchhandlung und Antiquariat. 1 letter, Berlin, 12 August 1886; in English. — Regarding the "Lögbók of 1578"; also referring to his work on Shakespeare.

Collins, Ellen. 1 note, New York City, 12 September [1882]; in English. — Donation for the relief fund of Iceland.

Cramer, M. J., American Legation in Copenhagen. 1 letter, Copenhagen, 19 December 1879; in English. — An answer to Fiske's inquiry about sailing-vessels bound to Iceland.

Davis, John V. 2 letters, New York, 3 October 1882; in English. — Contribution to the relief fund for Iceland. Enclosed; an anonymous note from Chefton, Cincinnati, 27 August 1882, regarding same.

Dey, John H., *New-York Evangelist.* 1 letter on behalf of Henry M. Field, editor, New York City, 26 August 1874; in English. — Bibliographical information concerning Iceland.

Ditlev Thomsen, 1867-1935. 4 letters, Copenhagen and Reykjavík, 22 October, 20 November, and 9 December (with letters from Grímur Thomsen) 1879; 25 June 1894; in Danish and English. — His trip on the steamer, Diana, from Iceland to Denmark in 1879; his schoolwork; expressing thanks for the calenders; on his life and activities since he wrote to Fiske as a fifteen-year-old boy; presenting Fiske with his publication.

Dufferin, Lord, 1826-1902. 2 letters, Government House, Ottawa, and

London, 10 March 1874; 10 November 1879; in English. — On projects concerning progress in Iceland.

Durfee, H. R., Mrs. 1 note, Palmyra, N.Y., 11 September 1882; in English. — Contribution to the relief fund for Iceland.

Edgren, Hjalmar, 1840-1903. 1 postcard, Malmö, 21 July 1874; in English. — Presenting his books to the National Library of Iceland.

Eðvald Friðriksson Møller, 1875-1960, the Icelandic Chess Society in Copenhagen. 1 letter, Copenhagen, 21 February 1902; in Icelandic. — Acknowledging the chess material sent by Fiske.

Edzardi, A[nton], 1849-1882. 1 letter, Leipzig, 30 November 1879; in German. — On donating books to Iceland.

Eggert Ó[lafur] Briem, 1811-1894, county justice. 2 letters, Reykjavík, 1 October 1891; 5 February 1892; in Icelandic. — His business with Fiske through Ólafur Davíðsson.

Eggert Laxdal, 1846-1923, merchant. 2 letters, Akureyri, 17 April 1880; 18 October 1901; in Icelandic. — Sending *Njála* to Fiske; on the policy and activities of Framfarafélag Akureyrar (the Society for Progress); regarding shipments to Grímsey; mentions acquaintances of Fiske in Akureyri. Enclosed: a report on Icelandic export to England and Denmark, dated 28 July 1879.

E[gill] Egilsson, 1829-1896, store manager. 1 letter, Reykjavík, 9 October 1879; in Icelandic. — A formal letter inviting Fiske and Arthur Middleton Reeves to a farewell party given by "farmers and farmers' friends."

Einar Benediktsson, 1864-1940 (the letters were written when he was a student). 7 letters, Reykjavík; Copenhagen; Kiel; Rome, etc., November 1879 - November 1903; in Icelandic and English. — Thanking for books sent to him by Fiske; relating activities of the students in the Junior College in Reykjavík; mentions the late Jón Sigurðsson; asking for a loan to enable him to finish his last year of studies in Copenhagen; commenting on Icelandic politics; his trip to Italy.

Einar Finnbogason, 1863-1944, Overseer. 1 letter, Þórisholt in Mýrdalur, 5

January 1903; in Icelandic. — On procuring of a chessboard for the Chess Society of the district.

Einar Þórðarson, 1818-1888, printer. 1 letter, Reykjavík, 12 February 1880; in Icelandic. — Sending the periodical *Máni;* criticizing the Icelandic parliament for neglecting the "technical culture" of the nation.

Eiríkur Bjarnason, blacksmith. 6 letters, Reykjavík, November 1879 - August 1891; in Icelandic. — Expressing thanks for the presents from Fiske; his studies and activities. Enclosed: a letter from B. P. Hjaltested, Eiríkur Bjarnason's foster father, undated, but included with the first letter.

Eiríkur Briem, the Rev., 1846-1929. 1 letter, Copenhagen, 29 December 1879; in Icelandic. — Expressing gratitude for Fiske's condolences to Icelanders because of the death of Jón Sigurðsson.

Eiríkur Magnússon, 1833-1913, librarian. 17 letters, Cambridge, England, May 1874 - July 1889; in English. — Appreciation for the effort to collect books for Iceland in 1874; the prosperity of the Icelandic nation, its culture and politics; the economic situation in Iceland and the need for improvement in every aspect of the society; the need for a polytechnic high school; about the late Jón Sigurðsson; Magnússon's translations and scholarly work; inviting Fiske to his home in Cambridge; biographical notes on Pjetur Guðmundsson, pastor in Grímsey; the "famine" in Iceland in 1882 and relief to aid the distressed areas; on the school at Möðruvellir; commenting on the bank laws of 1885, about his translation of a play by Shakespeare, and other topics. One of the letters is inserted in *Stormurinn, sjónleikur eftir William Shakespere* [sic!] I. Íslenzk þýðing eftir Eirík Magnússon, M.A. (Reykjavík: Sigm. Guðmundsson prentari, 1885).

E[iríkur] Þorbergsson, 1867-1949, photographer. 2 letters, Húsavík, 9 August 1902; 19 April 1903; in Icelandic. — On his trip to Grímsey to take photographs on behalf of Fiske; acknowledging payment; the forming of a Chess Society in Húsavík. Enclosed: an invoice; a list of books sent by Fiske to the Chess Society. See also a letter to Halldór Hermannsson.

Elínborg Thorberg. 1 letter, Copenhagen s.d.; in Icelandic. — Accepting an invitation. Also a greeting, undated, but "Aug. 79" added in pencil; with letters from Þorvaldur Thoroddsen.

Field, Cyrus W. 2 letters, New York City, 28 October 1874; 13 October 1879; in English. — The prospect of laying a telegraphic cable from the Shetland Islands to Iceland.

Field, Henry M. See **Dey, John H.**

Finnur Jónsson, 1858-1934, Professor. 3 letters, Copenhagen, 2 and 9 September (two letters) 1903; in Icelandic. — Describing the housing problems of the National Library in Reykjavík. Enclosed: a draft from Fiske to the Hon. James Bryce, concerning funds for a new library building in Reykjavík.

Folwell, William W. 1 letter, University of Minnesota, Minneapolis, 26 March 1900; in English. — Presenting Fiske with Victor Nilsson's thesis, *Loddfáfnismál. An Eddic Study* (Minneapolis: The University Press of Minnesota, 1898). The letter is inserted in the book.

Friðbjörn Steinsson, 1838-1918, bookbinder and bookseller. 11 letters, Akureyri, November 1879 - February 1902; in Icelandic. — Procuring books and periodicals for Fiske; brief news from Akureyri; acknowledging material sent to him and to the Reading Society of Akureyri; information on *Spilabók* by Jósep Grímsson; on chess in Iceland; commenting on the bad season and farming conditions in 1882; the establishment of the Chess Society of Akureyri. Enclosed: two invoices; a letter from J. Jónsson to Friðbjörn Steinsson concerning the Chess Society of Akureyri, 29 January 1902.

Friðjón Friðriksson, 1849-1913, merchant. 1 letter, Gimli, Manitoba, 8 September 1882; in English. — Procuring the periodical *Framfari* for Fiske; asking about a good encyclopedia.

F[riðrik] J[ónsson] Bergmann, 1858-1918. 2 letters, Winnipeg, 3 May 1892; 29 February 1904; in Icelandic and English. — Business matters on behalf of the Reverend Jón Bjarnason; sending material to Fiske; expressing thanks for *Mímir.*

Frímann [Arngrímsson] B. Anderson, 1855-1936, electrician. 1 letter, Cambridge, Mass., 29 June 1889; in English. — His résumé and plans to "awaken a greater interest in Scandinavian literature" in the United States.

Garrison, W. P., editor of *The Nation.* 1 postcard, New York City, 13 April 1875; a note, 23 September 1881; in English. — Publishing articles by Fiske in the paper.

Geir T[ómasson] Zoëga, 1857-1928 (the letters were written when he was a student). 6 letters and a postcard, Copenhagen, December 1879 - April 1880; in Icelandic. — On the death of Jón Sigurðsson and his funeral; replying to reference questions; the politics of Jón Sigurðsson; the affairs of Hið íslenzka bókmenntafélag; on a wool factory in Akureyri; referring to Icelandic scholars and their publications; a list of Icelandic students in Copenhagen; about Regensen (Garður), the student housing; commenting on Fiske's treatment of Gröndal in *Icelandic Notes.*

Gering, Hugo, 1847-1925. 1 letter, Halle, Germany, 18 December 1879; in German. — Mentioning Fornleifafélagið (the Antiquarian Society), the death of Jón Sigurðsson.

Geyr-Schweppenburg, Albert, von. 1 postcard, Copenhagen, 18 January 1900; in German; inserted in his *Meine Reise nach den Färöern* (Paderborn, Verlag von J. Esser, 1900). — Bibliographical information.

Gísli Brynjúlfsson, 1827-1888, Docent and poet. 4 letters, Copenhagen, 26 May 1863; 7 September 1873, with a postscript by Marie Brynjúlfsson, hoping that Fiske still is a New Churchman and about bringing the "truth" to people; 22 December 1879; 20 October 1882; in Icelandic and English. — Commenting on the Civil War in America; asking Fiske to return *Sciagraphia* by Hálfdan Einarsson; asking Fiske to submit an article (corrected if possible) by Mrs. Brynjúlfsson to *The New Jerusalem Messenger* in New York; commenting on Swedenborg's doctrines; about the nationality of Leifur Eiríksson; mentions the late Jón Sigurðsson; briefly on European politics; thankful for books and periodicals; his financial situation; asking for a loan. Enclosed: an invoice, paid by Boghandler Lind in Copenhagen, 5 November 1855; a list of new books and periodicals, printed in Icelandic in the years 1849 to 1852; on the first novels written in Iceland in the nineteenth century.

Gísli Einarsson, 1858-1938 (the letter was written when he was a student). 1 letter, Reykjavík, 28 November 1879. Icelandic. — Expressing thanks for a book sent by Fiske; brief news about friends and family.

Grímur Thomsen, 1820-1896, poet. 5 letters, Copenhagen and Bessastaðir, 28 November 1879; 8 February and 20 March 1880; 6 and 30 August

1895; in English and Icelandic. — Appreciating Fiske's goodwill towards Iceland; arguing against Fiske's theory that the Eddic poems originated from Hjaltland (Shetland Islands) and the Orkneys; advising Fiske not just to praise Iceland, but also criticize; pleased that Fiske likes his poetry; thanks for photographs of antique statues. (Probably the pictures now in Ljós- og prentmyndasafn at the National Museum of Iceland, No. 1684-1705. The first entry: "Finnur Sigmundsson landsbókavörður afhenti (líkl. úr dánarbúi dr. Gríms Thomsens á Bessastöðum...)"

Grossman, Karl. 1 letter, Continental Hotel, Cairo, 22 March 1898; in English. — Returning two books; commenting on an article in *Allgemeine Zeitung* and on a book about the "Færoes", sending some of his reprints; mentions his "lantern demonstration." Inserted in his "Across Iceland", an offprint from *The Geographical Journal*, 1894.

Guðbrandur Jónsson, 1888-1953. 1 postcard, Reykjavík, 9 July 1900; in Icelandic. — "Kveðja frá Þingvöllum."

Guðbrandur Vigfússon, 1827-1889, scholar. 2 letters and 2 postcards, Oxford and the Deanery, Winchester, 17 November 1874; 15 May 1879; 1 January 1880; 31 March 1887; in English and Icelandic. — On his scholarship; complimenting Fiske on his article on Vínland and on the "catalogue"; mentioning Charles Smith from Boston; a brief account of his own life and work.

Guðm[undur] Finnbogason, 1873-1944, librarian. 1 letter, Reykjavík, 17 June 1904; in Icelandic. — Book offered for sale; bibliographical information.

Guðmundur Guðmundsson, 1858-1924 (the letter was written when he was a medical student). 1 letter, Reykjavík, undated, but added in pencil "1895 or 96"; in Icelandic. — Asking for financial assistance in order to continue his studies.

Guðm[undur] Helgason, the Rev., 1853-1922. 1 letter and a postcard, Reykholt, Borgarfjörður, both dated 4 January 1901; in Icelandic. — Acceptance of a chessboard and books on chess.

Guðm[undur] Magnússon (pseud., Jón Trausti), 1873-1918, writer. 1 letter, Reykjavík, 16 March 1902; in Icelandic. — Sending his book of poems to Fiske; brief account of his life.

Guðrún Hjaltalín, 1833-1903. 1 letter, Copenhagen, 20 November 1896; in English. — Asking for a contribution to help those who suffered from the earthquakes in Iceland.

Guild, Reuben A., Library of Brown University. 1 letter, Providence, Rhode Island, 20 May 1874; in English. — The procuring of books for the National Library in Reykjavík.

Gunlögsen, Bertel. See **Bertel Gunlögsen.**

Hagander, A. G., Antiquary in Stockholm. 2 letters, Stockholm, 4 February 1898, and one undated; in Swedish. — A runic stick from Dalarna 1667 offered to Fiske for sale.

Hagen, S[ivert] N., the State University of Iowa. 1 letter, Iowa City, 28 march 1904; in English. — Asking for *Mímir;* sending his article on the origin of the term "Múspell."

Halldór Briem, 1852-1929, librarian. 3 letters, Möðruvellir; Gimli, Manitoba; Akureyri, 16 April 1887; 14 December 1879; 7 March 1904; in Icelandic and English. — Expressing gratitude for Fiske's goodwill towards Iceland and Icelanders; presenting Fiske with his publications; accepting books and pamphlets; sending his own publications in return. One of the letters is inserted in his book *Yfirlit yfir Goðafræði Norður-landa* (Akureyri: Prentsmiðja B. Jónssonar, 1886).

Halldór Hermannsson, 1878-1958, Curator of the Fiske Icelandic Collection. 127 letters and 39 postcards, Copenhagen and Florence, December 1899 - May 1904; in Danish, English, German, and Icelandic. Includes: 3 form letters in Halldór Hermannsson's hand, one signed by W. Fiske; newspaper clipping about chess; invoice of books; list of duplicates of Scandinavian chess books; an extract from a work by Professor Troels Lund, one sheet. — Primarily concerning his work at Fiske's library in Florence, Italy, for example, bibliographical infor-mation; the publishing of chess material; the establishing of a library, "Eyjarbókasafn", in Grímsey; purchasing books; collecting chess prob-lems from various sources; his research on chess in Scandinavia for Fiske's publications; ordering books from Scandinavia; providing an or-gan for Grímsey; work on *Bibliographical Notices* IV, and *Mímir.* Also giving his opinion on scholarly works on Old Norse and Icelandic mat-ters in numerous letters. See also Manuscript Material 54.

Halldór Jónsson. 1 letter, Hólar in Hjaltadalur, 18 April 1880; in Icelandic. — Thanking for the portrait photograph and newspapers sent by Fiske; mentions briefly his studies.

Hallgr[ímur] Melsteð, 1853-1906, librarian, the National Library of Iceland. 5 letters, Reykjavík, 31 May 1888; 17 July 1889; 3 December 1900; 13 September 1901; 22 October 1901; in Icelandic. — Listing books offered to Fiske for sale; appreciating Fiske's generosity towards the Library, asking for missing issues of different series.

Hannes Þorsteinsson, 1860-1935, the National Archives. 1 letter, Reykjavík, 1 October 1890; in Icelandic. — Job inquiry; about making a list of duplicates in the National Library.

Hans Christján Riis. See **Árni Riis.**

H[ans] Th. A. Thomsen, d. 1899, merchant. 2 letters, Reykjavík and Copenhagen, 20 November 1879; 10 December 1879, with letters from Grímur Thomsen; in Danish. — A list of laws and regulations in the year 1879; on the death of Jón Sigurðsson; mentions Tryggvi Gunnarsson and Arthur Middleton Reeves.

Hantzock, Bernh. 1 letter, Dresden, Plauen, 28 February 1904; in German. — His article on Grímsey.

Harvard College Library. 1 letter, Cambridge, Mass., 17 February 1883; signed by William C. Lane; in English. — Bibliographical inquiry.

Hayes, John J., American Geographical Society and the National Association of Wool Manufacturers. 3 letters, New York; Boston, 2 and 14 May 1874; 26 April 1880; in English. The second letter is a circular, headed, "The Iceland Millennial." — On his and Fiske's interest in Icelandic culture; the arrangements for his proposed trip to Iceland to attend the Millennial Celebration; mentioning an article by Fiske and sending his own publications to the Library.

Headley, P[hineas] C[amp], 1819-1903. 3 letters, Boston, 26 and 29 October, 3 November 1874; in English. — On the editing and publishing of *The Island of Fire; or a Thousand Years of the Old Northmen's Home. 874-1874* (Boston, 1875), asking for comments.

Helgi Jónsson. 2 letters, Winnipeg, 4 August 1884; 5 September 1885; in

Icelandic and English. — Acknowledging Fiske's subscription to his periodical *Leifur;* pleased that Fiske put so much effort into learning Icelandic; sending Icelandic periodicals and pamphlets published in Canada to Fiske.

Heman, John. 1 letter, Grafton, Dakota Territory, 24 June 1885; in Icelandic. — On his need for instruction in the English language.

Herdersche Verlagshandlung. 1 letter, Freiburg im Breisgau, 1 June 1901; in German. — Asking permission to reproduce Fiske's photographs of Iceland for Baumgartner's book *Island und die Faröer.*

Hess, J. W. 1 postcard, Basel, 14 September 1900; in German; inserted in his *Beschreibung der Insel Island* (Basel: Schweighauserische Buchdruckerei, 1864). — Bibliographical information.

Hetzel, J., & Cie. 1 postcard, Paris, 12 September 1900; in French. — Bibliographical information on Edmond Neukomm. Inserted at the end of his book *Les Dompteurs de la Mer* (Paris: J. Hetzel et Cie [1895]).

Heydenreich, W. 1 letter, Günzburg, Bayern, 19 March 1904; in German. — Commenting on *Mímir;* suggesting a publication of a periodical on the Icelandic language and literature.

Hilmar Finsen, 1824-1886, Governor of Iceland. 1 letter, Reykjavík, undated and unsigned, but the date, 27 August 1879, and the name, later added in pencil; in Danish. — Accepting an invitation.

Historical Society of Pennsylvania, The. 1 note, Philadelphia, 10 April 1874; in English. — Book donations to Iceland in 1874. With letters from Howard M. Rice.

Howell, Frederick W[illiam] W[arbreck]. 1 letter, Handsworth, Birmingham, England, 20 September 1900; in English. — A list of photographs taken in Iceland. Also a postcard, 11 May 1900; inserted in his *Icelandic Pictures. Drawn with Pen and Pencil* (London: The Religious Tract Society, 1893). — Offering Fiske ca. 200 photographs for sale. See Graphic Material, Boxes 1-3.

Hull, Charles H. 1 letter, Halle, Germany, 28 June 1891; in English. — Informing Fiske about titles of books on Iceland he has come across. Additional bibliographical data included on a separate sheet.

Indriði Einarsson, 1851-1939, playwright. 2 postcards, Reykjavík, 23 March 1881; 12 July 1900; in English. — Acknowledging receipt of chess boards; sending a copy of his play *Sverð og bagall;* statistical information concerning Icelandic export.

Ingvar Guðmundsson. 4 letters, Sveinagarðar in Grímsey, 10 July 1901; 2 February, 7 May 1902; 10 February 1903; in Icelandic. — On living conditions in Grímsey; appreciating presents from Fiske; the history of chess in Grímsey; the contemporary practice of chess in Grímsey. Numerous chess games played in Grímsey and chess problems are enclosed.

J[acob] V[aldimar] Havsteen, 1844-1920. 1 letter, the Royal Swedish and Norwegian Consulate, Akureyri, 6 November 1892; in English. — Books offered for sale.

Jakob Guðmundsson, the Rev., 1817 (or 1819)-1890. 1 letter, Sauðafell in Dalir, 10 March 1882; in Icelandic. — Brief account on members of his family; remarking on the school at Möðruvellir; the need for progress and good public education in Iceland.

Jakob Gunnlögsson, 1857-1926. 3 letters, Raufarhöfn and Copenhagen, 1 June 1890; 4 February 1894; 24 June 1896; in Icelandic. — Acknowledging *Bibliographical Notices;* notifying the establishment of a bookstore in Copenhagen; the founding of the periodical *Eimreiðin.*

Jessen [Carl Arnold] E[dwin]. 1 postcard, Copenhagen, 28 March 1900; in English. — Informing Fiske that he had translated the Icelandic "Sunsong" into English. Inserted in *Sol-Sangen. Et gammelt islandsk Kvad.* Extr.fr. (Hamilton's) *Nordisk tidskrift* (Lund, 1867).

J[óhann] Magnús Bjarnason, 1866-1945, writer. 1 letter, Winnipeg, 8 January 1892; in Icelandic. — Job inquiry.

Jóh[annes] Halldórsson, 1822-1904, school principal. 1 letter, Akureyri, 6 September 1875; in Icelandic. — Acknowledging books sent to the elementary school in Akureyri.

Jóhannes L[árus] L[ynge] Jóhannsson, 1859-1929. 1 letter, Kvennabrekka in Dalir, 14 March 1904; in Icelandic. — Appreciation of Fiske's goodwill towards Iceland; remembers meeting Fiske as a teenager while working in Einar Þórðarsson's printing shop in Reykjavík; his résumé; remarking on the project of establishing a university in Iceland; asking Fiske to suggest aid from Carnegie.

Jóhannes St. Stefánsson. 1 letter, Húsavík, 7 September 1880; in Icelandic. — Thanking for the presents from Fiske; brief account of Fiske's acquaintances in Húsavík.

Johnson, J. J. 1 letter, Irondale, Jeff. Co., Ohio, 12 December 1874; in English. — Reference question concerning the Norse discovery of America.

Johnston, A. W., Viking Club. 3 letters, London, 30 September and 4 November 1902; 8 February 1904; in English. — Business matters; informing Fiske he had been elected a member of the Viking Club.

Jón Árnason, 1819-1888, librarian, the National Library of Iceland. 3 letters, Reykjavík, 28 November 1879; 10 February 1880; 26 October 1882; in Icelandic. — About his book collection; the prospect of working on an English-Icelandic dictionary; commenting on Fiske's idea about a telegraph line between Iceland and Europe; the death of Jón Sigurðsson; the sale of Árnason's books; acknowledging books from Fiske to the National Library; remarking on the bad season in 1882.

Jón Bjarnason, the Rev., 1845-1914. 10 letters and 2 postcards, Decorah, Iowa; Winnipeg; other places in the United States and Canada, May 1874 - February 1900; in Icelandic and English. — Regarding his work as a pastor in different churches and views on their different doctrines; on his scholarly work and teachings; about Icelandic immigration to America; bibliographical information; the procuring of material for Fiske; the Icelandic Millennial Celebration in Milwaukee; relating his activities since arriving in the United States. Drafts of the first two letters were sent to the Fiske Icelandic Collection, along with letters from Fiske to Bjarnason, by Theodora Hermann, his foster daughter, Winnipeg, Manitoba, 7 September 1955. See Fiske in Miscellaneous Correspondents and Recipients of Letters. One of the postcards is inserted in his *Ísland að blása upp* (Reykjavík, 1888).

Jón Björnsson, the Rev., 1829-1892. 3 letters, Eyrarbakki and Copenhagen, 2 August 1890; 11 and 25 November 1891; a circular in English, 1 October 1891; in Icelandic. — Petition for financial aid to build a new church in Eyrarbakki. See also Jón Þorkelsson, Rector.

Jón Borgfirðingur [Jónsson], 1826-1912. 7 letters and one postcard, Reykjavík, September 1882 - April 1901; in Icelandic. — Additional bibliographical information on "The Living Authors of Iceland"; offering epitaphs and books for sale. Enclosed: bibliographical data, 22 sheets; a letter from Fiske, 21 March 1899, mainly a desiderata list.

Jón Á. Egilsen. 4 letters, Kornsá and Blönduós, 9 November 1879; 22 April and 21 August 1880; 21 January 1898; in Icelandic. — Thanking for presents from Fiske; brief account of mutual acquaintances; Egilsen's studies. In the last letter the correspondent relates a brief biographical account of the eighteen years since he first met Fiske.

Jón Finnsson, 1865-1940 (the letters were written when he was a student at the Junior College in Reykjavík). 2 letters, Reykjavík, 10 February and 28 November 1879; in Icelandic. — Acknowledging books sent by Fiske. A list of the students travelling on *Diana* along the coast of Iceland is included with the letter.

Jón Hermannsson, 1873-1960 (the letters were written when he was a student in Copenhagen). 5 letters, Copenhagen, 24 April and 3 May 1900; 16 March 1901; 22 and 29 March 1903; in Danish. — Bibliographical information; concerning parcel shipping to Iceland; message from Halldór Hermannsson, who lies sick in the hospital in Copenhagen.

J[ón] Hjaltalín, 1807-1882, Head Physician of Iceland. 3 letters, Reykjavík, 28 November 1874; 29 November 1879; 13 February 1880; in English. — Acknowledging books and pictures from Fiske.

Jón A[ndrésson] Hjaltalín, 1840-1908, school principal. 23 letters and one postcard, Advocates Library, Edinburgh and Möðruvellir in Hörgárdalur, February 1874 - July 1901; in English and Icelandic. — On libraries in Reykjavík; information on Icelandic publications; commenting on emigration from Iceland to America; a list of his scholarly work; appreciating Fiske's concern for Iceland; remarking on several scholars and their work; information on the mail-service to Iceland; commenting on Bugge's forthcoming book and giving an opinion on the relationship between Irish and Icelandic literature; describing the conditions at Möðruvellir and his work there; about publishing a textbook in English; criticizing the distress relief; the school policy in Iceland; on the constitutional struggle. Enclosed: an address of thanks to Fiske from students at the school at Möðruvellir, 2 March 1882, both in Icelandic and English.

Jón Jakobsson, 1860-1925, the National Library of Iceland. 2 letters, Reykjavík, 12 May 1897; 27, no month, 1900; in Danish and Icelandic. — Acknowledging receipt of plaster figures to the National Museum, and books to the National Library.

Jón Ólafsson, 1850-1916, editor. 13 letters, several places in the United States; Copenhagen; Reykjavík; Eskifjörður, April 1874 - May 1900; chiefly Icelandic, but also some Danish and English. — On his activities in America; stopping to visit Fiske in Ithaca; assisting Icelandic immigrants; sending material to Fiske; on the proposed Icelandic Colony in Alaska; commenting on the Icelandic government; on the dictionary by Cleasby and Vigfússon; the literary style of several Icelandic scholars and authors; the printing of *Alaska.* The letters written after he settles in Iceland again: Icelandic politics; commenting on Grímur Thomsen's poetry; the general situation in Iceland before and now. The last letter is in English and is mainly concerned with his family, their careers, and also his own literary activities. Included with the letters are a few poems by Jón Ólafsson, some on separate sheets, each individually dated: "Á Sierra Nevada", 5 stanzas, 10 September 1874; "Til kvöldstjörnunnar", 2 stanzas, 2 December 1873; "Leiðindi", 4 stanzas, 11 February 1874; "Eimreiðin", 3 stanzas, 7 September 1874; "Graf-letr yfir sjálfan mig", 7 stanzas, Christmas day 1874; "Veraldar-vísur. Eins ferðalangs. Skraddara-þankar um þennan heim", 17 stanzas, 10 November 1874; "Quaestio", 1 stanza, 11 November 1874. Also a specimen of a second proof of *Alaska.*

Jón Stefánsson, 1862-1952, scholar and teacher. 9 letters, London; Copenhagen; Aarhus, Jutland, October 1897 - August 1902; in English. — On his scholarly work; about finding documentary evidence for negotiations between England and Denmark concerning Iceland in 1518-19; Icelandic titles in Bruun's *Bibliotheca Danica* unreliable; expressing a wish to visit Fiske in Florence to compare his own bibliography with Fiske's catalogue; informing about the sale of Jón Pétursson's collection; recording titles of pamphlets he sent to Fiske; mentioning Hall Caine's production of a play on an Icelandic subject; remarking on his own work and publications; about the Clarendon Press sending books to the Junior College in Reykjavík to supplement their gift in 1874; appreciating *Mímir* and submitting additions to it.

Jón Þórarinsson, 1854-1926, school principal. 1 letter, Flensborg School, Hafnarfjörður, 26 September 1900; in Icelandic. — Acknowledging chess material sent to the school.

Jón Þorkelsson, 1822-1904, Rector of the Junior College in Reykjavík. 5 letters, Reykjavík, 10 April 1875; 29 November 1879; 10 February 1880; 11 September 1881; 15 September 1882; in Icelandic. — Acknowledging books sent to him, the school, and the National Library; informing Fiske that a report had been made of the books donated to the National Library on the occasion of the Millennial Celebration and sent to donors; presenting his publications to Fiske; on the study of Old Icelandic in America; commenting on Cleasby's dictionary; on procuring the publications of the schools at Bessastaðir and Reykjavík for Fiske; on his work and publications; remarking on the bad season in the year 1882. Enclosed: two letters certifying the petition of the church building in Eyrarbakki, 30 July 1890 and 1 October 1891.

Jón Þorkelsson, 1859-1924, archivist. 96 letters and 31 postcards, Copenhagen and Reykjavík, September 1886 - February 1903; in Icelandic. — Primarily on procuring books for Fiske and giving bibliographical information. Also on his trip to Sweden to visit libraries; his transcribing of *Gríshildar saga* and *Gríshildarrímur* for Fiske; remarking on some of Fiske's writings on Icelandic matters; corrections to Fiske's *Bibliographical Notices;* transcription of "iðrunarsálmar Petrarcha"; sending books to Fiske; commenting on Olsen's book about Rask; relating tidings from Iceland; on finding an assistant to Fiske — mentions Hannes Þorsteinsson, Ólafur Davíðsson, and the son of Jón of Gautlönd; checking the cost of off-printing at Pacht & Crone; selling a collection of occasional poetry to Fiske; expressing a concern for what will happen to the Icelandic book collection after Fiske is gone; about writing a review on Ólafur Davíðsson's book on games; reflecting on Arthur Middleton Reeves' accomplishments for Icelandic literature; his idea about a Society to publish "source material" after 1400; offering Fiske an Icelandic collection of autographs; his trip to Iceland; commenting on the situation in Viðey; about the establishment of an Icelandic university; mentions the periodical *Sunnanfari* briefly in several letters; literary announcements; his tutoring of James Morgan Hart, Professor at Cornell University, in Icelandic; sending a list of Arnljótur Ólafsson's manuscripts; death notices; making arrangements for his own manuscript collection; asking to borrow the vellum manuscript of *Jónsbók* for the University Library in Copenhagen on behalf of Ólafur Halldórsson; job inquiry; transcription of *Grímseyjarbók;* appreciating *Mímir* and commenting on it at the same time; additions and corrections to *Mímir* on three separate sheets. Enclosed: a letter from S. Einarsson, watchmaker, to Jón Þorkelsson, selling him *Passionis* (Hol. 1620), 19 January 1890. Bibliographical data, lists of books sent to Fiske, some with prices, desiderata lists, invoices and receipts, 51 sheets. See also Manuscript Material 33 and 168.

Jónas Björnsson, the Rev., 1850-1896. 1 letter, Sauðlauksdalur in Barða-strönd, 28 April 1887; in Icelandic. — Bibliographical information.

J[ónas] Jónassen, 1840-1910, Head Physician of Iceland. 1 letter, Reykjavík, 28 November 1889; a thank-you note, 20 October 1903; in Icelandic. — Sending a book to Fiske.

Jonsson, Dennan? 1 letter, Partille, Sweden, 18 December 1901; in Swedish. — On chess and *Í uppnámi.*

J[ulius] Havsteen, 1839-1915, District Governor. 1 letter, Akureyri, 25 February 1887; in Icelandic. — Sending a report on the District Library in Akureyri.

Kålund, Kr[istian], 1844-1919, librarian. 3 letters and a postcard, Copenhagen, 1 October 1898; 6 February and 1 June 1899; 7 June 1900; in Danish. — Bibliographical information; requesting *Bibliographical Notices* IV for the University Library. Also a note addressed to Kålund with bibliographical information on Lieut. V. Ohlsen. Possibly asked by Kålund on behalf of Fiske. The note is dated 28 September 1900 and is inserted in his *Bidrag til en historisk-topografisk Beskrivelse af Island* I (Copenhagen: Gyldendalske Boghandel, 1877). The postcard is inserted in vol. II (1879-82).

Katrín Einarsdóttir. 1 letter, Copenhagen, 16 July s.a.; in Danish. — Asking for financial aid to help pay for her son's hospitalization and medicine.

Kistler, P. C. 1 postcard, Kissingen, 3 October 1900; in English. — Bibliographical information. Inserted in Sohlern, Edgar von, *Baldurs Tod. Musikdrama in 3 Akten* 2. Auflage (Bad Kissingen: Verlag der Tagesfragen [1897]).

Klemming [Gustaf Edvard], 1823-1893, the Royal Library in Stockholm. 1 letter, Stockholm, 6 July 1889; in Swedish. — Letter of acknowledgment for *Bibliographical Notices,* with a personal note.

Kohtz, J. 2 letters and one postcard, Dresden, 30 December 1901; 7 and 28 January 1902; in German. — Pertaining to the publishing of *Í uppnámi.*

Königl. bibliothek. 1 postcard, Haag, 22 December 1899; the signature is illegible; in German; inserted in Johann Anderson, *Beschryving van Ysland, Groenland en de Straat Davis ...* Door J. D. J. (Amsterdam, Steven van Esveldt, 1750). — An answer to a query regarding a Dutchman with the initials J. G. J.

Koopman, H. L., the library of Brown University. 1 letter, Providence, Rhode Island, 19 March 1900; in English; pasted on back flyleaf of *Supplement to the Antiquitates Americanæ* Ed. under the auspices of the Royal Society of Northern Antiquaries by C. C. Rafn (Copenhagen, 1841). — Answering a reference question concerning Thomas Hopkins Webb. A clipping on Webb pasted on front flyleaf.

Kranita, Maria. 1 letter, Florence, dated Wednesday only; in English. — Thanking Fiske for the broadsides on Iceland.

Kr[istján] Jónasarson. 1 letter, Copenhagen, 20 March 1903; in English. — Offering his translation of *Peer Gynt* into Icelandic for sale.

Kristján Kristjánsson (sign. Christiansson), 1806-1882, District Governor of the North and East. 1 letter, Akureyri, 25 July 1879; in Icelandic. — Inviting Fiske and Arthur Middleton Reeves to breakfast.

Kr[istján] Ó[lafur] Þorgrímsson, 1857-1915, merchant. 7 letters, Reykjavík, November 1879 - February 1884; in Icelandic. — Book dealings, including 5 invoices.

Lára Bjarnason, d. 1921. 1 letter, Winnipeg, 4 September 1891; in Icelandic. — Seeking advice and assistance in establishing schools for Icelanders in the United States and Canada.

Lasa, H. v.d. 1 letter, Florence, 16 May 1892; in English. — On chess and Iceland.

Leverkühn, Paul, Direction des Institutions et Bibliothèque Scientifiques de S.A.R. le Prince de Bulgarie, Sofia. 1 letter, Sofia, 14 June 1898; in English. — Expressing interest in corresponding with Fiske about Iceland; plans to visit the island; willing to send his list of books on the natural history of Iceland.

Lindemann, J. Hegeman, Danish Minister at the Legation in Washington,

D.C. 1 letter, 17 March 1874; in English. — Replying to a question concerning a tentative visit of the Danish Crown Prince to Iceland in the summer.

Linderfelt, K. A. 1 letter, Milwaukee Public Library, 9 August 1890; in English. — Bibliographical inquiry.

Liverpool Public Library, 1 postcard, Liverpool, England, 14 September 1903; signed by Peter Howell, Chief Librarian; in English. — Bibliographical information. Inserted in Grossman, Karl, "Across Iceland", an offprint from *The Geographical Journal*, 1894.

Lorenzen, M[arcus], 1847-1928. 3 letters and one postcard, Copenhagen, 27 November 1885; 13 May 1886; 18 December 1889; 17 December 1895; in Danish. — Pertaining to the publications of Samfund til udgivelse af gammel nordisk litteratur.

Lounsbury, F. R. 1 letter, New Haven, 3 May 1874; in English. — Book donations to Iceland.

Lucas, E. V. 1 letter, London, undated; in English. — Bibliographical information. Inserted in *The Story of Burnt Njal.* Translated by Sir George Webbe Dasent (London: Grant Richards, 1900).

Lund, P. W. 1 letter, Bishop Hill, Henry County, Illinois, 2 January 1882; in English. — Asking for bibliographies of literature on Iceland.

M[agnús] Einarsson. 5 letters, Copenhagen, 28 and 29 January, 6, 9, and 19 February 1890; in Icelandic. — Book dealings with Fiske; list of Icelandic books he wants to sell.

Magnús M[agnússon] Smith, 1869 or 1871-1934. 8 letters, Winnipeg, August 1900 - February 1901 (one is incomplete); some Icelandic, but chiefly in English. — Offering to analyze the game of "valdskák" for Fiske; biographical accounts; his career as a chess-player; asking about Fiske's book on chess in Iceland; giving Fiske the liberty to use any of his games; selling Fiske's publications on chess; the establishment of an Icelandic Chess Society in Winnipeg. Enclosed are 18 sheets and 4 slips with chess diagrams and problems; 5 newspaper clippings; Magnús Smith's calling card.

Magnús Stephensen, 1836-1917, Governor of Iceland. 3 letters and one postcard, Reykjavík, 24 August 1879; 22 March and 16 October 1880; 14 September 1882; in Icelandic. — The change of location of the banquet to be given by members of the parliament in honor of Fiske and Arthur Middleton Reeves (see also Tryggvi Gunnarsson); appreciation of the goodwill towards Hið íslenzka bókmenntafélag (the Icelandic Literary Society); announcing the publications of same. Enclosed: a receipt from Hið íslenzka bókmenntafélag.

Markús Þorsteinsson, harnesser. 1 letter, Reykjavík, 3 December 1900; in Icelandic. — Book offered for sale.

Marsh, G[eorge P[erkins], 1801-1882. 1 letter, Rome, 3 April 1880; in English. — On Old Norse literature.

Matthías Eggertsson, the Rev., 1865-1955. 12 letters, Miðgarðar on Grímsey, July 1901 - March 1904; in Icelandic, one postscript in English. — Appreciation for the attention Fiske shows Grímsey; chess in Grímsey and in general; sending photographs from Grímsey; a trip to Húsavík and Flatey; about photographs taken by Eiríkur Þorbergsson (see his letters and also Graphic Material, Box 14); sending chess games played by people on the island; the fire in Húsavík; about the visit of the German, Bernhard Hantzsch, who was collecting bird's eggs; mentions also the previous visit of Dr. Thienemann.

Matthías Jochumsson, the Rev., 1835-1920. 16 letters and 2 postcards, Reykjavík and Akureyri, October 1874 - May 1904; in Icelandic and English. — Letters of appreciation; procuring *Þjóðólfur;* remarking on the general situation in Iceland; philosophizing on the prevailing principle in the world; commenting on Jón Ólafsson's plan concerning emigration to Alaska; mentions Carpenter, Jón Sigurðsson, and Guðmundur Hannesson; printing Fiske's article on Jón Sigurðsson in *Þjóðólfur;* the bad season in 1882; establishing a school in Oddi; writing to Fiske on behalf of Einar Hjörleifsson (Kvaran), Hannes Þorsteinsson, and the Reverend Jón Björnsson in Eyrarbakki; on poverty in Iceland; mentions his poem celebrating Fiske's goodwill towards Grímsey; about Grímsey; commenting on his poetics. Enclosed: typed copies of the letters in duplicate, with notes in the margin; a list of publications on Matthías Jochumsson, last year recorded is 1938; extracts from his letters to various recipients where Fiske is mentioned, taken from *Bréf Matthíasar Jochumssonar.* One of the letters is inserted in his *Ljóðmæli* (Reykjavík: Forlag Kristjáns Ó. Þorgrímssonar, 1884).

Maurer, Konrad von, 1823-1902, Professor. 12 letters and 2 postcards, Munich, November 1879 - June 1900; in German. — Letters about Iceland's condition and scholarly matters.

Maurer, Valérie von. 6 letters and 2 cards, Munich, February 1902 - February 1904; in German. — On the sale of Konrad von Maurer's library.

May, S. 1 postcard, Leicester, Mass., 29 May [1874]; in English. — On donating books to Iceland.

Mazel, Edward. 1 postcard, Kadetten Schule, Lemberg, Léopol-Autriche, s.d.; in English. — Requesting to exchange his own publications on chess for *Í uppnámi.*

McCarthy, S. 1 letter, Monroe County, N.Y., 10 November 1881; in English. — Reference questions concerning the history of Iceland.

Mellbye, Sophie (born Munch). 1 letter, Christiania, 28 May 1902; in English. — Thanking for the photographs of her father's monument in Rome; expressing a wish to meet Fiske as she and her family are going to spend the year in Italy; presenting a book about her father, written by her sister under a pseudonym.

Mikkelsen, Marie R. 1 letter, Copenhagen, 19 September 1901; in Danish; inserted in her translation of poems by Heine *Sangirnir úr Heinrich Heine: "Die Harzreise."* Týddir av M. M. (Tórshavn, 1901). — Presenting Fiske with an offprint of the translation.

Möbius, Th[eodor], 1821-1890. 1 letter and three postcards, Kiel, 20 November 1879; 21 February and 20 March 1880; 5 June 1888; in German. — Concerning scholarship in Icelandic literature; on his library. The postcard from 1888 is inserted in his *Catalogus librorum Islandicorum et Norwegicorum ætatis mediæ editorum versorum illustratorum. Skáldatal sive poetarum recensus Eddæ Upsaliensis* (Lipsiæ: W. Engelmann, 1856).

Montelius, Oscar, 1843-1921, 1 postcard, Stockholm, 25 April 1900; in Swedish; inserted in *Antiquités Suédoises, arrangées et décrites par Oscar Montelius* (Stockholm: P.A. Norstedt & Söner, 1873-75). — Bibliographical information.

Móritz Halldórsson, 1854-1911 (the letters were written when he was a medical student). 3 letters, Copenhagen, 8 and 20 February, 8 April 1880; in Icelandic. — About his intention to give his newspapers and periodicals to the National Library in Reykjavík by the end of every year; sending Icelandic publications to Fiske; criticizing Fiske's bibliography for not including Halldór Friðriksson and his work on linguistics; asking for Fiske's articles on Iceland for his collection of such material; remarking briefly on his work and studies.

Morten Hansen, 1855-1923, school principal. 1 postcard, Reykjavík, 26 September 1900; in Icelandic. — Acknowledging a chess board.

Murray, John, *The Quarterly Review.* 1 letter, London, 5 April 1899; in English. — Giving the name of T. Bowick as the author of "Iceland To-day", in *The Quarterly Review* No. 357, July 1894. The letter is inserted between pages 82 and 83 of the periodical.

Negus, S[amuel] G., W. I. & S. G. Negus, Hardware. 1 letter, New York, 20 October 1882; in English. — Reference question concerning the history of religion in Iceland.

New York Tribune, New York City. 1 letter, 3 August 1874; signed by Whitelaw Reid; in English. — Fiske's article on Iceland.

Newton, Alfred, 1829-1907. 1 postcard, Cambridge, England, 3 December 1886; in English. — On his publications relating to Iceland.

Nicholson, James Holme. 1 postcard, Cheshire 6 February 1900; in English; inserted in *Transactions of the Lancashire and Cheshire Antiquarian Society* Vol. IX (Manchester, 1892). — Bibliographical information.

Niles, Marston. 5 letters, Law Offices, New York City, 2 May and 1 April 1874; 23 January, 10 February, and 18 August 1882; in English. — The donation of books to Iceland in 1874; concerning Bertel Gunlögsson's translation of *De Charitate* into Icelandic for the Swedenborg Society; the problem of type for the Icelandic characters.

Noreen, Adolf [Gotthard]. 1 postcard, Uppsala, 24 May 1890; in German. — On Fiske's *Bibliographical Notices.* Inserted in his *Altisländische und altnorwegische Grammatik unter Berücksichtigung des Urnordischen* (Halle, 1892).

Oddur Björnsson. 1 letter, Copenhagen, 20 October 1899; in Icelandic. —
On the sale of his collection of occasional poetry. A receipt in English is
enclosed.

Office of the Chief Signal Officer, Washington, D.C. 1 letter, 19 March
1880; signed by Albert J. Myer; in English. — On a telegraphic cable
from Northern Europe to the Faeroe Islands and Iceland.

Ólafur Davíðsson, 1862-1903, scholar in Copenhagen. 43 letters and 9 postcards, Reykjavík and Copenhagen, November 1879 - April 1892; in
Icelandic. — Chiefly concerning the procuring of books, the recording
of latest publications, and bibliographical information. Also about lectures in Reykjavík in 1879-80; the evening activities of Icelandic people; riddles about chess; the funeral of Jón Sigurðsson; the scholarly
work of the teachers at the Junior College in Reykjavík; young promising authors and poets; comments on *Gríshildarrímur;* on Fiske's catalogue of old Icelandic books; a bibliography of Icelandic books before
1781 by Jón Árnason; on the business between Jón Árnason and
Rosenthal; Icelanders in Copenhagen; his research on games in Iceland;
Hið íslenzka bókmenntafélag; literary activities in Iceland; proof reading of Fiske's bibliography of books before 1844; bibliographical research on behalf of Fiske; the establishment of the periodical *Heimfari;*
his list of "Islandica" in Danish periodicals; suggesting a publication of
Icelandic bibliography; mentioning Bogi Th. Melsteð; his own literary
activities. Enclosed: "Áætlun um hvernig haga ætti íslenzku rithöfundatali, ritatali og skrá yfir útlend rit, sem snerta Ísland", 10 sheets, written
on both sides, dated 26 February 1892. Also numerous sheets of bibliographical data and bibliographies. See also Manuscript Material 78.

Ólafur Halldórsson, 1855-1930, director of the Icelandic Cabinet in
Copenhagen. 1 letter, 29 May 1899; in Icelandic. — Concerning Fiske's
vellum manuscript of *Jónsbók.*

Olmstead, F. L. 2 letters, New York City, 17 April, 30 March 1874; in
English. — Book donations to Iceland on the occasion of the Millennial
Celebration.

Otto Tulinius. 1 letter, Akureyri, 1 December 1902; in Icelandic. —
Informing Fiske he has been elected an honorary member of the Chess
Society of Akureyri.

Páll Briem, 1856-1904, Governor of the North and East. 1 letter, Akureyri, 31 December 1903; in Icelandic. — The prospect of Carnegie financing public libraries in Iceland.

Páll Melsteð (Pálsson), 1812-1910, historian. 1 letter, Reykjavík, 27 November 1879; in Icelandic. — The question of schools for women. Enclosed: a brief historical account of the women's high schools in Iceland.

Páll Þorkelsson, 1850-1936, goldsmith. 2 letters, Reykjavík and Copenhagen, 7 July 1887; 16 July 1902; in Icelandic. — Sending specimen proofs of his *Icelandic-French Dictionary* in order to get Fiske's opinion; on his invented international language, with some handwritten specimens, and transcribed letters of recommendation in Danish.

Patursson, Sigurd Olaff. 2 letters and one postcard, Copenhagen, 31 August, 10 and 14 November 1899; in Faeroese and Danish. — Needs donations to support a newspaper in the Faeroe Islands; on his work and financial difficulties.

Peet, S[tephen] D., *The American Antiquarian, and Oriental Journal.* 1 letter, Clinton, Wisconsin, 9 February 1882; in English. — An offer to send books for review. Enclosed: one form letter, dated Chicago, 24 November 1881.

Perkins, Henry A. 2 letters, Hartford, Conn., undated, but envelope postmarked 25 December 1902; 27 February 1904; in English. — Their shared interest in Iceland; sending photographs from his visit there in 1901; expressing delight about his meeting with Fiske and their conversation in Copenhagen.

Petersen, Julius Magnús, b. 1827. 1 letter, Copenhagen, 17 September 1900; in Danish. — His résumé.

Petersens, Carl af. 1 letter and one postcard, Thackeray Hotel, London, and Lund, 25 September 1899; 11 October 1902; in English and Swedish. — Accepting an invitation; bibliographical information.

Pettersen, Hjalmar. 11 letters and 11 postcards, the University Library, Christiania; various places in Italy, May 1891 - November 1903; in English and Danish. — Bibliographical matters; a visit to Villa Landor; his research and work.

P[étur] Pétursson, Bishop, 1808-1891. 1 letter, Reykjavík, 9 February 1880; in Icelandic. — Appreciating Fiske's account of his journey in Iceland which appeared in *Times;* sending Icelandic publications with W. H. Carpenter to Fiske.

Pétur Zophoníasson, 1879-1946, genealogist. 19 letters and 3 postcards, Reykjavík, May 1900 - July 1902; in Icelandic. — Bibliographical notices; procuring of books; compiling bibliographies of books donated to the National Library by Fiske; chess in Icelandic literature; on the sale of chess publications in Iceland; the Chess Society of Reykjavík; informing Fiske of his election as an honorary member. Included with the letters are invoices, desiderata lists, a list of subscribers to *Í uppnámi,* a record of the sale of same; the chess game of Pritzel and Þorkell Þorkelsson at Garður 20 May 1901; a solution to a chess problem; records of chess material sent to the Chess Society, financial report for 1900-1901, etc.

Pjetur [Þórðarson] Guðjohnsen, 1870-1900 (the letters were written when he was a student). 18 letters, Reykjavík and Copenhagen, October 1890 - March 1900; in Icelandic (one letter in Danish). — Mentioning Fiske's visit to Húsavík; offering to make "herbarium Islandicum" for Fiske; speaking briefly about his studies, his siblings; asking for financial assistance; learning to play a violin; inquiring about job prospects in Egypt; asking for help to seek health care. Enclosed: a letter from Pjetur Guðjohnsen's doctor confirming his state of health.

Playfair, Lyon, Baron, 1818-1898. 1 letter, London, 5 December 1879; in English. — About funds for Icelandic scholarship at the University in Edinburgh.

Poestion, J[osef] C[alasanz], 1853-1922. 16 letters, Vienna, April 1885 - November 1903; in German. — Remarking on his books on Iceland, their publication and reception in Europe and the United States; offering to send his books to Fiske; on his Scandinavian grammar publications; desiring an honorary doctorate from a university in the United States; his position in Vienna; mentions Fiske's publications; his family and their situation; appreciating Fiske's publications; trying to have his "Isländische Anthologie" published; bibliographical information on German-speaking scholars writing on Iceland; commenting on *Mímir* and giving additional information to the list of his publications; remarking on Icelandic politics (i.e. commenting on Valtýr Guðmundsson and Hannes Hafstein).

Post Office Department, Washington, D.C. 1 letter, 24 April 1873; signed by Joseph H. Blackfan; in English. — On postal service from the United States to Iceland.

Powell, F[rederick] Y[ork], 1850-1904. 1 letter, Oxford, 25 September 1896; in English. — Inability to find a copy of Oddur Gottskálksson's translation of the *New Testament* from 1540.

Press, Muriel Annie Caroline (b. Hoare). 1 postcard, Bristol, 28 October 1900; in English. — Giving her full name. Inserted in her translation of *Laxdæla saga* (London: J. M. Dent & Co., 1899).

Prior, Waldemar. 2 letters, Nassjö, Sweden, 19 December 1897; 31 December, s.a.; in English and Swedish. — Mainly acknowledging material sent to him by Fiske.

Pruyn, John N. L. See **Albany Institute.**

Quaritch, Bernard, bookseller. 1 letter, London, 19 March 1896; in English. — Offering an Icelandic manuscript of the *Elder Edda*, from about 1790, for sale.

Rafn, Carl Christian, 1795-1864. 17 letters and notes, Copenhagen, November 1850 - September 1854; in Danish. — Invitations; offering to introduce Fiske to young Icelanders in Copenhagen; on translating into English articles for *Mémoires de la Société royale des antiquaires du Nord;* letters of introduction to Carl Gustaf Styffe, in the Royal Archives in Stockholm, and another to Professor C. G. Bunius, Lund, Sweden; about Old Norse scholarship.

Rafn, Caroline. 7 letters, Copenhagen, March 1882 - April 1903; in Danish. — Mainly thanking for material sent by Fiske, Christmas greetings, a death notice, expressing pleasure at Fiske's visits, etc. Also sending her father's publications to Fiske. Enclosed: an undated Christmas card from the family Rafn, congratulating Fiske on the Order of Dannebrog.

Rafn, Dagmar. 3 letters, Copenhagen and Romden, 18 April 1893; 21 November 1894; 27 March 1895; in Danish. — Appreciation for the reception in Florence; presenting Fiske with C.C. Rafn's correspondence compiled by her and her sister, Caroline — see Manuscript Material 81;

mentioning George P. Marsh's biography by his wife. Also two Christmas cards, undated.

Reeves, Caroline M. 2 letters, s.l., 20 October 1890; 8 April 1891; in English. — Thanking for the basket of fruit for her journey; Responding to Fiske's letter of consolation. The letters, along with several newspaper clippings about her son's, Arthur M. Reeves', death, are placed in an envelope pasted to the back cover of *Biography and Correspondence of Arthur Middleton Reeves by W. D. Foulke* (London: Henry Frowde, 1895). The photograph of Reeves, Willard Fiske, Matthías Jochumsson, and Carpenter, is pasted to the verso of the back flyleaf.

Religious Tract Society, The. 1 letter, London, 26 February 1880; signed by Lewis Borrett White; in English. — About an illustration for a book.

Reusch, Hans. 2 letters, Vossevangen and Christiania, 26 August 1899; 3 June 1904; in English. — Welcoming Fiske to Norway and regretting not being in Christiania to meet him; on *Mímir*.

Rice, Howard M. 4 letters, English & Classical High School, Providence, 11, 14, and 25 May, 27 July 1874; in English. — Donating books to Iceland on the occasion of the Millennial Celebration in 1874.

Rodwell, G. F. 1 letter, Marlborough College, Wiltshire, England, 24 April 1880; in English. — On telegraphic communication of Iceland with America and Europe.

Sephton, J. 1 card, London, 24 May [before 1895]; in English. — About his poor travelling abilities; thanking Fiske for his appreciation of Sephton's work; on his translation of *Ólafs saga Tryggvasonar* [which was published in London in 1895.]

Shaw, Katherine M. B. 4 letters, Literary Office, Florence, 4 March [1901]; 29 May, 8 July, and 27 November 1901; in English. — Checking Icelandic papers and periodicals for Fiske's library; on proof reading of same.

Sheeleigh, M., the Rev. 1 letter, Whitemarsh, Montg. County, Pennsylvania, 22 August 1874; in English. — Reference question on translations of Luther's hymns into Icelandic.

Sheldon, H. S. 1 letter, Middlebury, Vermont, 23 February 1880; in English. — Concerning Icelandic coins.

Sherman, L. A. New Haven, 2 letters, 1 and 16 May 1882; in English. — Needing Scandinavian and Icelandic books for his paper on Scandinavian literature; observing that Yale's holdings are limited; suggesting book exchange.

Sigfús Blöndal, 1874-1950, librarian. 41 letters and 7 postcards, Copenhagen; Oxford; London, September 1898 - November 1903; primarily in English, but some Icelandic. — Job inquiry; on behalf of Guðmundur Tómasson; acting for Fiske in Copenhagen; Bjarni Jónsson's illness; desiderata; cataloguing books for Fiske's library; bibliographical problems; recommending Halldór Hermannsson as Fiske's assistant; receipt of material sent to Fiske to Copenhagen; on Dante translations into Icelandic; his illness; an inscription on a tankard; asking for letters of recommendation to literary people in Oxford; his activities in England; his work for Fiske in England; the late Guðbrandur Vigfússon's condition in Oxford; on *Mjög lítill skákbæklingur;* reading proofs of some of Fiske's publications; his engagement to Björg Thorláksson (see her letter); their summer holidays in Iceland in the summer 1902; commenting on Fiske's article on the Constitutional changes in Iceland; Blöndal's work on the Icelandic-Danish dictionary.

Sigfús Eymundsson, 1837-1911, bookseller. 4 letters, Copenhagen and Reykjavík, 3 February 1880; 6 May 1882; 27 April and 24 September 1901; in Icelandic. — Potential trade agreement between Iceland and the United States; on exporting horses to England; proposes to publish a book of photographs of various Icelandic scenes; sending the Icelandic translation of *Peer Gynt.* Enclosed: a circular announcing the publication of *Peer Gynt.*

Sigríður E[inarsdóttir] Magnússon, 1831-1915. 3 letters, Cambridge, England, 19 October 1882; 5 April 1886; 20 April 1892; in English. — Acknowledging contribution for the Icelandic relief fund; regretting inability to visit Fiske in Florence; about the establishment of a high school for girls in Iceland.

S[igurður] M[ethusalem] S[igurbjarnarson] Askdal, 1861-1918 (agent for books in Minneota, Minnesota). 1 letter, Minneota, 30 May 1886; in Icelandic. — Intends to go to Iceland to study Old Norse and asks Fiske to refer him to shipping companies.

Sigurður Jensson, the Rev., 1853-1924. 2 letters, Flatey in Breiðafjörður, 10 January 1887; 20 November 1900; in Icelandic. — Bibliographical problems; on the public library in Flatey.

Sigurður Jóhannesson, 1841-1923, poet. 1 letter, Halifax, Nova Scotia, 5 May 1880; in Icelandic. — Remarking on the general situation in Iceland, lack of roads, bad housing, agriculture, lack of working skills. Proposing to send timber to Iceland for building bridges.

Sigurður Jónsson, 1839-1909, jailer. 1 letter, Reykjavík, 6 December 1901; in Icelandic. — Appreciating the donations to the Chess Society of Reykjavík.

Sigurður Kristjánsson, 1854-1952, bookseller. 56 letters, one postcard, and a New Year's greeting, Reykjavík, February 1886 - June 1903; in Icelandic and Danish. — Business matters. Enclosed are numerous invoices, price lists, and lists of titles.

Skapti Jósepsson, 1839-1905, editor. 6 letters, Akureyri; Seyðisfjörður; Copenhagen, July 1874 - April 1892; in Icelandic. — A letter of recommendation on behalf of Fiske, addressed to "Kæri vin minn"; the newspaper *Norðlingur;* the affairs of "Framfarafélag Akureyrar"; sending his periodical *Austri;* the establishment of a library for the Eastern District of Iceland; asking for book donations. Enclosed: one sheet with musical notes by Sigríður Jósephsson, to the poem Matthías Jochumsson composed to honor Fiske.

Slater, Henry H., the Rev. 1 postcard, Thornhaugh Rectory, Wansford, England, 15 September 1903; in English. — Information relating to his book *Manual of the Birds of Iceland* (Edinburgh, 1901). The postcard is pasted on back end leaf of his book. See also postcard to Halldór Hermannsson from same.

Smith, E. J. 1 postcard, Brookhaven, N.Y., 12 October 1882; in English. — Contributing to the relief fund for Iceland.

Søkort-arkivet. 1 letter, Copenhagen, 28 October 1901; signed by C.B. Kilbe; in Danish. — Sending a colored sketch map of Grímsey, 12.8 x 12.3 cm. Enclosed: the same map, in black and white, 15.1 x 15.6 cm.

Solberg, Thorvald, 1852-1949, Library of Congress. 8 letters, Washington, D.C., November 1880 - June 1904; in English. — Asking for two circulars on Icelandic literature by Fiske, issued in Berlin; acknowledging publications sent by Fiske; his intention to compile a bibliography on literature pertaining to Iceland; sending proof-sheets of a list of the text-editions and translations of the Eddas in order to get opinion and suggestions to improve the work; recognizing corrections from Fiske; on his work; acknowledging *Bibliographical Notices* IV; his trip to Europe to collect bibliographical data; appreciation of *Mímir;* his second trip to Europe to do research on copyright matters.

[Sonzogno, Edoardo]. 1 postcard, Milano, 21 November 1902; in Italian. — Unsigned. Inserted in Ed. Edoardo Sonzogno *Storia dei Popoli Scandinavi* (Milano, 1893). Tipped in at the end of book.

Steenstrup, K. J. V. 1 postcard, Copenhagen, 5 February 1900; in Danish. — Bibliographical information. Inserted in his *Om Østerbygden* (Copenhagen, 1886).

St[efán] Guðjohnsen. 1 letter, Húsavík, 22 December 1903; in Icelandic. — Appreciating the article "Book-Collections in Iceland", sent to him by Fiske.

Stefán Þórðarson. See **Thordarson, Stephen.**

Stefansson, Vilhjalmur, 1879-1962. 4 letters, Cambridge, Mass. and "on way to New York", 31 August 1903; 18 May and 10 June (two letters) 1904; in English. — About translations of publications dealing with modern Icelandic literature; acknowledging *Mímir* and the pamphlet on the "libraries of Iceland"; suggesting additional names that should appear in *Mímir;* his proposed attempt at writing a book on modern Icelandic literature.

Steingrímur Thorsteinsson, 1831-1913, teacher at the Junior College in Reykjavík. 1 letter, Reykjavík, 12 February 1880; in English. — Thanking for the book sent by Fiske; commenting on Bugge's theories on Old Norse mythology.

Steinn Steinsson, farmer. 1 letter, Hvammur in Dalir, 9 March 1880; in Icelandic. — Remarking on the pleasure of having had Fiske as a guest in Hvammur; asking Fiske to select the book he is to receive, preferably on homeopathy.

Stetson, George R. 1 letter, Stuttgart, 3 March 1883; in English. — On the body found in the bog at Veile in Denmark.

Storm, Joh. 1 letter, Christiania, 6 April 1894; in Danish. — Presenting Fiske with Müller's translation of Dante's *Inferno;* appreciating the interest Fiske shows in Scandinavian literature.

Sunswick. 1 note, West Hampton Centre, Long Island, N.Y., 20 September 1882; in English. — Contribution to the relief fund to aid Icelanders.

Sveinbjörn Sveinbjörnsson, 1861-1924, teacher at the College in Aarhus. 1 note, Aarhus, 27 December 1896; in Italian.

Tatum, L. W. 1 letter, lumber dealers, Pittsburgh, Penn., 6 September 1882; in English. — Donations to the relief fund for Iceland.

Tegnér, Elof. 1 letter, the University Library in Lund, 22 January 1900; in Swedish. — Bibliographical information.

Thiele, L[ouise] F[rances] von. 1 postcard, Lintz, England, 26 November 1902; in English. — Bibliographical information on her work. Inserted at end of her "Through Iceland on a side saddle." Extr.fr. *Travel.* Vol. VI (London, 1901).

Thiele, Richard. 1 postcard, Erfurt, 2 June 1900; in English. — Giving his first name. The postcard is pasted on the back flyleaf of his *Die Insel Island* (Erfurt, 1894). See also letters to Halldór Hermannsson.

Thomas, Mary H. 1 letter, Union Springs, N.Y., 4 January 1883; in English. — Donation to the relief fund for Iceland.

Thompson, G. M. 1 letter, Gimli, Manitoba, 10 August 1895; in English and Icelandic. — Presenting to Fiske the Icelandic periodical *Svava,* and books published in Gimli.

Thor [Philip Axel] Jensen, 1863-1947, merchant. The letters were sent to Valdimar Stefánsson, who was writing a biography of Thor Jensen in 1939, by regular mail. He used them in the biography. He had been asked to return them, but apparently did not. See letters from Valtýr Stefánsson to Halldór Hermannsson.

Thóra [Pétursdóttir] Thoroddsen, d. 1917. 2 letters, Copenhagen, 2 January 1902; 20 November 1903; in Danish. — Thanking for the boxes of chocolates.

Thordarson, Stephen. 1 letter, Winnipeg, 2 December 1895; in Icelandic. — Pleading for donations to the church building in South Winnipeg.

Tidsskrift for Skak. 1 letter, Copenhagen, 15 November 1900; signed by Andr. Rosendahl; in Danish. — About the periodical, subscriptions, etc.

Tietgen, C. F. 1 letter, Copenhagen, 1 March 1880; in English. — On the North Atlantic Telegraph.

Torfhildur Þ[orsteinsdóttir] Hólm, 1845-1918, writer. 1 letter, Gimli, Manitoba, 13 December 1879; in Icelandic. — Thanking for the picture of "Friðriksgáfa"; appreciating Fiske's goodwill towards Iceland. Two copies of a photograph of "Friðriksgáfa" exist in the Fiske Icelandic Collection. See Graphic Material, 6.32.

Tryggvi Gunnarsson, 1835-1917, banker. 9 letters, Copenhagen and Reykjavík, January 1880 - October 1897; mainly Icelandic, but also some Danish. — Mentioning the prospect of a trade agreement between Iceland and the United States; presenting to Fiske the publications of Þjóðvinafélagið; about Ólafur Davíðsson; asking for dates from Fiske's life to publish in *Almanak Þjóðvinafélagsins.* Enclosed: a formal invitation from the parliamentary representatives to dinner, 20 August 1879. Signed by Magnús Stephensen, H. K. Friðriksson, and Tryggvi Gunnarsson. See also Magnús Stephensen.

Tweedie, Mrs. Alec [i.e. Ethel B. Harley]. 1 letter and a postcard, London, 26 January and 2 February 1900; in English. — Bibliographical information concerning her books. The postcard is pasted inside back cover of her *A Girl's Ride in Iceland* (London, 1889), and the letter is inserted at the end of the same book from 1895.

Tyler, M. C. 1 letter, Editorial Rooms, Christian Union, New York City, 3 September 1874; in English. — Regrets having to decline Hjaltalín's article because of its length.

Valdimar Ásmundsson, 1852-1902, editor. 10 letters and notes, and one postcard, Leirá in Borgarfjörður; Reykjavík, April 1880 - September 1900; in English and Icelandic. — Biographical account; his intention to go to the United States; desire to attend Cornell University; offering Oddur Gottskálksson's *New Testament* translation from 1540 and later also other titles from the sixteenth — eighteenth centuries.

Valgerður Þ[orsteinsdóttir] Gunnarsson, 1836-1917, Principal of the Women's School at Laugaland in Eyjafjörður. 1 letter, Laugaland, 1 March 1880; in Icelandic. — Acknowledging 12 issues of *Harper's Bazar* sent by Fiske to the school.

Valtýr Guðmundsson, 1860-1928, Professor. 5 letters and 2 postcards, Copenhagen, May 1890 - September 1903; in Icelandic, English, and Danish. — Acknowledging the receipt of *Bibliographical Notices;* reflecting on Arthur Middleton Reeves, his life and accomplishments, and their translation of *Laxdæla;* on the postal service from Europe to Iceland; on Fiske's obtaining *Eimreiðin* bound; sending the same periodical to Grímsey by the order of Fiske.

Vetter, Theodor, 1853-1922, teacher. 1 letter, Frauenfeld, 15 June 1887; a note of acknowledgment, 24 June 1887; in English. — Asking for letters of introduction on behalf of his brother, Dr. Ferdinand Vetter, Professor of Germanic philology at the University of Berne, who intended to go to Iceland to study the language.

Vilhjálmur Jónsson, 1870-1902, post office clerk. 4 letters, Reykjavík and Copenhagen, 10 February, 17 June, 26 September, and 18 October 1901; in Icelandic and English. — Job inquiry; asking for a letter of recommendation to the "Library School" in New York.

Vilhjálmur Stefánsson. See **Stefansson, Vilhjalmur.**

Waters, Edwin F. 1 letter, Boston, 25 June 1887; in English. — Referring to Mrs. Ole Bull's letter; on the Norse voyages to America. See Bull, Sara.

Welsch, F. C. 5 letters, Dresden, 22 June, 10 and 20 September 1891; 11 and 20 November 1892, with a postscript by Ada Welsch; in English. — Presenting to Fiske *Voyages Historiques de L'Europe par M. de B. F.,* which has 15 pages devoted to Iceland.

Westminster Review, The. 1 letter from the editors, Paris, 22 November 1890; in English; inserted in *The Westminster Review,* Nov. 1888, vol. CXXX, preceding "King Olaf Tryggvisson", p. 533. — Bibliographical information.

White, John G., counselor at law. 1 letter, Cleveland, 21 August 1901; in

English. — Dealing with chess. See also Manuscript Material 43 and 54.

Wilkinson, Garth. 3 letters, London, 6 March 1887; 19 May and 9 June 1898; in English. — A letter of introduction on behalf of Clement Wilkinson; spent the morning with *Völuspá* and Sveinbjörn Egilsson's *Lexicon Poeticum;* on Swedenborg's writings; sending *Völuspá* to Fiske. Last letter with a postscript by Florence Attwood-Mathews. See also a letter to Wilkinson from Fiske, Miscellaneous Correspondents and Recipients of Letters, and Manuscript Material 44.

Wilson, George. 1 letter, Lexington, Missouri, 2 November 1891; in English. — Reference question on books to study the Icelandic language; giving an account of his Icelandic books.

Winslow, Wilh. A note on the back of an envelope, Chicago, 19 October 1868; in English. — Mentioning Gísli Brynjúlfsson.

Wood, Francis H. 1 postcard, London, 1 May 1900; in English. — Bibliographical information. Inserted in Wilfred T. Grenfell, *Vikings of To-Day* (London, 1895).

Wroblewsky, Otto B. 1 postcard, Copenhagen, 30 June 1900; in Danish. Inserted in Købke, Peter, *Om Runerne i Norden* (Copenhagen: Otto B. Wroblewskis Forlag, 1890). — Bibliographical information.

Þóra Pétursdóttir Thoroddsen. See **Thóra P. Thoroddsen.**

Þ[órður] Guðjohnsen, 1844-1926, store manager. 2 letters, Húsavík, 10 January 1880; 29 December 1886; in English and Icelandic. — Thanking for the books to the children; mentioning Fiske's journey in Iceland; regretting inability to give information on old books on the list Fiske sent to him; giving references to Rector Jón Þorkelsson, and Þorleifur Jónsson, Skinnastaðir. Enclosed is a letter from Þórður Guðjohnsen Jr., 2 January 1880, thanking for the books, and mentioning his school work; another letter from same is pasted with letters from Ólafur Davíðsson, 6 September 1880; mentioning family and friends.

Þórður Þ[órðarson] Jónasson, 1825-1884. 1 letter, Reykjaholt, Borgarfjörður, 1 October 1879; in Icelandic. — Thanking for the books to the children and Fiske's photograph; asking for prices of a plough and a saddlery in the United States.

Þorkell Árnason. 1 letter, Sandvík on Grímsey, 9 May 1902; in Icelandic. — About chess on Grímsey.

Þorlákur Ó[lafsson] Johnson, 1838-1917, merchant. 4 letters, Reykjavík and Leith, 10 September 1876; 28 November 1879; 10 February and 23 March 1880; 23 April 1888; in Icelandic and English. — Sending his periodical *Útsynningur* to Fiske; remarking on progress in the United States and the prospect of trade between the countries; on behalf of Sigfús Eymundsson; the late Jón Sigurðsson; about translated articles by Fiske on Iceland and published; the idea of a commercial college in Iceland, with commentary on "the miserable state of Iceland's trade is one of the greatest drawbacks to our progress."

Þ[orleifur] J[ón] Bjarnason, 1863-1935 (the letters were written when he was a student at the Junior College in Reykjavík). 1 letter, Reykjavík, 29 November 1879; in Icelandic. — Thanking for the books sent by Fiske; briefly remarking on school work; a poem of two stanzas, "Norðurljósin", included with the letter.

Þórleifur Jónsson, the Rev., 1845-1911. 1 letter, Skinnastaðir, Þingeyjarsýsla, 7 July 1887; in Icelandic. — Thanking for *Bibliographical Notices* I; inability to remark on the printed list from Fiske on "Icelandic Books of the 16th Century."

Þorsteinn Br[ynjúlfur] Arnljótsson, the Rev., 1865-1921. 4 letters, Bægisá in Eyjafjörður, 5 November 1879; 2 March, 6 September 1880; 8 January 1887; in Icelandic. — Remarks on the school at Möðruvellir and the Women's School at Laugaland; his studies at home.

Þorsteinn Erlingsson, 1858-1914, poet. 1 letter, Copenhagen, 21 December 1890; in Icelandic. — Books offered for sale.

Þorvaldur Jónsson, 1837-1916, post office clerk. 12 letters, Ísafjörður and Copenhagen, June 1900 - August 1903; in Icelandic and one in Danish (written in Copenhagen). — Chiefly on chess matters and chess societies in Iceland; on parcel service between Leith and Iceland. One sheet of a chess problem enclosed. Also a letter of appreciation from the members of the Chess Club in Ísafjörður.

Þorvaldur Thoroddsen, 1855-1921, geologist. 17 letters and 2 postcards, Copenhagen; Möðruvellir; Reykjavík, February 1880 - September 1903; in Danish and Icelandic. — About research on Iceland's nature and geology; remarking on William Lee Howard's account of his journey in Iceland in 1881; complaining of lack of understanding from the government concerning geological research; sending his publications to Fiske; on his travels and research in Iceland; death notices, and other topics. Enclosed: a Christmas card from Þóra and Þorvaldur Thoroddsen, 1899. Also a list of his publications.

2. Letters to Halldór Hermannsson

Abraham, Peter. 1 letter, University of California, Los Angeles, 13 September 1940; in English. — Job inquiry on behalf of Robert Abraham, who had been teaching in Akureyri.

Aðalsteinn Kristjánsson, 1878-1949. 1 letter, Winnipeg, 27 February 1918; in Icelandic. — Bibliographical inquiry concerning "democracy."

Adam Þorgrímsson, the Rev., 1879-1924. See Manuscript Material 129.

Agnar Klemens Jónsson, 1909-1984, Icelandic Consul in New York. 2 letters, 10 May 1941; 31 May 1942; in Icelandic. — Reference question on sources relating to the Icelandic church on behalf of Thor Thors; news from Iceland; new Concul in New York.

Ágúst H. Bjarnason, 1875-1952, Professor at the University of Iceland. 3 letters, Reykjavík, 7 March 1914; 29 August and 18 December 1928; in Icelandic. — Plans for the new buildings at the University of Iceland in Reykjavík (on same topic see also letter from Carl Lorentzen); about proposed research grants from the Rockefeller Institution. See also: Raymond Pearl, Alan Gregg, Guðmundur Finnbogason, and Guðmundur Hannesson.

Alexander, J. 2 letters, Birmingham, England, 27 January and 17 February 1930; in English. — Thanking for the extract from Jón Grímsson's *Spilabók;* asking about interlibrary loan.

Alexander Jóhannesson, 1888-1965, Rector, University of Iceland. 1 letter, Reykjavík, 13 April 1940; in Icelandic. — Asking Halldór

Hermannsson to represent the University of Iceland at a celebration at the University, Philadelphia, Pennsylvania.

Allen, Jean Pennock (Mrs. Coe H. Allen). 1 letter, Bedford, Ohio, s.d., but postmarked 11 November 1935; in English. — Mentioning an English translation of an Icelandic saga, probably *Þorvalds saga víðförla.* Enclosed: a sheet with table of contents.

Allen, Ralph B., b. 1891. 5 letters, University of Pennsylvania, Philadelphia, 6 November 1933; 14 February, 30 April, and 15 May 1934; 16 September 1947; in English. — About translation of sagas; publication affairs.

American Business Magazine, New York City. 4 letters, 3 August, 3 and 27 October 1928; 22 January 1929; signed by M. A. Kesner, managing editor; in English. — Request for an article relating to Iceland's National Celebration in 1930.

American Geographical Society, New York City. 33 letters, September 1926 - November 1940; most are signed by Isaiah Bowman, some by G. M. Wrigley and others; 3 telegrams; copies of 2 letters from Halldór Hermannsson; in English. — The letters are chiefly from the year 1930, on the editing of Thorstina Walters' English translation of *Vínlandsferðirnar* by Matthías Þórðarson. See also letters from Thorstina Walters and Matthías Þórðarson.

American Historical Review, The, New York City. 2 letters, 3 March 1941; 8 May 1941; signed by R. L. Schuyler, managing editor; in English. — About a review of William G. Goodwin's *The Truth about Leif Ericsson and the Greenland Voyages.* Enclosed: a typescript of the review by Halldór Hermannsson for the periodical; two sheets.

American Numismatic Society, The, New York City. 2 letters, 2 December and 27 November 1918; signed by Sidney P. Noe; in English. — Request for the *Catalogue of Runic Literature*; receipt of same acknowledged.

American-Scandinavian Foundation, The, New York City. 67 letters, January 1915 - March 1946; mainly signed by Hanna Astrup Larsen, some by James Creese, J. B. C. Watkins, and Henry Goddard Leach and others; two telegrams; drafts and copies of 8 letters from Halldór Hermannsson; a note suggesting Cliff-Eyvind as a translation for Fjalla-

Eyvindur; in English. — Mainly on editing and translation problems, bibliographical inquiries, and requests for articles for the *American-Scandinavian Review*. Enclosed: a request for a book from Frick Art Reference Library, addressed to the Foundation and transferred to Halldór Hermannsson.

American Unitarian Association, Boston, Mass. 4 letters, 10 and 19 February, 7 March and 10 May 1923; in English. — The lecture tour of Professor Bjarnason of the University of Iceland.

Amtsbókasafnið í Stykkishólmi (The District Library). 1 letter, Stykkishólmur, 4 August 1908; signed by the librarian, Baldvin Bergvinsson; in Icelandic. — Reception of volumes of the Islandica series affirmed.

Anderson, S[ven] Axel, b. 1900. 2 letters, University of Vermont, Burlington, 14 February, 19 March 1931; in English. — Reference question; needs pictures to go with his article on Icelandic industries.

Anderson, John A. 1 letter, Grantsville, Utah, 26 November 1931; in English. — About learning Icelandic by correspondence.

Andersson, Aksel, 1851-1923, Uppsala University Library. 4 letters, 7 July, 7 September, and 6 November 1915; 23 February 1916; 2 postcards, 26 May 1906 and undated but postmarked 10 September 1915; in English and Swedish. — Bibliographical information. Enclosed: a list of "Icelandic 16th-century books in the Library of the Royal University of Uppsala." 1 folio sheet.

Arctic Institute of North America, Washington, D.C. 2 letters, 22 August and 17 September 1947; signed by Marie Tremaine; in English. — On Halldór Hermannsson's publication plans.

Arestad, Sverre. 1 letter, University of Washington, Seattle, 27 October 1941; in English. — About translating a lecture by Ejnar Munksgaard into English.

Árni B[jörn] Björnsson, 1896-1947, goldsmith. 1 letter, Reykjavík, 10 September 1944; in Icelandic. — A letter of introduction on behalf of Haraldur Árnason.

Árni Helgason, b. 1891, Icelandic Consul in Chicago. 1 letter, Wilmette,

Illinois, 5 August 1945; in Icelandic. — Informing Halldór Hermannsson of a collection of Icelandic books offered for purchase in Chicago.

Árni Þorvaldsson, 1874-1946, Akureyri. See Manuscript Material 92 and 93.

Arnljótur B. Olson. See **Olson, Arnljótur B.**

Arpi, Rolf. 1 letter, Uppsala, 24 November 1903; in Swedish. — Relating to the publication of *Mímir.* Enclosed: a bibliography of Swedish scholars writing on Icelandic matters, 47 sheets.

Arup, Erik, 1876-1951, historian, Copenhagen. See Manuscript Material 106.

Ása Guðmundsdóttir Wright. See **Wright, Ása Guðmundsdóttir.**

Austin, Winifred. 3 letters, the Ogontz School, Pennsylvania; Morton, Mass., 11 March 1914; 6 November 1933; 22 October 1944; in English. — Reference question on Old Norse matters.

Babcock, W[illia]m H[enry], 1849-1922, attorney at law. 2 letters, Washington, D.C., 8 and 15 November 1910; in English. — The Vinland question.

Bainton, Roland H., b. 1894. 2 letters, New Haven, 23 January and 16 February 1941; in English. — Calling for letters from George L. Burr to use in writing his memoirs.

Bakeless, John, b. 1894. 3 letters, Washington, D.C., 20 May, 22 and 26 August 1942; in English. — On the etymology of the name Marlowe; acknowledging answer.

Baker, George P., Professor, Harvard University. 1 letter, Cambridge, Mass., 2 April 1917; in English. — Expressing thanks for directions given by Halldór Hermannsson for the staging of Jóhann Sigurjónsson's play, *Eyvind of the Hills.* Enclosed: a review of the performance in *The Boston Evening Transcript,* March 1917.

Baldur Guðjohnsen. See **Gudjohnsen, Baldur.**

Baldvins, Otto J. 2 letters, Watertown, Mass., 13 and 17 March 1931; in English. — Books offered for sale (publications of Icelandic sagas).

Banks, Edgar J. 1 letter, Eustis, Florida, 11 March 1924; in English. — "Ancient Babylonian tablets" for sale.

Bardal, H. S. 30 letters and 3 postcards, Winnipeg, September 1905 - February 1918; two drafts of letters from Halldór Hermannsson, 21 July and 8 September 1905; in Icelandic. — Bardal was the Fiske Icelandic Collection's agent for Icelandic books published in Winnipeg. The main subject of the letters is regarding procuring of books and periodicals.

Barnason, Charles Frederick, Harvard University. 1 letter, Hingham, Mass., 19 March 1937; also a draft of a letter from Halldór Hermannsson, 15 April 1937; in English. — Pertaining to Barnason's dissertation topic; job inquiry.

Bartoli, Jane Fortescue. 4 letters, Pittsburgh, Pennsylvania; Concord, Mass., 8 August, 20 September, and 21 November 1942; one undated; in English. — Old Norse matters; reference questions; shipping problems to Iceland in 1942.

Bay, J. Christian, Librarian, John Crerar Library, Chicago. See Manuscript Material 64.

Beck, Thor J[ensen], b. 1882. 13 letters and one postcard, Copenhagen; Ithaca; New York; University of South Dakota, Vermillion; Emory, Virginia; Monticello, Arkansas, February 1924 - July 1939; two undated; in Danish and English. — Chiefly relating to his research on Old Norse literature. Enclosed: copy of a letter from Cornell University; copy of a letter from Otto Kinkeldey, Cornell University Librarian; copy of a letter from Halldór Hermannsson to Arthur Andrews on behalf of Beck; list of questions about Old Norse matters.

Bellows, H. A., b. 1885. 4 letters, Minneapolis, 21 and 28 October, 9 and 12 November 1935; in English. — Reference question regarding a new introduction to a second edition of his translation of the *Poetic Edda;* appreciating bibliographical information.

Bendes, Harold H[erman], b. 1882. 1 letter, Princeton, 30 December 1936; in English. — Acknowledging information on the etymology of the word "skijoring."

Benedikt Gröndal, b. 1924 (the letter was written when he was a student at Harvard University). 1 letter, Cambridge, Mass., s.d.; in Icelandic. —

Reference question and a request to Halldór Hermannsson to comment on Gröndal's thesis.

Ben[edikt] S. Þórarinsson, 1861-1940. 5 letters, Reykjavík, 26 October 1924; 14 November 1927; 12 September 1938; 19 June and 31 July 1939; in Icelandic. — Brief news from Iceland; childhood memoirs; request for volumes of the Islandica series.

Benson, Adolph B[urnett], 1881-1962, Yale University. 4 letters, New Haven, 15 and 23 October 1934; 21 May 1935; 1 February 1939; in English. — Submitting a paper for MLA in 1934; on illustration for the translation of Hjalmar Lindroth's book *Motsatsernas ö;* reference question.

Bergelin, O. P., University of Delaware. 1 letter, Newark, 16 May 1951; in English. — Reference question on the recovery of heat from hot springs.

Bergh, Johan Robert Hjalmar. 1 letter, Providence, Rhode Island, 8 March .1941; in English. — An appeal for advice concerning admittance to graduate school. Enclosed: his résumé and portrait photograph.

Bergson, Paul. 1 letter, Winnipeg, 10 July 1912; in Icelandic. — *Guðbrandsbiblía* offered for sale.

Bibliographical Society of America, Chicago. 7 letters, November 1917 - June 1918; signed by George Watson Cole; in English. — About "Fiske memorial meeting" of the Society.

Birgel, Henry F. & Sons, New York City. 2 letters, 2 April and 4 May 1943; signed by Andrew P. Birgel; copies of two letters from Halldór Hermannsson; in English. — Layout and binding of the edition of *Laxdœla.*

Bishof, Ruth. 3 letters, Rochester and Ithaca, N.Y., 8 February 1931; 14 June 1940; 21 August 1941; in English. — Request to Halldór Hermannsson to comment on her retelling of Scandinavian myths and to write an introduction for the publication of same; publication problems.

Bjarni Sæmundsson, 1867-1940, teacher at the Junior College in Reykjavík. See Manuscript Material 129.

Bjarni Þorsteinsson, the Rev., 1861-1938, Siglufjörður. See Manuscript Material 129.

Björgvin Vigfússon, 1866-1942, county justice. 1 letter, Efri-Hvoll in Rangárvellir, 8 April 1939; in Icelandic. — Concerning his writings on "organized social upbringing." Enclosed: operating estimate for a school in Rangárvallasýsla specializing in working skills, dated 30 April 1937, 5 sheets.

Björn G. Björnsson. 1 letter, Madison, Wis., 17 November 1919; in Icelandic. — Seeking titles to learn Icelandic on behalf of his English teacher.

Björn M[agnússon] Ólsen, 1850-1919, Rector at the Junior College in Reykjavík. 19 letters, 10 postcards, and 1 card, Reykjavík, December 1898 - March 1918; in Icelandic. — School matters; news from Iceland; Icelandic politics; on his research; on publication matters (Fiske's, Halldór Hermannsson's, and his own); comments and corrections to Islandica VIII; books to be purchased from Iceland; about Fiske's collection of Icelandic books. See also Manuscript Material 129.

Björn Sigurðsson, 1913-1959, University Laboratory. 1 letter, Reykjavík, 22 April 1944; in Icelandic. — Request for the first two printed catalogues of the Fiske Icelandic Collection, sending offprints of his publications.

Björn Þorsteinsson, 1918-1986, Professor, University of Iceland. 1 letter, Reykjavík, 8 November 1951; in Icelandic. — Publication of a pamphlet on place names.

Blankner, Fredericka. 15 letters and 2 postcards, Vassar College, New York; Chicago; Cleveland, June 1933 - October 1940; 10 of the letters are undated, but seem to be from about 1934; in English. — Regarding her translation of Giovanni Bach's *A History of Scandinavian Literatures,* and publication of same; bibliographical questions; request for editorial comments.

Boas, Harriet Betty (Mrs. Emil L. Boas). 4 letters, New York City and Wardman Park Hotel, Washington, D.C., 30 January, 5 February, and 19 April 1925; one undated; in English. — Asking for information about a manuscript of "Rímur af Úlfari sterka" she owns, written in 1751 by Árni Böðvarsson.

Boberg, Inger Margr[ethe], 1900-1957, Indiana University. 4 letters and 1 postcard, Bloomington; Mt. Kisco, N.Y., 10 April, 17 and 25 September 1946; 27 January 1947; one undated; in Danish and English. — On her research; housing in Ithaca.

Bogi Th[orarensen] Melsteð, 1860-1929, historian. 74 letters, 49 postcards, and 1 card, Copenhagen, January 1900 - May 1925; a few slips of paper with extra information, messages and inquiries; in Icelandic. — Arrangement for a trip to Italy; the prospect of getting Halldór Hermannsson either to Copenhagen or Reykjavík; the Arnamagnæan Institute; requesting material for publication by Fræðafélag. In numerous letters: news from Copenhagen and Iceland; Icelandic politics; on Melsteð's research and publications; his professional activities; bibliographical requests and information; general publications on Icelandic subjects; Hið íslenzka fræðafjelag, and more.

Bousios, Basil Nicholas Hellenagoras. 1 letter, New York City, 12 April 1940; in English. — Reference question on Hellenism in the Scandinavian world; "answered in the negative" is noted on the letter in Halldór Hermannsson's hand.

Brady, Caroline, b. 1905. 5 letters, University of California, Davis, 15 August 1940; 1 February, 7 and 21 July 1941; 8 October 1944; copy of a letter from Halldór Hermannsson, 9 September 1940; in English. — Reference questions; editorial problems regarding her edition of *Jarlmanns saga ok Hermanns*.

Brennan, Pauline. 1 letter, Pembina, North Dakota, 10 November 1935; copy of a letter from Halldór Hermannsson, 12 June 1939; in English. — Asking about the value of her Icelandic books.

Brewer, Gil. 1 letter, Canandaigua, N.Y., 6 April 1939; in English. — Reference question on Norse archaeological finds in Greenland.

Brewster, Paul G., University of Missouri. 1 letter, Columbia, 4 March 1939; in English. — Reference question dealing with comparative study on the ballad "The Two Sisters."

Brøndum-Nielsen, Joh[annes], 1881-1977. See Manuscript Material 140.

Brooklyn Museum, The, New York City. 1 letter, 21 March 1944; signed by

(Mrs) Grace W. Banker, Librarian; in English. — Appreciating the loan of facsimile pages of Icelandic manuscripts exhibited at the museum.

Bruderhausen, A. Domestic & Foreign Books. 2 letters, New York City, 3 May 1934; 16 September 1939; in English. — The value of Icelandic books in stock.

Buford, Albert H. 1 letter, Bell Buckle, Tenn., 9 March 1942; copy of the reply, 12 March 1942; in English. — Asking for reference to a grammar for the Scandinavian languages.

Burtness, O. B., congressman for North Dakota. 3 letters, 9 January, 9 and 18 February 1922; copies of 2 letters from Halldór Hermannsson; copy of a letter from Burtness to Hon. Wilbur J. Carr, Director of the Consular Service, Department of State; in English. — On establishing an American Consulate in Iceland. On same subject see: Jonas Hall, Jón Magnússon, and Ólafur Johnson.

Busch, Florence E. 2 letters, Verdugo City, Calif., 18 and 28 April 1927; in English. — Bibliographical inquiry concerning books in English on the Old Icelandic Constitution.

Cady, Putnam. 2 letters, Kingston, N.Y., 23 January and 5 February 1930; in English. — Asking about the National Celebration in Iceland in 1930.

Carlson, W[illia]m H., University of Arizona Library. 1 letter, Tucson, 7 April 1941; in English. — Requesting information on the holdings of Scandinavian material at Cornell University Library for an article on Scandinavian Collections in libraries of the United States.

Carlton, W. N. C., The Newberry Library. 1 letter, Chicago, 26 September 1919; in English. — Regretting not having a copy of his paper on the Icelandic sagas to send to Halldór Hermannsson.

Carmody, Francis, University of California. 1 letter, Berkeley, 1 May 1939; in English. — Concerning the edition of *The Icelandic Physiologus*.

Carnegie Institution of Washington. Department of Historical Research. 2 letters, Washington, D.C., 18 and 22 September 1924; signed by J. Franklin Jameson; in English. — On classifying Handritadeild hins íslenzka bókmenntafélags as a library.

Carpenter, William H. See **Columbia University Library.**

Carter, George Revile. 1 letter, Chicago, 9 July 1941; addressed to Cornell University Library; in English. — Reference question on Icelandic subjects.

Caverhill, Beverley, University of Oregon Library. 1 letter, Eugene, 31 December 1941; addressed to The President of the University; a copy of the reply from Office of the Dean, College of Arts and Sciences, Cornell University; in English. — Inquiry about Halldór Hermannsson's retirement.

Cawley, F[rank] S[tanton], d.1941. 1 letter, Cambridge, Mass., 26 March 1931; in English. — Requesting proof reading of his edition of *Hrafnkels saga.* Enclosed: a reply from his widow, Erica B. Cawley, to a letter of condolence, 28 February 1941.

Cheatham, Kitty (Catharine Smiley). 3 letters and one postcard, New York City, 3 February 1930; 12 December 1938; 2 September 1939; 21 September 1939; in English. — Primarily pertaining to her genealogy. Enclosed: reprints of articles about Iceland by Cheatham, published in American newspapers; reprint from the *Cyclopedia of American Biography.*

Cheney, Harry A. 1 letter, Hopkinton, Mass., 13 May 1938; copy of the reply, 16 May 1935; in English. — Claiming to have made prehistoric Norse discovery in New England.

Christensen, Claude H., Graduate Library School, University of Chicago. 1 letter, Chicago, 14 May 1932; in English. — Reference question about Icelandic libraries in the Middle Ages.

Clarendon Press, The, Oxford, England. 8 letters, some addressed to G. W. Harris, March 1915 - January 1918; copies of two letters from Halldór Hermannsson to the Clarendon Press; in English. — The publishing of the *Catalogue of Runic Literature.* See: Oxford University Press. Enclosed: two lists of addressees to which a copy of the catalogue is to be sent, 9 and 4 typewritten sheets.

Clark, Austin H., Smithsonian Institute. 1 letter, Washington D.C., 19 August 1943; in English. — Presenting an article on Iceland. Inserted in his *Iceland and Greenland* (Washington D.C.: Smithsonian Institute, 1943).

Clemens, John J. 1 letter, Aurora, Illinois, 2 October 1926; in English. — Asking for a reference to a bibliography of the introduction of Christianity into Iceland and on the Reformation.

Coblentz, Catherine Cate (Mrs. William Weber Coblentz), 1897-1951. 1 letter, Washington, D.C., 7 February 1941; in English. — Reference questions concerning the settlement of Icelanders in Greenland.

Collingwood, W[illiam] G[ershom], 1854-1932. 1 letter, Lanehead, Coniston, Lancashire, England, 12 July 1932; copies of two letters from Halldór Hermannsson, 11 and 14 July 1932; in English. — Granting Halldór Hermannsson permission to use his pictures of Oddi in the publication on Sæmund Sigfússon the learned.

Columbia University Library, New York City. 4 letters, 8 and 25 March 1918; 17 March 1919; 6 November 1922; signed by William H. Carpenter; in English. — Bibliographical matters.

Commonwealth Fund, The, New York City. 1 letter, 19 September 1931; signed by Whittemore Littell; in English. — Notifying the arrival of Miss Bertha Thompson, a Commonwealth Fund Fellow of 1931.

Cook, Albert S[tanburrough], 1853-1927, Yale University. 3 letters, New Haven, 3 letters, 6, 29, and 31 December 1919; in English. — Reference questions dealing with Old Norse subjects.

Cooper, Lane, 1875-1959, Professor, Cornell University. 1 letter, Ithaca, N.Y., 20 July 1939; in English. — Request for *The Icelandic Bestiary*.

Cormack, Maribelle, b. 1902. 6 letters, Department of Public Parks, Providence, Rhode Island, April 1935 - May 1941; in English. — Reference questions pertaining to her books on Vikings for young readers; bibliographical information on "popular Viking stories"; request for a letter of recommendation.

Cornell University, Ithaca, N.Y. Numerous letters, May 1905 - October 1947; in English. — Concerning Halldór Hermannsson's appointment as a curator of the Fiske Icelandic Collection and a teacher in the Scandinavian languages; regarding leave of absence, research grants, etc. Enclosed: letters concerning a proposed lecture by Dr. Hannah Rydh in the spring of 1938.

Cornell University Press, Ithaca, N.Y. 2 letters, 16 March 1943; 21 July

1943; in English. — On sales of Islandica; notices sent to Icelandic periodicals.

Cornellian Council of Cornell University, The. 1 letter, 16 October 1930; signed by Harold Flack; in English. Enclosed: form for filling out financial needs of departments.

Cotton, Chas W. 1 letter, Tolworth Rise, Surrey, England, s.d.; copy of a letter from Halldór Hermannsson, 30 October 1937; in English. — Presenting a book, *Iceland's Great Inheritance,* by Adam Rutherford. Enclosed: a flyer.

Council on Foreign Relations, New York City. 3 letters, 17 October 1940; 26 October and 3 November 1945; signed by Walter H. Mallory, and one by his secretary, A. Winning; in English. — Requesting a contribution for *Political Handbook of the World.* Enclosed: Halldór Hermannsson's articles, one dated 22 October 1945, the other undated.

Cox, Edward G[odfrey], 1876-1963, University of Washington. 1 letter, Seattle, 10 March 1927; in English. — Reference question pertaining to books on travel in Iceland.

Crabb, Edward L. 2 letters, Shoshoni, Wyoming, 14 January 1933; 15 January 1944; in English. — Reference questions concerning chronology in Icelandic history of the Middle Ages.

Craigie, W[illiam] A[lexander] [Sir], 1867-1957. 54 letters and 3 postcards, Oxford, December 1914 - December 1956; in English. — Letters of acknowledgment for volumes of Islandica with comments on most of them; the need for Icelandic grammar for foreigners; publication problems; on his research and publications on Icelandic literature; notations on Stefán Einarsson's proposed Icelandic dictionary. Enclosed: a transcript from "Rímur af Feracuth [rectè Fierabras] Balants syni, kveðnar af Guðmundi Bergþórssyni", the fifth ríma of 14 stanzas, 3 sheets.

Crissey, A. Elwell. 3 letters, Minneapolis, 4 and 27 September, 28 December 1946; in English. — Expressing a wish to meet Halldór Hermannsson; asking for assistance in selecting one masterpiece from the Old Norse literature.

Crowley, Dennis Wilfred. 1 letter, St. Francis Seminary, s.l., 11 April 1946; in English. — Needs reference to material on the commerce of Iceland.

Cruft, George T. 2 letters, Boston, 6 and 14 November 1924; in English. — Apparently an answer to an inquiry about Edward Cruft's commercial connection with Iceland in 1810.

Curran, J. W., *Sault Daily Star.* 1 letter, Sault Ste. Marie, Ontario, 13 August 1938; in English. — Reference question concerning the early history of Hudson's and James Bays.

Dasent, Arthur Irwin. 1 letter, Hampton on Thames, 26 April 1917; in English. — A reply to Halldór Hermannsson regarding a commemoration of Sir George Webbe Dasent's anniversary.

Davies, Arthur. 3 letters, the Victoria University of Manchester and the University of Leeds, 9 March and 21 April 1933; 29 January [1934]; in English. — Concerning John Cabot.

Davis, Herbert. 1 letter, Smith College, Northampton, Mass., 31 July 1941; in English. — On behalf of Erik Mesterton.

Delabarre, Edmund B[urke], b. 1863. 4 letters, Brown University, Providence, R.I., 4 May 1916; 14 January 1920, pasted on the front flyleaf of his book on the history of Dighton rock; 19 October 1931; 29 November 1932; in English. — Asking for research assistance for a bibliography of literature dealing with Dighton Rock; the Vinland question; reference questions pertaining to runes.

Department of State, Washington, D.C. 1 letter, 24 September 1948; signed by A. E. Weatherbee, Recruitment Section, Division of Foreign Service Personnel; a copy of Halldór Hermannsson's reply; in English. — Asking for a suggestion on a candidate to serve as secretary to the United States Minister at the Legation in Reykjavík.

Dickins, Bruce, b. 1889, Professor at the University, Leeds, England. 1 letter, Leeds, 14 December 1931; in English. — Asking for volumes of Islandica for the Melsteð Library.

Dictionary of American History, New York City. 3 letters, 23 March 1938; 15 June 1938; 1 December 1939; signed by T. R. Hay and R. V. Coleman; in English. — Requesting articles for the *Dictionary*. Enclosed: Halldór Hermannsson's typescript copies of "Norsemen in America" and "Vinland"; a typescript copy of the former article revised by the Dictionary.

Dilworth, Harry B., student at Princeton University. 1 letter, Princeton, N.J., 9 April 1947; in English. — Concerning Icelandic Arthurian romances translated into English.

District of Columbia, Public Library. 1 letter, Washington, D.C., 9 March 1935; signed by George F. Bowerman; a copy of the reply; in English. — Seeking pictures of Vikings for their collection of prints.

Donovan, T. L. 1 letter, Lexington, Virginia, 18 February 1922; in English. — Reference to textbooks in Old Icelandic and the Scandinavian languages, civilization, and history.

Donworth, Albert B[ernard], b. 1867, counselor at law. 2 letters, Houlton, Maine, 5 December 1939; 15 January 1940; copy of the reply, 17 January 1940; in English. — Requesting comments on his book *The Reason Why Columbus Sailed.*

Downing, Collins S. 1 letter, "Somewhere in New Guinea", 30 July 1944; in English. — Reference question concerning *Sturlunga saga* and the history of Iceland.

Duggan, Walter F., M.D. 2 letters, Utica 2, N.Y., 12 and 31 May 1945; in English. — Requesting a reference to a textbook and grammar of the Icelandic language; his collection of saga literature.

Duncan, Alice Jean. 2 letters, Princeton, Illinois, 3 September and 4 October 1930; in English. — On acquiring sagas in the original; needing reference to an Old Norse-English dictionary other than Zoëga's.

Dunham, Mary, Smith College Library, Northampton, Mass. 1 letter, Northampton, 29 October 1926; in English. — Regarding the Fiske Icelandic Collection's duplicates of Icelandic books for sale.

Eaton, J. W., University of Saskatchewan. 3 letters, Saskatoon, 1 November 1926; 20 February and 19 March 1928; in English. — Bibliographical inquiry; asking Halldór Hermannsson to suggest potential publishers of his work on the relations between German and Danish Literatures in the eighteenth century.

Eddison, Eric Rucker, 1882-1945. 4 letters, Campden Hill, London, 29 June and 19 October 1930; 3 July and 13 September 1931; in English. —

Letter of appreciation; the problem of translating sagas — mainly concerning style; his translation of *Egils saga;* an invitation to lunch.

Edwards, Richard I. 1 letter, s.l., 20 February 1931; in English. — Concerning leave of absence and his graduation.

Eggert Jóhannsson, b. 1860, clerk at the Land Titles Office, Winnipeg. See Manuscript Material 129.

Eiður S[igurðsson] Kvaran, 1909-1939. 1 letter, Greifswald, Germany, 21 January 1938; in Icelandic. — Presenting to the Fiske Icelandic Collection his dissertation and a translation of stories by Einar H. Kvaran.

Einar Benediktsson, 1864-1940, poet. 5 letters, New York City, 20 September, 7 and 22 October 1921; 4 and 8 November 1921; copies of two letters from Halldór Hermannsson, 31 October and 6 November 1921; in Icelandic. — Concerning his collection of books on Greenland and prehistoric Iceland; on the status of Greenland.

Einar Helgason, 1867-1935, the Farming Association of Iceland, Reykjavík. See Manuscript Material 129.

Einar Jónsson Committee, The. 1 letter, New York City, 30 October 1916; addressed to the subscribers to the *Einar Jonsson Fund;* in English. — The statue of Thorfinn karlsefni in Fairmont Park.

Einar P[áll] Jónsson, 1880-1959. 1 letter, Winnipeg, 25 September 1941; in Icelandic. — Request for an article in the Icelandic weekly *Lögberg.*

Eiríkur Þorbergsson, 1867-1949. 1 letter, Húsavík, 2 July 1902; in Icelandic. — Consenting to go to Grímsey to take photographs for Fiske. See also letters to Fiske.

Eliot, Christopher P. 1 letter, Cambridge, Mass., 2 March 1931; in English. — Request to Halldór Hermannsson to speak at a celebration of the Unitarian Historical Society — "replied in the negative" written on the letter.

Emerson, Justin V., student at Yale University. 2 letters, New Haven, 10 January 1937; 4 March 1938; in English. — Concerning the Kensington stone; request for recommendation.

Encyclopædia Britannica. 2 letters, London, 13 January and 21 February 1928; signed by Walter B. Pitkin; copies of two letters from Halldór Hermannsson; in English. — An article on the Pre-Spanish Voyages.

Encyclopaedia Sexualis. 1 letter, New York City, 16 February 1935; signed by Victor Robinson, M.D.; in English. — Request for an article. On the letter is written in Halldór Hermannsson's hand: "referred him to Stefán Einarsson."

Erhardt-Siebold, Erika von. 1 letter, Vassar College, 15 January 1941; in English. — On behalf of Dr. Vera Lachmann.

Erkes, Heinrich, b. 1864, librarian, the University at Cologne. 3 letters and 2 postcards, Cologne, 21 May 1923; 19 July 1923; 21 January 1924; 22 March 1924; 7 October 1924; in German and English. — Request for book exchanges; the publications of *The Society for the Advancement of Scandinavian Study.*

Evans, Austin P[atterson]. 4 letters, Columbia University, New York City, 9 and 25 July 1941; 13 February and 3 December 1942; in English. — An invitation to lead a discussion at a meeting of medievalists (see also Margaret Schlauch and Arpad Steiner); reference question on a translation of the longer *Magnús saga.*

Explorers Club, The, New York City. 2 letters, 9 May 1928; 30 April 1929; signed by Frederick A. Blossom, the librarian; in English. — Reference question on popular books describing Iceland, its resources, customs, etc.; sending for Islandica publications and the *Catalogue of Runic Literature.*

Farabee, W[illiam] C[urtis], 1865-1925, the University Museum, Philadelphia. 1 letter, 3 January 1921; in English. — Acknowledging information on Icelandic matters.

Feltyn, Alexander, University of Maryland. 1 letter, Baltimore, 19 April 1925; in Swedish. — Reference question on the existence of a literary work on the biblical *Judith* in Icelandic.

Fernald, M[erritt] L[yndon], b. 1873, Gray Herbarium, Harvard University. 1 letter, Cambridge, Mass., 25 June 1921; in English. — A reply to a question regarding his work on the Norse voyages to America.

Fife, Robert Herndon, Modern Language Association of America. 1 letter, New York, 11 May 1944; in English. — Reference question.

Finnur Jónsson, 1858-1934, Professor in Copenhagen. 24 letters and 9 postcards, Copenhagen, June 1900 - April 1932; photocopies of two letters from Halldór Hermannsson; in Icelandic. — Chess matters; on Icelandic politics; calling for, and commenting on some of Halldór Hermannsson's publications; on his own research and publications; news from Iceland and Denmark; Kålund's position; about Halldór Hermannsson taking a position in Copenhagen; affairs of the Arnamagnæan Institute; commentaries on scholarly publications on Icelandic history and literature; popular editions of Old Icelandic literature.

Finnur Jónsson. See **Johnson, Finnur.**

Finnur Sigmundsson, 1894-1982, the National Library of Iceland. 13 letters, Reykjavík, October 1944 - June 1951; in Icelandic. — The affairs of the National Library; the Fiske Icelandic Collection; the possibility of Halldór Hermannsson coming to Reykjavík to supervise the project of a bibliography of Icelandic publications; bibliographical information; replying to a reference question; Halldór Hermannsson's successor at the Fiske Icelandic Collection; birthday greetings; a parliamentary bill on compulsory depository copies to libraries; thanking for periodicals given to the library; news from Iceland; about a bibliography of eighteenth-century books; the vellum leaf from *Heiðarvígasaga.*

First Federated Church. 1 letter, Winnipeg, 5 June 1941; in Icelandic. — An invitation to the celebration of the church's 50th anniversary.

[Fischer, Joseph]. 1 postcard, Copenhagen, 21 September 1903; in German. — Giving the address of Professor Joseph Fischer. The note is unsigned. Inserted in his *Die Entdeckungen der Normannen in Amerika* (Freiburg im Breisgau: Herdersche Verlagsbuchandl., 1902).

Fiske, Christahl F., Vassar College. 1 letter, Poughkeepsie, New York, 2 June 1916; in English. — Reference question on Old Norse literature.

Fiske, Daniel Willard, 1831-1904. 78 letters and 56 postcards, Florence and London, 1900-1904; included are letters written on behalf of Fiske by Charles W. Alison, M. Monzecci, Ettore Sordi, and G. M. Wood; in English, Danish, and Italian; messages often added on the envelopes. —

Instructions to Halldór Hermannsson concerning his work at Fiske's library; regarding publication of *Í uppnámi,* and other chess matters; plans for a library at Grímsey; instructions concerning *Mímir* (in numerous letters). See also Manuscript Material 43. Enclosed: a list of names to appear in *Mímir,* 1 sheet.

Fleischhauer, Wolfgang, b. 1913, Professor at Ohio State University. 1 letter, Columbus, 9 May 1938; in English. — Needs his quotation from *Ólafs saga helga* checked against the publication.

Flemming, L. M., student at Queen's University. 1 letter, Kingston, Ontario, s.d., but postmarked Kingston, Ontario, 11 October 1912; in English. — About Icelanders in Canada.

Flom, George T[obias], 1871-1960, University of Illinois. 6 letters and 1 postcard, Urbana, April 1922 - May 1939; in English. — Requesting reviews and articles for *Journal of English and Germanic Philology;* reference question; interlibrary loan.

Florell, Edna M., University of Idaho. 2 letters, Moscow, Idaho, 1 March and 30 September 1931; in English. — Asking for a list of publications on Icelandic arts and crafts; Icelandic grammar in English or German.

Forbes, S. C., Monarch Electric Company, Kansas City, Missouri. 3 letters, 1 and 6 October; 30 December 1913; in English. — Ordering Islandica publications; reference questions on the Icelandic sagas.

Foyle, W. & G. Ltd., booksellers. 1 letter, London, 12 September 1932; in English. — Regretting not having found a copy of Haarhaus's *Maculaturalia.*

Fox, Walter H., M.D. 2 letters, Hartford, Michigan, 7 and 20 December 1914; in English. — Reference questions; interested in books about Icelandic history and literature; on his collection of Icelandic books and books about Iceland, and more.

Franzén, Gösta, b. 1906, Professor at the University of Chicago. 1 letter, Chicago, 2 October 1945; in English. — Reference question on *Jóns saga leikara,* which is to be edited by a student of his.

F[rímann] B[jarnason] Arngrímsson, 1855-1936. 8 letters, Akureyri, March 1915 - October 1929; in Icelandic and English. — Books offered for sale; reference questions; about electricity in Iceland; the periodical *Fylkir* presented to the Fiske Icelandic Collection. The last two letters are addressed to the Librarian at Cornell University.

Galbiati, Giovanni. See Manuscript Material 115.

Ganong, William Francis, 1864-1941, Professor, Smith College. 1 letter, Northampton, Mass., 1 March 1927; in English. — On the Vinland question.

G[eir] T[ómasson] Zoëga, 1857-1928, Rector, the Junior College in Reykjavík. 1 letter, Reykjavík, 14 November 1913; in Icelandic. — Acknowledging Islandica on behalf of the school library. See also Manuscript Material 129.

Gellhoff, G. A. 1 letter, Long Island, N.Y., 26 June 1945; in English. — Reference to books to learn Icelandic needed.

Georg Ólafsson, 1884-1941, banker. 1 letter, Reykjavík, 1 February 1927; in Icelandic. — Pertaining to a book published by the National Bank of Iceland in 1926, possibly *Iceland*, edited by Þorsteinn Þorsteinsson.

Gerould, J. T., the University of Minnesota Library. 3 letters, Minneapolis, 9 November, 4 and 16 December 1916; in English. — Book offered for sale on behalf of a family in Minneapolis.

Gestur Jóhannsson, b. 1850, postal clerk, Poplar Park, Manitoba. See Manuscript Material 129.

Gísli Brynjólfsson, M.D., 1861-1930. 43 letters and 10 postcards, Copenhagen, October 1904 - August 1930; in Icelandic and some Danish. — Pertaining to Hið íslenzka bókmenntafélag and Hið íslenzka Fræðafélag; on his work; news from Copenhagen and Iceland.

Gísli Jónsson, b. 1876. 1 letter, Winnipeg, 3 May 1942; in Icelandic. — Concerning articles by Halldór Hermannsson for *Tímarit Þjóðræknis-félagsins.*

Gjerset, Knut, 1865-1936. 1 letter, Decorah, Iowa, 28 March 1921; in English. — Interlibrary loan; concerning his writing on the history of Iceland.

Goblet, Y. M., Paris. Copy of a reply to Goblet from Otto Kinkeldey on be-half of Halldór Hermannsson. See Manuscript Material 140.

Goodenough, Ward H. 1 letter, New Haven, 17 July 1941; in English. — Requesting comments on his paper on the social factors contributing to the emergence of the Viking Age.

Goodmann, Kristinn. 1 letter, Blaine, Washington, 27 October 1933; in Icelandic. — Thanking for the article on the Icelandic printing presses; request for an estimate of the value of Icelandic books in his possession. A list of Icelandic books included.

Goodwin, William B., b. 1866. 17 letters, Hartford, Connecticut, September 1936 - January 1941; copy of a letter from Halldór Hermannsson, 28 October 1936; in English. — About his research on the history of Connecticut and the Vinland question; reference questions pertaining to same. Enclosed: notes concerning possible landfall in America and Iceland by the early Irish, a typescript copy of 8 sheets; photograph of an axe, supposedly of Norse origin.

Gookin, Frederick W. 1 letter, Chicago, 29 December 1919; in English. — Presenting a copy of *The Icelandic Sagas* by Carlton to the Fiske Icelandic Collection.

Gordon, E[ric] V[alentine], 1896-1938. 2 letters, Stockport, England, 4 October 1935; 16 August 1936; a typewritten copy of a letter to Ejnar Munksgaard from Gordon, 17 September 1935; in English. — Concerning a new series of Icelandic texts and translations to be pub-lished by Munksgaard; a request to Halldór Hermannsson to edit the *Vinland sagas.*

Gourlie, Norah D. 1 letter, s.l., 7 December 1946; in English. — Reference question; mentions W. P. Ker; Gourlie's stay in Iceland and reading of Icelandic literature.

Gray, John, the Rev. 1 letter, Edinburgh, 21 September 1916; in English. — About a bibliography of works in Icelandic.

Gregg, Alan, M.D., 1890-1957, the Rockefeller Foundation. 2 letters, New York, 19 November 1935; 29 December 1941; draft of 2 letters from Halldór Hermannsson, 21 June 1929, and 16 November 1935; in English. — Acknowledging books sent to him by Halldór

Hermannsson; his trip to Iceland, and meeting with Guðmundur Hannesson at the Medical School; fellowship for Icelanders to study with Dr. Raymond Pearl. See also letters from Ágúst H. Bjarnason, Guðmundur Finnbogason, Guðmundur Hannesson, and Raymond Pearl. Enclosed: a letter from A. R. Mann, Office of the Provost, Cornell University, 7 November 1935, requesting that Gregg be put on the list of recipients of Islandica.

Grey, Edward F., the British Consulate, Boston. 8 letters, January 1929 - January 1931; in English. — Reference questions; the Vinland question; on his research and publications.

Grimsson, Gudmundur, b. 1878, Judge. 2 letters, Rugby, North-Dakota, 28 February 1933; 1 December 1939; in English. — The statue of Leifur Eiríksson in Chicago; request for a list of the Islandica publications, with prices.

Grosjean, Paul. 1 letter, Société des Bollandistes, Bruxelles, 4 October 1928; in English. — Bibliographical inquiry.

Grundtvig, V., the National Library in Aarhus, Denmark. 3 letters, 15 October 1928; 19 June, 6 November 1930; copies of 6 letters from Halldór Hermannsson, mainly complaining about shipments from Aarhus that were unasked for; in Danish and English. — On book exchange between the Fiske Icelandic Collection and the library in Aarhus; purchasing of duplicates. Enclosed: a typewritten copy listing Icelandic duplicates. See also letters form Ejler Haugsted.

Gudjohnsen, Baldur. 1 letter, Seattle, January 1931; in Icelandic. — Manuscript offered for sale, *Edda Snorra Sturlusonar,* transcribed by Árni Böðvarsson in 1743. Enclosed: 5 photographs of pages of the manuscript, 15.2 x 11.3 cm.

Guðmundur G[uðmundsson] Bárðarson, 1880-1933, geologist, Kjörseyri, Strandasýsla. See Manuscript Material 129.

G[uðmundur] Björnsson, 1864-1937, head physician of Iceland. 2 letters, Reykjavík, 7 and 14 September 1914; in Icelandic. — Presenting his pamphlets to the Fiske Icelandic Collection; reflecting on the importance of the Fiske Icelandic Collection for Icelandic culture and literature, etc.

Guðmundur Finnbogason, 1873-1944, Librarian, the National Library of

Iceland. 21 letters and 1 postcard, Reykjavík; Minneapolis; Rauðará, November 1915 - March 1943; in Icelandic. A copy of a letter of introduction in English on behalf of Gerard B. Van Deene from Halldór Hermannsson, 18 April 1935. — On his work, research, and publications; about publishing articles by Halldór Hermannsson in Icelandic periodicals; relating tidings from Iceland; matters of the National Library in Reykjavík; Hið íslenzka bókmenntafélag in Reykjavík; a question concerning graduate studies at Cornell on behalf of Þórhallur Halldórsson; the prospect of fellowships from the Rockefeller Foundation for Icelanders to study genetics. (See also Ágúst H. Bjarnason, Raymond Pearl, Guðmundur Hannesson, and Alan Gregg). Enclosed: a list of terms applied to Icelandic clergymen in biographies; typewritten copies of "On the Establishment in Iceland of an Institute for the Study of Anthropology, Genealogy and Genetics", and "Notes on Icelandic Genealogy" by Hannes Thorsteinsson, 6 and 9 sheets. See also Manuscript Material 129.

Guðmundur Gamalíelsson, 1870-1953, bookseller. Numerous letters, Reykjavík, 1915 - 1946; in Icelandic. — Business matters. Enclosed: invoices; lists of books sent by Guðmundur Gamalíelsson; desiderata lists, etc.

Guðmundur Grímsson. See **Grimsson, Gudmundur.**

Guðmundur Hannesson, M.D., 1866-1946, Professor, University of Iceland. 7 letters, Reykjavík and Copenhagen, August 1924 - August 1933; in Icelandic. — Applying for a grant from the Rockefeller Foundation to build a National Hospital in Iceland, and inquiring about a scholarship for Icelandic students (see also letters from Ágúst H. Bjarnason, Raymond Pearl, Guðmundur Finnbogason, and Alan Gregg); brief news from Iceland; his research and publications; on Icelandic politics and general situation in Iceland. Enclosed: copy of a letter from the Faculty of Medical Science at the University of Iceland to the Rockefeller Foundation, in the hand of Halldór Hermannsson, and a copy of a letter from him to the President of the Foundation.

Guðmundur Kamban, 1888-1945, author. 2 letters, New York City, 21 and 24 May 1917; in Icelandic. — In need of photographs to use in an article, and in presenting a lecture.

Guðmundur Kristjánsson, tenor. 4 letters, Chicago, 20 August 1931; December 1934; 27 December 1934; 7 January 1936; a flyer on

Gudmundur Kristjánsson's career included with the letters; in Icelandic. Enclosed: a letter to Foster M. Coffin, Willard Straight Hall, four letters to Guðmundur Kristjánsson and three to Halldór Hermannsson from Coffin, all in December 1934 and January 1935. In English. — Mainly dealing with Kristjánsson's proposed performance at Cornell University.

Guðmundur Magnússon (Pseudonym **Jón Trausti**), 1873-1918, author. 4 letters and 5 postcards, Reykjavík, April 1915 - November 1918; in Icelandic and English. — On his articles in the *American-Scandinavian Review;* the translation of his literary works into English; brief tidings from Iceland; bibliographical information concerning him and his works; on his book collection; observations concerning *Icelandic Books of the Sixteenth Century;* acquiring books for the Icelandic Collection; material presented to same. Enclosed: draft of a letter of condolence from Halldór Hermannsson to Guðrún Sigurðardóttir, Guðmundur Magnússon's widow, undated.

Gunnar Gunnarsson, 1889-1975, author. 1 letter, Birkeröd, Denmark, 6 November 1933; in Icelandic. — Bibliographical information on his literary works.

Gustafson, Walter W. 3 letters, Upsala College, East Orange, New Jersey, 15 October 1924; 31 December 1940, date is with Halldór Hermannsson's hand; one undated; in English. — Reference questions; on his studies in Old Icelandic.

Guttormur J[ónsson] Guttormsson, 1878-1966. 1 letter, Icelandic River, Manitoba, 31 December 1922; in Icelandic. — On the possibility of presenting his plays to theaters in New York.

Hagedorn, Ralph, the University of Wisconsin Library. 1 letter, Madison, 8 January 1947; in English. — Pertaining to Sir Joseph Banks.

Hagen, S. N., Vanderbilt University and Gettysburg College. 2 letters, Nashville, Tenn. and Gettysburg, Pennsylvania, 10 February 1911; 21 March 1923; in English. — Presenting a reprint of an article to the Fiske Icelandic Collection; suggesting exchange of books between Vanderbilt library and the Collection; reference questions pertaining to Danish studies; expressing dissatisfaction with the periodical *Maal og Minne.*

Haight, William H. 2 letters, New York City, 1 June and 27 July 1945; a
copy of a letter from Halldór Hermannsson, 19 June 1945; in English.
— Seeking publishers for his writings on Iceland; his stay in Iceland;
his collection of publications in Icelandic and about Iceland. Enclosed:
newspaper clipping.

Hall, Jonas. 7 letters, Edinburg, North Dakota, May 1921 - August 1922; in
English. — Relations between Iceland and the United States of
America; on the establishment of an U.S. Embassy in Iceland.
Enclosed: 3 letters from congressman O. B. Burtness to Hall, and one
letter from John Prince at the American Legation in Copenhagen to
Burtness. On same topic see: Jón Magnússon, O. B. Burtness, and Ólaf-
ur Johnson.

Halldór Daníelsson, 1853-1929. 12 letters, Wild Oak, Manitoba, June 1909 -
May 1925; in Icelandic. — Request for *Bibliographical Notices,* comments on same; Icelandic politics; some description of "Big Point" in
Wild Oak, Manitoba; bibliographical information on various Icelanders,
etc.; reference questions; periodicals offered for sale; bits of knowledge
on various Icelandic matters. See also Manuscript Material 94.

Halldór Pálsson, b. 1911. 1 letter, New York City, 4 November 1944; in
Icelandic. — Presenting his dissertation to the Fiske Collection; on
Icelandic politics.

Halldór Pétursson, b. 1916. 1 letter, New York City, 21 September 1944; in
Icelandic. — His work on a lithograph-series of Icelandic hay-making;
mentioning a picture of Halldór Hermannsson he is working on.

Halldór Stefánsson, b. 1877, farmer at Hamborg, Fljótsdal. 1 letter, Eiðar,
29 March 1917; in Icelandic. Co-signed by Metúsalem Stefánsson,
School Principal, Eiðar. — Asking for assistance to obtain Orion Swett
Marden's permission to translate *Pushing to the Front* into Icelandic.

Hance, Helen. 1 letter, Graymoor, Garrison, New York, 5 May 1944; in
English. — The Vinland question.

Hannes Hafstein, 1861-1922, Reykjavík. See Manuscript Material 129.

Hannes, Robert H., Bengal-Union Paint Organization, New York City. 1 letter, 17 June 1938; copy of Halldór Hermannsson's reply; in English. —
Considering taking up residence in Iceland.

Hannes Þorsteinsson, 1860-1935, the National Archives, Reykjavík. 3 letters, 21 August 1924; 7 March 1925; 11 February 1933; copy from Halldór Hermannsson, 10 December 1924; in Icelandic. — Pertaining to the purchasing of a manuscript from Harvard University Library; answer to a reference question. See also Manuscript Material 142.

Hansome, Marius, b. 1887. 3 letters, New York City, 16 October 1929; 18 November 1934; 3 December 1947; in English. — Seeking a translator for Vilhelm Rasmussen's book *Verdens Udvikling;* bibliographical information on Icelandic authors for his book on proletarian culture; photographs of Iceland.

Haraldur Hannesson, economist. 4 letters, Reykjavík, 14 July, 4 August, and 29 September 1945; 3 December 1946; in Icelandic. — Requesting copies of articles about the author Nonni, i.e. Jón Sveinsson; about bibliographies and information on the literary works of Nonni; reproduction of photographs.

Haraldur Kröyer, b. 1921. 1 letter, Berkeley, 28 July 1944; in Icelandic. — About his thesis on the relation between Denmark and Iceland in 1918-44. Needs books through interlibrary loan.

Harold, Freda S. 2 letters, Hanover, New Hampshire, 3 February 1930; 23 September 1936; in English. — Reference question; about her plan to write a novel.

Harrassowitz, Otto. 1 letter, Leipzig, 7 April 1914; in English. — Requesting the *Catalogue of the Icelandic Collection;* proposing to act as an agent for the sale of the Islandica publications in Europe.

Harris, George W[illia]m, Librarian, Cornell University. 2 letters, 24 April 1905; 7 August 1907; in English. — Welcoming Halldór Hermannsson to the United States and advising him to spend some days in New York City before coming to Ithaca; publication problems.

Harvard College Library, Cambridge, Massachusetts. 15 letters, December 1922 - June 1945; copy of a letter from Halldór Hermannsson; in English. — Cataloguing problems and other library matters; bibliographical questions and information. The letters are from George Parker Winship, Walter B. Briggs, T. Franklin Currier, and K. D. Metcalf. Enclosed: list of corrections and additions to the *Catalogue of the Icelandic Collection.*

Harvard University Library, Cambridge, Massachusetts. 5 letters, 5 December 1924; 2 April 1925; 16 and 23 May and 7 June 1946; signed by Archibald Cary Coolidge and William A. Jackson, the Houghton Library; copies of three letters from Halldór Hermannsson; in English. — On sale of an Icelandic manuscript to the National Archives in Reykjavík; concerning an Icelandic translation of *Don Quixote.*

Haskin, Leslie L., 1882-1949. 1 letter, Brownsville, Oregon, 18 November 1942; in English. — Reference question on the Norse discovery of America.

Haugen, Einar, b. 1906. 2 letters, University of Wisconsin, Madison, 20 January and 8 March 1937; in English. — On improving Scandinavian publications in the United States.

Haugsted, Ejler, the State Library in Aarhus. 3 letters, 6 March 1929; 26 March 1930; 30 December 1930; in Danish. — On book exchange between the libraries. Enclosed: a desiderata list of Icelandic books wanted by the library at Aarhus. See also letters from V. Grundtvig.

Hausmann, Philip William. 4 letters, Albany, N.Y., 4 March and 5 April 1925; 1 February 1927; one undated; in English. — Asking for volumes of the Islandica publication; reference questions.

Haverhill Public Library, Massachusetts. 1 letter, 26 February 1930; signed by Donald Campbell; in English. — Asking for a suggestion on books about Iceland to purchase for the library. Enclosed: checklist of Icelandic books in the library at the time.

Helgi P. Briem, b. 1902, the Icelandic Consul in New York. 16 letters, New York, December 1942 - November 1946; in Icelandic. — News from Iceland; Icelandic newspapers; celebrating Halldór Hermannsson's 65th birthday; about a painting of Halldór Hermannsson by Halldór Pétursson to be presented to the National Library in Reykjavík, the Fiske Icelandic Collection owns a photograph of this painting. See Graphic Material, 12.16; the Vinland question. Enclosed: 4 snapshots of Halldór Hermannsson, 6.7 x 6.7 cm; 3 photographs of Halldór Hermannsson with a group of people, all formally dressed, gathered around a piano and singing, 12.6 x 18.2 cm.

Helgi Helgason, b. 1848, Wynyard, Saskatchewan. See Manuscript Material 129.

Helgi Konráðsson, the Rev., 1902-1959, the Library of Skagafjörður. 1 letter, Sauðárkrókur, 21 November 1937; in Icelandic. — Requesting the *Catalogue of the Icelandic Collection* and copies of Islandica publications for the library at Sauðárkrókur.

Helgi Valtýsson, 1877-1971, teacher, Flensborg high school, Hafnarfjörður. See Manuscript Material 129.

Hermann, M., Miss. 2 letters, Winnipeg, 5 and 18 October 1936; in English. — Books offered for sale. Enclosed: a list of Icelandic books; Halldór Hermannsson's reply.

Herrmann, Paul, 1866-1930. See Manuscript Material 140.

Herz, Charles. 1 letter, Gainsborough Galleries, Inc., New York, 29 December 1926; in English. — On Professor Theodor Wedepohl's exhibition. See also letters from Vilhjalmur Stefansson and Mrs. Theodor Wedepohl.

Hettlage, Dr. 1 letter, Münster i W., 17 November 1924; in German. — Book offered for sale.

Hið íslenzka fornritafélag, Reykjavík. 3 letters, 29 August 1942; 14 February 1944; 18 February 1947; signed by Jón Ásbjörnsson; copy from Halldór Hermannsson, 28 September 1943; in Icelandic. — The offset printing of *Laxdæla saga.*

Hiersemann, Karl W., bookseller. 2 letters, Leipzig, 19 March and 26 April 1924; copy of a letter from Halldór Hermannsson; invoice from Hiersemann; in English. — Business matters.

Hight, George Ainslie. 2 letters, Oxford, 11 December 1922; 10 August 1932; in English. — Seeking a publisher of his *Biographical Dictionary of the Icelandic Sagas.*

Hildur Blöndal, b. 1883. 1 letter, Copenhagen, 25 April 1950; in Icelandic. — A reply to a letter of condolence.

Hjörvarður Árnason, student at Princeton University. 5 letters, Princeton, 23 and 28 April, 15 July and 30 November 1935; 25 July 1944; in English. — Reference question; his research on Einar Jónsson's art; interest in manuscript illuminations. Last letter on head of Office of War Information.

Hofstead, John A. 1 letter, New York City, 20 March 1928; in English. — Reference question.

Holand, H[jalmar] R[ued], 1872-1963. 13 letters, Ephraim, Wisconsin and Baltimore, March 1920 - October 1941; copy of a letter from Halldór Hermannsson; in English. — Requesting a translation of a page from *Hauksbók;* reference questions; interlibrary loan; commenting on *The Problem of Wineland.* Enclosed: a printed copy of a letter to Holand from Gathorne-Hardy on the genuineness of the Kensington stone.

Hollander, Lee M., b. 1880, Professor at the University of Texas. 16 letters, Austin; Madison, Wisconsin, April 1915 - March 1946; a letter to Hollander from Hanna Astrup Larsen, 6 December 1944; copy of a letter from Halldór Hermannsson; in English. — Reference questions; on translating and publishing skaldic poetry for English speakers; his research and publications.

Hólmfríður Árnadóttir, 1873-1955, author. 1 letter, New York City, 12 May 1920; in Icelandic. — Reference question on textbooks to use in teaching Icelandic.

Honour, Margaret C. 2 letters, East Orange, New Jersey, 16 February and 22 March 1940; in English. — Inquiry about graduate work in Old Icelandic at Cornell University; a schedule of courses taken at Oxford University 1937-39.

Honti, John Th. 1 letter, Paris, 6 October 1938; in English. — About his work on Old Norse, his résumé, job proposal. Inserted in his "New Ways to Vinland Problems." In *Acta Ethnologica,* 1938.

Horcher, William. 1 letter, New York City, 19 October 1939; in English. — Reference question on wrestling in Iceland. Enclosed: Halldór Hermannsson's reply.

Hormanson, Kate McNobb. 1 letter, Baltimore, 22 October 1934; in English. — Seeking information about the name Hormanson — Hermannsson.

Horr, A[lfred] R[euel], b. 1875, the Cleveland Trust Company. 1 letter, 2

June 1947; in English. — Mentioning his trip along the Labrador; expressing interest in the Vinland question.

Horsford, Cornelia, b. 1861. 2 letters, Shelter Island, N.Y. and Boston, Mass., 7 August 1908; 16 April 1909; in English. — Promising some of her late father's books to the Fiske Icelandic Collection; about her work on "Vinland."

Høst, Andr. Fred. & Søn., Royal Danish Booksellers, Copenhagen. Letters and invoices, September 1910 - January 1931; copy of a letter from Halldór Hermannsson; copy from Cornell University Press, 26 December 1934, about transferring to Levin & Munksgaard the agency for the series Islandica; in Danish and English. — Business matters.

Hutton, James, Department of Classics, Cornell University. See Manuscript Material 127.

Indriði Einarsson, 1851-1939, playwright. 5 letters, Reykjavík, 14 September and 2 December 1911; 13 March and 17 December 1912; 30 November 1928; in Icelandic. — Request to express an opinion on Lee M. Hollander's translation of Einarsson's *Sverð og bagall* into English; information concerning his literary work.

Ingalls, Albert G., *Scientific American.* 1 letter, New York, 24 June 1941; in English. — Reference question. Enclosed: an article on the Vinland question by Hugh O'Neill Hencken published in the *Scientific American.*

Ingibjörg [Margrét Vilhjálmsdóttir] Jónsson (Mrs. Einar P. Jónsson) b. 1896. 1 letter, Winnipeg, 27 August 1948; in Icelandic. — Asking for the supplement catalogue of 1927 to use in listing her own book collection.

Ingvar Guðmundsson. 1 letter, Sveinagarðar on Grímsey, 10 February 1903; in Icelandic. — Information on the chess book by Jón Norðmann.

Iwan, Walter, d. 1945. 1 letter, Berlin, 6 March 1935; in English. — Submitting his work "Island, Studien zu einer Landeskunde", for publication in the Islandica series.

Jackson, Jess H[amilton]. 1 letter, the College of William and Mary,

Williamsburg, Virginia; Durham, North Carolina, 27 October 1934; a letter to Stefán Einarsson, 8 July 1934; in English. — Consenting to present a paper, "Editing Later Icelandic Manuscripts", at a MLA meeting.

Jacobsen, Anna. 2 letters, Ames, Iowa, 12 and 16 January 1920; in English. — Reference question concerning Icelandic dramatists; interlibrary loan.

Jacobson, Lis. 2 letters, Det Danske Sprog- og Litteraturselskab, Copenhagen, 4 January 1934; 6 February 1935; a copy of a letter from Halldór Hermannsson, 8 January 1934; in Danish. — Proposition to Halldór Hermannsson to participate in the Arnamagnæan Commission and to accept a position of a director of the Institute; a call for letters from Georg Brandes. Enclosed: a list of non-Scandinavian correspondents of Brandes; draft of a letter by Halldór Hermannsson concerning the matter.

Jacometti, Fabio. See Manuscript Material 115.

Jenks, A[lbert] E[rnest], 1869-1953. 1 letter, University of Minnesota, Minneapolis, 26 July 1943; in English. — Calling for evaluation of an Icelandic book.

Jewitt, Arthur R[ussell], b. 1904. 2 letters, Halifax, Nova Scotia, 19 February and 20 March 1946; in English. — Job inquiry; request for a letter of recommendation.

J[óhann] Magnús Bjarnason, 1866-1945, writer. 8 letters, Elfros, Saskatchewan, May 1931 - September 1944; 1 card, s.d.; Christmas card with a photograph of Bjarnason and his wife; in Icelandic. — Reference questions, f.ex. on Bishop Marteinn Einarsson; about Icelanders in England in sixteenth and seventeenth centuries; praising Halldór Hermannsson's *The Problem of Wineland;* requests for volumes of the Islandica publications and the printed catalogues. See also Manuscript Material 129.

Jóhann Kristjánsson, b. 1884, genealogist in Reykjavík. See Manuscript Material 129.

Jóhannes L[árus] L[ynge] Jóhannsson, 1859-1929. 7 letters, Reykjavík, January 1921 - April 1928; in Icelandic. — Regarding the Icelandic Dictionary, the project, financial difficulties, etc.; presenting his pamphlets to the Fiske Collection; about writing an Icelandic grammar in English.

Jóh[annes] Örn Jónsson, 1892-1960. 2 letters, Fagranes in Öxnadalur, 10 January and 15 September 1932; in Icelandic. — Books offered for sale; bibliographical information; description of pages from an old book. Enclosed: draft of Halldór Hermannsson's reply.

Jóhannes Páll Pálsson. See Palsson, Jóhannes Páll.

Jóhannes Sveinsson, the Rev. 2 letters, Seattle, 1 August and 17 December 1927; in English and Icelandic. — Asking for the *Catalogue of the Icelandic Collection;* needs reference to *Egils saga* in English translation on behalf of a friend.

John Carter Brown Library, The. 1 letter, Providence, Rhode Island, 6 February 1909; signed by Margaret B. Stillwell; in English. — Describing the 1757 edition of Westman's *Itinere priscorum Scandianorum in America* belonging to the John Carter Brown Library.

Johnson, Finnur, 1868-1955. 13 letters, Winnipeg, February 1918 - October 1924; in Icelandic. — Business matters, especially procuring of books and periodical.

Johnson, H. F., Smith, Kinloch & Johnson, Inc. 1 letter, Utica, New York, 3 December 1935; in English. — Asking about *Icelandic Illuminated Manuscripts of the Middle Ages.*

Johnson, Jakobina, b. 1883. 1 letter, Seattle, 18 May 1947; in English. — Asking for a bibliography on the history of the Fiske Icelandic Collection and the works of Fiske and Halldór Hermannsson.

Johnson, Sveinbjörn, 1883-1946. 50 letters, University of Illinois, Urbana; Johnson & Short, Chicago, June 1927 - December 1945; copy of a letter to Princeton University Press and a copy of a reply from same; in English. — Reference questions pertaining to Old Norse and Scandinavian law and modern Icelandic law; asking Halldór Hermannsson to read and comment on a translation of his; about his translation of *Grágás;* translation problems; the foundation of the American Scandinavian Legal Society.

Johnston, A. W., Viking Society for Northern Research. 1 letter, London, 28

December 1935; in English. — Puzzled by the forms of the place-names "Breiðabólstaður", and "at Forsi."

Johnstone, Harry Inge. 1 letter, New York City, 19 February 1928; in English. — Expressing gratitude for Halldór Hermannsson's course on Scandinavian culture; his plans to study at the Royal Academy of Fine Arts in Stockholm.

Jón Bjarnason, the Rev., 1845-1914, Winnipeg, Manitoba. See Manuscript Material 129.

Jón Borgfirðingur Jónsson, 1826-1912. See Manuscript Material 129.

Jón Friðfinnsson, 1865-1936, composer, Winnipeg, Manitoba. See Manuscript Material 129.

Jón Helgason, 1899-1986, Professor in Copenhagen. 3 letters, Copenhagen, 2 December 1924; Second of Easter 1927; 25 February 1948; in Icelandic. — Publications of Hið íslenzka bókmenntafélag; reference questions; regretting inability to provide the Fiske Icelandic Collection with the periodical *Frón;* remarking on his work; "the manuscript question."

Jón Jakobsson, 1860-1925, Librarian, the National Library of Iceland. 4 letters, Reykjavík, 21 November 1908; 9 May 1911; 25 January and 25 March 1921; in Icelandic. — Presenting his bibliographies to the Fiske Icelandic Collection; recognizing Halldór Hermannsson's observations on his bibliographies. See also Landsbókasafn Íslands, and Manuscript Material 129, 143, and 168.

Jón Jónasson, b. 1885. 1 letter, New York City, 4 September 1918; in Icelandic. — Requesting his identification certificate translated into English.

Jón Jónsson, the Rev., b. 1849, Dean. 1 postcard, Stafafell in Lón, 4 May 1917; in Icelandic. — On Iceland's Coat of Arms. See also Manuscript Material 129.

Jón Magnússon, 1859-1926, Minister of Iceland. 1 letter, Reykjavík, 22 August 1921; in Icelandic. — On establishing a Consulate of the United States in Reykjavík. Enclosed: a translation of the letter into English, in the hand of Halldór Hermannsson. On same topic see also letters from O. B. Burtness, Jonas Hall, and Ólafur Johnson.

Jón Ólafsson, 1850-1916, editor. See Manuscript Material 129.

Jón Runólfsson, 1861-1930, teacher at the Elementary School in Winnipeg, Manitoba. See Manuscript Material 129.

Jón Hj[altalín] Sigurðsson, 1878-1955, Rector of the University of Iceland. 1 letter, Reykjavík, 1 September 1944; in Icelandic. — Formal letter of gratitude to the Icelandic Collection and Cornell University for their contribution to Old Norse and Icelandic scholarship.

Jón Stefánsson, 1862-1952. 1 letter, Brit. Mus., 7 September 1934; in Icelandic. — Comment on *Icelandic Authors of To-Day* by Halldór Hermannsson; on Stefánsson's own scholarly work.

Jón Stefánsson, 1881-1962, artist. 2 letters, Reykjavík, 27 May and 24 August 1931; in Icelandic. — Plans for an exhibition at the International Art Center, Roerich Museum, New York. See also letters from Matthías Þórðarson, the Roerich Museum, Sveinn Björnsson, and Valtýr Stefánsson.

Jón Stefánsson. See Manuscript Material 129 and 160.

Jón Sveinsson (Mrs.) See Manuscript Material 129.

Jón Sveinsson (Nonni), 1857-1944. 1 letter, St. Andreas Kollegiet ved Charlottenlund, Denmark, 4 September 1903; in Danish. A list of Catholic priests in Iceland. See also Manuscript Material 129.

Jón Þórarinsson, b. 1854, Director of Education, Reykjavík. See Manuscript Material 129.

Jón Þorkelsson, 1859-1924, National Archivist. 12 letters and one postcard, Reykjavík, May 1905 - October 1918; in Icelandic. — Explaining the status of his business with Fiske; information on where Fiske obtained some of his books; bibliographical information; comments on Icelandic politics; Halldór Hermannsson's publications; requesting *Icelandic Authors of To-day* to be sent to Sighvatur Grímsson Borgfirðingur. Enclosed: a transcript of "Reikningar Guðbrands bps 1589", and also bits and pieces copied from books and manuscripts. See also Manuscript Material 112, 143, 168, and 178.

Jónas Jónasson, 1856-1918, pastor and author. 1 letter, Akureyri, 29

September 1909; in Icelandic. — Proposal for a book exchange between himself and the Fiske Icelandic Collection.

Jones, C[harles] H[ugh] L[ePailleur], b. 1876, Mersey Paper Company. 1 letter, Liverpool, Nova Scotia, Christmas 1934; including a letter of acknowledgment by F. N. Greenleaf, his secretary; in English. — Presenting his, and Thomas H. Raddall's, book, *The Markland Sagas,* to Halldór Hermannsson.

Jones, Gwyn, b. 1907, Professor. 2 letters, University College of Wales, Aberystwyth, 30 March 1943; 12 June 1944; in English. — Thanking Halldór Hermannsson for reading and correcting mistranslations on his manuscript of the *Vatnsdæla saga;* his former student, Frank Lewis', research on the origin of "tafl."

Josephson, Aksel G. S., the John Crerar Library. 1 letter, Chicago, 4 February 191[7]; in English. — Requesting a contribution from Halldór Hermannsson to a bibliography of Scandinavian literature in English translation to be published by the American-Scandinavian Foundation.

Kahle, B[ernhard], Professor, 1861-1910. 1 letter, Heidelberg, 10 December 1908; in German. — Bibliographical information, comments on Halldór Hermannsson's, *Bibliography of the Icelandic Sagas and Minor Tales* Islandica I (Ithaca: Cornell University Library, 1908).

Kålund, Kr[istian], 1844-1919. 5 letters and 2 postcards, Copenhagen, December 1905 - October 1916; in Danish. — Reference question; concerning Arngrímur Jónsson's *Crymogæa;* commenting on the *Bibliography of the Icelandic Sagas and Minor Tales;* announcing that the Arnamagnæan Commission will be presenting the Fiske Collection with its publications. Thanking for volumes of Islandica sent to the Arnamagnæan Institute; stanzas by Þorleifur Halldórsson copied from manuscripts in the Institute; inquiring on the publication date of Flom's edition of the *King's Mirror.* See also Manuscript Material 140.

Karl Strand, M.D., b. 1911. 1 letter, London, 15 July 1948; in Icelandic. — Requesting volumes of the Islandica publications and the catalogues of the Fiske Icelandic Collection.

Keller, Carl T. 2 letters, Boston, 28 March and 1 April 1932; also a letter to Sigurður Nordal asking for a list of the Norse and Icelandic sagas con-

sidered to be the most authentic, 17 March 1932; in English. —
Acknowledging the list of Norse and Icelandic sagas; origin of the name
Halfdan; commenting on Morris' translations of the sagas.

Kenworthy, Leonard S[tout], b. 1912. 1 letter, Coshocton, Ohio, 6 January
1946; in English. — Seeking names of outstanding persons in Iceland.

Keogh, Andrew, Yale University Library. 2 letters, New Haven, 31 October
and 13 November 1919; in English. — Asking Halldór Hermannsson to
examine and describe an Icelandic manuscript that was given to the library.

Kilty, Joan Gunlaugsson (Mrs. Reginald A.) 2 letters, Stillwater,
Minnesota, 27 February and 12 April 1938; in English. —
Bibliographical inquiry about titles of Icelandic literature.

Kindall, Louise J. 1 letter, Excelsior, Minnesota, 23 August 1909; in
English. — Needs photographs to use at a talk about Iceland.

Kindle, E[dward] M[artin], 1869-1940, Department of Mines, Canada
Geological Survey. 2 letters, Ottawa, 10 and 17 March 1922; copy of a
letter from Halldór Hermannsson, 7 March 1922; in English. — The geology of Labrador.

Klahre, Alfred C. 1 letter, New York City, 18 October 1932; in English. —
Reference question on Fiske and his work on chess.

Klodic, R. 2 letters, Ljublajana, Yugoslavia, 3 August 1947; 18 February
1948; copy from G. F. Shepherd, Jr. to Klodic; in English. — Asking
for volumes of the Islandica publication as a means to study the
Icelandic language, history, and literature.

Koht, Halvdan, 1873-1965. 2 letters, Norwegian Legation, Washington,
D.C., 27 March 1942; s.d.; a letter from Richard Robinson, Chairman
Committee on University Lectures; copy of a letter to Koht from
Halldór Hermannsson; in English. — Concerning a lecture to be given
at Cornell University by Professor Koht.

Kongelige Bibliotek, Det (The Royal Library), Copenhagen. 5 letters, 19
November 1924; 11 June 1929; 12 December 1932; 25 May 1939; 23
January 1946; signed by Carl S. Petersen, Holger Ehrencron-Müller,
and Richard Paulli; in Danish. — Business matters.

Korgen, Reinhard Lunde. 1 letter, Brunswick, Maine, 31 March 1936; in English. — Asking about a translation of *Grágás.*

Krenn, Ernst. 1 letter, Allentsteig, Austria, 23 May 1947; in Faeroese. — Submitting his work on the Faeroe Islands for publication in the Islandica series.

Kristinn Goodmann. See **Goodmann, Kristinn.**

Kristján Ásgeir Benediktsson, 1861-1924. 2 letters, Gimli and Winnipeg, Manitoba, 27 August 1913; 4 October 1917; in Icelandic. — Commenting on Halldór Hermannsson's *Icelandic Authors of To-day;* his meeting with Fiske and Reeves in Northern Iceland in 1879; books offered for sale.

Kristján Karlsson, b. 1922, Curator of the Fiske Icelandic Collection. 1 letter, Ithaca, N.Y., 3 August 1949; in Icelandic. — Expressing an opinion on Richard Beck's *History of Icelandic Poets: 1800-1940.*

Kristján Kristjánsson, 1873-1959, second-hand bookseller. 4 letters, Reykjavík, 26 January and 8 October 1919; 12 December 1920; 5 May 1924; in Icelandic. — Autobiographical sketch; proposing to act as an agent in Reykjavík for the Fiske Icelandic Collection; on book exchange; books listed for sale; offering his own library for purchase. Enclosed: a letter from Elizabeth S. Ingersoll, Accessions Division, Cornell University Library, 17 June 1925, about the shipment from Kristján Kristjánsson. A list of the books included with the letter, 13 sheets.

Krogh, Elva. 1 letter, University of Illinois Library, Urbana, 27 January 1936; in English. — Job inquiry.

Kungliga Biblioteket (The Royal Library), Stockholm. 1 letter, 28 January 1926; signed by Gustaf Adde; in Swedish. — Business matter.

Lacy, Charles E. 1 letter, London, 16 January 1906; in English. — A reply to a letter from Halldór Hermannsson to the late Russel-Jeaffreson concerning unidentified books.

LaGuardia, Fiorello, Mayor of New York City. 1 letter, 23 August 1944; in English. — Invitation to attend New York City's official reception to

President Sveinn Björnsson. Enclosed: newspaper clippings; invitation to dinner by the Icelandic Consul in New York; the printed menu included.

Lamont, William H. F. 3 letters, Rutgers University, New Brunswick, New Jersey, 23 November 1937; 21 February and 20 June 1946; in English. — Concerning a reading list of Scandinavian novels. Enclosed: a list of contemporary European novels.

Lancaster, H[enry] Carrington, 1882-1954. 1 letter, the Johns Hopkins University, Baltimore, 16 November 1944; in English. — Concerning the qualification of Stefán Einarsson for a promotion at Johns Hopkins University.

Lancaster Press, Lancaster, Pennsylvania. Letters and invoices, August 1924 - December 1945; copies of letters from Halldór Hermannsson; in English. — Concerning the publication of the Islandica series. See also Manuscript Material 115 and 143.

Landsbókasafn Íslands, Reykjavík. 1 postcard, 27 July 1921; signed by Jón Jakobsson; in English. — An acknowledgment for the gift of *Book of hours,* manuscript on vellum.

Lärdomshistoriska Samfundet, Uppsala, Sweden. 1 letter, 8 May 1946; signed by Johan Nordström; in English. — Asking for *The Icelandic Physiologus* to be reviewed in their annual, *Lychnos*.

Larsen, Henning. 2 letters, the University of Iowa, Iowa City and University of Illinois, Urbana, 4 May 1925; 8 May 1941; in English. — Submitting a book for the Islandica series; request for an article in *Scandinavian studies presented to George T. Flom by colleagues and friends.* Enclosed: an offprint from *Danske Studier*.

Larsen, Laurence M. 9 letters, University of Illinois, Urbana, March 1923 - August 1936; in English. — Bibliographical inquiries; reference and research questions; requesting contribution to the chapter on the Scandinavian countries in *Manual of Historical Literature.*

Leach, Henry Goddard, 1880-1970, the American-Scandinavian Foundation. 15 letters, New York City, October 1916 - March 1946; also to W. W. Lawrence from Leach, 22 June 1945; two letters from George H. Sabine, Committee on University Lectures, Cornell University, to Halldór Hermannsson, 30 November and 11 December 1939, concerning Leach's proposal for a lecture series at Cornell; his résumé and a list of proposed lecture subjects included with the letters; in English. — Request to Halldór Hermannsson to comment on Leach's work; reference questions; concerning his work at the American-Scandinavian Foundation and research on Icelandic literature; acknowledging volumes of the Islandica publication; on behalf of John B. C. Watkins; asking for suggestions on titles, and other related topics.

Leonard, William Ellery, 1876-1944. 2 letters, the University of Wisconsin, Madison, 7 October 1922; 9 January 1924; in English. — Bibliographical inquiries.

Lewis, Timothy. 1 letter, University College of Wales, Aberystwyth, 30 January 1930; in English. — Bibliographical inquiry.

Library of Congress, Washington, D.C. 7 letters, May 1908 - February 1933; 3 letters addressed to George Wm Harris concerning copyrights, and one from Harris to the Library of Congress; in English. — Chiefly on cataloguing problems.

Lidholm, Eiríkur, violin maker. 5 letters, St. Louis, Missouri, 23 February, s.d. (answered 14 March), 13 and 19 March 1920; 30 July 1921; in English and Icelandic. — Reference questions; the Icelandic alphabet; listing his Icelandic books.

Liggett, W. K. 1 letter, Columbus, Ohio, 20 January 1927; in English. — Reference question on contemporary Icelandic literature.

Lindemann, J. W. R., University of Buffalo. 1 letter, Buffalo, N.Y., 16 March 1937; in English. — On the etymology of his name.

Linderholm, Justus B. 1 printed letter, Port Arthur, Ontario, s.d., to the President's Office, referred to Halldór Hermannsson; a letter from A. B. Carman, President's Secretary, 5 January 1934, informing Linderholm that his letter had been forwarded; in English. — On transforming the Icelandic weekly *Lögberg* into an educational magazine of studying English in its relation to Norse, Anglo-Saxon, etc.

Lison, Thelma Reinke, St. Louis, Missouri. Copy of a letter from Halldór Hermannsson, 6 January 1940; in English. — Inability to suggest studies on the food value of rye.

Litzenberg, Karl, b. 1905. 4 letters, University of Michigan, Ann Arbor, 16 November 1931; 19 and 29 February 1932; 25 February 1934; in

English. — Requesting volumes of the Islandica publications; his work on English-Icelandic literary relations; on William Morris and Old Norse; bibliographical inquiry; reference questions.

Loftur L[oftsson] Bjarnason, b. 1913. 2 letters, Reykjavík and Palo Alto, California, 22 November 1937; 23 June 1941; copy of a letter from Halldór Hermannsson, 10 January 1938; in English. — Letter of introduction; reference questions concerning Lutheran sermons.

Loomis, Roger S. 2 letters, New York City, 5 January 1941; 31 October s.a.; in English. — Suggesting Ezio Levi-d'Ancona as George Hamilton's successor; a reference question.

Lorentzen, Carl C. 11 letters, New York, January 1912 - December 1922; in English. — Requesting someone to read and comment on his article on Iceland; photographs needed; "Mr. Russel's lantern slides"; reference question; about raising money for the University of Iceland's new buildings (see also letters from Guðmundur Hannesson); acknowledging volumes of Islandica. Enclosed: two newspaper clippings.

Los Angeles Public Library. 1 letter, Los Angeles, 6 February 1925; signed by Maryette G. Mackey; in English. — Cataloguing problems.

Lowrie, Walter, the Rev. 1 letter, Princeton, 6 March 1936; in English. — Suggesting Professor E. Geismar as a lecturer at Cornell University in 1936. Enclosed: a letter from G. Watts Cunningham, Committee on University Lectures, 28 January 1936, approving Geismar's lecture.

Lund, John J. 1 letter, Berkeley, 27 February 1936; in English. — Reference question concerning Sir Joseph Banks.

Luttrapp?, Sverker, D.M.D. 1 letter, Boston, 29 December 1910; in English. — Asking Halldór Hermannsson to read and comment on his translation of "Kråkas song" in *Ragnars saga loðbrókar* into English.

Macbeth, Donald, Artists Illustrators Ltd., London. Letters, a telegram, and an invoice, August 1913 - August 1931; in English. — Concerning rotograph extracts from manuscripts in the British Museum. See also Manuscript Material 115.

Macmillan Company, The, publishers. 3 letters, New York City, 1, 26, and 29 June 1945; application form, filled out, and granted, 26 June 1945; in

English. — Permission to use selections from W. P. Ker's *Epic and Romance* in the edition of *Þorgils saga ok Hafliða*, to be published in the Islandica series. Enclosed is a copy of Halldór Hermannsson's letter asking for a permission to quote the book, 29 May 1945.

Magnús Helgason, 1857-1940, the Teachers College of Iceland. 9 letters, Reykjavík, December 1916 - February 1933; in Icelandic. — Acknowledging volumes of Islandica; relating brief news from Iceland; presenting school-reports of the Teachers' College.

Magnús Jónsson, the Rev. 2 letters, Ísafjörður, 27 March 1916; 5 August 1916; in Icelandic. — Request for the printed catalogues of the Fiske Icelandic Collection for the District Library in Ísafjörður; some historical details about the library.

Magnús Jónsson, 1878-1934, Professor, University of Iceland. 1 letter, Reykjavík, 17 July 1946; in Icelandic. — Inquiring on the number of editions of the Icelandic book of hymns in America.

Magnús Kjaran, 1890-1962, general importer. 2 letters, Reykjavík, 12 December 1944 and 5 April 1945; Halldór Hermannsson's reply from 13 December 1944; in Icelandic. — Suggesting a publication of Gaimard's pictures of Iceland.

Magnús Markússon, b. 1868, real estate dealer, Winnipeg, Manitoba. See Manuscript Material 129.

Magnús Matthíasson. 1 letter, Winnipeg, 20 October 1915; in Icelandic. — On writing a pamphlet about Iceland for foreign travellers.

Magnús Pétursson. See Peterson, Magnus.

Magnús J. Skaptason, the Rev., 1857-1932, Souris, North Dakota. See Manuscript Material 129.

Magoun, Francis P[eabody]., Jr., b. 1895. 9 letters, Cambridge, Massachusetts, January 1941 - August 1954; in English. — Relating to his research on Old Norse and Scandinavian literature; reference and bibliographical questions; translation of Icelandic terms into English.

Makinson, Mary Atwater. 1 letter, Los Angeles, 18 January 1947; in English. — Seeking news of Dr. Anne Tjomsland; asking for a copy of Tjomsland's edition of *Hrafns saga Sveinbjarnarsonar*.

Malone, Kemp, 1889-1971, Professor at the Johns Hopkins University. 4 letters, Baltimore, 15 February 1928; 24 April, 7 and 10 December 1938; in English. — Donating some of his monographs to the Fiske Icelandic Collection; asking for an opinion on a manuscript submitted to the *Modern Language Notes;* Stefán Einarsson is mentioned.

Marden, Orison Swett. 1 letter, New York City, 10 May 1917; in English. — Granting permission for his book *Pushing to the Front* to be translated into Icelandic. See Halldór and Metúsalem Stefánsson.

Matthías Eggertsson, the Rev., 1865-1955. 2 letters, Miðgarðar on Grímsey, 26 June 1901; 11 September 1902; in Icelandic. — On the library on Grímsey; thankful to Fiske for the books to the library; recording his and Halldór Hermannsson's common genealogy.

Matthías Jochumsson, the Rev., 1835-1920. See Manuscript Material 129.

Matthías Þórðarson, 1877-1961, Curator of the National Museum in Reykjavík. 90 letters and 8 postcards, Reykjavík; Hafnarfjörður; Seljord, Norway; Copenhagen, etc., July 1900 - December 1954; in Icelandic. — Speaking of the Norwegian student, Johan Halmöy, and his drawing of Snorri Sturluson; a trip to Munich; relating news from Iceland and mentioning Icelandic politics in several letters; the affairs of Hið íslenzka bókmenntafélag in Copenhagen and Reykjavík; Icelanders in Copenhagen; sending textbooks in Danish; commenting on Old Norse and Icelandic scholarship; the Icelandic Student Society in Copenhagen; on his research; concerning boxes from the Fiske estate; the affairs of the National Museum in Reykjavík; asking for a painting of Fiske to be made for the museum; on the economic situation in Iceland; his cataloguing of church items in Iceland; on Iceland's Coat of Arms; trip to Scandinavian cities to catalogue Icelandic antiquities in museums; his work on Jónas Hallgrímsson; the prospect of getting Halldór Hermannsson to the University in Reykjavík; on a present to the Junior College in Reykjavík from their class; taxes in Iceland; the painting of Bishop Þórður by Hjalti Þorsteinsson; bibliographical information; on maps of Iceland by Lander; the manuscript question; on securing books from the United States; about the Arnamagnæan Institute; dealing with two poems by Jónas Hallgrímsson; the situation of Icelandic scholarship in Copenhagen; mentions Nína [Sæmundsson, 1892-1965] and "móðurást"; the Vinland question; his research and publications; asking Halldór Hermannsson to represent the Museum at a celebration at the Roerich Museum in New York; on Thorstina Walters' translation of his

Vínlandsferðirnar; plans for an exhibition of paintings by Icelandic artists (see also letters from Jón Stefánsson, Roerich Museum, Sveinn Björnsson, and Valtýr Stefánsson); on exhibitions of Icelandic art in Scandinavia and Europe; his trips around Iceland collecting and listing artifacts; Grettir and Drangey; commenting on Halldór Hermannsson's work, and other topics. Enclosed: an invitation from Roerich Museum to a celebration in 1929; letter from Halldór Hermannsson to Kinkeldey, 21 March 1938, on lending books for the exhibition at the World Fair in 1939; draft of a letter to Matthías Þórðarson agreeing to the request; to Louis L. Horch, Roerich Museum from Matthías Þórðarson. See also Manuscript Material 129, 135, 142, and 143.

McCauley, Leo T., Consul General of Ireland. 1 letter, New York, 18 December 1940; in English. — Accepting information on early emigration from Ireland to Iceland.

McConnell, Carl H., Biology Department, Hartwick College. 1 letter, Oneonta, N.Y., 23 January 1933; in English. — Inquiry about pamphlets for travellers in Iceland.

McGreal, Elizabeth I. 5 letters, Hancock, New Hampshire, 11 December [1939]; 11 March [1940]; 3 August 1940; 25 March and 2 September 1941; in English. — Reference questions regarding books on the Icelandic language; seeking fresh information on recent events in Iceland for her talk at the meeting of the Association of New Hampshire Librarians; asking Halldór Hermannsson to comment on her book *Climbing Higher;* presenting her book on Iceland, *Quest in the Northland;* requesting a translation of a review of her book from Icelandic into English.

McGreal, William. 1 letter, Hancock, New Hampshire, 13 May 1940; in English. — Seeking the text and music to the Icelandic national anthem.

Means, Philip Ainsworth, 1892-1944. 10 letters, Lenox, Massachusetts; Pomfret, Connecticut, October 1936 - July 1943; a letter of introduction on behalf of Means by Dr. Dyneley Prince; in English. — Primarily dealing with his work on the Norse voyages to Greenland and America; several reference questions; asking for volumes of the Islandica series; a response to Halldór Hermannsson's review of his book in the *Geographical Review.* Enclosed: 3 letters from the American Geographical Society, requesting a review of Means' book; an excerpt from the *Review.*

Medieval Academy of America, The, Cambridge, Massachusetts. 2 letters, 25 June 1938; 25 February 1941; signed by Allan Evans, review editor, and S. H. Cross; in English. — Requesting an opinion on an article by H. R. Holand, submitted to *Speculum.*

Meixner, Esther Chilstrom (Mrs. Warren B. Meixner), University of Pennsylvania. 4 letters, Philadelphia, 1 December 1939; 1 February and 29 March 1940; 24 February 1941. A questionnaire included with the letters; in English. — Asking about the teaching of the Scandinavian languages at Cornell.

Merriam, G. & C., Publishers of Webster Dictionaries. 1 letter, Springfield, Massachusetts, 4 February 1942; signed by J. P. Bethel; in English. — Recognizing comments on the Biographical section of *Webster's New International Dictionary;* asking for Icelandic names to be included in the dictionary.

Merrick, Maurine Robb. 1 letter, Palo Alto, California, 30 January [1947]; in English. — Asking for the latest news from Iceland; requesting pictures.

Merrill, W[illia]m Stetson, b. 1866, "formerly on the staff of the Newberry Library of Chicago." 1 letter, Oconomowoc, Wisconsin, 18 November 1948; in English. — Concerning his bibliographical manuscript on the Norse voyages to America.

Metúsalem Stefánsson, 1882-1953, School Principal, Eiðar. See **Halldór Stefánsson.**

Metzenthin, Esther. 2 letters, Chapel Hill, North Carolina, 24 July 1936; 1 June 1937; in English. — Asking for permission to use the Fiske Icelandic Collection.

Mezger, F. 1 letter, Bridgeport, Pennsylvania, 23 February 1947; in English. — Asking for a reference to a history of Iceland; inquiring about Halldór Hermannsson's publications.

Miller, Roscoe R. 2 letters, New Liskeard, Ontario, 15 August and 3 October 1931; in English. — Reference question concerning the name of Canada from Icelandic or Scandinavian sources.

Mitchell, P[hillip] M[arshall], b. 1916. 16 letters, Urbana, Illinois; France;

s.l., June 1940 - August 1951, including 6 v-letters; letter from Halldór Hermannsson, 23 September [1939]; in English. — About use of the Fiske Icelandic Collection; his studies in Scandinavian literature at the University of Illinois; reference question pertaining to a poem by K. G. von Leitner; on writing dissertation; wartime situation; Irmgard Schwarz's dissertation on Gräter being sent to the Fiske Icelandic Collection; inability to find Gräter's "Nachlass"; on a skaldic poem in *Þorgils saga*. One of the letters is inserted in his *Old Norse-Icelandic Literature in Germany, 1789-1849 with a Critical Bibliography. An Abstract of a Thesis* (Urbana, 1942).

Modern Language Association of America, The, New York City. 1 letter, 3 May 1934; signed by Percy W. Long; in English. — Concerning a secretary for the Scandinavian group.

Mollerup, A. J. W., National Museum in Copenhagen. See Manuscript Material 54.

Monlux, W. S., student at the Veterinary College, Cornell University. 1 letter, Ithaca, N.Y., 5 August 1937; in English. — Asking about a Scandinavian club on campus. Enclosed: a letter from Halldór Hermannsson to Mrs. Wood with information for Monlux.

Moore, Tom E. 1 letter, Canton, New York, 2 February 1946; in Norwegian and English. — Relating to his studies of Scandinavian languages.

Morgan, Arthur E[rnest], 1878-1975. 1 letter and 1 postcard, Yellow Springs, Ohio, 30 January, 12 February 1940; in English. — Reference question concerning utopian elements in Icelandic literature.

Morison, Samuel Eliot, 1887-1976, Harvard University. 1 letter, Boston, 24 January 1942; copy of a letter from Halldór Hermannsson, 2 February 1942; in English. — The Vinland question.

Morris, Elizabeth L. 2 letters, Sayreville, New Jersey, 23 February and 12 March 1931; in English. — Reference question pertaining to the history of education in Iceland.

Morrison, L. M., Nova Scotia Booth, Canadian Pavilion, New York's World's Fair. 1 letter, New York City, 18 August 1939; a copy of the reply; in English. — Reference question on the Norse discovery of America.

Munksgaard, Ejnar, 1890-1948, publisher. 95 letters, 2 telegrams, and 1 postcard, Copenhagen, September 1929 - October 1947; copies of 10 letters from Halldór Hermannsson; in Danish. — Business matters; publication of Icelandic manuscripts and Icelandic sagas in translation; bibliographical information. Enclosed: a letter from C. H. Thordarson, Chicago; from Nordisk Kunst- og Lystryk, Copenhagen; 3 letters from Wendt & Jensen, Reproduktionsanstalt, Copenhagen; copy of a letter to Munksgaard from Cornell University Press; copy from E. V. Gordon to Munksgaard, and from Munksgaard to Gordon; copy to Vilhjalmur Stefansson from Munksgaard, and to Munksgaard from Stefansson; copy from Munksgaard to Rolf Hassel; newspaper clippings; invoices.

Munn, W. A. 1 letter, St. John's, Newfoundland, 6 June 1931; in English. — Mentions his article on the Vinland question. Inserted in his *Wineland Voyages. Location of Helluland, Markland, and Vinland* (St. John's [1931]).

Munthe, Gustaf. 3 letters, Minneapolis; Los Angeles; New York City, 24 February, 15 and 20 March 1940; in English. — Concerning a lecture he is to deliver at Cornell University. Enclosed: his résumé.

Myrvaagnes, Kaspar O. 3 letters, Alfred, N.Y., 6 and 11 January, 23 December 1937; in English. — Concerning his examination and work. Enclosed: a letter from A. B. Faust, Department of German, Cornell University, 10 June 1935. About Myrvaagnes' continuation toward the Ph.D. degree.

National Geographic Society, Washington, D.C. 1 letter, 20 January 1938; signed by George W. Hutchison; in English. — Concerning maps to be sent to Karen S. Lyngbye by the request of Halldór Hermannsson.

National Library of Iceland. See **Landsbókasafn Íslands.**

Needham, Wilbur. 1 letter, Hinsdale, Illinois, 24 January 1924; in English. — Requesting a bibliography of translations from Icelandic into English.

Nelson, Frank G., Professor, University of Wichita. 1 letter, Kansas, 15 February 1939; in English. — Concerning his paper on *Trójumanna saga.*

Newark Public Library, New Jersey. 1 letter, 15 September 1927; signed by J. C. Dana; in English. — Asking for a suggestion on Icelandic books to purchase for the library.

Níels Steingrímur Thorláksson, the Rev., 1857-1943, Selkirk, Manitoba. See Manuscript Material 129.

Nielsen, Lauritz, b. 1881, the Royal Library, Copenhagen. 3 letters, 2 May 1922; 23 August 1927;. 14 March 1931; in Danish and German. — Interlibrary loan; bibliographical inquiries concerning sixteenth-century books. Enclosed: a letter from Staats- und Universitätsbibliothek, Hamburg, recording the title of an Icelandic book of prayers from 1576; bibliographic information noted by Halldór Hermannsson, 3 sheets.

Nissen, Kristjan. 1 letter, Tromsö, 11 April 1933; in Danish. — Pertaining to cartography.

Njáll Sigurjónsson. 1 letter, Pontiac, Michigan, 3 June 1928; in Icelandic. — Inquiring where best to study electrical engineering.

Noreen, Erik, 1890-1946. 1 letter, Lund, 2 March 1936; in Swedish. — About sending a copy of his review of Holand's *The Kensington Stone* in *Sydsvenskans Revy* to Halldór Hermannsson. The review is enclosed with the letter.

Norona, Delf, b. 1895, editor and publisher. 1 letter, Moundsville, West Virginia, 20 January 1946, copy of a letter from Halldór Hermannsson; in English. — The Vinland question.

Northfield, Sigrun Marlys. 1 letter, Rochester, N.Y., 24 August 1933; in Icelandic. — Reference question dealing with literature on Vikings; about using the Fiske Icelandic Collection.

Northwestern University Library. 1 letter, Evanston, Illinois, 20 November 1922; signed by Theodore Wesley Koch; in English. — On book exchange between the libraries.

Oddur Björnsson. See Manuscript Material 129.

Ófeigur Vigfússon, the Rev., 1865-1947. 1 letter, Fellsmúli, Landsveit, 5

November 1924; in Icelandic. — Asking for volumes of the Islandica series.

Office of War Information, New York City. 1 letter, 7 October 1943; signed by Virginia Meredith; in English. — Requesting biographical data about Judge A. B. Gislason and Mr. Bjorn Schram of Detroit. See also Manuscript Material 144.

Ogburn, William F[ielding], 1886-1959, University of Chicago. 1 letter, Chicago, 31 October 1928; in English. — Reference question on population statistics for Iceland.

Ögmundur Sigurðsson, 1859-1937, school principal. 2 letters, Hafnarfjörður, 20 December 1915 and 4 January 1917; in Icelandic. — Sending school reports; acknowledging the *Catalogue of the Fiske Icelandic Collection* and the Islandica publications on behalf of the school library.

Ólafur Johnson, 1881-1958, the Commercial Council of Iceland. 1 letter, Reykjavík, 29 August 1921; in Icelandic. — On establishing a Consulate of the United States in Reykjavík. Enclosed: translation of the letter into English by Halldór Hermannsson. On same subject: O. B. Burtness, Jonas Hall, and Jón Magnússon.

Ólafur Kjartansson. 1 letter, Meadville, Pennsylvania, 26 December 1914; in Icelandic. — Reference question on an English translation of *Fjalla-Eyvindur,* a play by Jóhann Sigurjónsson.

Ólafur Lárusson, 1885-1961, Professor, University of Iceland. 3 letters, Reykjavík, 30 January 1935; 12 December 1937; 3 October 1941; in Icelandic. — On problems regarding editions of *Jónsbók;* on behalf of Þorvarður Þórarinsson.

Ólafur (Óskar) Lárusson, M.D., 1884-1952. 1 letter, Brekka in Fljótsdalshérað, 24 September 1915; in Icelandic. — Reference questions on medical schools in the United States.

Ólafur S. Thorgeirsson, printer & publisher. 12 letters, Winnipeg, October 1928 - March 1935; copy from Halldór Hermannsson, 22 October 1928; invoices; in Icelandic and English. — Bibliographical inquiry; his proposed republication of Icelandic folk tales in English translation; business matters; requesting an article for his *Icelandic National Almanac.*

Oleson, Tryggvi J[ulius], 1912-1963. 4 letters, Winnipeg and Toronto, 29 January 1936; 4 April 1937; 10 December 1939; 6 April 1942; copy of a letter from Halldór Hermannsson, 6 February 1937; in English. — On Oleson's post graduate studies; his résumé; reference questions dealing with Old Norse. Enclosed: Prof. Kolsrud's suggestions on a topic for Oleson's thesis.

Oliver, Walter. 2 letters, Moosup, Connecticut, 7 and 14 May 1924; in English. — Arguing that the inhabitants of his native district in Scotland are descendents of Norse Vikings, based on onomastic evidence.

Olsen, Magnús, b. 1878, historian. 1 letter and one postcard, Oslo and Christiania, 12 October 1915; 12 April 1933; in Danish. — Bibliographical information on "Bjarnasonakvæði"; congratulating Halldór Hermannsson on his introduction to *Íslendingabók.*

Olson, Arnljótur B. 2 letters, Winnipeg, 31 March and 10 April 1934; in Icelandic. — Requesting the bibliography of his book collection returned. See also Sigurður Júl. Jóhannesson.

Olsson, Nils W., b. 1909. 3 letters, University of Chicago, 25 and 26 February 1941; 22 May 1946; in English. — Reference questions pertaining to *Vilmundar saga viðutans.* See also Manuscript Material 133.

Orton, Don A. 1 letter, University of Utah, Salt Lake City, 12 January 1948; in English. — The American-Scandinavian Foundation as a source of material for a doctoral dissertation in education.

Ostlund, George. 1 letter, New York City, 22 January 1946; in English. — Reference question, interested in reading about "fishes in Iceland."

Oswald, Victor A. Jr. 2 letters, New York City, 23 March 1935; 5 April 1936; in English. — Reference questions; his proposed doctoral dissertation on the development of the Modern Icelandic vocabulary.

Oxford University Press, London. 6 letters, August 1915 - March 1918; signed by F. J. Hall, and Humphrey Milford, of the Oxford University Press; a copy of a letter to Humphrey Milford from Horatio S. White, 22 December 1919; a letter to G. W. Harris from White, 4 May 1915; a stamped receipt from the Press; in English. — The publishing of the *Catalogue of Runic Literature.* See also the Clarendon Press and Manuscript Material 120.

Pacht & Crones Eftf., Copenhagen. Letters and invoices from February 1926 to November 1938; copies of letters from Halldór Hermannsson; in Danish. — Business matters. Enclosed: a letter from Generaldirektoratet for Post- og Telegrafvæsenet informing Pacht & Crones about registered mail to the United States.

Páll Á[sgeir] Ingvason. 8 letters, State College of Agriculture, Fort Collins, Colorado; Berkeley, Cal.; St. Paul, Minn., February 1915 - June 1922; in Icelandic. — Requesting Cornell University's publications on agriculture; on his studies in agricultural science; reference questions; asking to be introduced to L. H. Bailey; concerning reproductions of pictures of Icelandic horses for an article in a newspaper in Chicago; seeking information on irrigation systems in Medieval Iceland.

Páll Eggert Ólason, 1883-1949, Professor, University of Iceland. 12 letters and 1 postcard, Reykjavík, March 1915 - February 1930; copy of a letter from Halldór Hermannsson, 15 April 1929; in Icelandic. — Bibliographical information; matters of the National Library in Reykjavík; on his work; on the publication of *Diplomatarium Islandicum;* "the manuscript question." See also Manuscript Material 154.

Páll Sveinsson, 1878-1951, Sub-Rector at the Junior College in Reykjavík. 2 letters, Reykjavík, 9 September and 9 November 1929; in Icelandic. — Concerning his work on Icelandic poetry in Latin.

Palsson, J[óhannes] P[áll], M.D., b. 1881. 1 letter, Elfros, Saskatchewan, 31 March 1924; in English. — Reference question on the living conditions in Iceland in the latter part of the fifteenth century.

Parsons, Russell C., real estate dealer. 1 letter, Washington, D.C., 21 August 1945; in English. — Asking for the "most authentic" translations of the *Vinland sagas.*

Partridge, Harry B. 3 letters, Philippine Island, California, etc., 29 November 1944; 8 October 1945; s.d.; in English. — On his work. Enclosed: a newspaper clipping on the Icelandic sagas.

Paterson, T. G., Consul of Iceland. 1 letter, London, 21 May 1908; also a copy of a letter to the Library of Congress; in English. — Books offered for sale.

Paulsen, Gordon, student at the Graduate School of New York University. 1

letter, Yonkers, N.Y., 18 April 1942; in English. — Concerning Icelandic music in manuscripts.

Paulson, Stephen M. 2 letters, St. Michael's Parsonage, Mt. Airy, Philadelphia, 2 October 1917; 5 February 1921; in English. — Brief biographical account of himself; interested in the Reformation in Iceland; interlibrary loan request.

Pearl, Raymond, 1879-1940, the Johns Hopkins University. 7 letters, Baltimore and Paris, October 1927 - May 1929; copy from Halldór Hermannsson, 27 September 1928; in English. — Concerning Rockefeller Foundation grants to Icelanders for the study of human biology. See on same topic: Ágúst H. Bjarnason, Guðmundur Finnbogason, Guðmundur Hannesson, and Alan Gregg.

Pedersen, P. O. 1 letter, the Royal Technical College, Copenhagen, 21 December 1929; in Danish. — Formal letter of gratitude. Enclosed: letter of gratitude addressed to Cornell University, 20 December 1929; in English.

Peffers, David Hay, book and print seller. 1 letter, London, 23 July 1922; in English. — Seventeenth-century map of Iceland offered for purchase.

Peihl?, J. A. 1 letter, Wheaton, Illinois, 2 August 1924; in English. — Asking for information about how to procure the saga literature; mentions that he is engaged in writing papers on the "Goth people."

Peirce, James Harvey, Peirce Fisher & Clapp, law offices. 3 letters, Chicago, 22 November 1912; 8 January and 27 July 1913; in English. — Referring to letters from Fiske and Reeves.

Perkins, Henry A. 1 letter, Hartford, Connecticut, 22 February 1936; in English; pasted on the inside of the back cover of his translation of Gunnar Gunnarsson's *Trællen, The Serf.* This is the original typewritten copy of the translation, which was published in *Book Notes.* — Presenting the Fiske Icelandic Collection with the translation; mentions interest in travel literature.

Peterson, Aldis. 3 letters, Arborg, Manitoba, 17 March, 11 May, and 8 August 1945; copy of a postal order from Halldór Hermannsson, 23 August 1945; in Icelandic. — Books listed for sale.

Peterson, Carl C. 4 letters, YMCA, Scranton, Pennsylvania, 22 May 1921;

10, 17, and 23 February 1923; in English. — Seeking information about the Fiske Icelandic Collection; on the origin of the name of New York City. Enclosed: newspaper clipping.

Peterson, C[larence] Stewart, b. 1896. 1 postcard, Baltimore, 19 January 1945; in English. — Requesting an opinion on the Kensington stone.

Peterson, Frederick W. 2 letters, Ann Arbor, Michigan, 5 January 1932; 3 March 1934; in English. — Bibliographical inquiry.

Peterson, Magnus, bookseller. 7 letters, Norwood, Manitoba, November 1940 - May 1942; copies of two letters from Halldór Hermannsson; a receipt included with the letters; in Icelandic. — Business matters.

Peterson, Sigurd H. 2 letters, Oregon State Agricultural College, Corvallis, 30 September 1928; 21 February 1933; in English. — Asking for a suggestion on a dissertation topic; submitting his dissertation for publication in the Islandica series.

Pétur Jakobsson, 1886-1958. 1 letter, Reykjavík, 17 February 1939; in Icelandic. — Presenting his books of poetry to the Fiske Icelandic Collection.

Pétur Sigurgeirsson, b. 1919. 2 letters, Lutheran Seminary, Mt. Airy, Pennsylvania, 16 January [1945]; 3 February 1945; in Icelandic. — Interlibrary loan; his paper on Icelandic church history.

Pétur Zophoníasarson, 1879-1946. 3 letters, Reykjavík, 14 July 1915; 24 May 1916; 24 March 1920; in Icelandic. — About Pétur Zophoníasarson's work on the chess collection in the National Library in Reykjavík.

Phillpotts, Bertha S. 2 letters, Cambridge, England, 9 March 1926; 5 September 1930; in English. — Acknowledging the pamphlet on Eggert Ólafsson; regretting that Halldór Hermannsson could not come to Cambridge to see an exhibition of Icelandic books at the library.

Pierce, David H. 1 letter, John Adams High School, Cleveland, Ohio, 31 October 1940; a copy of the reply; in English. — Regarding inbreeding and insanity rate in Iceland.

Pierson, Dr. Frank F. 1 letter, Wilmington, Delaware, 11 June 1937; in English. — The Vinland question.

Pilcher, C. Venn, the Rev. 16 letters and 2 postcards, Wycliffe College, Toronto, and Sydney, Australia, August 1917 - April 1947; copy of a letter from Halldór Hermannsson, 16 June 1947; in English. — Request for an article; about his work on the seventeenth-century clergyman and poet Hallgrímur Pétursson; publication problems; about his work on Icelandic church history and translations of Icelandic hymns; interlibrary loan; reference questions.

Pjetur Sigurðsson, b. 1896, secretary at the University of Iceland. 4 letters, Reykjavík, 26 September 1928; 9 November 1936; 18 December 1944; 24 May 1945; in Icelandic. — Notations on *Icelandic books of the Seventeenth Century,* with additional titles; asking for volumes of Islandica for the University Library in Reykjavík; sending the University of Iceland's publications to the Fiske Icelandic Collection. See also Manuscript Material 133.

Place, Charles A. 5 letters, Sterling, Massachusetts, 7 and 11 December 1931; 16 March 1932; 17 November 1933; 4 March 1934; in English. — Reference questions pertaining to books on Lutheran worship in Iceland.

Plimpton Press, The, Norwood, Massachusetts. Numerous letters, November 1912 - October 1913; signed by William Dana Orcutt; in English. — The printing of the *Catalogue of the Icelandic Collection.* Enclosed: "Memorandum regarding the Icelandic Catalogue", 3 sheets; "Explanatory Notes", 6 sheets; copy of a letter from William Dana Orcutt to H. S. White.

Plummer, C[harles], 1851-1927. 2 letters, Corpus Christi College, Oxford, 6 December 1925; 19 December 1926; in English. — Thanking for volumes of Islandica, sending one of his publications; mentions briefly that his Icelandic has gotten rusty and he has gone over to Irish studies.

Poestion, J[osef] C[alasanz], 1853-1922. 3 letters and 11 postcards, Vienna, April 1910 - January 1921; in German. — Commenting on the *Bibliography of the Icelandic Sagas and Minor Tales,* and some other Islandica publications; expressing thanks for the receipt of same.

Pohl, Frederick J[ulius], b. 1889. 1 letter, New York City, 6 January 1940; in English. — Reference question on early Scandinavian voyages in English translation.

Polunin, Nicholas. 4 letters, Department of Botany, the University, Oxford;

London, 4 and 17 October 1938; 4 August and 10 October 1945; in English. — His discovery of plants supposedly brought from America to Greenland by the Norse expedition; arranging a date; reference question on a related topic.

Poor, Harry W., H. W. Poor & Co. 1 letter, New York City, 23 December 1905; in English. — On obtaining Icelandic publications.

Porterfield, Allen W. 1 letter, West Virginia University, Morgantown, 19 January 1935; in English. — Seeking a translation of an English sentence into Icelandic.

Price, Eleanor. 1 letter, Rochester, N.Y., 19 June 1937; in English. — About preserving leather bindings.

Pritchard, F. H., M.D. 9 letters, Colton, California, October 1919 - February 1931; in English. — Reference questions relating to Iceland.

Progressive Grocer, The, New York City. 1 letter, 29 November 1939; signed by L. Copeland, librarian; in English. — Seeking information on the source of an old Viking legend.

Prowse, G. R. F., Winnipeg, Manitoba. See Manuscript Material 183.

Pulling, Arthur C., Law School of Harvard University. 1 letter, Cambridge, Mass., 22 June 1943; in English. — Inquiry about Icelandic and Scandinavian legal bibliographies.

Quarterly Journal, The, the University of North Dakota. 2 letters, Grand Forks, 18 November and 7 December 1931; signed by F. E. Bump, Jr., editor; in English. — Requesting a review of Dr. Richard Beck's book, *Icelandic Lyrics*, for the journal.

Raddall, Thomas H., b. 1903. 1 letter, Liverpool, Nova Scotia, 13 January 1933; in English. — Bibliographical inquiry about books about the Norse discoveries of America.

Rambusch, Viggo F. E., St. Ansgar's Scandinavian Catholic League. 2 letters, New York City, 3 October and 10 November 1941; a copy of the reply; in English. — Reference question on books in English on medieval church history of Iceland.

Rannveig K[ristín] G[uðmundsdóttir] Sigbjörnsson, 1880-1963, author. 4
letters, Leslie, Saskatchewan, 4 January and 26 March 1934; 17 July
1935; 17 January 1936; copy of a letter from Halldór Hermannsson, 27
January 1936; in Icelandic. — Reference questions; asking Halldór
Hermannsson to read and comment on her paper on *Vídalíns postilla.*

Ray, Olaf E[dward], 1856-1943, counselor at law. 3 letters, Chicago, 10
February and 17 March 1935; 8 December 1937; in English. —
Reference questions concerning Leifur Eiríkson and the Vinland voyages. Enclosed: "The Memorial of Leif Erikson in America", a printed
leaflet by Olaf Ray.

Regan, John W. 3 letters, Halifax, Nova Scotia, 31 March, 12 April and 21
May 1934; in English. — The Vinland question.

Reman, Edward, 1887-1945. 1 letter, Los Angeles, 23 September 1944;
copy of Halldór Hermannsson's reply; in English. — The Vinland question.

Retzek, Henry, the Rev. 1 letter, St. Alexius Rectory, West Union,
Minnesota, 27 July 1936; in English. — On the Kensington stone.

Rhea, W. A., Professor at Southern Methodist University, Dallas, Texas. 2
letters, 12 and 27 February 1930; in English. — Asking for the runic
characters for "Law Speaker."

Richard Beck, b. 1897, Professor, University of North Dakota. 180 letters,
Grand Forks and Winnipeg, November 1921 - August 1958; in
Icelandic. — About his work on Icelandic literature; contemporary literature in Iceland; Icelandic literary politics; Old Norse and Icelandic
studies; reference questions, and related topics. Enclosed: Beck's résumé written by Halldór Hermannsson to J. E. Creighton, The Graduate
School, Cornell University; "Íslendingatal fyrir *Hver er maðurinn*", 2
sheets; copy of a letter from Beck to Bjarni Jónsson, Reykjavík, 20 July
1942; extract from a letter from Prof. Skúli Johnson to Beck; copy of
Halldór Hermannsson's review of Beck's *Icelandic Lyrics*, 4 sheets; extracts from letters remarking upon his book *History of Icelandic Poets,*
3 sheets; offprint from *The North Dakota Quarterly,* "Rolvaag,
Interpreter of Immigrant Life", by Beck.

Ries, H. 1 letter, Ithaca, N.Y., 24 January 1922; in English. —
Acknowledging a note from Halldór Hermannsson and sending the reference on a separate sheet, which is missing.

Riksarkivet (The National Archives), Stockholm. 1 letter, 14 February 1931; signed by Helge Almqvist; in English. — Replying to a request about maps.

Robb, Maurine, the Christian Science Publishing Society. 5 letters, Boston, 24 and 28 January, 27 and 31 March, and 2 October [1924]; a letter from Francis H. Snow of *Current History,* 28 June 1924, with a reference question on behalf of Miss Robb; in English. — Reference questions for her article on politics in Iceland.

Roberts, F. G. 4 letters, St. Albans, Herts, England, 29 September, 21 October, and 13 November 1930; 3 January 1931; copies of two letters from Halldór Hermannsson to Roberts, and a copy to O. Kinkeldey, Cornell University; in English. — Palladius' *Catechismus,* printed at Holar in 1576, listed for sale, and bought.

Rockefeller Foundation, The, New York City. 1 letter, 8 December 1924; copy of a letter to Prof. Guðmundur Hannesson, University of Iceland, from the Rockefeller Foundation, signed by George E. Vincent; in English. — Regarding aid to improve hospital facilities for the Medical School in Reykjavík. See also letters from Guðmundur Hannesson.

Roerich Museum, New York City. 4 letters, 11 December 1929; 17 February, 21 July, and 31 October 1931; signed by Adeline L. Atwater and Louis L. Horch; a copy of a letter from Halldór Hermannsson to the Museum; copies of two letters to Matthías Þórðarson, National Museum of Iceland, from the Museum; in English. — On a contemplated exhibition of Modern Icelandic Art at the Roerich Museum. See also letters from Jón Stefánsson, Matthías Þórðarson, Sveinn Björnsson, and Valtýr Stefánsson.

Rogers, Frank Sill. 2 letters, St. Peter's Church, Albany, N.Y., 3 and 11 November [1910]; in English. — Seeking a translation of two Icelandic songs into English, "Bára blá" and "Ólafur liljurós."

Rögnvaldur Pétursson, the Rev., 1877-1940. 16 letters and one telegram, Winnipeg; Boston; Ottawa, May 1931 - January 1937; in Icelandic and English. — On behalf of his son, Þorvaldur; request for an article for *Tímarit Þjóðræknifélagsins;* the translation of "Réttarstaða Íslands" by Ragnar Lundberg from German into Icelandic. Enclosed: a circular from the Committee for Iceland at the World's Fair in New York, 6 January 1939.

Roselius, Ludwig, Königl. Bulgarischer Generalkonsul. 1 telegram, Bremen, 23 March 1934; in German. — Invitation to participate in a conference to be held in Bremen in May 1934. Enclosed: the program for the conference; copy of a telegram from Halldór Hermannsson regretting inability to attend the conference.

Rosenthal, Jacques, bookseller. 1 letter, Munich, 9 February 1909; in German. — An old map of Iceland listed for sale.

Rosenthal, Ludwig. See Manuscript Material 154.

Rostan, Clare E. 1 letter, Vineland, New Jersey, 2 June 1944; in English. — Thanking for a loan of Icelandic books to an exhibition.

Rothery Pratt, Agnes (Mrs. Harry Rogers Pratt), 1888-1954. 1 letter, University Station, Charlottesville, Virginia, 15 December 1946; in English. — Requesting a bibliography of Icelandic literature in translation in order to prepare for a visit to Iceland and to write a book.

Royal Geographical Society, The, London. 1 letter, 25 October 1907; signed by J. Scott Keltic; in English. — Recognizing suggestions to the articles on Iceland in the *Statesman's Year-Book.*

Royal Ontario Museum of Archaeology, The, Toronto. 2 letters, 14 December 1937; 23 May 1938; signed by C. T. Currelly, Director and E. M. Greenaway, Assistant Director; a copy of Halldór Hermannsson's reply, 21 December 1937; in English. — The Vinland question. Enclosed: photograph of weapons supposedly from a Norse grave.

Rugg, Harold G., the College Library, Dartmouth College. 1 letter, Hanover, New Hampshire, 23 October 1930; in English. — Concerning publications on the botany of Iceland.

Runólfur Marteinsson, the Rev., 1870-1959. 8 letters, Wesley College, Winnipeg, Manitoba, November 1911 - March 1947; in Icelandic. — Inquiry about courses in Icelandic or Old Norse at Cornell, also about textbooks; reference questions pertaining to the Reverend Jón Bjarnason, his publications, genealogy, etc.; about Runólfur Marteinsson's trip to New York; asking information about Cornell University; on behalf of Joseph B. Skaptason.

Russell, W. S. C. 4 letters, Springfield, Massachusetts, 28 August 1914; 29

January, 9 and 17 February 1916; in English. — On the reception of his book, *Iceland;* his work on Old Norse literature; asking Halldór Hermannsson to examine his introduction to *Hænsa Þóris saga;* reference question regarding Old Norse matters.

Sæmundur Bjarnhéðinsson, M.D., 1863-1936, Reykjavík. See Manuscript Material 63.

Salverson, Laura Goodman, b. 1890. 1 letter, Edmonton, Alta, 22 May 1923; in English. — Reference question pertaining to her plans to write a novel based on the life of the seventeenth-century clergyman and poet Hallgrímur Pétursson.

Samuel, J[oseph] Bunford, b. 1853. 7 letters, Philadelphia, Pennsylvania; Sea Girt, Monmouth Co., New Jersey, August 1920 - March 1928; in English. — The dedication of the statue of Thorfinn karlsefni; sending a copy of his book about Thorfinn karlsefni; commenting on Cornelia Horsford's book *Leif's Home in Vineland.* Enclosed: newspaper clipping announcing Samuel as a Knight of the Order of the Icelandic Falcon. See also Manuscript Material 173.

Samzelius, Jonas L., b. 1886, librarian, Uppsala University. 3 letters, Uppsala, 29 August and 30 October 1921; 20 November 1923; in Swedish. — Information on Uppsala Library's holdings of publications by Rugman.

Sanders, Walter Frederick. 2 letters, Park College, Parkville, Missouri, 12 October and 4 December 1928; in English. — Bibliographical inquiry about Scandinavian literature.

Sarton, George, 1884-1956, ISIS, Harvard Library. 1 letter, Cambridge, Mass., 3 February 1943; in English. — Reference question pertaining to the introduction of decimal numbers into Scandinavia.

Scandinavia, Grand Forks, North Dakota. 4 letters, 30 October 1923; 4 February, 6 May, and 17 June 1924; signed by Georg Strandvold, editor; in English. — Request for an article on the Icelandic Library at Cornell University.

Scandinavian Club of the University of California. 1 letter, Berkeley, 9 September 1921; signed by S. Á. Bjarnason; in English. — Invitation to become a member.

Schach, Paul. 1 letter, North Central College, Naperville, Illinois, 6 March 1947; in English. — Acknowledging information on texts and translations of sagas.

Schacke, Erik. 1 letter, Leith, 6 June 1930; in English. — Books offered for purchase. Enclosed: a list of titles, 7 sheets.

Schaub-Koch, Prof. Emile, b. 1890. 1 letter, Geneva, Switzerland, 19 March 1941; in English. — Sending his own publications and asking for volumes of the Islandica series.

Schedin, Mrs. Lillian M. 1 letter, Schedin Studio, Leadville, Colorado, 30 November 1917; in English. — Reference question concerning literature on runic inscriptions.

Schepotieff, A., Minsk University. See Manuscript Material 140.

Scherer, Robert W. 1 letter, Fort Slocum, N.Y., 21 May 1948; copy of Halldór Hermannsson's reply; in English. — Reference question pertaining to his collection of stamps.

Schlauch, Margaret, b. 1898, Professor. 11 letters, New York and Warsaw, April 1933 - March 1946; in English. — Mentions books on Russian-Icelandic relations, proposing to write an article on the Fiske Icelandic Collection and Halldór Hermannsson for the *American-Scandinavian Review;* requesting Halldór Hermannsson to give a talk at a meeting of medievalists in New York, see also Austin P. Evans; translation problems, bibliographical information, etc. Enclosed: a copy of a plan for an Old Germanic Dictionary presented to the Scandinavian Group by Professor Mezger; letter to Cornell University Press, 8 January 1959, asking for *The Hólar Cato.*

Scholl, Walter. 2 letters, Berlin, 10 May and 14 July 1921; in German and English. — Bibliographical inquiry and information regarding Old Norse literature.

Schreiner, Thomas W. 2 letters, New York, 29 April and 6 May 1930; in English. — Asking for *Icelandic Manuscripts of the Middle Ages;* reference question.

Schumm, Donald. 1 letter, Three Rivers, Michigan, 18 June 1943; in English. — Reference questions pertaining to the "Passion Hymns" of Hallgrímur Pétursson.

Scott Polar Research Institute, Cambridge, England. 1 letter, 27 November 1933; signed by F. Debenham; a draft of Halldór Hermannsson's reply; in English. — Reference question pertaining to Eskimo kayaks.

Seawell, Octavia. 1 letter, Hampton, Virginia, 31 October 1940; in English. — Expressing interest in obtaining Old Norse sagas in the original.

Shaw, R. W., M.D. 11 letters, Grand Manitoulin Island, Ontario, June 1916 - November 1920; in English. — Reference questions; the meaning and pronunciation of Icelandic names; about his interest in Germanic studies and Icelandic literature; his work on the personal names of the Teutonic race. Enclosed: a list of Bishops of Greenland, 2 sheets.

Sigfús Blöndal, 1874-1950. 111 letters, 14 postcards, and 1 telegram, Copenhagen, January 1900 - November 1949; in Icelandic. — Bibliographical inquiries, information and reference questions in numerous letters; the affairs of Hið íslenzka bókmenntafélag in Copenhagen and Hið íslenzka fræðafélag; comments on various publications on Icelandic literature and history; commenting on his own work and the work of Halldór Hermannsson; news from Copenhagen; Icelandic politics in Copenhagen and Reykjavík; concerning a position at the Arnamagnæan Institute and at the University of Copenhagen, and other topics. Enclosed: a letter of appreciation to the President, Cornell University; "Spámaðurinn" by Púsjkin, translated into Icelandic by Sigfús Blöndal, 1 sheet. See also Manuscript Material 154 and 168.

Sighv[atur] Gr[ímsson] Borgfirðingur, 1840-1930. 7 letters, Höfði in Dýrafjörður, October 1919 - August 1928; in Icelandic. — Acknowledging publications sent by Halldór Hermannsson; sending pamphlets to the Fiske Icelandic Collection; about his work on biographies of pastors in Iceland. See also Manuscript Material 129 and 186.

Sigríður Einarsdóttir (Magnússon), 1831-1915. 1 letter, Cambridge, England, 12 March 1914; in Icelandic. — Books offered for sale. Enclosed: a list of Eiríkur Magnússon's books with descriptions in English, 14 sheets.

Sigurbjörn Sveinsson, b. 1878, Reykjavík. See Manuscript Material 129.

Sigurður Guðmundsson, 1878-1949. 10 letters, Copenhagen and Akureyri, January 1904 - April 1947; in Icelandic. — Icelandic politics in Copenhagen and Reykjavík; his work as a Rector at the Junior College

in Akureyri; on behalf of Haraldur Árnason; on the cemetery at Þingvellir.

Sigurður Július Jóhannesson, M.D., 1868-1956. 2 letters, Leslie,
Saskatchewan and Winnipeg Manitoba, 23 September 1933; 25 March
1934; in Icelandic. — Books offered for sale on behalf of A. B. Olson.
See also Arnljótur B. Olson and Manuscript Material 129.

Sigurður Kristjánsson, 1854-1952, bookseller. 46 letters, Reykjavík,
October 1905 - March 1928; copy of a letter from Halldór
Hermannsson, 18 November 1912; in Icelandic. Receipts included with
the letters. — Business matters; bibliographical information. See also
Manuscript Material 133.

Sigurður Nordal, 1886-1974, Professor, University of Iceland. 37 letters and
2 postcards, Reykjavík; Copenhagen; Stockholm; Harrogate;
Cambridge, Mass., etc., February 1925 - September 1956; in Icelandic.
— Commenting on his own work; numerous letters discuss Old Norse
and Icelandic scholarship in Iceland and abroad; about Professor Finnur
Jónsson; his travelling plans in Scandinavia; history of early modern literature; his lecture tour in the United States in 1932; the manuscript
question; the publishing of Icelandic literature by Munksgaard; comments on some of Halldór Hermannsson's work; on various publications on Icelandic literature and history; the economic and political situation in Iceland; his stay in England in 1932; about a conference in
Lund.

Sigurður Ólafsson, the Rev., 1883-1961. 2 letters, Selkirk, Manitoba and
Portland, Oregon, 30 December 1912; 19 June 1942; in Icelandic. —
Seeking an English translation of the hymn "Allt er eins og blómstrið
eina" by the seventeenth-century clergyman and poet Hallgrímur
Pétursson.

Sigurður Ólafsson, b. 1916, student at Philadelphia College of Pharmacy
and Science. 1 letter, Philadelphia, 21 December 1942; in Icelandic. —
Reference question on Icelandic literature in English translation.

Sigurður H. Pétursson. See **Peterson, Sigurd H.**

Sigurður Sigurðsson, 1864-1926, Reykjavík. See Manuscript Material 129.

Sigurgeir Einarsson, wholesale merchant. 4 letters, Reykjavík, 6 June 1944;

10 December 1948; 7 February and 6 March 1949; copies of 3 letters from Halldór Hermannsson; in Icelandic. — Concerning his donation to the Icelandic Collection. Enclosed: formal announcement of a gift to the Fiske Icelandic Collection from Sigurgeir Einarsson, 9 January 1949.

Skinner, Constance Lindsay, 1882-1939. 1 letter, New York, 17 February 1922; in English. — Reference question concerning publications on the Norsemen in Britain.

Skogberg, Georgine. 1 letter, Marinette, Wisconsin, 10 February 1940; a copy of the reply; in English. — Asking about graduate studies in the Scandinavian languages at Cornell University.

Slater, Henry H., the Rev. 1 postcard, Thornhaugh Rectory, Wansford, England, 4 February 1903; in English. — Information relating to his book *Manual of the Birds of Iceland* (Edinburgh, 1901). Pasted inside back cover of the book. See also postcard from same to Fiske.

Sloane, T. O'Conor. 2 letters, South Orange, New Jersey, s.d., but the reply is dated 10 November 1930. Cf. note on the first letter; in English. — Seeking titles of two modern Icelandic works of fiction; a letter of thanks for the reply.

Smart, T. G., Smart's Brokerage Co. 1 letter, Chattanooga, Tennessee, 16 October 1930; in English. — Reference questions on Icelandic matters.

Smith, J[oseph] Russel, 1874-1966, Professor at Columbia University. 3 letters, New York City, 2, 7, and 17 June 1920; in English. — Asking for a reference to books on Iceland.

Smith, Verle C., Mrs. 1 letter, Columbus, Ohio, 26 January 1940; in English. — Reference question pertaining to books on contemporary art in Iceland and Denmark.

Smithsonian Institution, Washington, D.C. 2 letters, 6 March and 1 April 1920; signed by Neil M. Judd, Curator, American Archeology; in English. — Reference questions pertaining to fragments of human bones, pierced by bronze arrowheads, possibly of Norse origin.

Snæbjörn Jónsson, b. 1887. 1 letter, Reykjavík, 17 April 1936; in Icelandic. — Acknowledging *Bibliographical Notices* presented to him by Halldór Hermannsson.

Snyder, Albert. 1 letter, Juniata College, Huntington, Pennsylvania, 22 September 1930; in English. — Reference question on an English translation of *Gunnlaugs saga ormstungu.*

Spargo, John W. 2 letters, Northwestern University, Evanston, Illinois, 10 November and 1 December 1937; in English. — Regarding the Modern Language Association.

Sparkes, Boyden. 2 letters, New York City, 30 September and 22 October 1941; in English. — Reference question concerning the Kensington stone.

Springer, Otto, b. 1905, Professor. 10 letters and one postcard, Wheaton College, Norton, Massachusetts, and University of Pennsylvania, Philadelphia, October 1934 - August 1946; in English. — Submitting a paper to be delivered at a meeting of the Modern Language Association; reference questions; proposing a bibliography of scholarly work on the *Elder Edda;* matters of the Modern Language Association.

Staples, Theodor. 1 letter, Washington, D.C., 9 November 1933; in English. — On acquiring modern Icelandic literature and newspapers.

Stechert, G. E. & Co., dealers in books and periodicals. 2 letters, New York City, 27 December 1906 and 8 January 1913; one postcard, 29 October 1915; in English. — Business matters.

Stefán Björnsson, Columbia Press, Winnipeg, Manitoba. 1 letter, 5 November 1912; in Icelandic. — Reference question answered; requesting articles by Halldór Hermannsson for publication in the Icelandic weekly *Lögberg.*

Stefán Einarsson, 1897-1972, Professor at the Johns Hopkins University. 125 letters and 14 postcards, Baltimore and Ithaca N.Y., January 1927 - July 1958; in Icelandic and English. — On meetings of the Scandinavian Group; numerous reference questions and bibliographical inquiries; on his research work (in numerous letters throughout the years); about using the Icelandic Collection in the summers; several requests for books through interlibrary loan; commenting on some of Halldór Hermannsson's publications, f.ex., *Sir Josept Banks, The Cartography of Iceland,* and *Sæmund Sigfússon and the Oddaverjar;* referring to letters by Jón Ófeigsson; about Icelanders in Baltimore; the necessity of reprinting Guðmundur Andrésson's *Dictionary;* about his review on Holand's *Kensington runestone* in *Speculum;* pertaining to publication matters; mentioning several scholars in the Old Norse and Icelandic field, their research, publications, and activities; the affairs of Johns Hopkins University; his work on the Icelandic dictionary (seeking advice on the layout); asking Halldór Hermannsson's opinion on the value of Ottesen's book collection; relating news from Iceland; mentioning contemporary Icelandic literature; his plans for the future; remarking on the discontinuation of the professorship in Scandinavian languages at Cornell; about Nordal's comments on the *History of Icelandic literature;* the manuscript question; his work for the American-Scandinavian Foundation. Enclosed: copy of a letter from Lancaster Press to John Warner, Cornell University Press, with an estimate on the printing of Stefán Einarsson's book, *History of Icelandic Prose;* 2 letters from Lancaster Press pertaining to Stefán Einarsson's book, 16 December 1946; copy of a letter of recommendation to the American-Scandinavian Foundation on behalf of Stefán Einarsson, and a letter acknowledging same from the Foundation, 15 February 1951. See also Manuscript Material 160.

Stefán Stefánsson, 1863-1921, high school principal. 1 letter, Akureyri, 3 November 1911; in Icelandic. — About sending the school reports from the high school in Akureyri, and receiving Islandica publications.

Stefán Jóhann Stefánsson, 1863-1921, the school at Möðruvellir. See Manuscript Material 129.

Stefansson, Vilhjalmur, 1879-1962. 62 letters and one telegram, American Geographical Society, New York; North Derby, Vermont, June 1920 - December 1954; copies of letters from Halldór Hermannsson; in English. — The letters are mainly on the Vinland question and related matters; the genuineness of the Kensington stone; on behalf of Dr. Raymond Pearl, who wants Halldór Hermannsson to call at the Rockefeller Foundation in Paris; Reference questions, f.ex. on Pythias' voyages, bibliography of the Norse voyages in the North Atlantic, publications on weather reports from Iceland, and on the Cabots; Ogden's *Basic English through Carl and Anna;* referring Dr. Lloyd Warner's question about the Brehon law school to Halldór Hermannsson; bibliographical information and inquiries; reference to Jón Dúason's manuscript on the discovery of Greenland; suggesting the making of a bibliography of sources on the discovery of the Faeroe Islands, Iceland, Greenland, and North America; asking for translation of words and phrases from Icelandic into English; whether to use commonwealth or republic for Medieval Iceland; the spelling of Leifur Eiríksson's name;

requesting books from the Icelandic Collection to exhibit at a lecture to be given at a meeting of the New York Historical Society; asking for opinions on various publications and theories on the Vinland question; asking permission to list Halldór Hermannsson as a consultant to the group working on a bibliography of exploration; about the prospect of pan agriculture in Iceland; maps of Iceland for the United States Navy; permission to quote Halldór Hermannsson's books; *Encyclopedia Arctica;* sundials on Icelandic mountain tops. Enclosed are copies of letters by Stefansson to: Gathorne-Hardy; Calvin Philips Jr., Seattle, Washington; Isaiah Bowman, American Geographical Society; Ásgeir Ásgeirsson, Reykjavík; Alexander J. Wall, New York Historical Society; John W. Regan, Halifax, Nova Scotia; William C. Darrah, Paleobotanical Laboratory, Cambridge, Mass.; Jón Dúason; Dr. William Hovgaard; Guðmundur Finnbogason; Wilhelm Munthe de Morgenstierne, Minister from Norway to the U.S.; Dr. Arthur E. Morgan, Yellow Springs, Ohio; Albert B. Donworth, and from Donworth to Stefansson; Miss Mina Brownstone, and from her to Stefansson; Leo T. McCauley, Consul General of Ireland, and from him to Stefansson, and to Halldór Hermannsson; J.A. Allis, Grace National Bank, New York; William Sloane, Henry Holt and Co., New York; Sivert N. Hagen, Franklin and Marshall College, Lancaster, Pennsylvania, and from him to Stefansson; Hans Olav, Royal Norwegian Embassy, Washington, D.C.; G. M. Wrigley, the *Geographical Review;* Dr. Lincoln Washburn, The Arctic Institute of North America; Adele Banvard, and from her to Stefansson. Also enclosed: letters and copies of letters to Stefansson from: Hjalmar R. Holand; A. H. Walker, Chicago; Tom Davin, Reference Department at the New York Public Library; G. S. Bryan, United States Navy. Letters to Halldór Hermannsson on behalf of Stefansson from Genevieve N. Shipman, 2 letters; Olive R. Wilcox, secretary, 3 letters; Evelyn Stefansson, 5 letters; Elaine McCaskill Popini, 1 letter. Also copy of Sigrid Undset's opinion on *Newport Tower* by Philip Ainsworth Means; report from a luncheon at the University Club, 16 February 1939 on the same book; 2 letters from Steingrímur Jónsson to Stefansson, translated into English, about the visibility of Greenland from Iceland, with calculations. See also Mrs. Theodor Wedepohl, Charles Herz, and Manuscript Material 133 and 153.

Steindór Steindórsson frá Hlöðum, b. 1902, teacher. 1 letter, Akureyri, 5 February 1944; in Icelandic. — Books and pamphlets offered for sale.

Steiner, Arpad. 1 letter, Hunter College, New York City, 22 February 1942; in English. — Pertaining to a lecture to be given by Halldór

Hermannsson at a meeting of the Mediaeval Group in New York City in April 1942. See also letters from Professor Margaret Schlauch and Austin P. Evans.

Steingrímur Arason, 1879-1951. 4 letters, Fort Tilden, New York, 4, 12, and 24 August 1942; 25 February 1943; in Icelandic. — Biographical information on Magnús and Barbara Árnason; regarding his and Vilhjalmur Stefansson's book on Icelandic for American soldiers; reference questions and translation problems concerning same.

Stenberg, Theodore T., State Normal School. 1 letter, Whitewater, Wisconsin, 3 December 1916; in English. — Letter of farewell from a former student.

Stet, J. H. 1 postcard, New York City, 4 August 1936; in English. — Bibliographical inquiry pertaining to Icelandic Bible translations.

Stewart, Bruce. 1 letter, Saginaw, Michigan, 27 January 1940; in English. — Request for deciphering of inscriptions on a wooden chest bought in Iceland in 1874. Enclosed: 2 photographs of the chest, 19.4 (18.3) x 25.2 cm.

Stewart, Joseph. 2 letters, University, Alabama, 10 May and 3 June 1941; in English. — Inquiring about studies in Germanic Philology at the University of Iceland, Reykjavík.

Stockholms Högskolas Bibliotek. 1 letter, Stockholm, 8 July 1930; signed by G. Philip; in Swedish. — Sending doctoral dissertations to the Fiske Icelandic Collection.

Straumfjord, John V., M.D. 2 letters, Portland, Oregon, 20 November and 9 December 1931; in English. — Reference question on the historical aspects of medical practice in Iceland.

Strömbäck, Dag, b. 1900. 12 letters, the University of Chicago, January 1937 - April 1938; in Swedish. — Arranging the date for his lecture at Cornell University. Enclosed: copies of 5 letters from Woodford Patterson, Cornell University, to the American-Scandinavian Foundation, and two letters to Halldór Hermannsson, a letter from Carleton C. Murdock, the Committee on University Lectures, and to him from Halldór Hermannsson, all pertaining to Strömbäck's lecture.

Students Book Department, University of Toronto. 1 letter, 19 January 1923; signed by G. E. L[aventure]; in English. — A textbook in Modern Icelandic needed.

Stutzenberger, Albert. 4 letters, Kentucky Military Institute, Lyndon, Kentucky, and Louisville, Kentucky, 1 August 1932; 10 March and 22 July 1933; 14 July 1941; in English. — On the advancement of his Icelandic studies; his translation of modern Icelandic short stories; translation problems; reference questions.

Sun Flame Appliances, Ltd., Ridgefield, New Jersey. 1 letter, 24 July 1944; signed by Charles T. Shears; in English. — A cataloguing problem at the local library.

Super, Charles W[illiam], b. 1842. 1 letter, Athens, Ohio, 19 January 1925; in English. — On translations of Homer into the Scandinavian languages.

Sveinbjörn Johnson. see **Johnson, Sveinbjörn.**

Sveinbjörn Sveinbjörnsson, 1847-1926, music teacher, Edinburgh. See Manuscript Material 129.

Sveinn Björnsson, 1881-1952, Iceland's Ambassador in Copenhagen and later the President of Iceland. 5 letters, Copenhagen and Reykjavík, 28 October and 10 December 1927; 22 September and 21 November 1928; 8 September 1944; in Icelandic. — Mentioning the manuscript question, Dr. Alan Gregg's visit to Reykjavík; recording the manuscripts that are to be returned to Iceland from Copenhagen, 6 sheets; plans for an exhibition of paintings by Icelandic artists (see also letters from Jón Stefánsson, Matthías Þórðarson, the Roerich Museum, and Valtýr Stefánsson). Appreciating kind reception by Icelanders in New York in the summer of 1944. See also the invitation from LaGuardia.

Sveinn Eiríksson. 1 letter, Edfield, Saskatchewan, 29 January 1932; in Icelandic. — Proposing to build a hall, modelled for Old Norse buildings, for the World Exhibition in Chicago 1933.

Swainson, Verne. 1 letter, New York City, s.d.; in English. — Requesting a catalogue of Icelandic books.

Swanson, C. L. 1 letter, Hastings, Nebraska, 19 June 1938; in English. — Concerning the best translation of the *Poetic Edda.*

Swanson, F. 1 letter, Atlantic City, New Jersey, 7 December 1934; in English. — A textbook in modern Icelandic needed.

Swedenborg Publishing Association, Minneapolis, Minnesota. 2 letters, 4 and 31 August 1911; in English. — Replying to Halldór Hermannsson's inquiry about Swedenborg's "New Jerusalem and Its Heavenly Doctrine", Icelandic translation.

Sweringen, Grace Fleming von, Professor, University of Colorado. 1 letter and a postcard, Boulder, 1 March 1911; 3 January 1914; in English. — A proposed trip to Iceland; needing information on steamers and accommodations in Reykjavík; asking about the Islandica publication; her hope to be able to carry her trip to Iceland through soon.

Symons, B[arend], b. 1853. 1 postcard, Groningen, Holland, 16 January 1921; in English. — Acknowledging the *Bibliography of the Eddas,* and sending some of his writings on the Eddic poems.

Teachers College Library, Columbia University, New York City. 1 letter, 2 June 1944; signed by Eleanor M. Witmer; in English. — Seeking information on a bibliography of Icelandic publications.

Telephone Almanac, The, New York City. 2 letters, 16 and 21 April 1936; signed by R. T. Barrett; in English. — Seeking historical data about Thorfinn karlsefni to use in *The Telephone Almanac.*

Thayer, Gordon W., Cleveland Public Library. 1 letter, 3 June 1942; in English. — Proposing to prepare a biographical dictionary of the characters in the sagas.

Thayer, John E[liot], 1862-1933. 1 letter, Thayer Museum, Lancaster, Massachusetts, 6 November 1922; in English. — Not interested in the collection Halldór Hermannsson wrote to him about. [Probably the collection of bird-drawings by Benedikt Gröndal. See Þórður Edilonsson].

Thiele, Richard. 1 postcard, Erfurt, 12 September 1903; pasted on the back flyleaf of his *Die Insel Island* (Erfurt, 1894); in German. — Providing his name and address. See also letters to Fiske.

Thompson, Lawrence S[idney], b. 1916. 1 letter, Ames, Iowa, 3 February 1942; in English. — Needs Halldór Hermannsson's *Joseph Banks and Iceland;* congratulating Halldór Hermannsson on his essay "Íslenzkar rímbækur og almanök."

Thor S. Benedikz. 1 letter, New York City, 25 November 1930; in Icelandic. — Inquiry about a job at Harvard University Library on behalf of Eiríkur and Þyri Benedikz.

Thor (Haraldur) Thors, 1903-1965, Consul of Iceland in New York City. 4 letters, New York and Washington D.C., 7 and 20 August 1941; 8 November 1943; 9 January 1946; in Icelandic. — Regarding Þorvaldur V. H. Þórarinsson's admittance to Cornell Law School; thanking for information regarding Albert Sigurðsson's proposed studies at Cornell University; asking assistance with Sibil Kamban's application to Cornell Medical School.

Thorlakson, Edward Julius. 8 letters, Northwestern University, Evanston, Illinois and New York City; September 1938 - June 1944; last two letters headed Office of War Information; in English. — On his research on Jón Sigurðsson's oratory; bibliographical inquiry; translation problems; Halldór Hermannsson's greeting to Icelanders via radio broadcasting in 1944. Enclosed: program of a concert on a poetic interpretation of the sagas held in the Theater at Brooklyn College.

Thorsteinn Jóhannesson, carpenter, Pembina, North Dakota. See Manuscript Material 129.

Thorvaldur Pétursson, b. 1904. 19 letters and 1 postcard, Winnipeg; Toronto; Clifton Springs, New York, May 1933 - June 1935; in English. — Regarding graduate studies in Old Norse at Cornell University; his treatment at the Clifton Springs Sanitarium and Clinic. Enclosed: 4 letters from the Clinic, and a number of invoices.

Tjomsland, Anne, M.D., b. 1880. 59 letters and one telegram, Jersey City, New Jersey; New York City; Ithaca, N.Y., October 1933 - May 1948; letter to Tjomsland from Henry E. Sigerist, the Johns Hopkins University; to Halldór Hermannsson from Cornell University Press, regarding Tjomsland's manuscript for *The Saga of Hrafn Sveinbjarnarson*, judgment on her work enclosed; in English. — Concerning research on the history of medicine in Iceland and Scandinavia; interlibrary loan requests; bibliographical inquiries; on her translation of *Hrafns saga Sveinbjarnarsonar,* and other topics.

Torfhildur Þ[orsteinsdóttir] Hólm, 1845-1918, author. See Manuscript Material 129.

Torgerson, O. C. 1 letter, Madison, Wisconsin, 26 March 1939; in English. — Asking about the graduate program in Scandinavian languages and an assistantship in the department. Enclosed: portrait photograph of Torgerson.

Traveller's Gazette. Thos. Cook & Son. 1 letter, London, 3 April 190?; in English. — Regretting inability to give bibliographical information. Inserted in Edwin Hodder, *All the World Over* Vol. I (London: Thomas Cook & Son, 1875).

Tregaskis, James and Sons, booksellers in London. 2 letters, 20 September 1932 and 5 April 1933; in English. — Books listed for sale. Enclosed: a description of two items relating to Iceland in each letter, i.e., Guð-brandur Þorláksson, *Kristileg undirvísun um ódauðleika sálarinnar* (Hólum, 1601), and Snorri Sturluson "Anecdotes of Olave the Black..." [Copenhagen], 1780; a 1644 edition of the Bible and a book by Percy about "runic poetry translated from the Icelandic language."

Trial, George T. 4 letters, Headquarters, U.S. forces in Iceland; s.l., 29 December 1943; 9 January and 26 May (a V-letter) 1944; s.d., but Halldór Hermannsson's reply is dated 16 December 1941; in English. — Reference questions about the teaching of Icelandic in the United States; his intention to write an essay on education in Iceland; offering to send Halldór Hermannsson a manuscript copy of his unpublished *History of Education in Iceland;* request for translation of an article in the Icelandic newspaper *Morgunblaðið.*

Tryggvi Gunnarsson, 1835-1917, banker in Reykjavík. See Manuscript Material 129.

Tuckerman, Charles Sanders. 1 letter, Boston, 14 April 1947; in English. — Expressing a wish to meet Halldór Hermannsson and view the Fiske Icelandic Collection.

Turville-Petre, Gabriel. 2 letters, Oxford and London, 11 December 1934; 20 October 1945; in English. — Asking for suggestions on potential publishers of his edition of *Víga-Glúms Saga;* expressing pleasure at Halldór Hermannsson's acceptance of his selection as a life member of the Viking Society for Northern Research.

Tuttle, Charles E., Old and Rare Books. 1 letter, Rutland, Vermont, 22 June 1938; in English. — Books offered for purchase. Enclosed: list of books on Iceland in stock.

Uggla, Arvid Hj., 1883-1964. 2 letters, the University Library, Uppsala, 28 July and 25 November 1921; in Swedish and English. — Bibliographical inquiries and information; sending Halldór Hermannsson his *Uppsala Universitetsbiblioteks Samling av Nyisländsk Litteratur* (Uppsala, 1921). Enclosed: A list of Uppsala Library's holdings of old Icelandic books. See also Manuscript Material 133.

Undset, Sigrid, 1882-1949, author. 1 letter, Lillehammer, Norway, 31 July 1946; in English. — Thanking for the copy of *Þorgils saga and Hafliði,* commenting on the lack of translations of the Icelandic sagas into English.

Universitäts-Bibliothek. 8 letters, Kiel, Germany, April 1929 - December 1931; signed by Christoph Weber, Librarian; in German. Copies of 3 letters by Halldór Hermannsson; letter by Dr. Jürgens, Berlin, asking for exchange of books between the Fiske Icelandic Collection and the University Library of Kiel, 30 May 1930; copy of Halldór Hermannsson's reply; letter from E. R. B. Willis, Cornell University Library, 13 June 1930, mentioning a list of duplicates of interest to the University Library of Kiel. In English and German.

University of California. 1 letter, Berkeley, California, 7 May 1945; signed by Arthur G. Brodeur, Professor of English and Germanic Philology; in English. — Searching for a teacher of Scandinavian languages for the University of California, asking for recommendations.

University of Chicago Libraries, The. 2 letters, Chicago, 1 and 9 October 1917; signed by J. C. M. Hansen; in English. — Cataloguing matters.

University of Edinburgh Libraries. See Manuscript Material 145.

University of Florida, College of Arts and Sciences. 1 letter, Gainesville, Florida, 4 March 1947; signed by Oscar F. Jones, Assistant Dean; in English. — Asking for suggestions on teachers in German for the University of Florida.

University of Minnesota Library. 2 letters, Minneapolis, 23 August and 1 October 1929; signed by Frank K. Walter, University Librarian; in English. — On acquiring government documents of Iceland for his library.

University of Notre Dame Library, The. 1 letter, Notre Dame, Indiana, 12 July 1948; signed by Paul R. Byrne; in English. — Reference question on behalf of a patron.

University of Toronto, Department of Geology. 2 letters, Toronto, 19 and 28 March 1934; signed by W. A. Parks; in English. — Requesting Halldór Hermannsson to give an examination in Danish to Helgi Johnson.

University Press: John Wilson and Son. 2 letters, Cambridge, Mass., 18 May and 26 July 1907; in English. — About corrections to proofs of *Bibliography of the Icelandic sagas and Minor Tales.*

Upplýsingaskrifstofa stúdenta, University of Iceland. 1 letter, Reykjavík, 4 June 1943; in Icelandic. — Requesting assistance to select an appropriate institution for Albert Sigurðsson to study comparative Germanic linguistics.

Uppvall, Axel J., b. 1872, University of Pennsylvania. 6 letters, Philadelphia, November 1924 - April 1936; in English. — Asking about the value of an Icelandic book; reference question; phonological subject; agreeing to have a picture made of the Thorfinn karlsefni monument.

Utley, Francis L., Ohio State University. 1 letter, Columbus, 13 August 1945; copy of the reply, 12 September 1945; in English. — Asking for contributions to a "Dictionary of Political Words and Phrases." Enclosed: a pamphlet explaining the project for the Dictionary.

Valborg Sigurðardóttir, Smith College. 2 letters, Northampton, Mass., 29 September and 6 October 1944; in Icelandic. — Requesting interlibrary loan and bibliographical information concerning her paper on high school education in Iceland.

Valdimar Erlendsson, M.D., 1879-1951. 1 letter, Frederikshavn, Denmark, 18 August 1946; in Icelandic. — Presenting books to the Fiske Icelandic Collection.

Valtýr Guðmundsson, 1860-1928, University of Copenhagen. 19 letters and 10 postcards, May 1904 - February 1927; in Icelandic. — About Halldór Hermannsson's articles for the periodical *Eimreiðin;* on the publishing of the periodical; remarking on Icelandic politics; Old Norse scholarship; on Valtýr Guðmundsson's work on Icelandic grammar, and other related topics.

Valtýr Stefánsson, 1893-1963, editor of *Ísafold* and later *Morgunblaðið.* 3 letters, Reykjavík, 14 February 1931; 17 January and 21 March 1939; copies of two letters from Halldór Hermannsson; in Icelandic. — Contemplated exhibition of paintings by Icelandic artists (on same see: Jón Stefánsson, Matthías Þórðarson, the Roerich Museum, and Sveinn Björnsson); request for articles for *Morgunblaðið;* about his research for the biography of Thor Jensen; asking about the letters of Thor Jensen to Fiske. Enclosed: transcripts of two letters between Fiske and Thor Jensen.

Vilhjálmur Þ. Gíslason, b. 1897. 2 letters, Reykjavík, 3 December 1923; 30 January 1924; in Icelandic. — Inability to meet Halldór Hermannsson in Copenhagen; the curatorship of the Icelandic Collection; about his studies.

Vilhjálmur Stefánsson. See **Stefansson, Vilhjalmur.**

Vilhjálmur Þór, b. 1899. 10 letters, New York and Reykjavík, November 1938 - September 1944; copy of a letter from Halldór Hermannsson; in Icelandic. — On the Icelandic book exhibition at the New York World's Fair in 1939, letter from Guðmundur Finnbogason, National Librarian, including a list of books to be exhibited; copy of a letter from Halldór Hermannsson, commenting on the exhibition; copy of a letter from Vilhjalmur Stefansson to Vilhjálmur Þór concerning the spelling of Leifur Eiríksson's name; a blue print; asking for information about the Hotel School at Cornell University on behalf of an Icelandic student; a farewell letter.

Vilmundur Jónsson, 1889-1972, Head Physician of Iceland. 3 letters, Reykjavík, 9 June 1943; 7 July 1944; 30 October 1945, copy of a letter from Halldór Hermannsson, 1 February 1937; in Icelandic. — Sending health reports and books from Ríkisútgáfa námsbóka; accepting Halldór Hermannsson's opinions on the editing of textbooks.

Vinland Publishing Co. 1 letter, Minneota, Minnesota, 26 March 1906; signed by Björn B. Jónsson; in Icelandic. — Regretting not having a spare copy of the issue of *Vinland* requested by Halldór Hermannsson.

Voynich, Wilfred M. 1 letter, New York City, 6 February 1924; in English. — Book offered for sale. See also Manuscript Material 11.

Vries, Jan de, 1890-1964. 1 letter, Leiden, Holland, 7 May 1934; in German. — Concerning his article "De Islandische Familiesaga."

Wallace, C. L. 1 letter, East Orange, New Jersey, 23 February 1936; in English. — Reference question about Icelandic coins.

Wallace, Donald. 3 letters, Boston, 11 July, 8 and 16 August 1936; in English. — Reference questions pertaining to Paul Egede's translation of the *New Testament* into Inuit.

Walters, Thorstina J[ackson]. 2 letters, New York City and Poughkeepsie, N.Y., 7 December 1944; 9 February 1946; in English. — Request for the hymn "Allt er eins og blómstrið eina" by the seventeenth-century clergyman and poet Hallgrímur Pétursson through interlibrary loan; reference question on a quotation from the *Poetic Edda.* Enclosed: newspaper clipping of an article, "Forges Closer U.S.-Icelandic Bonds", by Walters.

War Department, Army Map Service, Washington, D.C. 2 letters, 16 and 26 January 1943; a copy of the reply; signed by H. L. Hyndman, Jr; in English. — Map coverage information on Iceland needed.

War Department, Office of the Quartermaster General, Washington, D.C. 1 letter, 24 July 1942; signed by Earl P. Hanson; a copy of the reply; in English. — The procurement and nutritional value of the Icelandic dried fish.

Wardell, Harry C., University of Rochester. 1 letter, Rochester, N.Y., 7

March 1937; in English. — Reference question pertaining to museums in Iceland.

Warner, W[illiam] Lloyd, 1898-1970, Division of Anthropology, Harvard University. 2 letters, Cambridge, Mass., 13 October and 25 November 1932; in English. — Reference question on the old Brehon Law School at Kilfinora, County Clare.

Watkins, John, American-Scandinavian Foundation. 12 letters, New York City, January 1942 - March 1945; in English. — On his studies in Old Norse literature; about Icelanders in New York City; asking Halldór Hermannsson to look over some of his works; about Hollander's *The Scaldic Poets;* his own translation of episodes from *Sturlunga saga;* expressing an opinion on novels by Halldór Laxness.

Weber, Hilmar H. 1 letter, Berkeley, California, 1 September 1920; a copy of a letter from Halldór Hermannsson, 14 August 1920; a letter from Weber to Professor A. W. Boesche, 16 June 1920; from Boesche to Halldór Hermannsson, with a request to reply to Weber's question on his behalf; in English and German. — Acknowledging information about the translation of *Bolla þáttur Bollasonar;* his work on genealogical tables for the sagas.

Wedepohl, Theodor, Mrs. 7 letters, New York City, November 1931 - March 1932; in English. — On a contemplated traveling exhibit of Theodor Wedepohl's paintings from Iceland through the universities in the United States. Enclosed: copies of letters from Vilhjalmur Stefansson to Halldór Hermannsson, R. Mellors, and Emanuel Hahn, Toronto; a letter from Edward F. Hauch, Hamilton College, Clinton, New York, asking about the exhibition; portrait photograph of Professor Wedepohl, 8.2 x 6.1 cm. See also letters from Vilhjalmur Stefansson and Charles Herz.

Wells, H. Bartlett, American Consulate in Nicaragua. 2 letters, Managua, 23 February and 15 October 1938; a copy from Halldór Hermannsson, 31 October 1938; in English. — Bibliographical information needed.

Welty, Susan Fulton. 2 letters, Beloit, Wisconsin, 26 May and 9 June 1941; in English. — Reference question pertaining to a children's book she is writing.

Wendt, Theophil, Buffalo Museum of Science. 1 letter, Buffalo, N.Y., 14

November 1935; in English. — Reference question pertaining to Grieg's music.

Wentworth, Edward N[orris], 1887-1959. 1 letter, Chicago, 26 February 1946; in English. — Reference question on the history of swine in Norse literature.

Wessel & Vett, Booksellers. 1 letter, Copenhagen, 28 June 1930; in English. — Offering Icelandic books for sale. Enclosed: a list of same, 4 sheets.

Wessén, Elias, b. 1889, Professor. 2 letters, Stockholm and Ålsten, Sweden, 15 March 1930; 13 October 1933; Halldór Hermannsson's reply; in Swedish. — Suggesting book exchange between Stockholms Högskola and the Fiske Icelandic Collection; expressing thanks to Halldór Hermannsson and Munksgaard for sending him their publication(s).

Westerby, Erik, Landsretssagfører. 1 letter, Copenhagen, 8 December 1934; in Danish. — On Guðmundur Kamban's finances.

Westergård-Nielsen, Christian, b. 1910. 2 letters, Copenhagen, 19 December 1938; 24 February 1939; in Icelandic. — Asking for a photostat of the *Catechismus* from 1575 to use in his work on loanwords in sixteenth-century Icelandic literature.

Westermann, B., booksellers. 1 letter, New York City, 11 January 1935; in English. — Listing a collection of Icelandic books for sale.

White, H. C., University of Georgia. 2 letters, Athens, 6 and 11 May 1914; in English. — Requesting information to prepare a trip to Iceland.

White, Horatio Stevens, 1852-1934. 33 letters, Villa Landor, Florence; Copenhagen; Cambridge, Mass., November 1904 - April 1932; in English. — Arrangements for Halldór Hermannsson's curatorship at the Fiske Icelandic Collection; the preparations for the first printed Catalogue of 1914 and the Runic Catalogue of 1918; Islandica matters; on Fiske's biography, etc. Enclosed: a memorandum of an agreement between White and Milford of the University Press of Oxford on behalf of Clarendon Press, 4 sheets; a formal acknowledgment of the *Catalogue of Runic Literature* from the John Crerar Library, 24 April 1918. See also Manuscript Material 51.

Whitner, Mrs. Thos. C. 2 letters, Atlanta, Georgia, 1 and 19 November

1921; in English. — On arranging a program for her study group on Iceland; letter of appreciation of the suggestions of material to read.

Whitney, N. J., Syracuse University. 1 letter, Syracuse, N.Y., 10 July 1929; in English. — Seeking assistance in obtaining a permission to reprint selections from the *Arthurian Tales* published by the Norroena Society in 1906.

Wieder, Dr. F[rederik] C[aspar], b. 1874. 2 letters, Noordwijk, Holland, 12 August 1927; 8 January 1932; in English. — Giving a description of a map of Iceland; acknowledging *The Cartography of Iceland;* sending some of his own publications. See also Manuscript Material 115.

Wieselgren, O, the Royal Library in Stockholm. See Manuscript Material 16.

Wiggin, Blanton C. 1 letter, Newton Highlands, Massachusetts, 8 June 1947; in English. — Presenting maps to the Fiske Icelandic Collection.

Wigmore, John H[enry], 1863-1943, Northwestern University School of Law. 5 letters, Chicago, 26 and 31 July, 7 and 30 August and 17 October 1924, one of which is signed by Wigmore's secretary, S. B. Morgan; in English. — About reproduction of pictures of Þingvellir.

Wildman, E. Theresa, William Penn High School. 1 letter, Philadelphia, 5 November 1916; in English. — Reference question pertaining to books on Icelandic geography, people, commerce, etc., on behalf of her pupils.

Wilkers, J. Hanley. 5 letters, Haddon Hts., New Jersey, 3 December 1945; s.d., but apparently in sequence; 7 and 10 March 1946; 7 March 1947; in English. — Reference questions concerning Iceland in the eighteenth century; interlibrary loan.

Williams, Charles Allyn, University of Illinois. 3 letters, Urbana, 14 and 19 January 1916; 25 March 1946; Halldór Hermannsson's reply of 17 January 1916; in English. — Reference question concerning material on Icelandic immigration to Canada and the United States; sending to the Fiske Icelandic Collection correspondence received from Icelandic immigrants when he prepared a paper on Icelandic-American Publications in 1903. The letters are written by: I. J. Bergmann, lecturer in Icelandic Language and Literature, Wesley College, Winnipeg, 18 December 1901, 6 January 1902, and 6 February 1902; B. L. Baldwinson, Heimskringla News and Publishing Company, Winnipeg, 3 February and 4 August 1902, 12 August 1903; Jón Bjarnason, Winnipeg, 31 March 1902; Howard S. Johnson, barrister, Winnipeg, 9 April and 1 May 1902; G. M. Thompson, The Svava Printing & Publishing Co., Gimli, Manitoba, 3 July and 21 August 1902; Björn B. Jónsson, *Vínland,* Minneota, Minnesota, 18 August 1902 and 9 July 1903; Ólafur S. Thorgeirsson, printer & publisher, Winnipeg, 9 July 1903; S. B. Benedictsson, *Freyja,* Winnipeg, 11 August 1903; Frederic Swanson, *Dagskrá,* Winnipeg, 14 and 21 August 1903; M. Paulson, The Logberg Printing and Publishing Company, Winnipeg, 15 August 1903; Solon J. Buck, Minnesota Historical Society, Saint Paul, 6 March 1916; G. Arnason, The University of Chicago, 5 April 1916; Sveinbjorn Johnson, Grand Forks, North Dakota, 20 May 1916. Also enclosed: a letter to B. L. Baldwinson from Williams, 29 June 1903; to the publishers of *Vínland,* asking for a specimen number of the paper, 24 January 1916. The letter was sent back with a note written on it by Th. Thordarson, 3 February 1916.

Williams, Mary W., Goucher College. 1 letter, Baltimore, Maryland, 18 October 1917; in English. — Discussing her book on the social history of Scandinavia during the Viking Age; asking about interlibrary loan.

Willuweit, H., the Rev. 6 letters, Lexington, Nebraska, October 1929 - June 1932; in English. — Bibliographical inquiries pertaining to Greenland, Iceland, and church history.

Winfrey, L. E., student at Columbia University. 3 letters, New York City, 3 and 13 April, 8 May 1916; in English. — Asking for a suggestion on a subject for his doctoral dissertation; his résumé and future plans.

Winger, Björn. 1 letter, Indianapolis, Indiana, 4 February 1938; a copy of the reply; in English. — Inquiring about his prospects in securing a doctor's degree at Cornell.

Wisherd, Maude E., University Libraries, Lincoln. See Manuscript Material 140.

Wood, Frederic T[urnbull], University of Virginia. 2 letters, Charlottesville, 29 March and 3 May 1938; Halldór Hermannsson's reply; in English. — Asking for permission to use the Fiske Icelandic Collection in the summer of 1938, partly in order to collect titles to add to the Icelandic holdings at the University of Virginia Library.

Wormser, Richard S., book dealer. 1 letter, New York, 19 September 1945;

in English. — About the value of Þorlákur Skúlason's *Nøckrar Huggunar Greiner, og gledeleg Dæme wr Heilagre Ritningu ...* (Hoolum, 1652).

Wright, Ása Guðmundsdóttir. 2 letters, Reykjavík, 18 July 1945; s.d.; in English. — Trip to Iceland.

Wright, H. N. 1 letter, Holland Park, London, 27 November 1944; in English. — Trip to Iceland.

Yale University Library, New Haven, Connecticut. 3 letters, 18 and 24 February 1925; 3 November 1942; signed by Anna M. Monrad, Head Cataloguer; in English. — Classification problems. Enclosed: copy of the Library of Congress scheme for Runic-Norse, one sheet.

Þjóðræknisfélag Íslendinga í Vesturheimi, Winnipeg, Manitoba. 1 letter, 18 March 1923; signed by Gísli Jónsson; a copy of the reply, 6 April 1923; in Icelandic. — Asking for Halldór Hermannsson's expert opinion on Gjerset's *History of Iceland* before the Society decides to publish it.

Þorbjörn (sign. Thor) Bjarnarson, b. 1859. 1 letter, Pembina, North Dakota, 12 March 1916; in Icelandic. — Autobiographical information.

Þórður Edilonsson, M.D., 1875-1941. 2 letters, Hafnarfjörður, 25 September and 4 December 1922; in Icelandic. — Concerning the sale of Benedikt Gröndal's drawings of Icelandic birds.

Þórður Thorarensen, 1859-1944, goldsmith. 1 letter, Akureyri, 12 October 1916; in Icelandic. — Sending a book purchased by the Fiske Icelandic Collection.

Þórhallur Ásgeirsson, b. 1919. 1 letter, Washington, D.C., 21 January 1945; in Icelandic. — Acknowledging the receipt of *The Vinland Sagas.*

Þ[orkell] Þorkelsson, 1876-1961. 3 letters, Reykjavík, 16 October 1922; 9 and 18 November 1925; in Icelandic. — Suggestion on a gift from their class to the Junior College in Reykjavík; his work on Icelandic geometry and chronology.

Þorsteinn Erlingsson, 1858-1914, teacher and a poet in Reykjavík. See Manuscript Material 129.

Þorsteinn (Vilhjálmur) Gíslason, 1867-1938, editor of *Lögrétta* and other periodicals. 10 letters, Reykjavík, October 1898 - July 1932; in Icelandic. — About the position at the Fiske Icelandic Collection. See also Manuscript Material 129.

Þorsteinn Jóhannesson. See **Thorsteinn Jóhannesson.**

Þorsteinn Þorsteinsson, b. 1880. 1 letter, Reykjavík, 13 December 1928; in Icelandic. — Accepting Halldór Hermannsson's offer to compile the bibliography in the new edition of *Iceland,* published by the National Bank.

Þorsteinn Þ. Þorsteinsson, 1879-1955, Winnipeg, Manitoba. See Manuscript Material 129.

Þorvaldur Pétursson. See **Thorvaldur Pétursson.**

Þorvaldur Thoroddssen, 1855-1921, geologist. 27 letters and 6 postcards, Copenhagen, August 1903 - September 1920; in Icelandic. — About publishing an obituary on Fiske in *Illustrerede Tidende;* concerning the bibliography in *Landfræðisaga Íslands* IV, published 1904; Hið íslenska bókmenntafélag in Copenhagen; Icelanders in Copenhagen; his research and publications; Icelandic politics; commentaries on Old Norse and Icelandic scholarship; Bibliographical information; news from Iceland in the summer of 1920.

Þyri Benedikz. 1 letter, New York, 4 December 1930; in Icelandic. — On the cataloguing job at Harvard. See a letter from Thor S. Benedikz.

3. Miscellaneous Correspondents and Recipients of Letters

Bibliographical Notices. 47 postcards and one letter; orders and acknowledgements for *Bibliographical Notices, Chess in Iceland, the* Islandica series, and *the Catalogues of the Icelandic Collection,* from libraries, societies, and individuals.

Björn Þorsteinsson, 1918-1986, Professor, University of Iceland. 1 letter to "kæri vinur", probably Jóhann S. Hannesson, Reykjavík, 4 December 1953. — On Björn Þorsteinsson's work; news from Iceland.

Bleil, Charles, A. 1 letter, addressed to the President of Cornell University,

Philadelphia, 14 November 1891; in English. — Asking for the where-
abouts of Willard Fiske on behalf of Guðrún Sigurðardóttir.

Catalogue for the Icelandic Collection, orders for. See *Bibliographical*
Notices.

Chess in Iceland, orders for. See *Bibliographical Notices.*

Cockerell, S[ydney] C[arlyle] [Sir], 1867-1962. 1 letter addressed to W.
Brooke, London, 8 March 1898; another letter, London, 14 April 1898,
written by S. A. Peddie to W. Robinson, on behalf of Cockerell; in
English. Both letters are inserted in *The Story of Gunnlaug the*
Wormtongue and Raven the Skald. Printed at the Chiswick Press for
William Morris. Mdccclxli. An invoice from Francis Edwards Ltd.,
booksellers in London, 9 January 1940, addressed to Halldór
Hermannsson, is also inserted in the same book.

Edzardi, A[nton Philipp], 1849-1882. 1 letter addressed to "Verehrter Herr
Professor", Leipzig, 5 November 1878; in German; inserted in an offprint of his *"Die skaldischen Versmasse und ihr Verhältnis zur*
keltischen (irischen) Verskunst." — Comments on the article. The book
belonged to the Zarncke Library. Cf. Ex libris.

Einar Ólafur Sveinsson, 1899-1984, Professor at the University of Iceland.
3 letters to Jóhann S. Hannesson, 24 January 1957; 7 and 29 March
1958; in Icelandic. — About his work; coming to Ithaca; his lectures.
Also a copy of a letter to Einar Ólafur from Jóhann S. Hannesson, 19
March 1958.

Fiske, D[aniel] W[illard], 1831-1904. 1 draft of a letter to a German newspaper, "An den Redacteur der Allgemeinen Zeitung" [1879]; s.l.; in
German. — Sending an article on the late Jón Sigurðsson. On the back
side of the draft is an unfinished note in English on the *Elder Edda* (i.e.
the *Poetic Edda*), headed "Icelandic Literature 1878-9."

_____, 1 draft of a letter to [A. Carnegie], Copenhagen, 20 August 1903. —
Concerning building for the National Library in Reykjavík. The letter
mentions a note written by Sigfús Blöndal, at Fiske's instance, about the
matter. Two drafts of letters on same subject. In the letters Fiske refers
to Dr. Finnur Jónsson, and Dr. Thoroddsen, the geographer.

_____, 8 letters and a postcard to the Reverend Jón Bjarnason, Winnipeg,

Manitoba, May 1874 - December 1893; in English. — About American donations of books to Iceland in 1874 in commemoration of the millennial anniversary of Iceland's settlement; about American subscriptions to the Icelandic literary society; referring to letters from Jón A. Hjaltalín and Eiríkur Magnússon; mentions their work and the work of Guðbrandur Vigfússon; remarking on the project of an Icelandic colony; inviting Jón Bjarnason and his wife to stay with him in Ithaca during the summer holidays; asks that letters to him be written in Icelandic; regretting inability to go to Iceland in the summer of 1874; directions to Ithaca; his Icelandic class; charmed by Matthías Jochumsson's translation of Tegnér's *Frithiof saga;* mentions Jón Ólafsson and the "Alaska project"; the transporting of the cases of books donated by Americans to Iceland; mentions Icelandic publications he has received recently [in numerous letters]; trying to secure a position for Jón Bjarnason at Harvard; asking him to send copies of his sermon to scholars in Cambridge, Mass.; mentions Professor R. B. Anderson's work on Icelandic mythology; mentions Guðbrandur Vigfússon's project of editing *Sturlunga saga*; his own article for the *N.Y. Evening Post* on "Alaska and the Icelanders"; on procuring *Sameiningin;* commenting on his book collection; recently bought a fifteenth-century MS of *Jónsbók* in Madrid; mentions the revision of his catalogue of Islandica; asking for flyers and epitaphs printed in Winnipeg; sending money to procure various Icelandic publications in Winnipeg. Included with the letters are two sheets of desiderata and a receipt from H. S. Bardal, 15 May 1899, acknowledging payment for books and periodicals procured for Fiske. The letters were sent to the Fiske Icelandic Collection by Jón Bjarnason's foster daughter, Theodora Hermann, 27 September 1955. See also Manuscript Material 1.

______, 1 letter to Henry W. Longfellow, Ithaca, 30 December 1874. — Writing on behalf of the Reverend Jón Bjarnason, trying to secure him a teaching position. 1 letter from Jón Bjarnason to Fiske, Decorah, 8 November 1874; in Icelandic. — His speech at the Icelandic millennial celebration in Milwaukee; about Mr. Headly and his book on Iceland; about the Lutherans in Milwaukee, his position there, his and their disagreement on religious matters. This letter undoubtedly instigated Mr. Fiske in writing the letter to Longfellow. The Fiske Collection owns photocopies of these letters, the originals are at Harvard University.

______, 3 letters to Henry W. Longfellow, Ithaca, 24 December 1874; 7 July 1877; 16 June 1879. — Praising Professor's R. B. Anderson's work on Norse mythology; the books presented to Iceland in 1874; about

Svanhvít, a collection of translations of foreign verse into Icelandic by Matthías Jochumsson and Steingrímur Þorsteinsson; his plans for the trip to Iceland. The Fiske Collection owns photocopies of these letters, the originals are at Harvard University.

_____, 1 letter addressed to "My dear Sir", Berlin, 24 January 1880; in English. — Relating news about Icelanders in Copenhagen and Icelandic affairs; about Hið íslenzka bókmenntafélag (the Icelandic Literary Society); about the late Jón Sigurðsson, the arrangements for his funeral, his commemoration in Copenhagen, etc.; commenting on Gísli Brynjúlfsson's views on northern mythology; information about new publications; the Icelandic-Danish postal arrangements, with comment on the bad treatment of Icelanders by Danish steamer officers; praising Tryggvi Gunnarsson's abilities.

_____, 1 letter addressed to "Sehr geehrter Herr" (in triplicate), Bad Gastein, 12 August 1901; in German. — Asking for a contribution to *Í uppnámi*. All three copies are handwritten for Fiske by Halldór Hermannsson, one signed by Fiske, and one with Halldór Hermannsson's autograph.

_____, 1 letter to Garth Wilkinson, London, 30 September 1852; in English. — A letter of farewell; information on latest Icelandic publications; mentions Gísli Brynjúlfsson and suggests that Wilkinson might want to correspond with him about Icelandic matters.

Fiske Icelandic Collection, The. 17 postcards from different institutions and individuals on business matters, mainly acknowledging orders from Halldór Hermannsson and announcing material of possible interest to the Fiske Icelandic Collection.

Gils Guðmundsson b. 1914. 2 letters to Jóhann S. Hannesson, 24 January and 7 April 1956. — About Magnús Smith the chess player. Enclosed are newspaper articles about Magnús Smith and copies of 6 letters from 1956 to Gils Guðmundsson from Jóhann S. Hannesson.

Grimm, Jacob, 1785-1863. 1 letter to Leopold Karl Wilhelm August Freiherr von Ledebur, Cassel, 12 January 1828; with red seal; in German; inserted in *Lieder der alten Edda aus der handschrift herausgegeben und erklärt durch die Brüder Grimm*. Erster Band (Berlin: in Verlage der Realschulbuchhandlung, 1815). — Acknowledges the receipt of Ledebur's first book *Das Land und Volk der Brukterer* (1827). The letter was published by Halldór Hermannsson, "Two letters from

Jacob and Wilhelm Grimm" in the *Journal of English and Germanic Philology* Jan. 1918, No. 1. Vol. XVII.

Grimm, Wilhelm C., 1786-1859. 1 letter to Carl Christian Rafn, Cassel, 11 February 1824; in German; inserted in *Lieder der alten Edda aus der handschrift herausgegeben und erklärt durch die Brüder Grimm.* Erster Band (Berlin: in Verlage der Realschulbuchhandlung, 1815). — On Old Norse scholarship of Rafn and others. The letter was published by Halldór Hermannsson, see Grimm, Jacob, above.

Grímur Thomsen, 1820-1896, poet. 1 letter to Herr Boghandler Carl B. Lorck, Danish publisher in Leipzig, Copenhagen, 17 October 1848; in Danish. — Consents to contribute articles, but demands anonymity. The letter was bought at an auction in Copenhagen in 1923. Cf. note by Halldór Hermannsson.

Halldór Hermannsson, 1878-1958. A copy of a letter to Rochelle Girson, *Saturday Review of Literature,* 5 February 1943. — Declining to review a book by William B. Goodwin; commenting on Goodwin's scholarship. Inserted in Goodwin's *The Ruins of Great Ireland in New England* (Boston: Meador publishing company, 1946).

____, to Mr. Hohne, 10 April 1921. — On the Icelandic genre, "þulur", or "string of rhymes."

____, *Icelandic Letter-Book. Begun July, 1915. Finished Oct., 1917.* A black letter-book with red spine and corners; 28 x 23 cm. A few leaves have been excised at the beginning; title-page is numbered 16; stamped numbering of leaves, 16-300, leaves 39-41, 116, 161, 215-16, 259, and 282-296, excised. Alphabetized index at beginning of book. Chiefly procuring of books, answering reference questions, publishing of Islandica, and other business matters. The recipients of the letters include, i.a., Dr. Andersson, ll. 18, 35, 68, and 84, about sixteenth-century Icelandic books; "Kæri vinur", l. 51, his article on the constitutional question, his scholarly work; Magnús Matthíasson, Winnipeg, ll. 55-58, Icelandic politics; "Kæri vinur", ll. 85-87, about sixteenth-century books; Mr. Hart, ll. 25, 99-101, and 105-6, on the meaning of the terms South-Danes and North-Danes in "King Alfreð's geography", on King Alfred's work in relation to Old Norse literature; Library of Congress, l. 107, on classification of Icelandic books; Dr. Leach (and Miss H. A. Larsen) ll. 140-41, 147, 162-3, 196, 219, and 223, advice on the translation of Jóhann Sigurjónsson's drama *Fjalla-Eyvindur;* the staging of the play in Boston (concerning the costumes, etc.); Sigurður Kristjánsson, bóksali, ll. 153-4, about sending books overseas during the war; Dr. R. W. Shaw, ll. 224-5 and 270-71, on the etymology of Icelandic names; Páll Á. Ingvason, ll. 244-5, on Iceland's trading with the United States; Halldór Daníelsson, ll. 247-8, on sixteenth-century books; "Kæri vinur", ll 253-5, answering critic on *Icelandic Books of the Sixteenth Century,* Islandica IX, 1916; "Kæri vinur", ll. 279-80, about *Þjóðólfur.*

_____, *Letter-book of the Fiske Icelandic Collection. Begun October 1917.* [From 31 October 1917 to 8 October 1927]. Black book with red spine and corners; 31 x 27 cm.; alphabetized index in front; leaves numbered in stamp, 1-458. The recipients of the letters include, i.a., H. S. White, l. 6, about a paper on Fiske and his work as a collector of Icelandic books Halldór is going to present at a meeting of the Bibliographical Society of America; F. Johnson, Winnipeg, ll. 12-15, about procuring books in Canada; Aðalsteinn Kristjánsson, ll. 17-18, about democracy; Halldór Daníelsson, l. 28, mentions the war; Guðmundur Magnússon, ll. 29-30, procuring of pamphlets, the history of printing in Iceland; Sigurður Kristjánsson, l. 34, mentions the war and an ironic remark about the struggle against alcohol; Halldór Daníelsson, l. 36, about errors in the printed catalogue; Páll Eggert Ólason, ll. 42-3, about the war, lack of coal, politics, the independence question; Guðmundur Magnússon, ll. 44-5, 46-7, about Icelandic books from the sixteenth century; Sigurður Júl. Jóhannesson, Winnipeg, ll. 64-5, Icelandic politics, the eruption of the volcano Katla, lack of coal, bad economy, etc.; Mr. Winship, l. 71, Halldór Hermannsson's article about Fiske; Sighvatur Grímsson Borgfirðingur, l. 101, praising Sighvatur Borgfirðing's scholarly work; Sigurður Júl. Jóhannesson, ll. 110-111, about a paper Halldór Hermannsson intends to write on Vínland for *Tímarit þjóðrækni-félagsins;* Dr. Jón Þorkelsson, ll. 160 and 165, about the photographs of *Tungubréf* (see Manuscript Material 13; Sigurður Kristjánsson, l. 191, mentions the prohibition law; Páll Eggert Ólason, l. 197, about the roto-graphy of *Catonis Disticha;* Mr. White, l. 210, suggests the passage in *Mímir* pp. 70-73 was written by Fiske himself; Knut Gjerset, ll. 249 and 276, about Gjerset's writing of the history of Iceland, bibliographical in-formation; Lúðvík Guðmundsson, l. 265, about student exchange to be supported by the American-Scandinavian Foundation; Mr. Winship, ll. 342-345, a description of Winship's copy of Moller's *Soliloqvia,* 1677; Prof. Pilcher, ll. 349-51 and 396, about Pilcher's plan to write the histo-ry of Christianity in the Scandinavian countries, bibliographical infor-mation; Knut Gjerset, l. 353, comments on Gjerset's manuscript of *History of Iceland;* Miss Jackson, l. 354, comments on her father's work on the history of Icelandic settlements in America; Samuel A. Eliot, ll. 359-60, about the planned visit of Prof. Bjarnason; Mr. Creese, ll. 361-2, same subject; Mr. Peterson, l. 363, about the meaning of York in the seal of New York City; Mr. Eliot, l. 366, Prof. Bjarnason and a lecture he is to present at Cornell University; Sigurður Kristjánsson, ll. 399 and 451-2, brief comment on the economic situation in Iceland, about prices of books, the custom of publishing numbered editions with the author's autograph.

_____, [Letter-book, starting 29 November 1927]; no title; grey hardcover letter-book; 31 x 27 cm; 1-53 numbered leaves, rest of book is blank, one unnumbered leaf between ll. 22 and 23. The recipients include, i.a., Vilhjalmur Stefansson, l. 18, criticizing the Icelanders in Canada for their application to the Provincial Government for grants to go to Iceland to participate in the 1930 National Celebration, calling it "emigration propaganda."

Harris, George William, Cornell University Library. Numerous letters to Harris (mainly from the years 1906-7), concerning matters of the Fiske Icelandic Collection and its publications. The correspondents include, i.a., H. L. Koopman, the Library of Brown University. 1 letter, Providence, Rhode Island, 24 March 1914. — Congratulating Harris on the publication of the *Catalogue of the Icelandic Collection,* and commenting on the uniqueness and usefulness of the publication. Wallace Notestein, Department of History, Yale University. 1 letter addressed to "Dear George", New Haven, 30 April 1937. — On behalf of Theodor Mommsen who plans to work on Petrarch in Ithaca in the summer 1937. The letter was apparently answered by Halldór Hermannsson. Cf. note in pencil on the letter in his hand. H. S. White, 2 letters, 13 October and 3 December 1907. — On matters of the Fiske Icelandic Collection.

Hermann, Theodora. 1 letter to Jóhann S. Hannesson, Curator of the Fiske Icelandic Collection, Winnipeg, 27 September 1955; in Icelandic. — Presenting letters from Fiske to her foster father, Dr. Jón Bjarnason in Winnipeg. This letter is placed in a folder with the letters from Fiske to the Reverend Dr. Jón Bjarnason.

Hollander, Lee M. 15 letters to Jóhann S. Hannesson, May 1953 - February 1957; in English. — Reference questions about Old Norse matters. Enclosed are 11 copies of letters from Jóhann S. Hannesson to Hollander.

[*Invoices*]. 1871-1904. Numerous invoices to Willard Fiske from book-dealers, institutions, and individuals in various places in Europe and the United States. Also acknowledgements and orders for Fiske's publications, and other business matters. Placed in a separate box.

Irish Folklore Commission, University College, Dublin. 2 letters to George H. Droste, Cornell University Library, 2 April and 13 May 1948; signed by S[èamus] Ó. Duilearga and I. H. Delargy; in English. — Acknowledging receipt of Islandica and promising to provide the journal *Béaloideas* for Cornell University.

Islandica, orders for. See *Bibliographical Notices.*

Islandica-correspondence. Numerous letters from publishing companies and printing presses; copies of letters by Halldór Hermannsson concerning the publications; "Income Fiske Icelandic Publications Fund", 1 July 1929, one sheet; a list of recipients of review copies of Stefán Einarsson's *History of Icelandic Prose writers: 1800-1940,* Islandica Vol. 32-33, 1948, two sheets.

Johnston, A. W. Viking Club, Society for Northern Research. 2 letters to H. S. White, London, 10 February and 15 November 1904. — Acknowledging *Mímir;* asking for a notice of Willard Fiske's life and work for their *Proceedings;* supposing *Mímir* will be continued. Enclosed is H. S. White's reply, Florence, 25 November 1904. — Contact George Harris, Cornell University, about the continuing publication.

Jón Sigurðsson, 1811-1879. 1 letter to [Carl Christian Rafn], s.d., s.l., probably ca. 1850; in Danish. — Concerns Fiske's financial needs for a planned trip to Iceland in 1852.

Kahl? 1 draft of a first part of a letter, Uppsala, 10 October 1851; in Swedish; inserted between pp. 172 and 173 in *Förteckning öfver Kongl. Bibliothekets i Stockholm. Isländska Handskrifter.* Utgifven af Adolf Iwar Arwidsson (Stockholm, 1848). — A letter of recommendation addressed to "Herr doktor Kahl" on behalf of Herr Wm E. Dillson. The letter is unsigned, but possibly by Fiske.

Kristján Eldjárn, 1916-1982. 1 letter to Vilhjálmur Bjarnar, Reykjavík, 3 September 1980. — Asking Bjarnar to translate his introduction to the Fiske-Collection brochure about the Viking exhibition into English.

Enclosed is a typed copy of the introduction in Icelandic, 3 sheets, and 3 additional sheets with Vilhjálmur Bjarnar's translation.

Landsbókasafn Íslands. Numerous letters from the staff of the National Library to Jóhann S. Hannesson and Vilhjálmur Bjarnar. The letters date from 1953-1983.

Landsbókasafn Íslands. A Card to Cornell University Library, Reykjavík, 27 July 1921; signed by Jón Jakobsson, Librarian; in English. — Thanking for the gift of the vellum manuscript *Book of Hours.*

Magon, Leopold, the University of Greifswald. 1 copy of a letter from Otto Kinkeldey, Librarian at Cornell University, 19 October 1934. — Accepting book exchange between Greifswald and Cornell University Libraries, offering Magon the publications of the Fiske Icelandic Collection.

Mímir. Numerous letters and postcards with information about addresses and scholarly publications relating to Iceland for *Mímir,* some are replies from scholars and institutions to Fiske's inquiries, others are corrections and additions to *Mímir.* Also orders and acknowledgements for *Mímir* from libraries, societies, and individuals. Enclosed with the letters are notes for the publication by Willard Fiske and Halldór Hermannsson, and several slips of paper with information for a planned second issue of *Mímir* in 1904. It was never published.

Mitchell, P[hillip] M[arshall], b. 1916. Letters and bibliographies from Icelandic authors and others replying to Mitchell's inquiries about publications of Icelandic literature translated into various languages and works written by Icelanders in other languages. The information was used in P. M. Mitchell and Kenneth H. Ober, comp., *Bibliography of Modern Icelandic Literature in Translation. Including Works Written by Icelanders in Other Languages.* Islandica XL (Ithaca and London: Cornell University Press, 1975). The letters are written in Icelandic, English, and the Scandinavian languages. The correspondents are: Ármann Kr. Einarsson, s.d.; Einar Bragi [Sigurðsson], 15 March 1974; copy of a letter to Einar Bragi from Mitchell, 8 March 1974; Einar Ól[afur] Sveinsson, 23 January 1970; Elías Mar, 9 January 1970; Friðjón Stefánsson, s.d.; Guðmundur Böðvarsson, 18 December 1969; Guðmundur Daníelsson, 16 December 1969; Gunnar M. Magnúss, s.d.; Halldór Stefánsson, s.d.; Hannes Sigfússon, 23 December 1969 and 17 March 1974; Hildur Blöndal, 14 October 1962; Indriði G. Þorsteinsson,

16 December 1969; Jakobína Johnson, 25 June 1962, 11 November 1962, 1 February and 4 March 1963; Jóhann Hjálmarsson, December 1969, addressed to Ólafur Hjartar at the National Library; Jóhannes Helgi, 8 January 1970; Jón Björnsson, 12 January 1969; Jón Dan, 1 January 1970; Jón Óskar, s.d.; Jón úr Vör, s.d.; Margrét Thordarson, 1 January 1970; Mekkin S. Perkins, 27 November 1962; Nína Björk Árnadóttir [December 1969], another s.d.; Ólafur F. Hjartar, 23 December 1969; Ólafur Jóhann Sigurðsson, 17 December 1969; Sigurður A. Magnússon, s.d.; Snorri Hjartarson, s.d.; Stefán Hörður Grímsson, s.d.; Þórleifur Bjarnason, 22 December 1969.

Parcel post service to Iceland. Numerous letters in English, Danish, and German, regarding parcel post to Iceland, dated from July to October 1900, from Jón Hermannsson, the Icelandic Cabinet, Copenhagen, two letters; the Head Postmaster, Copenhagen; General Post Office, Edinburgh, also two acknowledgments of the receipt of Fiske's letters; Kaiserliches Postamt, Cologne; general post office, London, two letters; "Ministeriet for Offentlige Arbejder, Generaldirektoratet for Postvæsenet", Copenhagen. Enclosed: draft of a letter from Fiske to the General Post Office in Copenhagen; 2 letters and a postcard to Messers Parkins and Gotto, London, with instructions to send chess boards to various addressees in Iceland.

Schach, Paul, University of Nebraska, Lincoln. Numerous letters to Jóhann S. Hannesson and Vilhjálmur Bjarnar; in English. — On publishing scholarly articles or monographs in English in Iceland, and more. Enclosed is: a list of "Potential Publication outlets in Iceland", 2 sheets; typewritten manuscript of "Magnús Ketilsson's Orthography and the Hrappsey Press" by Sidney Rufus Smith, University of North Carolina, Chapel Hill, 15 sheets.

Sigurður Nordal, 1886-1974, Professor at the University of Iceland. 4 letters to Vilhjálmur Bjarnar, Reykjavík, 11 February 1963; 29 July 1964; 21 September 1965; 25 April 1966. — About Bjarnar's translation of *Íslensk Menning* by Nordal; about the teaching of Old Norse abroad. Also copies of 6 letters from Vilhjálmur Bjarnar to Sigurður Nordal from November 1962 - June 1967, about the same translation.

Stefán Einarsson, 1897-1972. Numerous letters to Jóhann S. Hannesson and Vilhjálmur Bjarnar from ca. 1952-1966. Enclosed: "Ættleggr of Nine", a typewritten manuscript of 29 sheets; "Formáli að *Íslenskri Menningu*," 3 handwritten sheets. See also Manuscript Material 106.

Williams Book Store, Boston, Mass. See Manuscript Material 133.

Wolf-Rottkay, W. H. 1 letter to Stefán Einarsson, Munich, Germany, 14 April 1947; in Icelandic. — Announcing the publication of his doctoral dissertation. Included is his résumé and an abstract from his dissertation, 8 numbered typewritten sheets.

III. DIPLOMAS AND HONORS

1. Cornell University Library

Gagnfræðaskólinn á Akureyri. Formal letters of gratitude from the high school of Akureyri, 23 March 1910 and 14 March 1912; signed by the principal, Stefán Stefánsson; in Icelandic.

Hið íslenzka bókmenntafélag, Copenhagen. A membership diploma, 17 May 1905; signed by Bogi Th. Melsteð. Also a formal letter that accepts Cornell University Library as a member of the Society, 17 May 1905; signed by Bogi Th. Melsteð and Hafsteinn Pjetursson; in Icelandic.

2. Daniel Willard Fiske

Framfarafélag Eyjafjarðar (The Progressive Society of Eyjafjörður). A formal letter to Fiske regarding the investment of foreigners in Icelandic industry, 6 February 1879; signed by several members of the Society; in Icelandic.

Hið íslenzka bókmentafélag, Copenhagen. A diploma conferring the selection of Fiske as an honorary member of the Society and a formal letter informing Fiske of the honor, both 26 May 1875; signed by Jón Sigurðsson; in Icelandic.

Lestrarfjelagið Íþaka. Formal letters of gratitude from Lestrarfjelagið Íþaka

(The Reading Society of the Junior College in Reykjavík), 28 November 1879; 27 June 1885; 13 May 1895; 14 October 1895; some signed by the board of directors, others by several members of the Society. Also a formal letter, 29 May 1904; signed by Guðbrandur Jónsson and Pétur Halldórsson; with illuminated capitals, some words in red and gold, and bound with a pink string; title-page: Til Herra prófessors Dr. phil. Willard D. Fiske R. af Dbr. p.p.; in a brown and yellow marbled hardcover folder, with black spine and corners, blue label on front cover with same heading; 3 folio sheets; in Icelandic.

The Order of Dannebrog. A diploma conferring the Order of Dannebrog on Fiske, September 1902; signed by Prince Hans of Glücksborg; in Danish. Enclosed: an envelope with red seal. Also a letter advising Fiske that he is to be receiving the Order of Dannebrog, 8 October 1902; signed by F. Reventlow, at the Danish Legation in Rome; in French. Enclosed: an envelope with black seal.

Stiptsbókasafn Íslands (the National Library of Iceland). A formal letter advising Fiske that books were to be presented to him by Stiptsbókasafn Íslands, 7 October 1879; signed by the directors of the library; in Icelandic.

Taflfélag Reykjavíkur. A formal letter of gratitude sent to Fiske by the Chess Society of Reykjavík, printed and dated MDCCCC; signed by Sigurðr [sic!] Jónsson, Sturla Jónsson, and Pétur Zóphóníasson; bound in red hardcover; in Icelandic.

3. Halldór Hermannsson

American Geographical Society. A certification that acknowledges Halldór Hermannsson as a fellow of the Society, 25 January 1927.

Bóksalafélag Íslands. A letter from Guðmundur Gamalíelsson advising Halldór Hermannsson of his selection as an honorary member of Bóksalafélag Íslands, 2 April 1947; a telegram acknowledging same; also a letter conferring the honor, 14 August 1947; signed by members of the board of directors; two resolutions, one about the honorary membership and the other about discounts of book sales to the Fiske Icelandic Collection; both dated 31 March 1947; unsigned. Also a draft of a letter of acceptance from Halldór Hermannsson. In Icelandic.

Hið íslenzka bókmentafjelag, Copenhagen. A diploma of a regular membership from the Society; signed by Ólafur Halldórsson, 18 April 1899; also a formal letter announcing the acceptance of Halldór Hermannsson to the Society, 24 April 1899; signed by Ólafur Halldórsson. In Icelandic.

Hið íslenzka bókmentafjelag, Reykjavík. A diploma presenting Halldór Hermannsson with an honorary membership, 17 June 1927; signed by Guðm[undur] Finnbogason and Matthías Þórðarson; in Icelandic.

Hin íslenzka fálkaorða. A diploma awarding Halldór Hermannsson the Knighthood of the Order of the Icelandic Falcon; signed and acknowledged by King Christian X; also a formal letter advising Halldór Hermannsson that he is to be receiving the honor, 7 December 1923; signed by J. Sveinbjörnsson. In Icelandic.

Hin íslenzka fálkaorða. A diploma awarding Halldór Hermannsson the Order of the Icelandic Falcon of the first degree, 1 December 1935; signed by King Christian X; also a formal letter, 1 December 1935; signed by J. Sveinbjörnsson.

Hin íslenzka fálkaorða. A diploma conferring the Order of the Icelandic Falcon with a star on Halldór Hermannsson, 17 June 1939; signed by King Christian X; also a formal letter, 17 June 1939.

Det kongelige nordiske Oldskrift-Selskab. A diploma acknowledging the membership of Halldór Hermannsson, 17 November 1925; signed by C. Neergaard; in Danish.

Letter of introduction, written on behalf of Halldór Hermannsson by Albert W. Smith, Acting President of Cornell University, 31 May 1921; addressed: "To whom it may concern."

Viking Society for Northern Research, The. A letter awarding Halldór Hermannsson a life membership, 31 January 1945; signed by G. Turville-Petre; in English.

Vísindafélag Íslendinga. A diploma conferring Halldór Hermannsson's selection as a corresponding fellow, 19 May 1923; signed by Jón Helgason and Jón Ófeigsson; in Icelandic.

Þjóðræknisfjelag Íslendinga í Vestrheimi. A diploma from the Society conferring an honorary membership on Halldór Hermannsson, 23 February

1921; signed by Rögn[valdur] Pétursson and Gísli Jónsson. Also a formal letter advising Halldór Hermannsson about the honor, 24 June 1921; signed by J. A. Sigurðsson and Gísli Jónsson. In Icelandic.

IV. GRAPHIC MATERIALS

1. Boxes 1-3

Collection of photographs from Iceland
by Frederick Howell and others

Howell, Frederick W[illiam] W[arbreck]. 6 albums containing 376
black and white photographs from Iceland and 11 from the Faeroe
Islands, of natural scenery, houses, people, etc. Black leather covered
albums; "Photographs" in gilded letters on front covers; marked i.-vi. on
slips pasted on front covers; title-pages; 18.3 x 28.5 cm. The photographs were taken during the last decade of the nineteenth century.
Album vi contains also photographs by Henry A. Perkins, Hartford,
Connecticut, and Magnús Ólafsson, Reykjavík. In Box 3 is another album (album vii) with 14 black and white photographs of paintings by
Icelandic artists. This album is without covers.

The albums were compiled by Halldór Hermannsson ca. 1923, and
identified in white beneath the pictures. Catalogued in *Catalogue of the
Icelandic Collection Bequeathed by Willard Fiske. Additions 1913-26*
(Ithaca: Cornell University Press, 1927). See also reference in the Fiske
Icelandic Collection's Accession Book, entry No. 12377, and a postcard
from Howell to Fiske.

Dimensions are given in centimeters rounded off to the next whole centimeter up.

Album i. Box 1.

[1]   Title-page: *I. Reykjavík — Þingvellir.*

[2]   *B[enedikt] Gröndal's Millennial card 1874.* 1 photoprint; 14 x 10 cm.

[3]   *S/S"Vesta".* 1 photoprint; 15 x 11 cm. Man working on deck.

[4]   *Reykjavík Bay and British training squadron. Esjan in the distance.* 1 photoprint; 11 x 15 cm.

[5]   *Reykjavík from the sea.* 1 photoprint; 11 x 15 cm. See also Box 18, lantern slide 3.

[6]   *"Jason", Reykjavík.* 1 photoprint; 11 x 15 cm. In the foreground: women washing fish on the shore.

[7]   *Reykjavík. Cathedral and Parliament House.* 1 photoprint; 11 x 15 cm. See also Box 4, No. 4.

[8]   *Reykjavík. Governor's House.* 1 photoprint; 11 x 16 cm. View of Austurstræti and Bankastræti to the right.

[9]   *Reykjavík. From the Tjörn.* 1 photoprint; 11 x 15 cm.

[10]   *Reykjavík. Thorvaldsen's monument.* 1 photoprint; 10 x 15 cm.

[11]   *Reykjavík. The mayor's (bæjarfógeti) House.* 1 photoprint; 11 x 15 cm. See also Box 18, lantern slide 1.

[12]   *Central Reykjavík from Governor's House.* 1 photoprint; 11 x 15 cm.

[13]   *Reykjavík. A loaded pack-train.* 1 photoprint; 11 x 15 cm. See also Box 18, lantern slide 12.

[14]   *Reykjavík. Aðalstræti.* 1 photoprint; 11 x 15 cm.

[15]   *Reykjavík. Vesturgata.* 1 photoprint; 11 x 15 cm. Man pulling a cart loaded with fish.

[16]   *Reykjavík. National celebration, 1898.* 1 photoprint; 11 x 15 cm.

[17]   *Reykjavík. Fish drying and shark oil station.* 1 photoprint; 11 x 15 cm.

[18]   *Fish drying. Reykjavík.* 1 photoprint; 8 x 10 cm.

[19]   *Angelica in Governor's garden, Reykjavík.* 1 photoprint; 11 x 15 cm.

[20]   *In older Reykjavík. House covered with chamomile.* 1 photoprint; 11 x 16 cm.

[21]   *Reykjavík. Unloading a hay-boat.* 1 photoprint; 15 x 11 cm.

[22]   *Ponies for export. Reykjavík.* 1 photoprint; 8 x 10 cm.

[23]   *Reykjavík. Interior of Cathedral. The font of Thorvaldsen.* 1 photoprint; 15 x 11 cm.

[24]   *Old wooden boxes. Archeol. Museum, Reykjavík.* 1 photoprint; 11 x 15 cm.

[25]   *Old chair from Rauðisandur. Nat[ional] Museum, Reykjavík.* 1 photoprint; 15 x 11 cm.

[26]   *Ancient carved church posts. Nat. Museum, Reykjavík.* 1 photoprint; 16 x 11 cm.

[27]   *Boxes. Nat. Museum, Reykjavík.* 1 photoprint; 11 x 15 cm.

[28]   *Reredos from Reynistaður. Nat. Museum, Reykjavík.* 1 photoprint; 11 x
       15 cm.

[29]   *Alabaster Reredos from Reynistaður. Archeol. Museum, Reykjavík.* 1
       photoprint; 11 x 15 cm.

[30]   *Ancient pulpit. Nat. Museum, Reykjavík.* 1 photoprint; 15 x 11 cm.

[31]   *Old loom. Nat. Museum, Reykjavík.* 1 photoprint; 15 x 11 cm.

[32]   *Reykjavík. The natural laundry, from which the place takes its name.
       The boiling water rises through the cold water of a stream.* 1 photo-
       print; 11 x 15 cm. Women working and laundry spread on the ground.

[33]   *Reykjavík Bay. Eiderducks.* 1 photoprint; 11 x 15 cm.

[34]   *The Church and Stiptamtmann's House, Viðey.* 1 photoprint; 11 x 15
       cm.

[35]   *Ruins of the Bishop's Palace, Laugarnes, Reykjavík, now [i.e. later]
       used as the foundations of the Leper Hospital.* 1 photoprint; 11 x 15
       cm.

[36]   *Elliðaá (Salmon river) near Reykjavík.* 1 photoprint; 11 x 15 cm.
       Showing a bridge made from cut rock and wood. See also Box 18,
       lantern slide 11.

[37]   *Bessastaðir Church, Álptanes.* 1 photoprint; 11 x 15 cm.

[38]   *Bessasaðir Church. Interior.* 1 photoprint; 11 x 15 cm.

[39]   *Hafnarfjörður.* 1 photoprint; 11 x 15 cm.

[40]   *Hafnarfjörður Bay. Evening.* 1 photoprint; 11 x 16 cm.

[41]   *The lava gap. Kaldá near Hafnarfjörður.* 1 photoprint; 8 x 11 cm.

[42]   *Þingvellir. Almannagjá (down).* 1 photoprint; 15 x 11 cm.

[43]   *Þingvellir. Almannagjá (up).* 1 photoprint; 15 x 11 cm.

[44]   *Þingvellir. The new bridge over Öxará.* 1 photoprint; 11 x 16 cm. See
       also Box 4, No. 9.

[45]   *Þingvellir through the Rift.* 1 photoprint; 9 x 7 cm.

[46]   *Þingvellir from Almannagjá.* 1 photoprint; 11 x 15 cm. See also Box 4,
       No. 2.

[47]   *Þingvellir. Church, lava and Hrafnabjörg.* 1 photoprint; 11 x 15 cm.

[48]   *Þingvellir. Almannagjá and Hotel.* 1 photoprint; 11 x 15 cm. See also
       Box 4, No. 13.

[49]   *Þingvellir. The Murderesses' Pool.* 1 photoprint; 11 x 15 cm.

[50]   *Þingvellir. The traditional Lögberg.* 1 photoprint; 11 x 15 cm.

[51]   *Þingvellir from the parsonage.* 1 photoprint; 11 x 16 cm.

[52]   *Þingvellir. Nikulásargjá.* 1 photoprint; 11 x 15 cm.

[53]   *Þingvellir. Ropy lava.* 1 photoprint; 11 x 15 cm.

[54]   *Þingvellir parsonage.* 1 photoprint; 11 x 15 cm.

[55]   *The loom. Þingvellir.* 1 photoprint; 7 x 10 cm.

[56]   *Þingvellir. Rift in lavabed near new Hotel.* 1 photoprint; 15 x 11 cm.

[57]   *Jökulkvísl gorge, near Kerlingarfjöll.* 1 photoprint; 15 x 11 cm.

[58] *Þingvellir. Falls of Öxará.* 1 photoprint; 11 x 15 cm. See also Box 4, No. 7.

[59] *Þingvellir. Hrafnagjá.* 1 photoprint; 11 x 15 cm.

[60] *Þingvallavatn from Hrafnagjá.* 1 photoprint; 11 x 15 cm.

[61] *The hornito above Gjábakki (near Þingvellir); first descended by F. W. W. Howells, 40 feet deep. A rent in the lava stream. Bell-shaped. Note the solidified jet on the left.* 1 photoprint; 11 x 15 cm.

[62] *Kaldárhöfði, near Sog. (Grímsnes).* 1 photoprint; 10 x 15 cm. A farm-house.

[63] *An Iceland laundry. Washing in the stream, Kaldárhöfði, S[outh] of Þingvallavatn.* 1 photoprint; diam. image 7 cm, on sheet 9 x 11 cm. Two women in the foreground.

[64] *Hengill, from Kaldárhöfði.* 1 photoprint; 11 x 15 cm.

[65] *Hengill from Ölkelduháls.* 1 photoprint; 10 x 14 cm.

[66] *Hengill. The hot spring (new in 1896).* 1 photoprint; 11 x 15 cm.

[67] *Sog ferry, S[outh] of Þingvallavatn.* 1 photoprint; 10 x 15 cm.

[68] *Villingavatn farm (in Grafningur). After the earthquake 1896.* 1 photoprint; 16 x 11 cm.

Album ii. Box 1.

[1] Title-page: *II. Geysir — Gullfoss — Hekla.*

[2] *Kálfstindar from Laugarvatnshellirar.* 1 photoprint; 11 x 15 cm.

[3] *Laugarvatn farm. The road Þingvellir to Geysir.* 1 photoprint; 11 x 15 cm.

[4] *Haystacks roofed with sods. Laugarvatn.* 1 photoprint; 10 x 8 cm.

[5] *Laugarvatn. Memorial tablet.* 1 photoprint; 16 x 11 cm.

[6] *Angelica. Mosfell, near Apavatn.* 1 photoprint; diam. image 7 cm, on sheet 8 x 11 cm.

[7] *Kitchen fire place. Mosfell near Apavatn.* 1 photoprint; rectangle image 8 x 6 cm, on sheet 11 x 9 cm.

[8] *Woods near Efstidalur. Hot springs (Reykir) and Hekla in distance. The road to Geysir.* 1 photoprint; 11 x 15 cm.

[9] *Laugarvatn farm, roof.* 1 photoprint; 7 x 10 cm.

[10] *Washing clothes, hot spring, Laugarvatn. The South Christians' baptizing place 1000 A.D.* 1 photoprint; 11 x 15 cm.

[11] *The way side, Þingvellir to Geysir, near Brúará.* 1 photoprint; 11 x 15 cm.

[12] *Woods (skógar) near Brúará.* 1 photoprint; 16 x 11 cm.

[13] *Stepping stones in brook near Brúará.* 1 photoprint; 11 x 15 cm. See also Box 18, lantern slide 16.

[14] *Brúará from above.* 1 photoprint; 7 x 10 cm.

[15] *Brúará down from the bridge.* 1 photoprint; 11 x 15 cm.

[16] *Brúará.* 1 photoprint; 11 x 15 cm. Horses crossing the river. See also Box 4, No. 12.

[17] *Brúará (up) from the bridge.* 1 photoprint; 15 x 11 cm.

[18] *Austurhlíð under Bjarnarfell.* 1 photoprint; 11 x 15 cm. A farmhouse.

[19] *Steinunn Hjartardóttir, í Austurhlíð, with faldur.* 1 photoprint; 10 x 7 cm. Wearing a national costume.

[20] *Haukadalur. Are Frode's home.* 1 photoprint; 11 x 16 cm.

[21] *Geysir from Haukadalur.* 1 photoprint; 11 x 16 cm.

[22] *Haukadalur. Lower set, hot springs, below Strokkur.* 1 photoprint; 11 x 15 cm.

[23] *Geysir, with Haukadalur (to the left).* 1 photoprint; 11 x 15 cm. See also Box 18, lantern slide 34.

[24] *Geysir mound. 1896.* 1 photoprint; 10 x 14 cm.

[25] *The tube of Geysir after an eruption. Diameter of basin 56 feet. Diameter of tube 16 feet.* 1 photoprint; 10 x 15 cm. See also Box 4, No. 6.

[26] *Geysir; eruption, 2^d shot.* 1 photoprint; 16 x 11 cm.

[27] *Geysir; eruption, 3^d shot.* 1 photoprint; 15 x 11 cm.

[28] *Geysir. Overflow; boiling waterfall.* 1 photoprint; 11 x 15 cm.

[29] *Geysir mound and Blesi deposit. After the earthquakes of 1896.* 1 photoprint; 11 x 15 cm.

[30] *Blesi (up) and Laugarfjall.* 1 photoprint; 11 x 15 cm.

[31] *Cooking in Blesi.* 1 photoprint; 11 x 15 cm.

[32] *The semi-defunct Strokkur, and lower set of hot springs.* 1 photoprint; 11 x 15 cm.

[33] *The grave of Strokkur. (Haukadalur).* 1 photoprint; 7 x 9 cm.

[34] *Geysir from Tungufljót.* 1 photoprint; 11 x 15 cm.

[35] *Skálholt.* 1 photoprint; 11 x 15 cm. The farmhouse.

[36] *Skálholt Church. Entrance.* 1 photoprint; 15 x 11 cm.

[37] *Skálholt. The pyx-lid. Silver filigree.* 1 photoprint; 10 x 15 cm.

[38] *Gullfoss.* 1 photoprint; 11 x 15 cm. See also Box 18, lantern slide 28, and Box 4, No. 5.

[39] *Gullfoss. The rush at the corner.* 1 photoprint; 7 x 9 cm.

[40] *Gorge of Hvítá, below Gullfoss.* 1 photoprint; 16 x 11 cm.

[41] *Basalt in gorge below Gullfoss.* 1 photoprint; 11 x 15 cm. See also Box 4, No. 1.

[42] *Basalt dyke in gorge below Gullfoss.* 1 photoprint; 11 x 15 cm.

[43] *Gorge of Hvítá, near Brattholt, below Gullfoss.* 1 photoprint; 16 x 11 cm.

[44] *Hvítá, below Brattholt, near Gullfoss.* 1 photoprint; 11 x 15 cm.

[45]   *Family at Brattholt, near Gullfoss.* 1 photoprint; 11 x 16 cm.

[46]   *Hvítá above Kópsvatn ferry.* 1 photoprint; 14 x 10 cm.

[47]   *Hruni. Church and parsonage.* 1 photoprint; 11 x 16 cm.

[48]   *A camp in church. Hruni.* 1 photoprint; 11 x 15 cm.

[49]   *The "pony fold" at church. Stórinúpur.* 1 photoprint; 7 x 10 cm.

[50]   *Þjórsá ferry near Stórinúpur.* 1 photoprint; 11 x 16 cm.

[51]   *Y[tri] Rangá from the inland, near Hekla.* 1 photoprint; 11 x 15 cm.

[52]   *Waterfall at Galtalækur.* 1 photoprint; 11 x 16 cm.

[53]   *Group at Galtalækur. The old woman was living there in 1845, but says she saw nothing of the lava decending, because of smoke, ashes and steam.* 1 photoprint; 11 x 15 cm.

[54]   *Galtalækur and Hekla. (a new hay-house, bottom half-sunk, galvanized iron roof, now being introduced everywhere).* 1 photoprint; 11 x 16 cm.

[55]   *Hekla from Galtalækur. Wool drying in the foreground. Under the snow is the 1846-7 lava.* 1 photoprint; 11 x 15 cm.

[56]   *Selsund. Pumice from Hekla.* 1 photoprint; 11 x 15 cm.

[57]   *Hekla. Corded lava near Næfurholt.* 1 photoprint; 10 x 15 cm.

[58]   *Hekla.* 1 photoprint; 8 x 10 cm.

[59]   *Hekla. Ponies' stopping place.* 1 photoprint; 11 x 15 cm.

[60]   *Hekla from below last snow. Looking up. July 25, 1899. 9.50 p.m.* 1 photoprint; 10 x 14 cm.

[61]   *Hekla. Lava and snow half way up snowslope.* 1 photoprint; 7 x 10 cm.

[62]   *Ancient lava stream edge; way up Hekla.* 1 photoprint; 8 x 10 cm.

[63]   *Hekla. The lava hand.* 1 photoprint; 7 x 9 cm.

[64]   *Hekla. A rest on the snow.* 1 photoprint; 7 x 10 cm.

[65]   *En route down Hekla.* 1 photoprint; 7 x 9 cm.

[66]   *True summit of Hekla from 1ˢᵗ or western peak.* 1 photoprint; 8 x 10 cm.

[67]   *View from the summit of Hekla (c).* 1 photoprint; 11 x 15 cm.

[68]   *Hekla summit from an old lava-stream on its flanks.* 1 photoprint; 7 x 9 cm.

[69]   *Hekla. The crater of 1845. A small sulphurous rent occurs in the top center of the dark part where the snow has been thawed, partly by the rent in question.* 1 photoprint; 11 x 15 cm.

[70]   *View S.W. from Hekla.* 1 photoprint; 11 x 15 cm.

[71]   *An old crater, Rauðukambar. (Hekla).* 1 photoprint; 11 x 16 cm.

Album iii. Box 2.

[1]   Title-page: *III. Sunnlendingafjórðungur. (Krísuvík — Þórsmörk — Öræfajökull, etc.)*

[2]   *Ponies crossing the pass to Krísuvík.* 1 photoprint; 11 x 15 cm. See also Box 18, lantern slide 2.

[3]   *Krísuvík. The maccalub or mud volcano.* 1 photoprint; 11 x 15 cm.

[4]   *Krísuvík. Big sulphur spring.* 1 photoprint; 11 x 15 cm. See also Box 18, lantern slide 33.

[5]   *Krísuvík.* 1 photoprint; 11 x 15 cm.

[6]   *Hjalli, in Ölves [i.e. Ölfus]. The farm site threatened by the lava that flowed during the Christianity debate in the Althing 1000 A.D.* 1 photoprint; 11 x 16 cm.

[7]   *Hlíðarendi in Ölfus.* 1 photoprint; 11 x 15 cm.

[8]   *Drift wood. Herdísarvík, near Krísuvík.* 1 photoprint; 8 x 10 cm.

[9]   *Lava fall, Herdísarvík, near Krísuvík.* 1 photoprint; 11 x 15 cm.

[10] *Strandakirkja. An old votive church.* 1 photoprint; 11 x 15 cm.

[11] *Coast and gulls near Strandakirkja.* 1 photoprint; 11 x 15 cm.

[12] *An Icelandic pack train crossing the bridge over Elliðaá, near Reykjavík.* 1 photoprint; 11 x 15 cm.

[13] *A lava sheet. Road from Reykjavík to Ölfusá.* 1 photoprint; 11 x 14 cm.

[14] *Lava arch. Road from Reykjavík to Kolviðarhóll. Hengill.* 1 photoprint; 11 x 15 cm.

[15] *Litli Geysir in eruption.* 1 photoprint; 15 x 11 cm.

[16] *Litli Geysir in eruption.* 1 photoprint; 7 x 10 cm.

[17] *Ölfusárbrú.* 1 photoprint; 11 x 15 cm.

[18] *Hraungerði. Minister and his family. (Rev. Ólafur Sæmundsson with his wife and mother).* 1 photoprint; 11 x 15 cm.

[19] *Hraungerði. The reredos.* 1 photoprint; 14 x 10 cm.

[20] *Þjórsá bridge.* 1 photoprint; 11 x 15 cm. See also Box 18, lantern slide 24.

[21] *Reyðarvatn.* 1 photoprint; 11 x 15 cm. See also Box 18, lantern slide 6.

[22] *Hof. Mörð's home near Stórólfshvoll.* 1 photoprint; rectangle image 5 x 8 cm, on sheet 8 x 11 cm.

[23] *Stórólfshvoll. The ponies' supper.* 1 photoprint; 11 x 16 cm. See also Box 18, lantern slide 29.

[24] *Stórólfshvoll Church.* 1 photoprint; 11 x 15 cm.

[25] *Pictures in Stórólfshvoll Church.* 1 photoprint; 15 x 11 cm.

[26] *Stórólfshvoll Church. Bowl, etc.* 1 photoprint; 11 x 15 cm.

[27] *Stórólfshvoll. Tombstone with Latin inscription.* 1 photoprint; 11 x 14 cm.

[28] *The fairy chalice of Breiðabólsstaður, Fljótshlíð. (Said to have been stolen or restored from the fairies).* 1 photoprint; 10 x 15 cm.

[29] *Hlíðarendi, Fljótshlíð.* 1 photoprint; 11 x 15 cm. The farmhouse.

[30] *Hlíðarendi. Gunnar's mound.* 1 photoprint; 11 x 15 cm.

[31] *Lunch under Hlíðarendi.* 1 photoprint; 11 x 15 cm.

[32] *Merkjárfoss, near Hlíðarendi.* 1 photoprint; 15 x 11 cm.

[33] *Barkarstaðir (Fljótshlíð). The glen.* 1 photoprint; 15 x 11 cm.

[34] *Mid - Markarfljót valley.* 1 photoprint; 16 x 11 cm.

[35] *Fording Markarfljót.* 1 photoprint; 11 x 15 cm. See also box 18, lantern slide 23.

[36] *Atmospheric denudation, lower Markarfljót, a hill half of which has been blown away.* 1 photoprint; 8 x 10 cm. See also Box 18, lantern slide 25.

[37] *Tent.* 1 photoprint; 11 x 15 cm.

[38] *Camp in Þórsmörk.* 1 photoprint; 11 x 15 cm.

[39] *Þórsmörk. A side valley. Sunset.* 1 photoprint; 11 x 14 cm.

[40] *Þórsmörk. Head of Krossárdalur.* 1 photoprint; 15 x 11 cm.

[41] *Þórsmörk. Natural bridge (eroded tufa).* 1 photoprint; 11 x 15 cm.

[42] *Þórsmörk. The 1st cave. Entrance.* 1 photoprint; 8 x 10 cm.

[43] *Þórsmörk. The Arch.* 1 photoprint; 11 x 15 cm.

[44] *Þórsmörk. 'Estinguisher' Hill.* 1 photoprint; 7 x 9 cm.

[45] *Þórsmörk. Rocks on arête. Head of Stóriendi.* 1 photoprint; 11 x 15 cm.

[46] *Þórsmörk. Crevasses, Krossárjökull.* 1 photoprint; 11 x 15 cm.

[47] *Þórsmörk. Krossárjökull descending from Goðalandsjökull.* 1 photoprint; 11 x 16 cm.

[48] *Gorge cutting into Eyjafjallajökull; the eastern branch of the gorge ends in a perfectly perpendicular wall-like shaft 3 or 4 hundred feet deep down which pours the waterfall which made it.* 1 photoprint; 16 x 11 cm.

[49] *Eyjafjallajökull from Þórsmörk.* 1 photoprint; 11 x 15 cm.

[50] *Þórsmörk. Glacier descending from Eyjafjallajökull.* 1 photoprint; 11 x 15 cm.

[51] *Gorge in angle between Goðalandsjökull and Eyjafjallajökull.* 1 photoprint; 16 x 11 cm.

[52] *An Icelandic hayfield, S. coast, near Eyjafjallajökull.* 1 photoprint; 11 x 14 cm. See also Box 18, lantern slide 10.

[53] *A farm house bed. South coast.* 1 photoprint; rectangle image 6 x 8 cm, on sheet 8 x 11 cm.

[54] *Basalt pavement, Kirkjubær (Síða). Said to have been used as monastery kitchen floor in Rom. Cath. days.* 1 photoprint; 7 x 9 cm.

[55] *The family at Holt, near Kirkjubær. (in Síða).* 1 photoprint; 7 x 10 cm.

[56] *The Skaptá lava. Largest stream in Europe.* 1 photoprint; diam. image 7 cm, on sheet 8 x 11 cm.

[57] *Núpsvötn and west end of Skeiðarárjökull.* 1 photoprint; rectangle image 6 x 8 cm, on sheet 8 x 10 cm.

[58] *Skeiðarársandur. Icehole.* 1 photoprint; 7 x 10 cm. See also Box 18, lantern slide 14.

[59] *Lower ice-fields west of Öræfajökull.* 1 photoprint; 8 x 10 cm.

[60] *Öræfajökull. South cone.* 1 photoprint; 7 x 10 cm.

[61] *Upper snowfields above Sandfell, Öræfajökull.* 1 photoprint; 7 x 10 cm.

[62] *Glaciers descending from Öræfajökull between Hof and Sandfell.* 1
      photoprint; 7 x 9 cm.
[63] *In the ice-fields, Öræfajökull.* 1 photoprint; 8 x 10 cm.
[64] *Breiðamerkurjökull, medial moraine and Öræfajökull.* 1 photoprint; 8 x
      10 cm.
[65] *Breiðamerkurjökull. Evening.* 1 photoprint; 7 x 10 cm.
[66] *Ponies on Breiðamerkurjökull.* 1 photoprint; 7 x 10 cm.
[67] *Ice cones on Breiðamerkurjökull.* 1 photoprint; 7 x 10 cm.
[68] *The Atlantic from the Breiðamerkurjökull.* 1 photoprint; 8 x 10 cm.
[69] *Svínafell. Flosi's home.* 1 photoprint; 8 x 10 cm.
[70] *Woods (Skógar) west of Öræfajökull, near Svínafell.* 1 photoprint; 8 x
      10 cm.
[71] *Reynivellir, near Breiðamerkurjökull.* 1 photoprint; 8 x 10 cm. A farm-
      house.
[72] *The chained church at Kálfafellsstaður.* 1 photoprint; 8 x 10 cm.

Album iv. Box 2.

[1]   Title-page: *IV. Austfirðinga- and Norðlendingafjórðungar. (Eskifjörður
      — Seyðisfjörður — Vopnafjörður — Jökulsá á Brú — Jökulsá í
      Axarfirði — Mývatn — Húsavík — Akureyri, etc.)*
[2]   *Eskifjörður.* 1 photoprint; 11 x 15 cm. See also Box 4, No. 8.
[3]   *Eskifjörður. Sýslumann's home.* 1 photoprint; 8 x 10 cm.
[4]   *Hólmafjall, Eskifjörður. "The pride of Eskifjörður."* 1 photoprint; 7 x
      10 cm.
[5]   *Fish washing. Eskifjörður. Icelandic and Faeroe girls.* 1 photoprint; 7 x
      10 cm.
[6]   *Pumice section. Eskifjörður.* 1 photoprint; 7 x 9 cm.
[7]   *Norðfjörður, near Eskifjörður. (weighing the anchor).* 1 photoprint; 12
      x 16 cm.
[8]   *Entrance to Seyðisfjörður.* 1 photoprint; 11 x 16 cm.
[9]   *Seyðisfjörður.* 1 photoprint; 11 x 15 cm.
[10] *Seyðisfjörður (up) from Vestdalsfoss.* 1 photoprint; 11 x 16 cm.
[11] *Seyðisfjörður. Evening. (underexposed)* 1 photoprint; 15 x 11 cm.
[12] *(Seyðisfjörður). An Icelander and his steed.* 1 photoprint; 11 x 15 cm.
      See also Box 18, lantern slide 18.
[13] *In Seyðisfjörður.* 1 photoprint; rectangle image 6 x 8 cm, on sheet 8 x
      11 cm. Houses.
[14] *Family fish washing. Seyðisfjörður.* 1 photoprint; 11 x 15 cm.
[15] *The remnants of whale, Seyðisfjörður.* 1 photoprint; 11 x 15 cm.
[16] *Seyðisfjörður. Waterfalls.* 1 photoprint; 11 x 15 cm.

[17] *Seyðisfjörður. Vestdalsfoss.* 1 photoprint; 16 x 11 cm.

[18] *Vopnafjörður. The creeping of the sea-fog.* 1 photoprint; 11 x 15 cm.

[19] *Vopnafjörður.* 1 photoprint; 11 x 15 cm. See also Box 4, No. 3.

[20] *Vopnafjörður. Fish washing.* 1 photoprint; 11 x 15 cm.

[21] *Milking the ewes at Valþjófsstaður.* 1 photoprint; 7 x 9 cm.

[22] *Skógar. Jökulsá above Valþjófsstaður. Lagarfljót.* 1 photoprint; 8 x 10 cm.

[23] *Haymaker and tent above Valþjófsstaður.* 1 photoprint; diam. image 7 cm, on sheet 8 x 11 cm.

[24] *An ordinary Icelandic road and glaciated rocks. (Lagarfljót).* 1 photoprint; 8 x 10 cm.

[25] *The highest trees in Iceland. Birch 29 feet high. Hallormsstaðaskógur, E. Iceland.* 1 photoprint; 8 x 10 cm.

[26] *Hengifoss.* 1 photoprint; 8 x 10 cm.

[27] *Hot springs near Aðalból (Hrafnkelsá — Jökulsá á Brú).* 1 photoprint; 7 x 9 cm.

[28] *A wall of sheeps' bones, Vaðbrekka (Jökulsá á Brú., E. Iceland).* 1 photoprint; 7 x 9 cm.

[29] *Jökulsá á Brú, near Brú.* 1 photoprint; rectangle image 6 x 8 cm, on sheet 7 x 11 cm.

[30] *Jökulsá á Brú. Kláfur, or wire rope bridge.* 1 photoprint; 8 x 10 cm. See also Box 18, lantern slide 21.

[31] *Brú. Basalt column for horse pole. (Jökulsá á Brú).* 1 photoprint; 7 x 10 cm.

[32] *Horns in Shepherd's hut (kofi), near Snæfell.* 1 photoprint; oval image 5 x 7 cm, on sheet 8 x 11 cm.

[33] *Snæfell.* 1 photoprint; 7 x 10 cm.

[34] *Retirement of Brúarjökull, N. of Vatnajökull, since the jökulhlaup.* 1 photoprint; 7 x 10 cm.

[35] *Ice cave in Brúarjökull. Source of Kverká.* 1 photoprint; 7 x 10 cm.

[36] *The headwaters of Kreppá, N. of Vatnajökull.* 1 photoprint; oval image 5 x 7 cm, on sheet 8 x 10 cm.

[37] *Rauðagnúpur, N. Iceland.* 1 photoprint; 8 x 9 cm.

[38] *The "fan." Basalt. Hljóðaklettar near Ásbyrgi.* 1 photoprint; 11 x 15 cm.

[39] *Dettifoss. The monarch of European falls.* 1 photoprint; 11 x 15 cm.

[40] *Gorge of Jökulsá, below Dettifoss.* 1 photoprint; 11 x 15 cm. See also Box 18, lantern slide 17.

[41] *Ponies by Jökulsá below Dettifoss.* 1 photoprint; diam. image 7 cm, on sheet 8 x 11 cm.

[42] *Cup and ball basalt, Jökulsá below Dettifoss.* 1 photoprint; diam. image 7 cm, on sheet 8 x 11 cm.

[43] *Basalt at Hljóðaklettar, near Dettifoss. "The triple staircase."* 1 photoprint; 11 x 15 cm.

[44] *Mývatn. Duck's eggs and nest, on island covered with marsh marigold.* 1 photoprint; 11 x 15 cm.

[45] *Reykjahlíð, north of Mývatn.* 1 photoprint; 7 x 10 cm.

[46] *Húsavík. Cottage; or site of house of Garðar Svavarsson, the first house built in Iceland.* 1 photoprint; 11 x 15 cm.

[47] *Þórður Guðjohnsen, Húsavík, with his children.* 1 photoprint; 11 x 15 cm.

[48] *Eyjafjörður. The Rimar group. (Rimar the loftiest peak in North Iceland).* 1 photoprint; 11 x 15 cm.

[49] *Eyjafjörður from Akureyri.* 1 photoprint; 11 x 16 cm. See also Box 18, lantern slide 20.

[50] *Akureyri from the fjord.* 1 photoprint; 11 x 15 cm.

[51] *Akureyri from the South.* 1 photoprint; 11 x 15 cm.

[52] *Akureyri (Oddeyri) Beach.* 1 photoprint; 7 x 9 cm.

[53] *Akureyri. An arctic garden.* 1 photoprint; 11 x 15 cm.

[54] *Glerárfoss, near Akureyri.* 1 photoprint; 15 x 11 cm.

[55] *Glerárbridge, near Akureyri. Vindheimajökull.* 1 photoprint; 15 x 11 cm.

[56] *"Pot"-holes, Glerá, near Akureyri.* 1 photoprint; 15 x 11 cm.

[57] *Grund, above Akureyri. (Bales of stockings for export).* 1 photoprint; 11 x 15 cm.

[58] *The new spinning mill, near Akureyri.* 1 photoprint; 11 x 15 cm.

[59] *Herringbone walling. Grund above Akureyri.* 1 photoprint; 10 x 15 cm.

[60] *Saurbær church, above Akureyri.* 1 photoprint; 11 x 15 cm. See also Box 4, No. 10.

[61] *Down Eyjafjarðardalur from the northern end of Vatnahjallavegur, the now forsaken way that skirts the north of Arnarfellsjökull.* 1 photoprint; 11 x 16 cm.

[62] *The valley of Eyjafjarðará above Akureyri. A crouching farm in the foreground.* 1 photoprint; 11 x 15 cm.

[63] *Looking down Eyjafjarðardalur from Tjarnir.* 1 photoprint; 11 x 15 cm. An Icelandic sheepdog in the foreground.

[64] *The head of Eyjafjarðardalur from Vatnahjalli.* 1 photoprint; 10 x 14 cm.

[65] *Siglufjörður.* 1 photoprint; 7 x 10 cm.

[66] *Mælifell.* 1 photoprint; 11 x 15 cm. Farmhouse and a church.

[67] *Silfrastaðir.* 1 photoprint; 11 x 15 cm. Farmhouse and a church.

[68] *An Icelandic kitchen. Silfrastaðir.* 1 photoprint; 11 x 15 cm.

[69] *Kotár gorge, near Silfrastaðir, Norðurárdalur, Skagafjörður.* 1 photoprint; 14 x 11 cm.

In an envelope pasted inside back cover: "Panorama photographs by Howell."

[—] *Atmospheric denudation, lower Markarfljót. A hill half of which has been blown away.* 1 photoprint; 9 x 11 cm.

[part A] *Bláfellsjökull and Hvítárvatn.* "Panoramic with B and C." 1 photoprint; 11 x 15 cm.

[part A] *Blesi and Geysir.* "Panoramic with B." 1 photoprint; 12 x 13 cm.

[part A] *Eyjafjallajökull from Þórsmörk.* "Panoramic with B." 1 photoprint; 11 x 14 cm.

[part A] *Woods by Rangá, Hekla.* "Panoramic with B." 1 photoprint; 11 x 16 cm. See also Box 18, lantern slide 26.

[part B] *Blesi and Geysir.* "Panoramic with A." 1 photoprint; 12 x 13 cm.

[part B] *Eyjafjallajökull from Þórsmörk.* "Panoramic with A." 1 photoprint; 11 x 14 cm.

[part B] *Rangá near Hekla.* "Panoramic with A." 1 photoprint; 11 x 16 cm.

[part B] *Skriðufell and Hvítárvatn.* "Panoramic with A and C." 1 photoprint; 11 x 15 cm.

[part C] *Icefall from Langjökull and Hvítárvatn.* "Panoramic with A and B." 1 photoprint; 11 x 15 cm.

[—] *Ísafjörður.* 1 photoprint; 11 x 15 cm.

Album v. Box 3.

[1] Title-page: *V. Vestfirðingafjórðungur, etc. (Hvalfjörður — Borgarfjörður — Mýrar — Snæfellsnes — Flatey — Ísafjörður, etc.)*

[2] *Svínaskarð. Ponies waiting.* 1 photoprint; 11 x 15 cm.

[3] *Svínaskarð, near Hvalfjörður.* 1 photoprint; 11 x 15 cm.

[4] *An Icelander's pet. Fossá, Hvalfjörður.* 1 photoprint; diam. image 7 cm, on sheet 8 x 11 cm.

[5] *Þyrilsnes, Hvalfjörður. Geirshólmi is just out of the picture, to the right.* 1 photoprint; 7 x 9 cm.

[6] *Draghály and Svínavatn, Hvalfjörður.* 1 photoprint; 11 x 15 cm.

[7] *Old drift-head of Hvalfjörður. West of Litli-Botn.* 1 photoprint; 11 x 15 cm.

[8] *Litli-Botn and Hvalfell. Hvalfjörður.* 1 photoprint; 11 x 14 cm. See also Box 18, lantern slide 4.

[9] *Rocks above Þyrill, Hvalfjörður.* 1 photoprint; 15 x 11 cm.

[10] *Glymur, Hvalfjörður. 1200-1500 feet deep.* 1 photoprint; 16 x 11 cm.

[11] *Akranes. North Bay.* 1 photoprint; 7 x 10 cm.

[12] *Akranes Church.* 1 photoprint; 7 x 9 cm.

[13] *Fish drying boards. Akranes.* 1 photoprint; 7 x 9 cm.

[14] *The head of Skorradalsvatn.* 1 photoprint; 11 x 15 cm.

[15] *Grund (in Skorradal).* 1 photoprint; 11 x 16 cm. A farmhouse.

[16] *Family group at Grund, Skorradalur.* 1 photoprint; 7 x 9 cm. See also Box 18, lantern slide 7.

[17] *Reykholt.* 1 photoprint; 7 x 9 cm. A farmhouse.

[18] *Reykholt. Snorri's bath. (Snorralaug).* 1 photoprint; 11 x 15 cm.

[19] *Snorri's bath, Reykholt.* 1 photoprint; 7 x 9 cm.

[20] *Tunguhver, Reykholtsdalur, with Icelanders bathing.* 1 photoprint; 7 x 10 cm.

[21] *Hot springs at Kroppur, Reykholtsdalur.* 1 photoprint; 7 x 10 cm.

[22] *Mountain avens carpeting the Heiði near Kroppur, lower Reykholtsdalur.* 1 photoprint; 8 x 10 cm.

[23] *Barnafoss on (N.) Hvítá, near Gilsbakki and Hraunsás.* 1 photoprint; 11 x 15 cm. See also Box 4, No. 14.

[24] *Waters of part of Norðlingafljót, old branch coming from under lava-stream into Hvítá, near Gilsbakki.* 1 photoprint; 11 x 15 cm. See also Box 18, lantern slide 32.

[25] *Water of Norðlingafljót (old branch) flowing into (N.) Hvítá from under a lava stream.* 1 photoprint; 7 x 9 cm.

[26] *Kalmanstunga.* 1 photoprint; 11 x 15 cm. A farmhouse.

[27] *Ok from Kalmanstunga.* 1 photoprint; 11 x 16 cm.

[28] *The ice-curtain in Surtshellir. (The largest lava-cave in the world).* 1 photoprint; 16 x 11 cm. See also Box 4, No. 15.

[29] *Ice pinnacles (ice stalagonites) in Surtshellir.* 1 photoprint; 11 x 15 cm.

[30] *Surtshellir. Iceicles (Ice stalagonites).* 1 photoprint; diam. image 7 cm, on sheet 8 x 11 cm.

[31] *Eldborg and the lava from the North.* 1 photoprint; 11 x 15 cm.

[32] *Búðahraun, S.E. from Snæfellsjökull, from the pass.* 1 photoprint; 11 x 15 cm.

[33] *Búðir near Snæfellsjökull, S.W.* 1 photoprint; 10 x 14 cm. With a group of people.

[34] *Coast from Búðir, and Tröllkarl. East of Snæfellsjökull.* 1 photoprint; 11 x 16 cm. Stacks of timber in the foreground.

[35] *On the S. coast of Snæfellsnes, near Búðir. Whale's remains.* 1 photoprint; 11 x 15 cm.

[36] *Fróðá (N. Snæfellsnes).* 1 photoprint; 11 x 15 cm. A farmhouse.

[37] *Tröllháls. N. coast Snæfellsnes.* 1 photoprint; 11 x 15 cm.

[38] *Mountain opposite Tröllaháls. N. coast, Snæfellsnes.* 1 photoprint; 11 x 15 cm.

[39] *Berserkjahraun in distance. N. coast, Snæfellsnes.* 1 photoprint; 11 x 14 cm.

[40] *Hraun. Styr's home.* 1 photoprint; 11 x 15 cm. Family standing outside farm. See also Box 4, No. 11.

[41] *Stöðin ("Ligkisten") and Kirkjufell ("Sukkertoppen") N. coast of Snæfellsnes.* 1 photoprint; 10 x 14 cm.

[42] *Ljósufjöll and Drápuhlíð, from road between Stykkishólmur and Hraun.* 1 photoprint; 11 x 14 cm.

[43] *Grundarfoss. N. coast Snæfellsnes.* 1 photoprint; 11 x 15 cm.

[44] *The "Hof"-site near Stykkishólmur.* 1 photoprint; 11 x 14 cm.

[45] *Helgafell (Snæfellsnes). Farm and hill.* 1 photoprint; 11 x 15 cm.

[46] *Stykkishólm Bay. Snæfellsnes.* 1 photoprint; 11 x 15 cm. See also Box 4, No. 16.

[47] *Stykkishólmur from the sea.* 1 photoprint; 11 x 15 cm.

[48] *Rev. Sigurður Gunnarsson with his family, Stykkishólmur.* 1 photoprint; 10 x 14 cm.

[49] *Breiðafjörður from Flatey. Evening.* 1 photoprint; 11 x 15 cm.

[50] *Cottage at Flatey. "Melur" (wild oats on roof).* 1 photoprint; 11 x 15 cm.

[51] *Flatey. The reef sheltering the harbor.* 1 photoprint; 11 x 15 cm.

[52] *Flatey Church, Breiðafjörður.* 1 photoprint; 7 x 9 cm.

[53] *Dýrafjörður.* 1 photoprint; 11 x 15 cm.

[54] *Ísafjörður, from the Hill.* 1 photoprint; 11 x 15 cm. See also Box 18, lantern slide 8.

[55] *Ísafjörður from the whale fishing station, or the 'spit'.* 1 photoprint; 11 x 15 cm.

[56] *Ísafjörður. Fishing station from the steamer.* 1 photoprint; 11 x 15 cm.

[57] *The cliff edge above Ísafjörður.* 1 photoprint; 15 x 11 cm.

Album vi. Box 3.

[1] Title-page: *VI. Central-Iceland. (Hveravellir — Langjökull, etc.). —* Includes also photographs by others.

[2] *N. Geitlandsjökull from Kalmanstunga.* 1 photoprint; 11 x 15 cm.

[3] *Geitlandsjökull from Vestri-Skarðsheiði.* 1 photoprint; 11 x 15 cm.

[4] *Geitlandsjökull over Kaldidalur.* 1 photoprint; 11 x 16 cm.

[5] *The last lunch on the 1st crossing of Langjökull.* 1 photoprint; 8 x 10 cm.

[6] *The ice 'moat' around nunatak piercing Langjökull above Hvítárvatn; thawed in the glacier by refraction and radiation from the tufa cone about 150 feet wide, 100 feet deep.* 1 photoprint; 11 x 15 cm.

[7] *"Bloc", Hvítárvatn. One of the 'orts' of Langjökull.* 1 photoprint; 8 x 10 cm.

[8]   *Bláfell.* 1 photoprint; 11 x 15 cm.

[9]   *Gorges in tufa under Bláfell, west side.* 1 photoprint; 11 x 15 cm.

[10] *Icefall on Hrútafell.* 1 photoprint; 16 x 11 cm.

[11] *Kjalfell (in distance) from Hrútafell. The route from Þjófadalur to Gránanes crosses picture left to right. Some of the sources of Fúlakvísl.* 1 photoprint; 15 x 11 cm.

[12] *The moraine of Hrútafell, Central Iceland.* 1 photoprint; 11 x 15 cm.

[13] *Skriðufell from Bláfellsjökull.* 1 photoprint; 8 x 10 cm.

[14] *Skriðufell from Hvítárvatn.* 1 photoprint; 11 x 15 cm.

[15] *Hrútafell from Þjófadalur.* 1 photoprint; 11 x 15 cm.

[16] *Arnarfellsjökull from the North. Hóp.* 1 photoprint; 11 x 14 cm. See also Box 18, lantern slide 30.

[17] *Details of glacier descending from Geitlandsjökull (South) towards Kaldidalur.* 1 photoprint; 11 x 15 cm.

[18] *Skriðufell, under Langjökull. Photographed July 5, 1900, at 12,o midnight.* 1 photoprint; 11 x 16 cm. See also Box 18, lantern slide 27.

[19] *Fúlakvísl. S.E. Langjökull.* 1 photoprint; 11 x 15 cm.

[20] *Ice cornice. Eyjabakkajökull, N.W. of Vatnajökull. The ice was thrust forward by the great jökulhlaup, and therefore the river is thrown against the land slope.* 1 photoprint; 7 x 10 cm.

[21] *Fording Hvítá near Bláfell.* 1 photoprint; 11 x 15 cm.

[22] *Kerlingarfjöll from Bláfell.* 1 photoprint; rectangle image 5 x 8 cm, on sheet 8 x 11 cm.

[23] *Kerlingarfjöll. Big hot spring in the valley of Ásgarðsá.* 1 photoprint; 11 x 15 cm.

[24] *Kerlingarfjöll (centre). Looking south.* 1 photoprint; 11 x 15 cm.

[25] *Kerlingarfjöll (E).* 1 photoprint; 11 x 15 cm.

[26] *The fight of frost and fire, Kerlingarfjöll, in the upper valley of Ásgarðsá. Glaciers advancing to hot sulphur ruts which thaw caves in the aggressor.* 1 photoprint; 11 x 16 cm. See also Box 18, lantern slide 35.

[27] *Gránanes camp and Kerlingarfjöll.* 1 photoprint; 11 x 15 cm.

[28] *Hveravellir. Eyvindarhver.* 1 photoprint; 8 x 10 cm.

[29] *Hveravellir. The hot cascade.* 1 photoprint; 8 x 9 cm.

[30] *Hveravellir, Central Iceland. Hot springs.* 1 photoprint; 11 x 15 cm.

[31] *Hveravellir. Hot springs, terraces. (with Daniel Bruun, the Danish captain and archaeologist).* 1 photoprint; 11 x 15 cm.

[32] *Bláhver, at Hveravellir.* 1 photoprint; 11 x 15 cm.

[33] *Hveravellir. Gamli Strokkur (the old churn). Tepid water.* 1 photoprint; 7 x 9 cm.

[34] Title-page: *Photographs from the Faeroes, by Frederick W. W. Howell.*

[35] *Tórshavn from the sea.* 1 photoprint; 11 x 15 cm.

[36] *Tórshavn from the rear.* 1 photoprint; 11 x 14 cm.

[37] *A street in Tórshavn.* 1 photoprint; 15 x 12 cm.

[38] *Tórshavn. Goat on house top. (a characteristic picture for the Faeroes or Iceland).* 1 photoprint; 11 x 16 cm.

[39] *Kirkebø near Tórshavn.* 1 photoprint; 11 x 15 cm.

[40] *Ruins of an unfinished R.C. Church Kirkebø near Tórshavn.* 1 photoprint; 11 x 15 cm.

[41] *Trangisvaag, Church and village.* 1 photoprint; 11 x 15 cm.

[42] *Trangisvaag (west).* 1 photoprint; 12 x 16 cm.

[43] *Group of Faroe people at Trangisvaag.* 1 photoprint; diam. image 8 cm, on sheet 9 x 11 cm.

[44] *Klaksvik.* 1 photoprint; 11 x 15 cm.

[45] *Klaksvik. The whale head wall. Skulls of globiceps.* 1 photoprint; 11 x 15 cm.

Perkins, Henry A. Photographs from Iceland taken during the summer of 1900. 17 black and white photoprints. See letters to Daniel Willard Fiske from Perkins.

[46] Title-page: *Icelandic Photographs by Henry A. Perkins, Hartford, Conn.*

[47] *Vestmannaeyjar.* 1 photoprint; 8 x 10 cm.

[48] *Reykjavík. Austurvöllur.* 1 photoprint; 8 x 11 cm.

[49] *Þingvellir. Almannagjá.* 1 photoprint; 8 x 11 cm.

[50] *Kalmanstunga looking toward Geitlandsjökull.* 1 photoprint; 8 x 10 cm. See also Box 18, lantern slide 9.

[51] *River above Eyjafjörður.* 1 photoprint; 8 x 10 cm. See also Box 18, lantern slide 31.

[52] *Near Ljósavatn.* 1 photoprint; 8 x 10 cm.

[53] *Mývatn.* 1 photoprint; 8 x 10 cm.

[54] *Church near Mývatn.* 1 photoprint; 10 x 8 cm.

[55] *Litla Víti.* 1 photoprint; 8 x 10 cm.

[56] *Litla Víti, near Reykjahlíð, Þingeyjarsýsla.* 1 photoprint; 10 x 8 cm.

[57] *Goðafoss.* 1 photoprint; 8 x 10 cm.

[58] *Goðafoss.* 1 photoprint; 10 x 8 cm.

[59] *Dettifoss.* 1 photoprint; 10 x 8 cm.

[60] *Dettifoss.* 1 photoprint; 8 x 10 cm.

[61] *Vopnafjörður.* 1 photoprint; 8 x 10 cm.

[62] *Seyðisfjörður.* 1 photoprint; 8 x 10 cm.

[63] *"Le pecheur d'Islande." In Eskifjörður.* 1 photoprint; 10 x 8 cm.

Magnús Ólafsson, 1862-1937. Photographs taken during the first and second decades of the twentieth century. 13 black and white photoprints.

[64] Title-page: *Icelandic Photographs by Magnús Ólafsson, Reykjavík.*
[65] *Reykjavík. Crowd at the inauguration of the Jón Sigurðsson statue in 1911.* 1 photoprint; 11 x 16 cm.
[66] *Reykjavík. The Athletic Field. Wrestling match.* 1 photoprint; 11 x 16 cm.
[67] *A foreign tourist starting from Reykjavík.* 1 photoprint; 11 x 16 cm.
[68] *Fish washing indoors. Reykjavík.* 1 photoprint; 12 x 17 cm.
[69] *Fish drying. Reykjavík.* 1 photoprint; 11 x 16 cm.
[70] *A mail train (póstlest).* 1 photoprint; 11 x 16 cm.
[71] *Hafravatnsrétt, Mosfellssveit.* 1 photoprint; 11 x 16 cm.
[72] *Ölfusár-bridge.* 1 photoprint; 10 x 14 cm.
[73] *Holt undir Eyjafjöllum. Parsonage.* 1 photoprint; 11 x 16 cm.
[74] *Creamery (Rjómabú) at Seljaland (Eyjafjöll).* 1 photoprint; 11 x 16 cm. See also Box 18, lantern slide 22.
[75] *Dyrhólar, in Mýrdalur.* 1 photoprint; 12 x 16 cm. See also Box 18, lantern slide 5.
[76] *Binding of hay.* 1 photoprint; 14 x 11 cm.
[77] *A hay train (heylest).* 1 photoprint; 10 x 14 cm.

Album vii. Box 3.

[1] Title-page: *Photographs of paintings by Icelandic artists.*
[2] *"Þingvellir."* Painting by Ásgrímur Jónsson. 1 photoprint; 7 x 17 cm.
[3] *Hekla.* Painting by Ásgrímur Jónsson. 1 photoprint; 8 x 18 cm.
[4] *Bp. Hallgrímur Sveinsson.* Painting by Ásgrímur Jónsson. 1 photoprint; 15 x 12 cm.
[5] *Icelandic thicket."* Painting by Eyjólfur Jónsson. 1 photoprint; 10 x 17 cm.
[6] *"An Icelandic village."* Painting by Jón Þorleifsson. 1 photoprint; 13 x 15 cm.
[7] *"Icelandic village."* Painting by Jón Þorleifsson. 1 photoprint; 13 x 15 cm. A different picture from 6.
[8] *"Portrait of a woman."* Painting by Júlíana Sveinsdóttir. 1 photoprint; 16 x 12 cm.
[9] *"Women washing fish in Siglufjörður."* Painting by Kristín Jónsdóttir. 1 photoprint; 11 x 14 cm.
[10] *Akureyri.* Painting by Kristín Jónsdóttir. 1 photoprint; 11 x 16 cm.

[11] *"The midnight sun."* Painting by Kristín Jónsdóttir. 1 photoprint; 11 x 15 cm.

[12] *"The midnight sun."* Painting by Kristín Jónsdóttir. 1 photoprint; 11 x 15 cm. Same as 11.

[13] *Icelandic landscape.* Painting by Þórarinn Þorláksson. 1 photoprint; 9 x 16 cm.

[14] *Icelandic landscape.* Painting by Þórarinn Þorláksson. 1 photoprint; 8 x 16 cm.

[15] *Icelandic landscape.* Painting by Þórarinn Þorláksson. 1 photoprint; 8 x 16 cm. Same as 14.

[16] *"Esjan."* Painting by Þórarinn Þorláksson. 1 photoprint; 11 x 16 cm.

2. Box 4

Collection of photographs from Iceland

Dimensions are given in centimeters rounded off to the next whole centimeter up.

4.1   16 loose photographs by Frederick W. W. Howell, duplicates of photographs in the albums. Captioned in pencil on verso.

1) *Hvítárgljúfrið, fyrir neðan Gullfoss.* 1 photoprint; 11 x 15 cm. "3410" on verso. See album ii, 41.

2) *Þingvellir, sjeð úr Almannagjá, mót suðri.* 1 photoprint; 11 x 15 cm. "3411" on verso. See album i, 46.

3) *Vopnafjörður.* 1 photoprint; 11 x 15 cm. "3412" on verso. See album iv, 19.

4) *Dómkirkjan og alþingishúsið í Reykjavík.* 1 photoprint; 11 x 15 cm. "3414" on verso. See album i, 7.

5) *Gullfoss í Hvítá, eina mílu frá Geysi.* 1 photoprint; 11 x 15 cm. "3415" on verso. See album ii, 38.

6) *Geysisgígurinn, eptir nýafstaðið gos.* 1 photoprint; 11 x 15 cm. "3416" on verso. See album ii, 25.

7) *Öxarárfoss, þar sem Öxará fellur ofan í Almannagjá.* 1 photoprint; 11 x 15 cm. "3417" on verso. See album i, 58.

8) *Eskifjörður.* 1 photoprint; 11 x 15 cm. "3418" on verso. See album iv, 2.

9) *Öxarárbrúin, þar sem Öxará fellur niður úr Almannagjá.* 1 photoprint; 11 x 15 cm. "3419" on verso. See album i, 44.

10) *Saurbæjarkirkja í Eyjafirði.* 1 photoprint; 11 x 15 cm. "3420" on verso. See album iv, 60.

11) *Hraun í Eyrarsveit. Þar bjó Styr (sjá Eyrbyggju).* 1 photoprint; 11 x 15 cm. "3421" on verso. Family outside the farm. See album v, 40.

12) *Brúará. Myndin sýnir fólk á ferð yfir brúna, en hún liggur yfir gjá í botni árinnar.* 1 photoprint; 11 x 15 cm. "3422" on verso. See album ii, 16.

13) *Þingvellir, mót norðri, Valhöll til hægri, Almannagjá til vinstri, Ármannsfell í fjarska.* 1 photoprint; 11 x 15 cm. "3423" on verso. See album i, 48.

14) *Hvítá fyrir norðan Barnafoss. Myndin sýnir óteljandi smálæki, sem koma fram undan hraunhellunni og fossa niður í ána. Eru það kvíslar úr Norðlingafljóti sem hverfa niður í hraunið 2-3 mílum ofar.* 1 photoprint; 11 x 15 cm. "3425" on verso. See album v, 23.

15) *Ísdrangar í botninum á Surtshelli.* 1 photoprint; 11 x 15 cm. "3517A" on verso. See album v, 28.

16) *Frá Stykkishólmi mót norðri.* 1 photoprint; 11 x 15 cm. "3518" on verso. See album v, 46.

4.2   16 loose photographs from Iceland by an unknown photographer. The first 5 are identified on a separate slip of paper, undated and unsigned. At the end: "All poor, I regret to state."

1) *Brúará or Bridge River.* 3 identical photoprints: albumen, sepia toned; 14 x 19 cm.

2) *Plain of Thingvellir, with the tents erected at the Millenial Celebration 1874.* 2 identical photoprints: albumen, sepia toned; 14 x 19 cm.

3) *Reykjavík Harbor.* 3 identical photoprints: albumen, sepia toned; 14 x 19 cm.

4) *Thorvaldsen's statue, our house in the 2 story of which we live.* 2 identical photoprints: albumen, sepia toned; 14 x 19 cm.

5) *Portion of Reykjavík.* 3 identical photoprints: albumen, sepia toned; 14 x 19 cm. Pond, cathedral, etc.

6) [*Dettifoss*]. 1 photoprint: albumen, sepia toned; 14 x 19 cm.

7) [*Farm and a church*]. 1 photoprint: albumen, sepia toned; 14 x 19 cm.

8) [*Farm and a church*]. 1 photoprint: albumen, sepia toned; 14 x 19 cm.

9) [*Geysir*]. 2 photoprints: albumen, sepia toned; 14 x 19 cm.

10) [*Gullfoss*]. 1 photoprint: albumen, sepia toned; 14 x 19 cm.

11) [*Hekla*]. 1 photoprint: albumen, sepia toned; 14 x 19 cm.

12) [*Icelandic landscape*]. 4 different photoprints: albumen, sepia toned; 14 x 19 cm.

13) [*Reykjavík*]. 2 different photoprints: albumen, sepia toned; 14 x 19 cm.

14) [*Unidentified village*]. 1 photoprint: albumen, sepia toned; 14 x 19 cm.

15) [*Unidentified village*]. 1 photoprint: albumen, sepia toned; 14 x 19 cm.

16) [*Þingvellir. Camping*]. 2 photoprints: albumen, sepia toned; 14 x 19 cm.

4.3   31 unmounted photographs from Iceland. Images somewhat faded. Identified on verso. Possibly the photographs from Björn Pálsson in Ísafjörður, mentioned in a letter to Fiske in February 1904. See letters to Daniel Willard Fiske.

1) *Akranesskagi.* 1 photoprint; 7 x 19 cm. A village. "054" on verso.

2) *Geirseyri við Patreksfjörð.* 1 photoprint; 7 x 19 cm. "074" on verso. Bottom right corner broken off.

3) *Kauptúnið Flateyri við Önundarfjörð. Hvalveiðastöð í nærsýn.* 1 photoprint; 12 x 19 cm.

4) *Siglufjörður.* 1 photoprint; 12 x 19 cm. "2856" on verso.

5) *Kauptúnið Flatey á Breiðafirði.* 1 photoprint; 12 x 19 cm. "059" on verso. Boats on the fjord.

6) *Altaristaflan í kirkjunni á Hólum í Hjaltadal.* 1 photoprint; 12 x 19 cm. "056" on verso.

7) *Kirkjan á Hólum í Hjaltadal.* 1 photoprint; 12 x 19 cm. "055" on verso.

8) *Hvalur á skurðarpalli við hvalveiðastöðina í Veiðileysufirði.* 1 photoprint; 12 x 20 cm.

9) *S/S "Skálholt." Strandferðabátur vestanlands á svæðinu milli Reykjavíkur og Akureyrar.* 1 photoprint; 6 x 8 cm. "2793" on verso. Right part broken off.

10) *Sjálfgjörð skipakví við Flatey á Breiðafirði.* 1 photoprint; 10 x 15 cm. "016" on verso.

11) *Nokkur hluti af Stykkishólmi.* 1 photoprint; 11 x 15 cm. "06" on verso.

12) *Blönduós, sjeð frá bakkanum norðan við Blöndu.* 1 photoprint; 11 x 15 cm. "2859" on verso.

13) *Borðeyri við Hrútafjörð. Sjeð frá suð-vestri til norð-austurs.* 1 photoprint; 11 x 15 cm. "2795" on verso.

14) *Brúin yfir Blöndu í Húnavatnssýslu.* 1 photoprint; 11 x 15 cm. "2809" on verso.

15) *Seyðisfjörður. "Aldan" í nærsýn Búðareyri fjær, sunnan við fjörðinn. Vestdalseyri, sem er norðan við fjörðinn sjezt ekki á þessari mynd.* 1 photoprint; 11 x 15 cm. "3545" on verso.

16) *Akureyri, með Oddeyri í fjærsýn. Sjeð frá suð-vestri til norð-austurs.* 1 photoprint; 11 x 15 cm. "3544" on verso.

17) *Sauðárkrókur við Skagafjörð. Sjeð frá suð-vestri til norð-austurs. Í fjærsýn eru Þórðarhöfði til hægri, þá Málmey, og Drangey til vinstri.* 1 photoprint; 11 x 15 cm. "2812" on verso.

18) *Hólmavík við Steingrímsfjörð, nýlega löggilt kauptún. Einn af viðkomustöðum strandferðabátsins "Skálholt."* 1 photoprint; 11 x 15 cm. "2810" on verso.

19) *Reykjafjarðar kauptún í Strandasýslu sjeð frá suð-vestri til norð-austurs.* 1 photoprint; 11 x 15 cm. "2811" on verso.

20) *Meleyri, hvalveiðastöð í Jökulfjörðum. Myndin er tekin í síðari parti maímánaðar. Snjór bráðnar þar aldrei með öllu vegna þess hve sólargangurinn er stuttur. Sjeð frá suðri til norðurs.* 1 photoprint; 11 x 15 cm.

21) *Hnífsdalur, fiskiver nálægt Ísafirði.* 1 photoprint; 11 x 15 cm. "2632" on verso.

22) *Ísafjarðarkaupstaður. Sjeð frá norð-vestri til suð-austurs. Handan við "Sundið" er Kirkjubólshlíð með djúpri skál ("Gryden" = "Potturinn") í fjallshlíðina.* 1 photoprint; 11 x 15 cm.

23) *Þingeyri við Dýrafjörð, sjeð frá vestri til austurs. Í fjarsýn til hægri, handan við fjörðinn er Framnes. Þar er stór hvalveiðastöð.* 1 photoprint; 11 x 15 cm.

24) *Árnesstapi. Klettur í sjónum nálægt Árnesi í Trjekyllisvík. Auðvitað eru ýmsar sögur um það, að klettur þessi hafi í fornöld verið lifandi vera. En sögunum greinir nokkuð á um það, hvernig á því stendur, eða með hvaða hætti það varð, að hann er nú aðeins dauður klettur að ýmsu leyti með manns mynd.* 1 photoprint; 11 x 15 cm. "2647" on verso.

25) *Vatneyri við Patreksfjörð.* 1 photoprint; 11 x 15 cm. "076" on verso.

26) *Meleyri, hvalveiðastöð í Jökulfjörðunum. Myndin er tekin í síðari parti maímánaðar. Snjór bráðnar þar aldrei með öllu vegna þess hve stuttur sólargangurinn er. Sjeð frá norðvestri til suðausturs.* 1 photoprint; 11 x 15 cm. "2807" on verso.

27) *Vestdalseyri við Seyðisfjörð. Búðareyri og Aldan hinumegin.* 1 photoprint; 11 x 15 cm. "3413" on verso.

28) *Bóndi á leið úr kaupstað (með kaupstaðarvarning). Er að fara út á brúna yfir Elliðaárnar nálægt Reykjavík.* 1 photoprint; 11 x 15 cm. "3409" on verso.

29) *Hvalveiðabáturinn "Nordenskjöld" kom inn á Ísafjarðarhöfn til að sýna hina fyrstu veiði sína.* 1 photoprint; 11 x 15 cm. "3160" on verso.

30) *Nokkur hluti af kauptúninu Stykkishólmur.* 1 photoprint; 11 x 15 cm. "05" on verso.

31) *Ísafjarðarkaupstaður ("Tanginn"). Sjeð frá Hafrafellinu, norðan yfir Skutulsfjörðinn. Snæfjallaströndin í fjærsýn. Arnarnesið til hægri. Þar er nú viti sem lýsir nærri því um allt "Djúpið" og út úr Djúpkjaptinum.* 1 photoprint; 11 x 15 cm.

3. Box 5

Miscellaneous Prints

19 lithographs, drawings, engravings, and etchings. Treated and framed by mats by the conservation department, Cornell University in 1991. The pictures include portraits of Icelanders, scenes from Iceland by various artists, a map of Iceland, figures from the Faeroe Islands, pictures from the Gaimard expeditions to Iceland, and scenes from Old Norse mythology.

Portraits of Icelanders. Arranged in alphabetical order by subject.

5.1   ***Finnus Iohannæus*** *S.S. Theol. D. & Episc. Skalholt. Nat. 16. Ian, 1704. anno æt. 50. Symb. Fide justus salvator* [i.e. Bishop Finnur Jónsson, 1704-1789]. Meno Haas, 1752-1833, sc. 1778. Print: engraving; oval image in frame with text 16.7 x 11.1 cm, on mat 25.3 x 20.2 cm.

5.2   ***Skulius Thordi Thorlacius*** [i.e. Skúli Þórðarson Thorlacius, 1741-1815]. "Ætatis 74" beneath the name; stanza of 6 lines in Latin with the initials B. T. below the image; J. Fyhn pinx. [i.e. Jens Jørgen Fyhn, 1788-1866]; O. Bagge sc. Print: engraving; oval image 8.2 x 6.5 cm, on mat 25.3 x 20.2 cm.

5.3   ***Thormodus Torfæus*** [i.e. Þormóður Torfason, 1636-1719]. *Assessor Consistorii Historiographus Regni Norvegiæ Nat. 27 Maji 1636. Ob. 31 Jan 1719.* Imp.sc: s.n. Print: engraving; oval image in frame with text 16.6 x 12.5 cm, on mat 25.3 x 20.2 cm.

Miscellaneous scenes from Iceland; a map; pictures from the Faeroe Islands. The pictures by Emanuel Larsen were probably painted in 1845, when he went on a trip to Iceland and the Faeroe Islands. See also Box 6. Ref.: *Dansk Biografisk Lexikon* ed. C. F. Bricka (Copenhagen: Gyldendalske Boghandels Forlag, 1896). Arranged in alphabetical order by artist.

5.4   **Durocher, J.** *Géologie des Iles Feröe.* Dessiné par J. Durocher; gravé par Himely; Arthus-Bertrand éditeur; imp. de Bougeard; Fig. 1-3. Print: etching; 31 x 24.8 cm, on mat 59.7 x 38.2 cm.

5.5   **Frisak?** *Prospect af Gaarden_Bœrn_Götheborg eller Helgestad i Island hvorfra man til venstre har Udsigt til Reidarfjord og til hoire til Eskefjorden. Man seer Handelskibe seile ind ad fjorden og fiskerbaade roe udaf fjorden. Optegned efter Naturen den 21^d julii 1812 og eftertegned den 1te martii 1822 af Mons. Frisak kaptain i norsk tjeneste. Tilsendt det Kongelige Sø Kaart Arkiv fra Hr. Major Schéel den 19 Marts 1822.* Lower case letters a-g written in ink on the picture for identification on verso. Drawing: ink wash; 16 x 19.3 cm, including text, on mat 30 x 48.2 cm.

5.6   **Larsen, Emanuel**, 1823-1859. *Geysir.* [1845]. Emanuel Larsen del.; E. Vesterberg lith.; printed and published by Em. Bærentzen & co. Print: lithograph; image 28.4 x 22.6 cm, on mat 59.7 x 38.2 cm. See same picture in Box 6.

5.7   ____, *Hekla den 23 Juli 1846 Emanuel Larsen.* Sign. Drawing: iron gold ink; 16.8 x 23 cm, on mat 30 x 48.2 cm.

5.8   **Quad, Matthias**, 1557-1613. *Islandia* (map of Iceland). Picture of King Christian IV at bottom right corner (dedication); some information on Iceland printed on the backside. This is a diminished reproduction of Ortelius' map (original made by Bishop Guðbrandur Þorláksson). Print: etching; image 22.5 x 29 cm, on mat 35.5 x 45.6 cm. Ref.: Haraldur Sigurðsson, *Kortasaga Íslands frá lokum 16. aldar til 1848* (Reykjavík: Bókaútgáfa Menningarsjóðs og Þjóðvinafélagsins, 1978), pp. 25-26.

5.9   **Schytte, H. H.** *Domkirken i Reikjavik.* H. H. Schytte del.; trykt i Em. Bærentzen & Co. Print: lithograph; image 21.8 x 39 cm, on mat 38.2 x 59.7 cm.

Pictures made by members of a French expedition to Iceland in 1835-1836 under the leadership of Paul Gaimard. Some were made at a later date. In M. Paul Gaimard, *Atlas historique lithographié d'après les dessins de M. A. Mayer* vols. I-II (Paris: Arthus-Bertrand, éditeur [1842]) and *Voyage en Islande et au Groenland. Atlas Zoologique, Médical et Géographique* (Paris: Arthus-Bertrand, éditeur [1850]). Jón Árnason, librarian and folklorist was responsible for the distribution and sale of these pictures in Iceland. Reference: *Íslandsmyndir Mayers 1836* (Reykjavík: Örn og Örlygur, 1986).

5.10 **Lassallé, Emile.** *Steingrímur Jónsson. Evêque d'Islande.* Emile Lassallé 1838, pr. sign.; imp. de Lemercier, Bernard et Cie; Arthus-Bertrand éditeur. Print: lithograph; image ca. 25 x 24 cm, on mat 59.7 x 38.2 cm. In *Atlas historique* vol. I., No. 23.

5.11 **Lottin V[ictor].** *Plan de Skálholt en 1784.* Par Mr V. Lottin d'après un manuscrit communiqué par M. Steingrímur Jónsson, Evêque d'Islande; gravé par Ambroise Tardieu; Arthus-Bertrand éditeur. Print: engraving; sheet 35.5 x 55.2 cm, on mat 38.2 x 59.7 cm. In *Atlas Zoologique,* No. 4.

5.12 ____, *Plan de Skálholt en 1836.* Par V. Lottin. Géographie No. 5. Print: engraving; sheet 35.5 x 55.2 cm, on mat 38.2 x 59.7 cm. In *Atlas Zoologique,* No. 5.

5.13 **Mayer, A[uguste].** *Croix en bois et Ecce homo en albâtre (Temple de Vallanes).* Dessiné par A. Mayer; lith. par Guiaud; imp. Lemercier, Benard et Cie; Arthus-Bertrand éditeur. Print: lithograph; image 28.5 x 23.2 cm, on mat 59.7 x 38.2 cm. In Gaimard *Atlas historique* vol. I, No. 3.

5.14 ____, *Etablissement Danois à Húsavik.* Dessiné par A. Mayer; lith. par Guiaud; Arthus-Bertrand éditeur; imp. Lemercier, Benard & Co. Lithograph printed in color; image 22.1 x 32.5 cm, on mat 38.2 x 59.7 cm. In *Atlas historique* vol. II, No. 120.

5.15 ____, **and Bévalet, [Louis].** *Plat Baptismal en airain du Temple de Reykjahlíd. Fonts baptismaux du Temple de Hólar.* Dessiné par Mayer et Bévalet; lith. par A. Mayer; imp. Lemercier, Benard et Cie; Arthus-Bertrand éditeur. Print: lithograph; images 37 x 26.5 cm, on mat 59.7 x 38.2 cm. In *Atlas historique* vol. I, No. 16.

Pictures portraying scenes from Old Norse mythology.

5.16 **Arbo, P[eter] N[icolai],** 1831-1892. *Sigurd Ranessön underkaster sig Kong Sigurd Jorsalafarers dom.* Efter tegning af P. N. Arbo [187?]; udgivet og forlagt af Asbj. Knutsen; Hoffensberg, Jespersen & Fr. Trap[s]. Lithograph printed in color; 28 x 37 cm, on mat 38.2 x 59.7 cm. Possibly a part of a series of drawings he published in 1876-1879, *Billeder af Norges Historie for Skolen og Hjemmet*, with Asbjørn Knudsen, Kristiania. Ref.: *Norsk Biografisk Leksikon* Edv. Bull, et.al. (Kristiania, 1923).

5.17 **Pauelsen, E[rik],** 1749-1790. *Rolf Krage og hans Stridsmænd ... 1782.* Malet af E. Pauelsen; dedicated to King Christian the VII; stukken af Meno Haas 1782; trÿkket af Bruun. Print: engraving; sheet 40 x 54 cm, unmatted. "See St. og gode Handl. af Danske Norske og Holstenere Pag. 350."

5.18 **Winge, M[årten] E[skil],** 1825-1896. *Hvorledes Loke bliver straffet.* Efter Maleri af M. E. Winge. Udgivet og forlagt af Asbj. Knutsen; Hoffensberg, Jespersen & Fr. Trap[s]. Lithograph printed in color; 37 x 28.7 cm, on mat 59.7 x 38.2 cm.

5.19 ____, *Thor i Kamp med Jötunerne.* Efter Maleri af M. E. Winge. Udgived og forlagt af Asbj. Knutsen; Hoffensberg, Jespersen & Fr. Trap[s]. Lithograph printed in color; 35 x 27.2 cm, on mat 59.7 x 38.2 cm.

4. Box 6

Miscellaneous Prints,
Including Photographs and Process Prints

Lithographs, engravings, and photographs. Scenes from Iceland by Emanuel Larsen (see also Box 5) and others. Also pictures from the Faeroe Islands.

6.1 **Blefkenius, Didthmar.** "From the ed. of Blefken's book in: De aanmerkenswaardigste ... Zeeen Landreizen der Portugeezen, Spanjaarden, Engelsen en allerhanden Nation VII. Deel. Leyden (Pieter vander Ana) 1727. fol. (This picture is also in the 1706-ed.)" in pencil in Halldór

Hermannsson's hand. Print: wood engraving; image 12.9 x 17.8 cm; clipping 18 x 24.6 cm. Picture of a volcano erupting, seen from the sea.

6.2 ***Der Grosse Geyser am Hekla.*** DCCCXVII. Aus d. Kunstanst. d. Bibl. Instit. in Hildbhsn. Print: steel engraving; plate mark 14.3 x 19.3 cm.

6.3 **Larsen, Emanuel,** 1823-1859. *Almanagjau ved Tingvalla paa Island.* Emanuel Larsen. 1849. No. 3. Print: etching; 9.7 x 12.9 cm, mounted on stiff paper 16.5 x 27.6 cm. "908" lower left corner. The original is at Statens Museum for Kunst, Copenhagen. Ref.: Frank Ponzi, *Nineteenth-century Iceland* (Reykjavík: Almenna bókafélagið, 1986), p. 60.

6.4 ____, *Geysir.* Emanuel Larsen del. [1845]; E. Vesterberg lith.; Em Bærentzen & Co. lith. Inst. Lithograph printed in color; image 28.4 x 22.5 cm, on sheet 37.8 x 28.3 cm. See also Box 5.

6.5 ____, *Goðafoss.* Emanuel Larsen del. [1845]; A. Nay lith.; Em Bærentzen & C°. lith. Inst. Lithograph printed in color; image 19.3 x 27.3 cm, on sheet 28.3 x 37.8 cm.

6.6 ____, *Hecla paa Island.* Emanuel Larsen. 1849. No. 2. Print: etching; 10.2 x 13 cm, mounted on stiff paper 23 x 26.2 cm. "906" lower left corner. The original is at Statens Museum for Kunst, Copenhagen. Ref.: Frank Ponzi, *Nineteenth-century Iceland* (Reykjavík: Almenna bókafélagið, 1986), p. 60.

6.7 ____, *Parti af "Almannagjá" med Udsigt til "Þingvallavatn" (Thingvallesö).* Emanuel Larsen del. [1845]; E. Vesterberg lith.; Em. Bærentzen & C°. lith. Inst. Lithograph printed in color; image 19.4 x 28.5 cm, on sheet 28.3 x 37.8 cm. A second copy.

6.8 ____, *Parti ved Hekla. Seet fra Selsund.* Emanuel Larsen del. [1845]; J. Hellesen lith.; Em. Bærentzen & Co. lith. Inst. Lithograph printed in color; image 18.8 x 27.8 cm, on sheet 28.3 x 37.8 cm.

6.9 ____, *Snæfellsjökull.* Emanuel Larsen del. [1845]; E. Vesterberg lith.; Em. Bærentzen & Co. lith. Inst. Lithograph printed in color; image 19.4 x 29.6 cm, on sheet 28.3 x 37.8 cm.

6.10 **Locher, Carl,** 1851-1915. *Offjelds jökel paa Island. (Danske Billeder fra Land og Sö).* Carl Locher pinx.; F. Larsen lith.; Hoffenberg & Trap[s] Etabl., Copenhagen. Reproduced from a painting by Carl Locher. Print:

chromo lithograph?; image 18 x 25.7 cm, on sheet 32 x 41.8 cm. Probably painted in 1907 when he travelled to Iceland. Ref.: *Dansk Biografisk Leksikon*, 3rd ed., Sv. Cedergreen Bech ed. (Copenhagen: Gyldendal, 1981).

6.11 ***Reykjavík.*** F. E. Bording[s] Bog & Stentr.; Nordisk Billed-Magazin. "1869-78" in pencil. Process print: line block; sheet 17.3 x 26.5 cm.

6.12 ***Reykjavik Kirke.*** Print: wood engraving; cutting 11.5 x 15.5 cm, mounted on stiff paper 21.6 x 26.6 cm.

6.13 ***Thingvalla Kirke.*** Print: wood engraving; cutting 9.9 x 15.2 cm, mounted on stiff paper 18.8 x 25.6 cm.

6.14 **Witschel.** Pr. sign. *Núpstaður (með torfkirkju)*. Captioned in pencil on verso. Print: etching; plate mark 17.6 x 23.8 cm, on sheet 28.3 x 38 cm.

Icelandic costumes.

6.15 **Hansen N. C.?** *Pige fra Island. Fille de l'Ile d'Islande.* Made by Hansen & Weller, Copenhagen. Photoprint of a painting; in color; on cabinet card. Same on a carte-de-visite mount. Made by N. C. Hansen & Schou., Copenhagen.

6.16 **Lund, F. C.** *En Pige fra Øfjord. Jeune Fille d'Øfjord. A Girl from Øfjord.* Nyt dansk Forlagskonsortiums Forlag. Hoffensberg & Trap[s]. Etabl. Process print of a painting by F. C. Lund; in color; image 26.2 x 18.1 cm, on sheet 37 x 27.9 cm.

6.17 **Lund, Solveig.** *Hilsen fra Norden. Brud, Island.* Process print of a painting; in color; image 14.2 x 10 cm. A woman dressed in a national costume holding a drinking horn.

Photographs, mostly by Sigfús Eymundsson, Reykjavík (or Daníel Daníelsson, who worked for Sigfús Eymundsson). Taken sometime between 1868 and 1909. Ref.: *Ljósmyndir Sigfúsar Eymundssonar*. Compiled by Þór Magnússon (Reykjavík: Almenna bókafélagið, 1976). The pictures are mounted on sheets 25.2 x 31.8 cm, and identified in pencil on verso.

6.18 **Sigfús Eymundsson,**1837-1911. *Bordeyri, a small place north country Iceland.* Photoprint: sepia toned; image 15.2 x 20.5 cm. Borðeyri by Hrútafjörður.

6.19 ____, *Children-waterfall (Barnafoss).* Photoprint: sepia toned; image 15.2 x 19.8 cm.

6.20 ____, *Clergymens* [i.e. man's] *House Thingvalla.* Photoprint: sepia toned; image 15.2 x 20.6 cm.

6.21 ____, *Farmhouse on the border of one of the best salmon rivers. Splendid place of resort for all tourists fishing salmon. Place called Hvítarvellir.* Photoprint: sepia toned; image 15.2 x 20.7 cm. In Mýrasýsla.

6.22 ____, *The Hanging Rock-Almannagjá.* Photoprint: sepia toned; image 15.2 x 20.5 cm. Þingvellir.

6.23 ____, *Harbor of Reykjavík.* Photoprint: sepia toned; image 13.9 x 18.3 cm.

6.24 ____, *View of Reykjavík.* Photoprint: sepia toned; image 15.2 x 20.7 cm. Cathedral, pond, etc.

6.25 ____, *View of Reykjavík and harbor.* Photoprint: sepia toned; image 14.9 x 20.5 cm.

6.26 ____, [*The statue of Bertel Thorvaldsen at Austurvöllur, Reykjavík*]. Photoprint: sepia toned; image 13.8 x 17.6 cm, on sheet 21.3 x 26.5 cm.

6.27 ____, *The valley of Marardal — very fine place near Reykjavík.* Photoprint: sepia toned; image 15.2 x 20.6 cm. In Árnessýsla.

6.28 ____, *View of Reykjavík in winter.* No. 2. Photoprint: sepia toned; image 15.2 x 20.5 cm.

6.29 ____, *View of Thingvalla.* Photoprint: sepia toned; image 15.2 x 20.5 cm.

6.30 *Akureyri.* Identified in pencil below image. Unidentified photographer. Photoprint; image 10.7 x 15.2 cm, on board 15.8 x 22.2 cm; "fjörtíu ára" in pencil on verso.

6.31 *Almannagjá.* Printed in italics beneath the picture. Unidentified photographer. Photoprint: sepia toned; image 11.4 x 14.8 cm, on sheet 21.3 x 27.1 cm.

6.32 [*"Friðriksgáfa" at Möðruvellir in Hörgárdalur*]. Unidentified photographer. 2 photoprints: sepia toned; 11.9 x 16.2 cm. The residence of the Governor of the North and East. The building burned in 1874. Ref.: Einar Laxness, *Íslandssaga* (Reykjavík: Bókaútgáfa Menningarsjóðs og Þjóðvinafélagsins, 1974).

The Faeroe Islands.

6.33 **Müller, H. C.** *Thorshavn. Fareoish Antiquities. Prob. coll. by W. Fiske in 1879.* Identified on an envelope in Halldór Hermannsson's hand. 5 photoprints on carte-de-visite: sepia toned; ca. 10 x 6.2 cm. One is titled *Bispestol* in pencil beneath the picture.

6.34 _____, *Thorshavn.* Photoprint: sepia toned; image 14.5 x 18.6 cm, mounted on sheet 23.5 x 31.8 cm.

6.35 _____, *Thorshavn.* A different view from the one above. Photoprint: sepia toned; image 14.5 x 18.5 cm, mounted on sheet 23.5 x 31.8 cm.

6.36 **Seidelin, P., Capt.** *Thorshavn. (Færöerne.)* Capt. P. Seidelin del.; E. Vesterberg lith.; Em. Bærentzen & Co. Print: lithograph in color; image 19.1 x 27.5 cm, on sheet 28.5 x 38.7 cm.

6.37 *Thorshavn.* Identified in pencil on verso. No photographer. Photoprint: sepia toned; image 15.2 x 19.7 cm, on sheet 24.2 x 32 cm.

Pictures of Viking antiquities.

6.38 *Antiquities [from the Viking ship of Gokstad*]. By O. Væring, Christiania. 5 different photoprints: sepia toned; ca. 17 x 22 cm. and smaller.

6.39 *The Viking ship of Gokstad.* By O. Væring, Christiania. 3 different photoprints: albumen, sepia toned; ca. 17 x 22 cm and smaller.

6.40 [*Viking ship*]. Taken by O. Væring, Christiania. 1 photoprint: albumen, sepia toned; 16.5 x 21 cm. Photograph of a painting of a Viking ship.

5. Box 7

Miscellaneous Prints,
Including Photographs and Process Prints

Portraits (and monuments) of Icelanders and Scandinavians. Arranged in alphabetical order by subject. Also group photographs of Icelanders.

7.1   [*Arngrímur Jónsson*]. Print: engraving on metal; plate mark 13.1 x 10.8 cm, on sheet 20.4 x 17 cm. A poem in Latin by Georg Dedehen (b.1564) beneath the image. A. J. met him in 1602. According to inscription the picture must have been made when the subject was 24 years old, i.e. 1592-3. This is then a reproduction, made 1602 or later. Ref.: Arngrímur Jónsson, *Crymogæa*. Translated with introduction and notes by Jakob Benediktsson (Reykjavík: Sögufélag, 1985).

7.2   *Á[rni] Helgason* [*the Rev.*] Pr. sign. Em. Bærentzen & Co. lith. Inst. Print: lithograph; image ca. 13.2 x 13.5 cm, on sheet 34.4 x 26.1 cm; head and shoulders portrait. In margin in pencil: "Str. 1104", "M 1598a", and "1674."

7.3   [*Árni Magnússon*]. Made by J[ulius] Magnus P[etersen] after 1869, after a drawing by Hjalti Þorsteinsson, a contemporary of Árni Magnússon. Print: engraving, china-collé; plate mark 7.2 x 9.5 cm, on sheet 27.1 x 30.8 cm. Ref.: Finnur Jónsson, *Ævisaga Árna Magnússonar* (Copenhagen: Hið íslenzka bókmenntafélag, 1930), p. 196. "M. 2454" in pencil, "2652" on verso.

7.4   *Árni Thorsteinsson, landfógeti.* Identified in pencil beneath the picture. Photoprint: sepia toned; oval image 16 x 13.2 cm, mounted on stiff green board 29.6 x 24.2 cm; head and shoulders portrait.

7.5   *Baldvin Einarsson* Pr. sign. Em. Bærentzen & Cº. lith. Inst. Print: lithograph; image ca. 10.3 x 9 cm, on sheet 36 x 27.7 cm; head and shoulders portrait.

7.6   *Benedikt Sveinsson,* Sheriff. *Boðsbrjef.* Print: wood engraving; sheet 27 x 23 cm; half-length portrait. Printed mirror image on verso where the date 1888 appears.

7.7   *B[jörn] Gunlögsen* [i.e. Gunnlaugsson]. Pr. sign. Sigurdr Gudmundson del. [i.e. Sigurður Guðmundsson málari, 1833-1874]; I. W. Tegner &

Kittendorff[s] lith. Inst. Print: lithograph; image 17.5 x 15 cm, on sheet 40 x 28.4 cm; head and shoulders portrait. The original in the National Museum of Iceland, No. 164. Ref.: *Sigurður Guðmundsson málari*. Jón Auðuns edited (Reykjavík: H.f. Leiftur, 1950).

7.8   [***Bogi Th. Melsteð***]. *Herbergi, vinnustofa Boga Th. Melsteðs í Ole Suhrsg. 18.* Taken by Svend Jensen, Copenhagen in 1914. Photoprint: sepia toned; 12 x 16.9 cm, on mount 21.8 x 29.8 cm. Inscription in ink on verso, besides title, by Melsteð: "Til Halldórs Hermannssonar, bókavarðar, með kærri kveðju frá B.Th.M.", and "Mynd þessi er tekin 30. decbr. 1914."

7.9   ***Briem*** [i.e. either Gunnlaugur Briem, 1773-1834, or Eggert Briem, 1811-1894]. E. Westerberg lith.; Em. Bærentzen & C°. lith. Inst. Print: lithograph; image 12.4 x 11 cm, on sheet 33.8 x 24.8 cm. "Syssilmand i Øfiórd=syssil paa Island", and "M564", in pencil bottom right corner, "587", upper right, and "SI 403" bottom center. Head and shoulders portrait of Briem as a young man. A second copy.

7.10 ***Cineribus Ericianis Sacrum*** [i.e. Jón Eiríksson's monument]; Made 1794. O. Olavsen [i.e. Ólafur Ólafsson, 1753-1832] inv. & posuit; [Joh. Christoffer] Seehusen sc.; text in Latin by S[kúli] Thorlacius. Print: etching; plate mark 31 x 23.2 cm, on sheet 37.5 x 28.3 cm. "186" on verso, partly cut off. Ref.: Matthías Þórðarson *Íslenzkir listamenn* II (Reykjavík: Prentsm. Gutenberg, 1925), pp. 28 and 33-4.

7.11 ***E[yjólfur] Einarsson***. Pr. sign. Sigurdr Gudmundson del. 1858; I. W. Tegner & Kittendorff[s] lith. Inst. Print: lithograph; image ca. 25 x 21.5 cm, on sheet 48.8 x 34.5 cm. In bottom right corner "M 1014" and on verso "1088." The original in the National Museum of Iceland, No. 4361. Ref.: *Sigurður Guðmundsson málari*. Jón Auðuns edited (Reykjavík: H.f. Leiftur, 1950).

7.12 ***Finn Magnússen*** [i.e. Finnur Magnússon]. Pr. sign. Made by C[hristian] A[lbrecht] Jensen, 1792-1870; Em. Bærentzen & C°. lith. Inst. Print: lithograph; image 22.5 x 17.9 cm, on sheet 34.9 x 26.1 cm; head and shoulders portrait. "450" upper left margin. A second copy with "363 fiske" on upper right margin. A third copy.

7.13 ***Finnur Jónsson [Bishop]*** *16 Januar 1704 - 23 Juli 1789.* Pr. sign. Th. Bergh[s]. lith. Inst. Print: lithograph; image ca. 13 x 12 cm, on sheet 33 x 25.2 cm; head and shoulders portrait.

7.14 [*Guðbrandur Þorláksson, Bishop*]. *Effigies Reverendissimi pietate et Doctrina Clarissimi Patris Domini Gvdbrandi Thorlacii Islandiæ Borealis Episcopi Meritissimi Anno Christi 1618 Ætatis Vero 77*. H. P. Hansen sc. Print: wood engraving; image 9.5 x 7.8 cm, on sheet 35.4 x 27 cm.

7.15 *Guðbrandur Þorláksson byskup, 1623, ætat(is) 83 GT*. Print: wood engraving; image 14.9 x 10.4 cm, on sheet 30.4 x 22.1 cm. Plate from the National Museum of Iceland, No. 446. Ref.: Arngrímur Jónsson, *Crymogæa*. Translated with introduction and notes by Jakob Benediktsson (Reykjavík: Sögufélag, 1985).

7.16 *Gunnar Gunnarsson*. Ernst Hansen, 1892-1968. Del. 1911; Johs. Britze sc. Print: etching, pencil manner; plate mark 15.8 x 10.2 cm, on sheet 27.5 x 21 cm; profile portrait. Edition 2/100.

7.17 *Guttormur Pálsson, Sira*, *Prófastur, Sóknarprestur að Vallanesi*. Printed signature beneath the printed name; E. Fortling lith.; Em. Bærentzen & C°. lith. Inst. Print: lithograph after a daguerreotype; image ca. 16 x 12.7 cm, on sheet 35.6 x 27.5 cm; half-length portrait.

7.18 *Helgi Hálfdánarson, Séra*. *Forstöðumaður prestaskólans í Reykjavík. (F. 19. Ágúst 1826)*. Process print; image 10.9 x 8 cm, on sheet 35.8 x 26.8 cm; head and shoulders portrait.

7.19 *Jóhann Sigurjónsson*. Harald Slott-Møller del. 1918. Johs. Britze sc. Print: etching in pencil manner; plate mark 15.8 x 10.6 cm, on sheet 27.6 x 21.8 cm. Edition 63/100.

7.20 *Jón Guðmundsson*. Identified on verso in pencil. Photoprint: sepia toned; oval image 12.8 x 9.2 cm, on sheet pasted on stiff board 34.9 x 28.9 cm; head and shoulders portrait. On verso: "Bought of Scandinavisk Antiquariat 1910. Kr. 1.-", and "115." Taken in Copenhagen 1848-49 when he was 41 years old. Ref.: Einar Laxness *Jón Guðmundsson alþingismaður og ritstjóri. Þættir úr ævisögu* (Reykjavík: Ísafoldarprentsmiðja, 1960).

7.21 *Jón Sigurðsson* [from Gautlönd]. 2 prints: wood engravings; image ca. 12 x 8 cm, on sheet 23.1 x 14.8 cm.

7.22 *J[ón] Þ[órðarson] Thoroddsen*. Pr. sign. and inscription. Sigurðr Guðmundsson 1853; Em. Bærentzen & C°. lith. Inst.; 11/2 1855. Print:

lithograph; image 7.5 x 6.5 cm, on sheet 18.9 x 12.6 cm. In margin: "2906", and "2751"; head and shoulders portrait. The inscription, "Með vorinu máttu skrifa mig í Haga", is from a letter to Gísli Brynjúlfsson. Ref.: Jón Thóroddsen *Kvæði eptir Jón Thóroddsen sýslumann* (Copenhagen: Hið íslenzka bókmenntafélag, 1871).

7.23 *J[ónas] Hallgrímsson.* Pr. sign. Process print; sheet 23.2 x 18.2 cm; profile portrait.

7.24 *Magnus Eirikssons Monument. Paa Garnisons Kirkegaard.* Efter Tegning af Arkitekt Alf[red] J[ensen] Råvad, 1848-1933. Print: woodcut; taken from a book; image 15.5 x 10.3 cm, mounted on sheet 29.6 x 24.1 cm.

7.25 *Magnús M. Smith.* Identified in pencil. Process print, sheet 18.5 x 13.9 cm; head and shoulders portrait.

7.26 *Matth[ías] Jochumsson.* Process print from *Fylgiblað "Unga Íslands"* nr. 6. Prentsm. Gutenberg — 1916; sheet 35.6 x 26.9 cm.

7.27 *Páll Melsteð.* Process print; sheet 21.8 x 14.5 cm; head and shoulders portrait.

7.28 *Pétur Pétursson, bishop.* Identified in pencil in Halldór Hermannson's hand. Photoprint: sepia toned; oval image 12.5 x 10.2 cm, on sheet 26.5 x 21.1 cm; head and shoulders portrait.

7.29 *R[asmus] Rask*, pr. sign.; *A[rni] Helgason*, pr. sign.; *F[innur] Magnússon*, pr. sign.; *B[jarni] Thorsteinsson*, pr. sign. Em. Bærentzen & C° lith. Inst. Print: lithograph sheet with 4 oval insets; images 5.9 x 4.9 cm, on sheet 27.8 x 22.3 cm. "M33" in lower right margin and "sp. 31" on verso.

7.30 *Sigfús Blöndal.* Sign. in ink. *Interiør fra et privatbibliotek i Hørsholm.* Print of a cut made from a photograph; image 12.3 x 9.3 cm, on sheet 29.3 x 22.8 cm. Sigfús Blöndal sitting at his desk.

7.31 *[The statue of Bertel Thorvaldsen].* Made after 1874. Cf. Matthías Þórðarson *Íslenzkir listamenn* II (Reykjavík: Prentsm. Gutenberg, 1925), p. 16. Print: steel engraving; image 17 x 23.1 cm, on sheet 21.8 x 28 cm. "1061" in pencil bottom right.

7.32 *S[tefán] Thorarensen* [i.e. Þórarinsson]. Print: lithograph; image 7.4 x 5.8 cm, on sheet 22 x 14.1 cm. Lower right corner "Amtmand paa Island" and "SI 2963."

7.33 *S[veinbjörn] Egilsson*. Pr. sign. Em. Bærentzen & Cº. lith. Inst. Print: lithograph; image 7.7 x 7 cm, on sheet 22.6 x 14.1 cm; head and shoulders portrait. "Str. 722" and "M1003a" in pencil at bottom margin, "1078" on verso.

7.34 *Thora Melsted.* Process print; sheet 21.8 x 14.5 cm; head and shoulders portrait.

7.35 *Thormod Torfesen* [i.e. Þormóður Torfason]. Efter et Kobberstik af J[ohan] M[artin] Preisler, 1715-1794; Em. Bærentzen & Cº. lith. Inst. Print: lithograph; oval image in a square frame 13.4 x 12 cm, on sheet 37 x 20.2 cm. "694" in blue pencil upper left margin.

7.36 *Þorkell Eyjúlfsson, prestur á Staðastað.* Process print; oval image 13.2 x 9.2 cm, on sheet 35.2 x 26.2 cm; head and shoulders portrait.

7.37 *Þ[orvaldur] Jónsson, læknir á Ísafirði.* Identified in pencil lower left corner. Process print: sheet 18.5 x 13.9 cm; head and shoulders portrait.

Portraits of Scandinavians.

7.38 *Daa, Ludvig Kristensen.* Pr. sign. R. Hartnack lith.; Hoffensberg Jespersen & Fr. Trap's Etabl.; Udgivet af Chr. Tönsberg. Process print from a lithograph on sheet 27.8 x 18 cm. Accompanied by a printed sheet with biographical account.

7.39 *Keyser, Rudolf.* Pr. sign. R. Hartnack lith.; Hoffensberg Jespersen & Fr. Trap's Etabl.; Udgivet af Chr. Tönsberg. Process print from a lithograph on sheet 26.9 x 17.5 cm. Accompanied by a printed sheet with biographical account.

7.40 *Lange, Christian Christoph Andreas.* Pr. sign. R. Hartnack lith.; Hoffensberg Jespersen & Fr. Trap's Etabl.; Udgivet af Chr. Tönsberg. Process print from a lithograph on sheet 27.7 x 18.1 cm. Accompanied by a printed sheet with biographical account.

7.41 *Peringsköld, Johan. född 1654. död 1720.* Joh. Cardon 1841; Tr. hos Spong & Cardon. Print: lithograph; sheet 44.4 x 31.3 cm.

7.42 ***Rudbeck, Olof d.ä.*** J. S. Samson lith.; Tr. hos Gjöthström & Magnusson. Print: lithograph; sheet 36.5 x 27.3 cm. A note on him in pencil at bottom of sheet.

7.43 ***Suhm, P[eter] F[rederik]***, 1728-98. G[erhard] L[udvig] Lahde, 1765-1833, ad Vivum del. & sc. 1795. Print: etching; plate mark 14.1 x 9.4 cm, pasted on marine col. paper; oval image; profile portrait. Upper left margin: "Lab. No. 40", bottom right: "Str. 2836 b."

Group photographs.

7.44 [***A class reunion, 30 June 1948***]. Photoprint; 11.1 x 22.7 cm. Upper row from left, Ólafur Jónsson, Matthías Þórðarson, Matthías Einarsson, Jón Hj. Sigurðsson. Second row from left, Ari Arnalds, Þorkell Þorkelsson, Bjarni Jónsson. On verso: "Beztu kveðjur", "30.VI.1948", and "29139." Furthermore, on verso: the subjects' autographs, excluding Ari Arnalds'.

7.45 ***Icelandic students in Copenhagen, in the spring of 1899.*** In ink in Halldór Hermannsson's hand on verso. Identified on a sheet pasted on back of picture: Sigurður Jónsson; Gísli Skúlason; Sigfús Einarsson; Ásgeir Torfason; Eggert Claessen; Magnús Jónsson; Halldór Hermannsson; Björn Bjarnason; Ari Jónsson; Karl Nikulásson; Gunnar Hafstein; Sveinn Hallgrímsson; Matthías Þórðarson; Steingrímur Matthíasson; Þorkell Þorkelsson; Jón Hj. Sigurðsson; Matthías Einarsson; Tómas Skúlason; Jón Þorláksson; Halldór Gunnlaugsson; Bjarni Jónsson; Halldór Steinsson; Haraldur Þórarinsson; Georg Georgsson; Árni Þorvaldsson; Sigfús Blöndal; Sigurður Eggerz; Einar Jónasson; Ólafur Dan Daníelsson; Bjarni Þorl. Johnson; Eðvald Möller; Ágúst Bjarnason. Photoprint; image 24.5 x 29 cm, on mount 35 x 46.8 cm. Made by Fred. Riise, Copenhagen.

7.46 ***Lærisveinar hins lærða skóla í Reykjavík vorið 1873.*** Photoprint: sepia toned; 6 insets 8.5 x 8.5 and 8.4 x 9.5 cm, on mount 24.5 x 32.5 cm. 6 different classes of the Junior College in Reykjavík in the year 1873.

7.47 ***Stúdentar frá 1881.*** In pencil in Halldór Hermannsson's hand. Photoprint: sepia toned; image (arched at top) 8.8 x 8.1 cm, on stiff mount 12 x 10.5 cm.

6. Box 8

Collection of Portrait Photographs

Portrait photographs (mostly of Icelanders) by various identified and unidentified photographers, including Sigfús Eymundsson, P. Brynjúlfsson, Ólafur Magnússon, and Árni Thorsteinsson. The photographs are from the collections of D. W. Fiske and Halldór Hermannsson. Arranged alphabetically by subject.

8.1 ***Bjarni Jónsson?*** Sigfús Eymundsson, Reykjavík. Photoprint: carte-de-visite; 10.5 x 6.3 cm; head and shoulders portrait. As a young man.

8.2 ***Bjarni Jónsson?, Halldór Hermannsson, and Tómas Skúlason.*** Sigfús Eymundsson, Reykjavík. Photoprint: carte-de-visite; 10.5 x 6.3 cm; full-length portrait. As young men.

8.3 ***Bjarni Jónsson*** *(from Unnarholt, bank manager in Akureyri).* Identified in pencil on verso. Chr. Neuhaus Eftfh: Oluf W. Jörgensen, Copenhagen. Photoprint: carte-de-visite; 10.5 x 6.4 cm; head and shoulders portrait. Plate No. 72818.

8.4 ***Bjarni Thorarensen.*** Identified in pencil on verso. Joh. Crone, Copenhagen. Photoprint: cabinet; 16.3 x 10.5 cm; head and shoulders portrait. A note on a separate sheet by Bogi Th. Melsteð: "Mynd þessi af Bjarna Thorarensen er tekin eptir myndinni í ferðabók Gaimard's, eptir henni er einnig myndin framan við Kvæðin (Kmhöfn 1884) tekin, og sjest best við samanburð hvílík ómynd sú mynd er" [i.e. taken from a lithograph from Gaimard's book]. Another copy of same picture, but different mount; unmarked. Photoprint on cabinet card; 16.5 x 10.7 cm.

8.5 ***Björn M. Ólsen.*** 1900. Date written on the photograph. Atelier Populær, Copenhagen. Photoprint: cabinet; 16.5 x 10.7 cm; head and shoulders portrait.

8.6 ***Bogi Th. Melsteð.*** 21/3 1900. Inscription: "Til prófessors Willard Fiske með þakklæti Bogi Th. Melsteð." Christensen & Morange, Copenhagen. Photoprint: cabinet; 16.6 x 10.6 cm; head and shoulders portrait.

8.7 _____, O. Gjørup & Co., Copenhagen. Photoprint: cabinet card; 16.5 x 10.5 cm; head and shoulders portrait.

8.8   ____, Emil Clausen, Copenhagen. Photoprint: carte-de-visite; 14 x 7.5 cm; head and shoulders portrait.

8.9   ____, Even Neuhaus, Copenhagen. Photoprint: carte-de-visite; 10.5 x 6.4 cm; head and shoulders portrait. Plate No. 13295.

8.10 *Einar Benediktsson.* Identified in ink on photograph. Sigfús Eymundarson [sic!], Reykjavík. Photoprint: carte-de-visite; 10 x 6.2 cm; head and shoulders portrait.

8.11 *Einar M. Jónasson, Sheriff.* Identified in pencil on verso. Johnny Johansen, Copenhagen. Photoprint: carte-de-visite; 9.7 x 6 cm; head and shoulders portrait.

8.12 *Guðbjörg Hermannsdóttir Thorstensen (the wife of the Rev. Jón Thorstensen at Þingvellir).* Identified in pencil on verso. Pétur Brynjulfsson, Reykjavík. Photoprint: carte-de-visite; 10.3 x 6.3 cm; head and shoulders portrait.

8.13 *Guðrún Hermannsdóttir (the wife of the Rev. Eggert Pálsson at Breiðabólsstaður, to the right).* Identified in pencil on verso. Gudm. J. Olafsson, Reykjavík. Photoprint: carte-de-visite; 10.4 x 6.3 cm; full-length portrait. Another woman to the left unidentified.

8.14 *Hermann Thorstensen* (the son of the Rev. Jón Thorstensen). Identified in ink on verso. S. Eymundsson, Reykjavík. Photoprint: carte-de-visite; 10.3 x 6.3 cm; full-length portrait. A child.

8.15 *Hermanníus Johnson (Sheriff at Vellir).* Identified in pencil on verso. Photoprint: carte-de-visite; 10.5 x 6.3 cm. "Gleðileg jól" printed beneath the photo. Halldór Hermannsson's father, sitting by a desk.

8.16 *Hilmar Finsen (Governor of Iceland).* 14/10 [18]79. Identified in ink on verso. Georg E. Hansen, Copenhagen. Photoprint: cabinet; 12.6 x 8 cm; half-length portrait.

8.17 *Inga and Ásta Thorarensen.* Identified in pencil on verso. Pétur Brynjólfsson, Reykjavík. Photoprint: carte-de-visite; 6.2 x 10.4 cm; half-length portraits. Halldór Hermannsson's nieces.

8.18 *Ingunn Halldórsdóttir.* Identified in pencil on verso. Photoprint: carte-de-visite; 10.5 x 6.3 cm; head and shoulders portrait, oval image.

"Gleðileg jól" printed beneath the image. Halldór Hermannsson's mother.

8.19 _____, sitting, and her daughter, **Kristín Hermannsdóttir** *(from Reynivellir in Kjós),* standing to the left. Identified in pencil on verso. Sigfús Eymundsson, Reykjavík. Photoprint: carte-de-visite; 10.4 x 6.3 cm; full-length portrait.

8.20 **Jón Hermannsson.** Identified in pencil on verso. Gunhild Thorsteinsson & Co., Reykjavík. Photoprint: carte-de-visite; 10.4 x 6.4 cm; half-length portrait. Halldór Hermannsson's brother.

8.21 _____, [*to the left, and*]**Halldór Hermannsson.** Dec 1899. Identified in pencil on verso. Peter L. Petersen, Copenhagen. Photoprint: carte-de-visite; 10.5 x 6.3 cm; head and shoulders portrait.

8.22 **Jón Þorkelsson, Dr.** *(with his wife and their son).* July 1900. Identified in ink on verso. Sigfús Eymundsson, Reykjavík. Photoprint: cabinet; 16.1 x 10.6 cm; full-length portrait.

8.23 **Kristín Eyjólfsdóttir** *(from Reynivellir).* Identified in pencil on verso. Ólafur Magnússon, Reykjavík. Photoprint: carte-de-visite; 10.3 x 6.4 cm; head and shoulders portrait. Plate No. 16777.

8.24 **Kristín Hermannsdóttir** *(the wife of the Rev. Halldór Jónsson at Reynivellir).* Identified on verso. Árni Thorsteinsson, Reykjavík. Photoprint: carte-de-visite; 10.3 x 6.3 cm; head and shoulders portrait. Halldór Hermannsson's sister.

8.25 _____, *and the younger Kristín.* Identified in pencil on verso. Pétur Brynjólfsson, Reykjavík. Photoprint: carte-de-visite; 10.6 x 6.4 cm; full-length portrait.

8.26 **Matthías Jochumsson.** Inscription on photo: "Prof. W. Fiske from M. Jochumsson" [18..] Hallgrímur Einarsson, Seyðisfirði. Photoprint: carte-de-visite; 10.2 x 6.2 cm; head and shoulders portrait.

8.27 **Matthías Þórðarson.** Spring 1909. Identified in ink on verso. Pétur Brynjólfsson, Reykjavík. Photoprint: carte-de-visite; 10.3 x 6.3 cm; half-length profile portrait.

8.28 _____ 1909. Identified in ink on verso. Pétur Brynjólfsson, Reykjavík. Photoprint: carte-de-visite; 10.3 x 6.3 cm; half-length portrait.

8.29 **Maurer, Konrad.** Identified in pencil on verso. Friedrich Müller, München. Photoprint: carte-de-visite; 10.3 x 6.4 cm; half-length portrait.

8.30 ____ Identified in pencil on verso. F[riedrich] Müller, München. Photoprint: carte-de-visite; 10.3 x 6.3 cm; half-length portrait.

8.31 **Oddur Hermannsson.** Identified in pencil on verso. Árni Thorsteinsson, Reykjavík. Photoprint: carte-de-visite; 10.5 x 6.3 cm; head and shoulders portrait. Plate No. 5832. [Halldór Hermannsson's brother].

8.32 ____, 1906. Inscription on separate slip of paper: "Höfn 23./6. '06. Frater Kær! Hjer hefur þú mynd af meistara Oddi í Kaupinhafnarútgáfu. þinn O. H." Albert Schou junr., Copenhagen. Photoprint: carte-de-visite; 10.3 x 6.3 cm; half-length portrait.

8.33 **Oddur Hjaltalín** *(head physician).* S. Eymundson, Reykjavík. Photoprint taken from an engraving: carte-de-visite; 10.5 x 6.3 cm; head and shoulder portrait.

8.34 **Pétur Guðjónsson.** Identified in ink on verso. Inscription on back: "Til vinar míns W. Fiske. P. Guðjónsson 23 ára gamall." A. P. Weishaupt, Copenhagen. Photoprint: cabinet; 16.7 x 10.8 cm; full-length portrait.

8.35 **Poestion, J. C.** 1898. Inscription on back of card: "Hern Professor W. Fiske in Verehrung J. C. Poestion, Wien, 17.VI.99." Photographie Olga, Wien. Photoprint: cabinet; 16.3 x 10.8 cm; half-length portrait.

8.36 **Richard Beck.** Photoprint on a postcard: sepia toned; 13.5 x 8.4 cm. A thank you note from Beck on verso. A graduation photograph of Richard Beck.

8.37 **Sigfús Blöndal.** Identified in pencil on verso, also "Meðtekið 4/6 1911." Oluf Borup, Copenhagen. Photoprint: carte-de-visite; 10.4 x 6.4 cm; half-length portrait.

8.38 ____ Inscription in ink on back of card: "Með kærri kveðju frá S.B., 29/1 1915." Oluf Borup, Copenhagen. Photoprint: carte-de-visite; 10.6 x 6.6 cm; half-length portrait.

8.39 ____, *and Björg Þorláksdóttir Blöndal.* Identified in ink on verso. Photoprint: carte-de-visite; 10.5 x 6.3 cm; half-length portrait.

8.40 ***Sighvatur Grímsson Borgfirðingur.*** 1912. Inscription on back of card: "Sighv. Gr. Borgfirðingur. mindin er tekin 6. Apríl, 1912." Pétur Brynjólfsson, Reykjavík. Photoprint: cabinet; 16.6 x 10.5 cm; half-length portrait. Plate No. 20624.

8.41 ***Steingrímur Matthíasson.*** Before 1933. Hallgrímur Einarsson, Akureyri. Photoprint on a postcard; 13.8 x 8.8 cm. A note to Halldór Hermannsson on verso, dated Akureyri 29/1 1933.

8.42 ***[Unidentified child].*** Sigfús Eymundsson, Reykjavík. Photoprint: carte-de-visite; 10.3 x 6.4 cm; full-length portrait.

8.43 ***[Unidentified young woman].*** Sigfús Eymundsson, Reykjavík. Photoprint: carte-de-visite; 10.5 x 6.3 cm; half-length portrait.

8.44 ***[Unidentified young woman].*** Föjer Eslöf? Photoprint: carte-de-visite; 7.9 x 4.9 cm; half-length portrait.

8.45 ***[Unidentified elderly man with a stick].*** Photoprint on cabinet card: sepia toned; 16.6 x 10.7 cm; full-length portrait.

8.46 ***[Unidentified elderly man].*** 1921. Elfelt kgl. dansk Hoffotograf, Copenhagen. 2 photoprints on carte-de-visite mounts: sepia toned; 10.5 x 6.4 cm; half-length portrait.

8.47 ***[Unidentified elderly man].*** Guðjón August Gudmundsson, Reykjavík. Photoprint: sepia toned; oval image on carte-de-visite; 10.4 x 6.3 cm; head and shoulders portrait.

8.48 ***Þóra*** *(the wife of Oddur Hermannsson).* Identified in pencil on verso. Pétur Brynjólfsson, Reykjavík. Photoprint: carte-de-visite; 10.5 x 6.3 cm; head and shoulders portrait.

8.49 ***Þorsteinn Björnsson*** *(úr Bæ).* Identified in pencil on verso. Sigfús Eymundsson, Reykjavík. Photoprint: carte-de-visite; 10.5 x 6.3 cm; full-length portrait. As a young man.

8.50 ____ Identified in pencil on verso. Sigfús Eymundsson, Reykjavík. Photoprint: carte-de-visite; 10.5 x 6.3 cm; same occasion, sitting.

8.51 ***Þorvaldur Jónsson.*** Sign. 1899. Written on back in pencil "Icelandic Chess-player and District Physician." Björn Pálsson, Ísafjörður.

Photoprint: cabinet; 16.7 x 10.7 cm; head and shoulders portrait. Plate No. 2882.

8.52 **Þorvaldur Thoroddsen.** 1887. Inscription on back of card: "Til herra próf. W. Fiske með virðingu og vinsemd frá Þorvaldi Thoroddsen. 9/6 87." Sigfús Eymundsson, Reykjavík. Photoprint: cabinet; 16.6 x 10.7 cm; half-length portrait.

8.53 ____, *with his wife and daughter.* Identified in ink on verso. Søstrene Schiøtz, Copenhagen. Photoprint: cabinet; 16.5 x 10.6 cm; full-length portrait.

7. Box 9

Collection of Portrait Photographs: Album 1

39 portrait photographs collected by Willard Fiske, compiled in a brown leather covered album, embossed in metal, with a metal clasp; foredges gilded; ca. 15 x 12 cm. The photographs are matted in such a way that it is impossible to identify the photographers and the exact sizes of the prints, exposed area is ca. 8 x 5 cm.

[1] *Jón Þorkelsson, rektor.* Photoprint on carte-de-visite: sepia toned; oval image; head and shoulders portrait.

[2] *Eiríkr Magnússon, M.A.* Photoprint on carte-de-visite: sepia toned; full-length portrait.

[3] *Matthías Jochumsson.* Photoprint on carte-de-visite: sepia toned; oval image; head and shoulders portrait. As a young man.

[4] *Steingrímur Thorsteinsson.* Photoprint on carte-de-visite: sepia toned; full-length portrait. Sitting with a child in his lap.

[5] *Árni Thorsteinsson.* Photoprint on carte-de-visite: sepia toned; half-length portrait.

[6] *Jón Egilsen.* Photoprint on carte-de-visite: sepia toned; oval image; half-length portrait.

[7] *Bogi Th. Melsteð.* Photoprint on carte-de-visite: sepia toned; full-length portrait. Sitting in a chair; as a young man.

[8] *Geir Zoëga.* Photoprint on carte-de-visite: sepia toned; oval image; head and shoulders portrait.

[9] *Þorvaldur Björnsson.* Photoprint on carte-de-visite: sepia toned; oval image; head and shoulders portrait.

[10] *Benedikt Sveinsson.* Photoprint on carte-de-visite: sepia toned; oval image; head and shoulders portrait.

[11] *Eiríkur Bjarnason.* Photoprint on carte-de-visite: sepia toned; full-length portrait. As a boy.

[12] *Björn M. Ólsen.* Photoprint on carte-de-visite: sepia toned; head and shoulders portrait. As a young man.

[13] *Margrét Magnúsdóttir (Ólsen).* Photoprint on carte-de-visite: sepia toned; full-length portrait. Sitting in a chair.

[14] [*Unidentified young woman*]. Photoprint on carte-de-visite: sepia toned; half-length portrait.

[15] [*Unidentified young man*]. Photoprint on carte-de-visite: sepia toned; oval image; half-length portrait.

[16] *Eggert Laxdal.* Photoprint on carte-de-visite: sepia toned; oval image; half-length portrait.

[17] *Rannveig Laxdal.* Photoprint on carte-de-visite: sepia toned; oval image; half-length portrait.

[18] *Bernharð Laxdal.* Photoprint on carte-de-visite: sepia toned; full-length portrait. A child.

[19] *Jóhannes D. Ólafsson.* Photoprint on carte-de-visite: sepia toned; oval image; half-length portrait.

[20] *Þorlákur O. Johnson.* Photoprint on carte-de-visite: sepia toned; full-length portrait.

[21] *Guðrún Ólafsdóttir.* Photoprint on carte-de-visite: sepia toned; oval image; head and shoulders portrait.

[22] [*Unidentified girl*]. Photoprint on carte-de-visite: sepia toned; full-length portrait.

[23] [*Unidentified woman*]. Photoprint on carte-de-visite: sepia toned; full-length portrait.

[24] [*Unidentified woman*]. Photoprint on carte-de-visite: sepia toned; full-length portrait.

[25] [*Unidentified woman*]. Photoprint on carte-de-visite: sepia toned; half-length portrait.

[26] [*Unidentified woman*]. Photoprint on carte-de-visite: sepia toned; full-length portrait.

[27] [*Unidentified woman*]. Photoprint on carte-de-visite: sepia toned; half-length portrait.

[28] [*Unidentified woman*]. Photoprint on carte-de-visite: sepia toned; oval image; half-length portrait.

[29] *Þorsteinn Daníelsson.* Photoprint on carte-de-visite: sepia toned; full-length portrait. Sitting in a chair.

[30] *Eiríkur Kúld.* Photoprint on carte-de-visite: sepia toned; oval image; half-length portrait.

[31] *Brynjólfur Kúld.* Photoprint on carte-de-visite: sepia toned; half-length portrait. A young man.

[32] *Jón Ólafsson.* Photoprint on carte-de-visite: sepia toned; half-length portrait.

[33] *Árni Riis.* Photoprint on carte-de-visite: sepia toned; half-length portrait.

[34] *Mrs. Friðbjörn Steinsson.* Photoprint on carte-de-visite: sepia toned; half-length portrait.

[35] *Friðbjörn Steinsson.* Photoprint on carte-de-visite: sepia toned; half-length portrait.

[36] *[Unidentified young boy sitting in a chair].* Photoprint on carte-de-visite: sepia toned; full-length portrait.

[37] *[Unidentified young man].* Photoprint on carte-de-visite: sepia toned; half-length portrait.

[38] *Konrad Maurer.* Photoprint on carte-de-visite: sepia toned; half-length portrait.

[39] blank.

[40] *[Unidentified young woman].* Photoprint on carte-de-visite: sepia toned; oval image; half-length portrait.

8. Box 10

Collection of Portrait Photographs: Album 2

A mixed carte-de-visite and cabinet album dressed in purple velvet, with metal clasp, heavily embossed in metal, including 2 silver plates on front cover with inscription. Upper plate: "Prófessor W. Fiske", lower plate: "Frá lestrarfélaginu Íþöku í Reykjavík." Ca. 30 x 23 cm. The album was compiled by students at the Junior College in Reykjavík and presented to Fiske. See letters to Daniel Willard Fiske from Björn M. Ólsen, 31 May 1885 and 27 June 1885. The photographs were matted in such a way that it is impossible to identify the photographers and exact sizes. Many of the sheets carry four photographs each, with exposed images ca. 8.5 x 5 cm, here counted from upper left. Head and shoulders portraits unless otherwise identified.

[1] *Rektor Jón Þorkelsson dr. R. af Dbr.* Photoprint on cabined card: sepia toned; exposed image 13.5 x 9.5 cm.

[2] *5. bekkr 1883-84.* Photoprint on cabined card: sepia toned; exposed image (lengthwise) 9.5 x 13.5 cm. A class picture.

[3]   *3. bekkr 1883-84.* Photoprint on cabinet card: sepia toned; exposed image (lengthwise) 9.5 x 13.5 cm. A class picture.

[4]   *Brúará.* Photoprint: sepia toned; exposed image (lengthwise); 9.5 x 13.5 cm. Crossing the river on horses.

[5]   *Halldór Kr. Friðriksson R. af Dbr., Halldór Guðmundsson, Steingrímur Thorsteinsson, and Páll Melsteð.* 4 carte-de-visite photoprints: sepia toned; oval images, except for the first one.

[6]   *Dr. Björn M. Ólsen, Sigurðr Sigurðarson, Björn Jensson, and Geir Zoëga.* 4 carte-de-visite photoprints: sepia toned; the first two oval images. Sigurðr Sigurðarson's autograph, partly hidden by mat.

[7]   *Ólafr Davíðsson, Guðmundr Magnússon, Oddr Jónsson, and Klemens Jónsson.* 4 carte-de-visite photoprints: sepia toned; oval images.

[8]   *Sigurðr Hjörleifsson, blank, Pálmi Þóroddsson, and Gísli Brynjúlfsson.* 3 carte-de-visite photoprints: sepia toned; oval images. Pálmi Þóroddsson's autograph, partly hidden by mat.

[9]   *Unidentified, Unidentified, Þorsteinn Erlingsson, and Sigurðr Jónasson.* 4 carte-de-visite photoprints: sepia toned; oval images; the second and third are half-length and full-length portraits. Sigurðr Jónasson's autograph, but hidden by mat.

[10] *Björn Ólafsson, Skúli Skúlason, Jón Finnsson, and Arnór Árnason.* 4 carte-de-visite photoprints: sepia toned; oval images. The first is a half-length portrait. Skúli Skúlason's autograph, but hidden by mat.

[11] *Bjarni Pálsson, Ólafur Magnússon, Lárus Árnason, and unidentified.* 4 carte-de-visite photoprints: sepia toned; oval images; the fourth is a full-length portrait. Ólafur Magnússon's autograph.

[12] *Bjarni Thorsteinsson and Guðmundr Scheving, Sveinbjörn Egilsson, Magnús Ásgeirsson, and Halldór Torfason.* 4 carte-de-visite photoprints: sepia toned; oval images. The first is a full-length portrait. Sveinbjörn Egilsson's and Magnús Ásgeirsson's autographs, partly hidden.

[13] *Reykjavík.* Photoprint on cabinet card: sepia toned; exposed image 9.5 x 13.5 cm.

[14] *1. bekkr 1883-84.* Photoprint on cabinet card: sepia toned; exposed image 9.5 x 13.5 cm. A class picture.

[15] *Akreyri.* Photoprint: sepia toned; exposed image 9.5 x 13.5 cm.

[16] *Hvítá í Borgarfirði.* Photoprint: sepia toned; exposed image 9.5 x 13 cm.

[17] *Ólafr M. Stephensen.* Photoprint on carte-de-visite: sepia toned; oval image. The other three spaces are blank.

[18] *Jón Steingrímsson, Ólafr Pálsson, Jón Arason, Andrés Gíslason.* 4 carte-de-visite photoprints: sepia toned; oval images; the second is a full-length portrait. Jón Steingrímsson's, Jón Arason's, and Andrés Gíslason's autographs, partly hidden by mat.

[19] *Ólafr Petersen, Magnús Magnússon, and Ríkarðr Torfason.* The first
     space is empty. 3 carte-de-visite photoprints: sepia toned; oval images.
[20] *Hálfdan Guðjónsson, Kristján Jónsson, Einar Friðgeirsson, and Björn
     G. Blöndal.* 4 carte-de-visite photoprints: sepia toned; oval images.
     Einar Friðgeirsson's autograph, partly hidden.
[21] *Árni Bjarnarson, Georg Pétr Hjaltesteð, Lárus Bjarnason, and Þórðr
     G. Ólafsson.* 4 carte-de-visite photoprints: sepia toned; oval images.
     Lárus Bjarnason's and Þórðr G. Ólafsson's autographs, partly hidden.
[22] *Gísli Einarsson, Sigurðr Jónsson, Guðlögr Guðmundsson, and Bjarni
     Einarsson.* 4 carte-de-visite photoprints: sepia toned; oval images, ex-
     cept the fourth. Gísli Einarsson's and Guðlögr Guðmundsson's auto-
     graphs, partly hidden by mats.
[23] *Magnús Bjarnarson, Magnús Bl. Jónsson, unidentified, and Guðmundr
     Helgason.* 4 carte-de-visite photoprints: sepia toned; oval images, ex-
     cept the second and the fourth.
[24] *Hannes Þorsteinsson, Stefán Stefánsson, Jóhannes Jóhannesson, and
     Kjartan Helgason.* 4 carte-de-visite photoprints: sepia toned; oval im-
     ages; the third is a full-length portrait. Hannes Þorsteinsson's, Stefán
     Stefánsson's, and Kjartan Helgason's autographs, partly hidden by
     mats.
[25] *Almannagjá.* Photoprint on cabinet card: sepia toned; visible image
     (lengthwise) 9.5 x 13.2 cm.
[26] *Austrvöllr (Reykjavík).* Photoprint on cabinet card: sepia toned; visible
     image (lengthwise) 9.5 x 13.2 cm.
[27] *Kirkjubrú (Reykjavík).* Photoprint on cabinet card: sepia toned; visible
     image (lengthwise) 9.5 x 13.2 cm.
[28] *Þingvallabær.* Photoprint on cabinet card: sepia toned; visible image
     (lengthwise) 9.5 x 13.3 cm.
[29] *Ólafr Finnsson, Árni Jóhannesson, Jósep Hjörleifsson, and Jóhannes
     Lynge.* 4 carte-de-visite photoprints: sepia toned; oval images, except
     the second photograph. Ólafr Finnsson's and Jóhannes Lynge's auto-
     graphs, partly hidden by mat.
[30] *Sigfús Jónsson, Páll Einarsson, Jón Guðmundsson, and Jón Helgason.*
     4 carte-de-visite photoprints: sepia toned; oval images, except for the
     second photo, which also is full-length portrait. Jón Helgason's auto-
     graph, hidden by mat.
[31] *Eggert Pálsson, Þorvaldr Jónsson, Jón Pálsson, and Mads A. V.
     Jacobsen.* 4 carte-de-visite photoprints: sepia toned; oval images. Þor-
     valdr Jónsson's autograph, hidden by mat.
[32] *Hallgrímr Thorlacius, Theodór Jónsson, and Benedikt Eyjúlfsson.* The
     fourth space is empty. 3 carte-de-visite photoprints: sepia toned; oval
     images. Theodór Jónsson's autograph, hidden by mat.

[33] *Guðmundr Bjarnarson and Jóhannes Daníelsson.* Three and four blank. 2 carte-de-visite photoprints: sepia toned; the first oval image.

[34] *Eggert Briem, Guðmundr Hannesson, and Magnús Jónsson.* The third space is empty. 3 carte-de-visite photoprints: sepia toned; the first is oval imaged, the second full-length, and the third half-length portrait.

[35] *Halldór Bjarnason, Þórðr Guðjohnsen, Þórðr Þórðarson, and Geir Sæmundsson.* 4 carte-de-visite photoprints: sepia toned; oval images.

[36] *Ólafr Thorberg, Einar Stefánsson, Ólafr Sæmundsson, and Jón Árnason.* 4 carte-de-visite photoprints: sepia toned; the first and third oval images.

[37] *Strokkr.* Photoprint on cabinet card: sepia toned; exposed image (lengthwise) 9.5 x 13 cm. A geyser.

[38] *Stykkishólmr.* Photoprint on cabinet card: sepia toned; exposed image (lengthwise) 9.5 x 13.3 cm. Village.

[39] *Hruni.* Photoprint on cabinet card: sepia toned; exposed image (lengthwise) 9.5 x 13.4 cm. Farmhouse and church.

[40] *Við Vestmannaeyjar.* Photoprint on cabinet card: sepia toned; exposed image (lengthwise) 9.4 x 13.3 cm.

[41] *Jóhann Pétrsson, Einar Thorlacius, Ólafr Helgason, and Fritz Zeuthen.* 4 carte-de-visite photoprints: sepia toned; the first two oval images; third and fourth full-length portraits.

[42] *Vilhelm Knudsen, Sigurðr Magnússon, Björgvin Vigfússon, and Einar Þórðarson.* 4 carte-de-visite photoprints: sepia toned; the second one oval image; the first and third full-length portraits. Sigurðr Magnússon's autograph, partly hidden by mat.

[43] *Guðmundr Jónsson, Jón Þorvaldsson, Þorsteinn Skúlason, and Hallbjörn Oddsson.* 4 carte-de-visite photoprints: sepia toned; third and fourth oval images, the first two full-length portraits. Þorsteinn Skúlason's autograph, partly hidden by mat.

[44] *Eyjúlfr Eyjúlfsson, Kjartan Jónasson, Ólafr Finsen, and Ludvig Knudsen.* 4 carte-de-visite photoprints: sepia toned; first two oval images, the other two full-length portraits.

[45] *Halldór Árnason, Bjarni Hjalltesteð, Jón Jónsson, and Runúlfr M. Jónsson.* 4 carte-de-visite photoprints: sepia toned; first and third oval images. Halldór Árnason's autograph, partly hidden by mat.

[46] *Bjarni Jónsson, Gísli Ísleifsson, G. Emil Guðmundsson, and Þorvarðr Brynjúlfsson.* 4 carte-de-visite photoprints: sepia toned; the first oval image.

[47] *Bjarni Sæmundsson.* Three empty spaces. Photoprint on carte-de-visite: sepia toned; full-length portrait.

[48] *Kristján Jónasson and Friðrik Hallgrímsson.* Two empty spaces. 2 carte-de-visite photoprints: sepia toned; full-length and half-length portraits.

9. Box 11

Daniel Willard Fiske and Jennie McGraw

11.1 [*Three men, Fiske in the middle*]. Reproduced from a group photograph of "Players at the first American Chess Congress, 1857" printed (By Courtesy of the Manhattan Chess Club, New York) in *Chess Tales & Chess Miscellanies* by Willard Fiske (London: Longmans, Green, and Co, 1912), p. 314. Photoprint; image 12.7 x 18 cm, mounted on cardboard (left corners broken off) 24.9 x 27.3 cm.

11.2 [*Fiske, Reeves, Matthías Jochumsson, and Carpenter in a group photograph taken in Iceland in the summer 1879*]. Photoprint; image 15.5 x 12.2 cm, mounted on grey cardboard 28 x 20.1 cm. Another copy loose.

11.3 [*Fiske*]. [1893]. Schemboche, Florence. Photoprint: sepia toned; image ca. 9 x 7 cm, on sheet 22.9 x 16.4 cm; head and shoulders portrait. Verso in pencil "(Use my autographed one)", and "21a"; beneath the picture: "return to Fiske Icelandic Collection. c. 1890." Ref.: *Willard Fiske Life and Correspondence. A Biographical Study* by Horatio S. White (London: Oxford University Press, 1925).

11.4 [*Fiske, in a robe with a beret late in life*]. G. Lékégian & Co., Cairo (Egypt). 2 photoprints on cabinet cards: sepia toned; 16 x 10.7 cm; half-length portraits.

11.5 [*Fiske*]. April 1904. Giacomo Brogi, Florence. 6 photoprints on cabinet cards; 16.4 x 10.5 cm; half-length portraits. Enclosed: a top of a cardboard box from the photographer: "Photos of W. F. April 1904", with list of names of recipients of the photograph in pencil.

11.6 [*Fiske's library at Villa Landor*]. Photoprint on cabinet card: sepia toned; 10.9 x 16.6 cm.

11.7 [*McGraw, Jennie*]. Frear, Ithaca, N.Y. 2 photoprints on carte-de-visite: sepia toned; 10.3 x 6.2 cm; head and shoulders portrait.

11.8 ____, Photoprint: sepia toned; on card 20.9 x 10.1 cm; profile portrait.

10. Box 12

Halldór Hermannsson,
Collection of Portraits and Snapshots

Studio portraits of Halldór Hermannsson. Arranged in chronological order as possible.

12.1   [*Halldór Hermannsson*]. Taken by Sigfús Eymundsson, Reykjavík. Photoprint on carte-de-visite: sepia toned; 10.5 x 6.3 cm; head and shoulders portrait. As a young man in Reykjavík.

12.2   _____, 1902. Taken by Emil Clausen, Copenhagen. Photoprint on carte-de-visite; 11 x 5 cm; full-length portrait. Dated in ink on verso.

12.3   _____ Taken by Elfelt, Copenhagen. Photoprint on cabinet card; 16.6 x 10.8 cm; head and shoulders portrait. Printed in P. M. Mitchell, *Halldór Hermannsson*. Islandica XLI (Ithaca: Cornell University Press, 1978), p. 24.

12.4   [*Halldór Hermannsson and Oddur Hermannsson*]. Sept. 1910. Albert Schou jun., Copenhagen. Photoprint on cabinet card; 16.5 x 10.5 cm; full-length portrait.

12.5   [*Halldór Hermannsson*]. Nov. 1914. Albert Schou jun., Copenhagen. 3 photoprints on cabinet cards: sepia toned; 16.6 x 10.4 cm; head and shoulders portrait. A fourth photograph, same occasion, but profile portrait.

12.6   _____ Made by Robinson, Ithaca, New York. 2 photoprints (different poses): sepia toned; 13.8 x 8.6 cm, mounted on sheet 30.6 x 20.8 cm; head and shoulders portraits.

12.7   _____ White Studio, New York. 2 photoprints: sepia toned; image 15.2 x 9.5 cm, printed on sheet 25.1 x 14.6 cm; head and shoulders portrait.

12.8   _____ Elfelt, Copenhagen. Photoprint: sepia toned; 14.2 x 10 cm, mounted on sheet 27 x 19.4 cm; profile head and shoulders portrait. Another half-length portrait 14.4 x 10.3 cm, on same kind of sheet.

12.9   _____ Albert Schou jun, Copenhagen. Photoprint; 15.1 x 10.5 cm, on mount 24.7 x 17.5 cm; half-length portrait. Another profile portrait.

12.10 ____ [1936] Trevor Teele, Ithaca, New York. 2 photoprints; 16.4 x 11.4 cm, framed by mat 27.8 x 19.3 cm; head and shoulders portrait. Printed in P. M. Mitchell, *Halldór Hermannsson*. Islandica XLI (Ithaca: Cornell University Press, 1978), p. 100.

12.11 ____ The Robinson studio, Ithaca, New York. 5 photoprints; 16. x 10.8 cm, on mat 23.9 x 15.5 cm; head and shoulders portraits.

Photographs of Halldór Hermannsson, including group photographs.

12.12 [*Halldór Hermannsson in the Icelandic Collection*]. Around 1930. Photoprint on glossy paper; 25.5 x 20.1 cm.

12.13 [*Halldór Hermannsson*]. 10 July 1926. By Bain News Service, New York. Photoprint on glossy paper; 25.8 x 20.3 cm. A photograph of Halldór Hermannsson in New York.

12.14 ____ 10 July 1926. By Bain News Service, New York. Photoprint on glossy paper; 25.8 x 20.3 cm. Holding a cigarette in one hand and his hat in the other.

12.15 [*Halldór Hermannsson crossing City Hall Square, Copenhagen*]. 11 August 1928. 3 photoprints in a row; images 5.6 x 7.4 cm, taped on stiff paper 27.8 x 12.2 cm. Printed in P.M. Mitchell, *Halldór Hermannsson*. Islandica XLI (Ithaca: Cornell University Press, 1978), p. 79.

12.16 [*Halldór Hermannsson*]. Photoprint on glossy paper; 17.3 x 13.3 cm; half-length portrait. Photograph of a painting made by Halldór Pétursson in 1943. The picture is taken of the painting in the National Library of Iceland by the photograph department.

12.17 ____ Taken by P. M. Mitchell in 1946. Photoprint; 25.3 x 18.7 cm. Printed as a frontispiece in P. M. Mitchell, *Halldór Hermannsson*. Islandica XLI (Ithaca: Cornell University Press, 1978).

12.18 [*Halldór Hermannsson in the Icelandic Collection*]. Around 1930. Photoprint; 25.2 x 20.1 cm.

12.19 [*The Icelandic Collection*]. Photoprint; 25.2 x 20.2 cm.

12.20 [*Halldór Hermannsson standing on a bridge*]. Photoprint on glossy paper; 20.5 x 25.3 cm.

12.21 [*Touring Washington*]. Photoprint: sepia toned; image 12.9 x 17.9 cm, on mount 20.2 x 25.2 cm. Halldór Hermannsson sitting in the centre of the back row of an automobile coach.

12.22 [*Graduation from the Junior College in Reykjavík*]. 1898. Made by Sigfús Eymundsson, Reykjavík. Photoprint; image 13.8 x 18.7 cm, on mount 20.1 x 25.3 cm. Halldór Hermannsson is in the top row, second from right.

12.23 [*In Junior College, Reykjavík*]. Ca. 1896. Made by Árni Thorsteinsson, Reykjavík. Photoprint on cabinet card: sepia toned; 10.7 x 16.7 cm. Printed in P. M. Mitchell, *Halldór Hermannsson*. Islandica XLI (Ithaca: Cornell University Press, 1978), p. 14. In the class room.

Snapshots of Halldór Hermannsson (and others); passport photographs.

12.24 [*Halldór Hermannsson*]. 18 passport photoprints: black and white and sepia toned. Some are dated on verso: 1921, 1923 (3), 1925 (2), 1930 (2), 1931 (3), 1938, and 6 (3 types) additional, all later than the last one dated. Two of the photos from 1923 are autographed.

12.25 ____, Oct. 1913. Photoprint; 10.6 x 8.2 cm. Dated on verso. Standing in front of a house.

12.26 *Oak avenue 120*. [191?] Photoprint; 8.5 x 6 cm. Captioned on verso. Halldór Hermannsson with an unidentified friend.

12.27 *On board S/S Albania [in] June 1921*. Photoprint; 8.8 x 6 cm. Captioned on verso. Halldór Hermannsson with an unidentified man.

12.28 *Um borð í E/S "Island", í sept. 1921*. Photoprint: sepia toned; 87.5 x 9 cm. "15" written in pencil on verso. Captioned on verso. Halldór Hermannsson with a group of people.

12.29 *Tivoli 1932*. A silhouette of Halldór Hermannsson made in Tivoli (the amusement park) in Copenhagen. Captioned on verso. According to P. M. Mitchell it was presumably made in 1923 and not 1932. 12.9 x 8.4 cm.

12.30 [*Halldór Hermannsson and Halldór Sigurðsson on horseback in Iceland in 1927*]. 2 photoprints; 6.4 x 8.8 cm. Different poses.

12.31 *Hafnarfjörður, 1927.* Photoprint; 5.8 x 8.5 cm. Captioned on verso.

12.32 [*On board Gullfoss*]. 5 photoprints; 5.7 x 8.3 cm. (One 8.3 x 5.7 cm.) 5 different snapshots of Halldór Hermannsson and others on board *Gullfoss* 14-17 June 1927, taken by Árni Helgason.

12.33 [*Halldór Hermannsson with a group of men in Iceland in 1928*]. Photoprint; 8 x 10.9 cm. Dated on verso. "3" written in pencil on verso. Some of the men are identified on verso: Bjarni Jónsson, Jón Hj. Sigurðsson, Sigfús Einarsson, Matthías Einarsson, Matthías Þórðarson, and Þorkell Þorkelsson.

12.34 [*Halldór Hermannsson with a group of men in Iceland in 1928*]. Photoprint; 8.2 x 10.3 cm. Dated on verso. "3" written in pencil on verso. Matthías Einarsson is one of the group, identified on verso.

12.35 *15. aug. 1930 Gullfossferð.* Photoprint; 8 x 5.5 cm. Captioned on verso. "2" written in pencil on verso. Halldór Hermannsson in Iceland.

12.36 *Copenhagen Aug., 1932.* Photoprint; 8.7 x 13.8 cm. Captioned on verso. Halldór Hermannsson and Guðmundur Finnbogason sitting by a water fountain.

12.37 *Halldór og Helen Gilleleje [in] Sept 1932.* Photoprint; 10.5 x 8.1 cm. Captioned on verso.

12.38 *Copenhagen January 1934.* 3 snapshots in a row; 18 x 6.9 cm. Captioned on verso. "16256" stamped on verso. Halldór Hermannsson walking in Copenhagen.

12.39 *Fountainbleu, N.Y. 2 Aug 1936.* 6 different photoprints; 7.1 x 5.2 cm. "57" stamped on verso of all photoprints. Most are of Halldór Hermannsson alone, one with Stefán Einarsson and Richard Beck, one of Richard Beck.

12.40 [*Halldór Hermannsson in Ithaca*]. February 1937. Photoprint; 9.5 x 6.9 cm. Dated on verso.

12.41 [*Halldór Hermannsson, Grace Radcliffe, and others*]. 6 different photoprints; 8.2 x 10.8 cm. The snapshots were enclosed in a letter from Grace Radcliffe, Marlboro St., Philadelphia. Taken 7 July 1938 on board a ship.

12.42 *With Sigurður Nordal, in Denmark.* 30 July 1939. 3 snapshots in a row; 8 x 18.2 cm. "11205" and dated on verso. Halldór Hermannsson and Sigurður Nordal walking.

12.43 [*Garden party in Denmark*]. August 1939. 3 different photoprints; 7.9 x 11.4 cm, and 7 different photoprints; 5.9 x 8.8 cm. Dated on verso. Possibly from two different parties with much the same people. Identified are: Halldór Hermannsson, Sigurður Nordal, and Anne Holtsmark.

12.44 [*Halldór Hermannsson*]. 3 September 1939. 2 photoprints; 17.3 x 12.6 cm, and 10.5 x 8 cm. Dated on verso. Standing in front of a car at Korsør, Denmark.

12.45 *Mr. Mackail, correspondent of "The Scotsman."* Photoprint; 5.7 x 8.9 cm. Halldór Hermannsson and Mr. Mackail, apparently sometime in the thirties.

12.46 *Clifton Springs July 27, 1941.* 3 different photoprints; 5.8 x 8.3 cm. Captioned on verso. "209" and "211" stamped on verso. Halldór Hermannsson with unidentified people at Clifton Springs.

12.47 [*Fountainbleu and Watkins Glen*]. 4 different photoprints; 8.2 x 11.6 cm, and 7 x 10 cm. Snapshots of Halldór Hermannsson, Stefán Einarsson, and others in the summers 1941 and 1942.

12.48 [*Halldór Hermannsson and a group of men*]. 1943. 2 different photoprints; 8.2 x 10.8 cm. Dated on verso. The same group of four men on both photos, besides Halldór Hermannsson, Stefán Einarsson is identified.

12.49 [*With Barði Guðmundsson and Sigurður Einarsson?*] 1939 in Copenhagen. Photoprint; 7 x 6.5 cm. "74929" written in pencil on verso. Identified on verso.

12.50 *July 1943 by Vedberg.* Photoprint; 10.1 x 7.4 cm. A snapshot of Halldór Hermannsson.

12.51 [*Halldór Hermannsson*]. 3 different photoprints; 11.2 x 7.9 cm, and 7.9 x 11.2 cm. Taken in January 1946 by P. M. Mitchell. Two in his office, one on campus.

12.52 [*Halldór Hermannsson*]. Photoprint; 15 x 10 cm. A snapshot taken by Kjartan Ó. Bjarnason in the summer of 1955. "221" stamped on verso.

11. Box 13

Collection of Photographs:
Icelanders in America

Icelanders in America.

13.1   ***Hjörtur Þórðarson, Chicago.*** Taken by William Louis Koehne, Chicago. Photoprint; mat 26 x 21 cm. Sitting with two books in front of him.

13.2   ***Hjörtur Þórðarson, með Coverdale Bible.*** Photoprint; 23.3 x 19.3 cm. On verso is written in pencil: "C. H. Thordarson, leading electrical manufacturer. Case contains many priceless books, some centuries old. He holds a copy of the first edition of the Myles Coverdale Bible, printed 1535, and even rarer than the famous Gutenberg Bibles. His copy is one of the finest known to exist." Also "Mrs May (T. D.) Collins" and "3631."

13.3   [***Hjörtur Þórðarson***]. *Photographs from Rock Island, the property of H. Thordarson.* 11 black and white photoprints; 9 x 14.6 cm.
Also 6 photographs of buildings and a model of a building. Rock Island?
1-2) "Icelandic Hall. Outside measurements 200 ft long, 70 ft wide, main building 48 ft high, water tower 64 ft high." 2 photoprints; 14.9 x 24.2 and 14.8 x 24 cm, on mount 23 x 31.5 cm.
3) "Green bay side" Photoprint; 14.6 x 24.1 cm, on mount 23 x 31.5 cm.
4) "Flower house 85 ft long, limestone pebbles, granite boulders, green [.....], Spanish tile roof." Photoprint; 14.4 x 23.5 cm, on mount 23 x 31.5 cm.
5) "Boat house '75 feet wide, 115 feet long, 12 feet of water inside, will hold 2 boats 80 ft long, foundation resting on limestone ledge, "finest boat house on the Great lakes." Photoprint; 14.8 x 24.3 cm, on mount 23 x 31.5 cm.
6) "B… hall walls 3 ft thick, 22 ft high, center of floor to ceiling 40 feet, red Spanish tile roof 100.000 lbs." Photoprint; 14.3 x 24 cm, on mount 23 x 31.5 cm.

13.4   ***Nína Sæmundsson and Vilhjalmur Stefansson.*** Photo by Vang Studio. Photoprint on glossy paper; 18 x 24.7 cm. Vilhjalmur Stefansson posing for a bust.

13.5   ***Stefán Einarsson, Prof. & Mrs.*** Inscription in Stefán Einarsson's hand.

Made by Cornellian Studios. Photoprint; visible image 23.8 x 17.7 cm, on mat 35.3 x 26.3 cm; half-length portrait.

Group photographs, arranged chronologically.

13.6 ***Modern Language Association of America.*** Drake Hotel Chicago, 29 December 1937. Flash photo Co. Photoprint; 30.4 x 50.7 cm. Dinner party.

13.7 ***Testimonial Dinner to Mr. & Mrs. Vilhjalmur Thor by Iceland Club.*** Hotel Shelton. 21 October 1939. Empire photographers, New York City. Photoprint; 30.3 x 50.7 cm. Plate 23972.

13.8 ***Dinner of welcome in honor of Mr. Thor Thors Consul General of Iceland.*** Hotel Shelton. 26 October 1940. Empire photographers, New York City. Photoprint; 25.4 x 50.6 cm. Plate 25770.

13.9 ***Reception. The Icelandic Government Trade Delegation.*** Hotel Savoy-plaza, New York City, 18 October 1941. Standard Flashlight Co., Inc., New York City. Photoprint; 30.4 x 50.9 cm. Plate 42851.

13.10 ***Dinner given in honor of his excellency Sveinn Björnsson President of Iceland and his excellency Vilhjálmur Thor Foreign minister of Iceland tendered by the Consul General of Iceland and Mrs. Helgi P. Briem.*** The Waldorf-Astoria, New York City, 27 August 1944. Photo by Drucker-Hilbert Co., New York. Photoprint; 27.6 x 35.5 cm. Plate 4880.

13.11 [***Group of Icelandic men at Waldorf-Astoria Hotel,*** 27 August 1944]. ACME Newspictures, Inc., New York. Photoprint on glossy paper; 20.5 x 25.4 cm. "124" in pencil on verso. From left: Thor Thors; Árni Helgason; Stefán Einarsson; Richard Beck; Halldór Hermannsson; Sveinn Björnsson; Vilhjálmur Þór; Gunnar Björnsson; Vilhjalmur Stefansson; Sveinbjörn Johnson?; Guðmundur Grímsson; Helgi P. Briem.

Photographs of statues.

13.12 ***Leifur Eiríksson, the statue of.*** Taken by Óskar [Gíslason, Reykjavík].

3 photoprints; 15 x 10.8 cm, on mount 23.2 x 14.7 cm. From three different angles.

13.13 ***Þorfinnur karlsefni, the statue of.*** Made by Ph. B. Wallace Photography, Philadelphia. 3 photoprints on glossy paper; 25.7 x 20.3 cm. The photos are taken from 3 different angles. The statue of Thorfinn Karlsefni by Einar Jónsson in Fairmont Park, Philadelphia. A fourth picture of the statue; 19 x 14 cm, background is black and "Thorfinn Karlsefni" is printed below image.

12. Box 14

Collection of Photographs from Grímsey

14.1 ***Guðný Guðmundsdóttir,*** *Miðgarðar. (born 29th of April 1869, the photograph taken in July 1901) mother of D. W. F. Matthíasson.* Taken by Anna M. Magnúsdóttir. Photoprint on carte-de-visite card; 10.1 x 6.1 cm; half-length portrait.

In the summer of 1902 Fiske hired Eiríkur Þorbergsson from Húsavík to go to Grímsey and take photographs of people and places. The photographs were taken in June. Cf. letters from the photographer to Daniel Willard Fiske and Halldór Hermannsson. Also from the Rev. Matthías Eggertsson to Fiske, 4 August 1902, where he talks about the project, describes the places, etc.

14.2 **E. Thorbergsson** [i.e. Eiríkur Þorbergsson], Húsavík. Photographs made for Fiske on Grímsey.

1) *Miðgarðakirkja að innan.* 3 photoprints: sepia toned; on card 12.9 x 15.8 cm. One of the bookcases given by Fiske is to the left of the pulpit, marked: "Eyjarbókasafnið. I."
2) *Á bjargi.* "Það er verið að binda sigamann í "augað". Auga er nefnt poki sá, sem bundinn er utan um sigamanninn að aptan svo að hann sárni ekki undan festinni. Augað sjest bezt á myndinni no. 3." 2 photoprints: sepia toned; on card 12.9 x 15.8 cm.
3) *Á bjargi.* "Bjargmaðurinn er kominn upp á brúnina með fuglaprikið í hendinni og er að losa sig við skegluungana, sem hann hefur tínt á sig niðri í bjarginu; sjónarbjargsmaður stendur þar uppi yfir honum og fes-

tarmennirnir aðrir þar fyrir ofan." 2 photoprints: sepia toned; on card 12.9 x 15.8 cm.

4) *Á bjargi.* "Sigamaðurinn kemur upp á brúnina með skegluungakippu." Photoprint: sepia toned; on card 12.9 x 15.8 cm.

5) *Á bjargi.* "Sigamaðurinn kemur upp á brúnina með skegluungakippu." Closer look. 1 photoprint: sepia toned; on card 12.9 x 15.8 cm.

6) *Á bjargi.* "Sigamaður er kominn nokkuð á leið ofan í bjargið og er að snara fugl; á bjargbrúninni sjer á "stokkinn" og "trossurnar." 1 photoprint: sepia toned; on card 12.9 x 15.8 cm.

7) [*Á bjargi, from a distance*]. 1 photoprint: sepia toned; on card 12.9 x 15.8 cm.

8) *Almannagjá.* 2 photoprints: sepia toned; on card 12.9 x 15.8 cm. Almannagjá in Grímsey. A man climbing.

9) *Kaldagjá og Hafsúlustapi.* 1 photoprint: sepia toned; on card 12.9 x 15.8 cm.

10) *Af eyjarfætinum, útsjór yfir Básana.* 1 photoprint: sepia toned; on card 12.9 x 15.8 cm.

11) *Eyjarfóturinn að austanverðu. Maður stendur uppi á hæsta hnjúknum á eynni.* 2 photoprints: sepia toned; on card 12.9 x 15.8 cm.

12) *Borgahöfðinn og Borgaskerin. Skip sjást á höfninni.* 2 photoprints: sepia toned; on card 12.9 x 15.8 cm.

13) *Sandvíkurgjögrar.* 2 photoprints: sepia toned; on card 12.9 x 15.8 cm.

14) *Aratópt og Grenivíkurnar.* 2 photoprints: sepia toned; on card 12.9 x 15.8 cm. A farmhouse.

15) *Básar.* 2 photoprints: sepia toned; on card 12.9 x 15.8 cm. A farmhouse, the family posing outside.

16) *Baðstofan í Aratópt. Það sjest í moldargaflinn, baðstofan er ópiljuð.* 2 photoprints: sepia toned; on card 12.9 x 15.8 cm.

17) *Baðstofan í Aratópt. Barn sefur í rúminu.* 1 photoprint: sepia toned; on card 12.9 x 15.8 cm.

18) [*Baðstofan í Aratópt*]. Same motif as 17, but from a greater distance. 1 photoprint: sepia toned; on card 12.9 x 15.8 cm.

19) *Eldhúsið í Aratópt.* "Belgurinn, sem sjest vinstra megin á myndinni, er til þess að blása með undir þegar brennt er kolum á hlóðunum. Á gólfinu liggur kippa af skegluungum." 2 photoprints: sepia toned; on card 12.9 x 15.8 cm.

20) *Sandvíkin. Sjeð frá skipi á höfninni.* 1 photoprint: sepia toned; on card 12.9 x 15.8 cm.

21) *Grenivíkurgjögrar.* 1 photoprint: sepia toned; on card 12.9 x 15.8 cm.

22) *Grenivíkurgjögrar og Hlíðarstapi.* 1 photoprint: sepia toned; on card 12.9 x 15.8 cm.

23) *Grenivíkurgjögrar.* 1 photoprint: sepia toned; on card 12.9 x 15.8 cm.

24) Missing.

25) *Grenivíkurgjögrar og Hlíðarstapi.* 2 photoprints: sepia toned; on card 12.9 x 15.8 cm.

26) *Aratópt.* 2 photoprints: sepia toned; on card 12.9 x 15.8 cm. A farmhouse. Sheep on the roof. A woman standing in the doorway.

27) *Búrið í Aratópt.* "Það er steinkolahrúga, sem stampurinn stendur á. Efst á myndinni sjást raptarnir ganga ofan á vegginn." 1 photoprint: sepia toned; on card 12.9 x 15.8 cm.

28) *Lendingin í Sandvík.* "Bærinn, sem sjest hægra megin á myndinni, er Efri-Sandvík." 1 photoprint: sepia toned; on card 12.9 x 15.8 cm.

29) [*Útsjón yfir Grenivíkurgjögra og Flesjar. Maður í handvað*]. 2 photoprints: sepia toned; on card 12.9 x 15.8 cm. Same motif as No. 30, but taken a little earlier.

30) *Útsjón yfir Grenivíkurgjögra og Flesjar. Maður í handvað.* 2 photoprints: sepia toned; on card 12.9 x 15.8 cm.

14.3 Photographs from Grímsey on cabinet cards. By same photographer. Lists of subjects on separate sheets, compiled by the Reverend Matthías Eggertsson, 4 August 1902. Headings: "Grúppumyndirnar úr Grímsey", and "Skýring á myndunum."

1) *Karlmenn sem tefla* [i.e. men who play chess]. 3 photoprints on cabinet cards: sepia toned; 10.6 x 16.6 cm. Identified on Matthías Eggertsson's list.

2) *Konur sem tefla* [i.e. women who play chess]. 1 photoprint on cabinet card: sepia toned; 10.6 x 16.6 cm. Identified on Matthías Eggertsson's list.

3) *Myndir af ungum drengjum* [i.e. young boys]. 1 photoprint on cabinet card: sepia toned; 10.6 x 16.6 cm. Identified on Matthías Eggertsson's list.

4) *Myndir af ungum telpum* [i.e. young girls]. 1 photoprint on cabinet card: sepia toned; 10.6 x 16.6 cm. Identified on Matthías Eggertsson's list.

5) *Ingvar Guðmundsson, Sveinagörðum.* Identified on back of picture. 2 photoprints on cabinet cards; sepia toned; head and shoulders portrait; 16.6 x 10.6 cm.

6) *Sjera Matthías* [*Eggertsson*]. 2 photoprints on cabinet cards: sepia toned; head and shoulders portrait; 16.6 x 10.6 cm.

7) *Miðgarðar.* 1 photoprint on cabinet card; 10.6 x 16.6 cm. A farmhouse, the home of the Reverend Matthías Eggertsson.

8) *Sandvíkurbær.* 1 photoprint on cabinet card; 10.6 x 16.6 cm. A farm-house.

9) *Miðgarðabjarg.* 1 photoprint on cabinet card; 10.6 x 16.6 cm.

10) *Grenivíkurbjörg og Hlíðarstapi.* 1 photoprint on cabinet card; 10.6 x 16.6 cm.

11) *Handfestargjá.* 1 photoprint on cabinet card; 10.6 x 16.6 cm.

12) *Sandvík. Eiðar. Sveinstaðir. Miðgarðar. Sveinagarðar.* In ink beneath the picture. On back: "Mynd af byggðinni í Grímsey, því af henni sem komið varð á eina mynd. Klettarnir eru Borgasker." 2 photoprints: sepia toned; mounted on card 24 x 33 cm.

13. Box 15

Stereoscope Pictures from Iceland

Magnús Ólafsson, 1862-1937. The pictures were made by Magnús Ólafsson and Ljósmyndastofa Magnúsar Ólafssonar, Reykjavík. 213 photoprints in a black box. All the photoprints are stereographs on stereo cards; 9 x 18 cm (centimeters rounded off to the next centimeter up).

1   *Reykjanesvitinn gamli.*
2   *Kaþólska kirkjan að innan. Reykjavík.*
3   *Biskupsvíxla síra Þórhalla í Reykjavíkurdómkirkju.*
4   *Kapella í Landakotsspítala.*
5   *Þjóðmenningardagur í Reykjavík. Minni Vestur-Íslendinga.*
6   *Landakotsspítali. Reykjavík.*
7   *Landakotsskóli. Reykjavík.*
8   *Stjórnarráðsskrifstofur í Reykjavík. Afhjúpun Jóns Sigurðssonar.*
9   *Afhjúpun Jóns Sigurðssonar líkneskis, Reykjavík.*
10   *Fólk að skemmta sér við Elliðaárnar, Reykjavík.*
11   *Botnvörpuveiði.*
12   *Fiskaðgjörð um borð í Trollara.*
13   *Slippurinn í Reykjavík.*
14   *Dómkirkjan og Alþingishúsið í Reykjavík.*
15   *Seglskip á fiskiveiðum.*
16   *Telpur læra sund í Reykjavíkurlaugum.*
17   *Íþróttamót í Reykjavík 1911. Ísland í rúmsjármyndum.*
18   *Íþróttamót í Reykjavík 1911. Kúluvarp (Sigurjón). Ísland í rúmsjár-myndum.*

19 *Á Íþróttamótinu í Reykjavík 1911. Ísland í rúmsjármyndum.*
20 *Íslandsglíman 1910. Norðlingar glíma.*
21 *Íslandsglíman 1910. Sigurjón Pétursson.*
22 *Gullfundurinn í Vatnsmýrinni í Reykjavík.*
23 *"Dilkur" í Hafravatnsrétt, Mosfellssveit.*
24 *Hafravatnsrétt, Mosfellssveit.*
25 *Íslenskir hestar í vetrarbúningi.*
26 *Konungsgos Geysis. Ísland í rúmsjármyndum.*
27 *Konungsfylgdin við Gullfoss. Ísland í rúmsjármyndum.*
28 *Konungsfylgdin á Sandskeiði.*
29 *Hagavík við Þingvallavatn.*
30 *Á Hagavíkurhlaði (við Þingvallavatn).*
31 *Nesjaklumba við Þingvallavatn.*
32 *Jórukleif.*
33 *Arnarfell við Þingvallavatn.*
34 *Sogið í nánd við Kaldárhöfða.*
35 *Silungsveiði í Soginu.*
36 *Írufoss í Soginu.*
37 *Ingólfsfjall. Brúin á Alviðru við Sogið.*
38 *Reyniviðartré við Sogið. Ingólfsfjall.*
39 *Vatnsgjá við gamla Lögberg á Þingvöllum. Ísland í rúmsjármyndum.*
40 *Meyjarsæti og Hofmannaflötur.*
41 *Útsýn til Skjaldbreiðar úr Brunnum.*
42 *Hestvík í Grafningi við Þingvallavatn.*
43 *Tröllafoss í Leirvogsá.*
44 *Gljúfur við Tröllafoss, Mosfellssveit.*
45 *Lest í Almannagjá.*
46 *Partur úr Almannagjá.*
47 *Hraundrangur norðan til í Almannagjá.*
48 *Norðurhluti Almannagjár.*
49 *Öxarárfossinn við Þingvelli.*
50 *Öxará og Þingvallavatn.*
51 *Útsýn vestur yfir Þingvallavatn.*
52 *Gestir við Öxará, Þingvöllum.*
53 *Gamla Lögberg á Þingvöllum.*
54 *Útsýn til Valhallar af gamla Lögbergi.*
55 *Á leið út á gamla Lögberg.*
56 *Útsýn til Ármannsfells af gamla Lögbergi.*
57 *Flosagjá, Þingvöllum.*
58 *Galtinn við Galtarfell, Gnúpverjahreppi. Ísland í rúmsjármyndum.*
59 *Stuðlaberg í Galtarfelli, Gnúpverjahreppi. Ísland í rúmsjármyndum.*
60 *Útsýn til Heklu úr Þjórsárdal.*

61   *Klettagöng í gjá í Þjórsárdal. Ísland í rúmsjármyndum.*
62   *Bergsnös í "Gjá" í Þjórsárdal. Ísland í rúmsjármyndum.*
63   *Illagil við Bláfell, Árnessýsla.*
64   *Þjórsárbrú.*
65   *Ölfusárbrúin.*
66   *Stórólfshvoll í Hvolhreppi. Ísland í rúmsjármyndum.*
67   *Útsýn yfir Þverá frá Teig í Fljótshlíð.*
68   *Smáfossar í Gjá í Þjórsárdal. Ísland í rúmsjármyndum.*
69   *Stuðlaberg í Gjá í Þjórsárdal.*
70   *Gjáarfoss í Þjórsárdal.*
71   *Foss í Hjálp í Þjórsárdal. Ísland í rúmsjármyndum.*
72   *Háifoss í Þjórsárdal. Ísland í rúmsjármyndum.*
73   *Hlíðarendakirkja, Fljótshlíð.*
74   *Gluggafoss í Fljótshlíð.*
75   *Á Gunnarshólma (Stóri Dímon frá Gunnarshólma).*
76   *Útsýn úteftir Þórsmörk. Ísland í rúmsjármyndum.*
77   *Móbergshausinn á Þórsmörk. Ísland í rúmsjármyndum.*
78   *Ferðamenn á Þórsmörk. Ísland í rúmsjármyndum.*
79   *Þórsmörk, tekið úr Stangarskógi.*
80   *Upprekstrarmannabæli á Þórsmörk. Ísland í rúmsjármyndum.*
81   *Fjárhellir á Þórsmörk. Ísland í rúmsjármyndum.*
82   *Þrengslin í Goðalandsgjá, Þórsmörk. Ísland í rúmsjármyndum.*
83   *Innst inni í Stakkholtsgjá við Þórsmörk.*
84   *Goðalandsgjá á Þórsmörk. Ísland í rúmsjármyndum.*
85   *Stakkholtsgjá við Þórsmörk.*
86   *Útsýn þvert suðuryfir Þórsmörk. Ísland í rúmsjármyndum.*
87   *Þórsmörk, Eyjafjallajökull. Ísland í rúmsjármyndum.*
88   *Markarfljótsvarnargarðurinn undir Eyjafjöllum.*
89   *Undir Eyjafjöllum. Seljalandsmúli. Ísland í rúmsjármyndum.*
90   *Seljalandsmúli og Drífandi undir Eyjafjöllum.*
91   *Dettifoss undir Eyjafjöllum.*
92   *Gljúfrabúinn undir Eyjafjöllum. Ísland í rúmsjármyndum.*
93   *Seljalandsrjómabú undir Eyjafjöllum.*
94   *Undir Eyjafjöllum (Hvammur). Ísland í rúmsjármyndum.*
95   *Undir Eyjafjöllum, Hvammsnúpur. Ísland í rúmsjármyndum.*
96   *Hvammsnúpur undir Eyjafjöllum. Ísland í rúmsjármyndum.*
97   *Eyjafjallajökull og Holtsnúpur.*
98   *Útsýn til Holtsnúps undir Eyjafjöllum. Ísland í rúmsjármyndum.*
99   *Holt undir Eyjafjöllum og Holtsnúpur.*
100 *Útsýn til Eyjafjallajökuls frá Holtsengjum.*
101 *Þorvaldseyri undir Eyjafjöllum. Ísland í rúmsjármyndum.*
102 *Undir Eyjafjöllum, Hrútafell. Ísland í rúmsjármyndum.*

103   *Skógafoss undir Eyjafjöllum.*
104   *Mýrdalsjökull og Jökulsá á Sólheimasandi. Ísland í rúmsjármyndum.*
105   *Jökulsá á Sólheimasandi og Mýrdalsjökull. Ísland í rúmsjármyndum.*
106   *Jökulsá á Sólheimasandi. Ísland í rúmsjármyndum.*
107   *Úr Hornafirði.*
108   *Fáskrúðsfjörður (fiskvinna).*
109   *Hafís á Fáskrúðsfirði.*
110   *Ís á Fáskrúðsfirði.*
111   *Franska spítalaskipið inni frosið á Fáskrúðsfirði.*
112   *Síldarafli á Fáskrúðsfirði.*
113   *Síldin tekin úr "lásnum", Fáskrúðsfirði.*
114   *Partur af Seyðisfirði.*
115   *Foss í Fjarðará, Seyðisfirði.*
116   *Fjarðará, Seyðisfirði.*
117   *Vetrarmynd frá Seyðisfirði.*
118   *Gatnaskógur við Lagarfljót.*
119   *Dilkur hjá dauðri móður sinni á Fljótsdalsheiði.*
120   *Birkitré innst inni í Ásbyrgi.*
121   *Hafragilsárgljúfrin í Jökulsá, Axarfirði.*
122   *Hafragilsfoss í Jökulsá.* Made by E. Thorbergsson [i.e. Eiríkur Þor-
        bergsson], Húsavík.
123   *Dettifoss í Jökulsá, Axarfirði. Ísland í rúmsjármyndum.*
124   *Hjálp í Þjórsárdal. Ísland í rúmsjármyndum.*
125   *Brúin yfir Jökulsá í Axarfirði.*
126   *Vaðlar í Mývatni.*
127   *Kálfastrandarstrýpar við Mývatn.*
128   *Skútustaðakirkja við Mývatn.*
129   *Reykjahlíð við Mývatn.*
130   *Reykjahlíðarfjall (úr Slútnesi við Mývatn). Ísland í rúmsjármyndum.*
131   *Heyvinna við Mývatn, Reykjahlíð.*
132   *Stargresi við Mývatn.*
133   *Kálfastrandarvogar við Mývatn. Ísland í rúmsjármyndum.*
134   *Kálfastrandarstrýpur við Mývatn. Ísland í rúmsjármyndum.*
135   *Vítishver við Mývatn.*
136   *Vítishver við Mývatn.*
137   *Vítishver að innan (við Mývatn).*
138   *Gljúfrin við Skjálfandafljótsbrú.*
139   *Hansensgat við Skjálfandafljót.*
140   *Goðafoss í Skjálfandafljóti.*
141   *Húsavík.*
142   *Í Hálsskógi í Fnjóskadal.*
143   *Í Hálsskógi í Fnjóskadal.*

144   *Kirkjan á Akureyri og Gróðrarstöð.*
145   *Oddeyri við Eyjafjörð.*
146   *Gata á Oddeyri.*
147   *Síldarsöltun á Oddeyri.*
148   *Síldaruppskipun á Oddeyri.*
149   *Hraundrangar í Öxnadal, Eyjafjarðarsýslu.*
150   *Víðivellir, Skagafjarðarsýslu.*
151   *Valagilsárgljúfrin, Skagafirði.*
152   *Sauðárkrókur, Drangey í fjarsýn.*
153   *Blönduós, Húnavatnssýslu. Ísland í rúmsjármyndum.*
154   *Dragferjan á Héraðsvötnum.*
155   *Við Skriðuvað í Vatnsdalshólum, Húnavatnssýslu.*
156   *Heylest á Blöndubrú, Húnavatnssýslu.*
157   *Borðeyri við Hrútafjörð.*
158   *Svartárdalur í Húnavatnssýslu.*
159   *Partur af Ísafirði.*
160   *Sandfell í Dýrafirði.*
161   *Vatnseyri við Patreksfjörð.*
162   *Æðarfugl á Breiðafirði.*
163   *Kirkjufell í Grundarfirði, séð frá Bryggjum. Ísland í rúmsjármyndum.*
164   *Grund í Grundarfirði, Snæfellsnesi.*
165   *Hestaútskipun í Stykkishólmi.*
166   *S/S Sterling við bólverkið í Stykkishólmi.*
167   *Æðarhreiður.*
168   *Æður í hreiðri.*
169   *"Baðstofan" við Hellna, Snæfellsnesi. Ísland í rúmsjármyndum.*
170   *Sjávartraðir við Hellna, Snæfellsnesi.*
171   *"Sjávartröð" við Hellna. Ísland í rúmsjármyndum.*
172   *Búlandshöfði og Máfahlíð, Snæfellsnesi. Ísland í rúmsjármyndum.*
173   *Háarif og Rifsá, Snæfellsnesi.*
174   *Snæfellsjökull "heiman úr Staðarsveit."*
175   *Við Sönghelli á Snæfellsnesi. Ísland í rúmsjármyndum.*
176   *Berserkjahraun. Ísland í rúmsjármyndum.*
177   *Stapahöfn á Snæfellsnesi. Ísland í rúmsjármyndum.*
178   *Lóndrangar á Snæfellsnesi. Ísland í rúmsjármyndum.*
179   *Músagjá við Arnarstapa.*
180   *Arnarstapi, Snæfellsnesi.*
181   *Gatklettur við Arnarstapa. Ísland í rúmsjármyndum.*
182   *Stapafell á Snæfellsnesi. Ísland í rúmsjármyndum.*
183   *Tröllakirkja við Dritvík, Snæfellsnesi.*
184   *Drangurinn við Dritvík á Snæfellsnesi. Ísland í rúmsjármyndum.*
185   *Tökin við Dritvík. Ísland í rúmsjármyndum.*
186   *Djúpalón við Dritvík. Ísland í rúmsjármyndum.*

187   *Lendingin í Dritvík á Snæfellsnesi. Ísland í rúmsjármyndum.*
188   *Bergbúinn við Dritvík. Ísland í rúmsjármyndum.*
189   *Vigið í Surtshelli.*
190   *Ísstöplar í Surtshelli. Ísland í rúmsjármyndum.*
191   *Ísfossinn í Surtshelli. Ísland í rúmsjármyndum.*
192   *Steinsvalirnar í Surtshelli.*
193   *Okjökull úr Geitlandinu.*
194   *Geitlandsjökull af Skúlaskeiði.*
195   *Bláfell við Hvítárvatn.*
196   *Útsýn til Hofsjökuls yfir Hvítárvatn ofan af Langjökli.*
197   *Skriðjökull úr Langjökli við Hvítárvatn.*
198   *Geitlandsjökull af Skúlaskeiði, Kaldadal.*
199   *Útsýn til Strúts og Eiríksjökuls, Borgarfjarðarsýslu.*
200   *Langjökull séð af Kaldadal. Ísland í rúmsjármyndum.*
201   *Uppi á Skarðsheiðarhorni, Borgarfjarðarsýslu.*
202   *Karl og kerling í Selgili við Húsafell.*
203   *Fossbúinn í Selgili við Húsafell, Borgarfjarðarsýslu.*
204   *Útsýn yfir Hvítá af Hraunsási.*
205   *Deildartunguhver.*
206   *Vellindishver í Reykholtsdal.*
207   *Vígsla Norðurárbrúar, Borgarfjarðarsýslu.*
208   *Hraunfossarnir við Gilsbakka (Hvítá). Ísland í rúmsjármyndum.*
209   *Brúarhlaðadrangurinn í Hvítá.*
210   *Brúarhlaðagljúfrin við Hvítá.*
211   *Geldingaá Leirársveit, Borgarfjarðarsýslu.*
212   *Reykholt í Borgarfirði.*
213   *Snorralaug í Reykholti, Borgarfirði.*

14. Box 16

Lantern Slides from Iceland 1

A wooden box containing 98 lantern slides made by different photographers. From the National Celebration in 1930, Icelandic landscape: Geysir, Hekla, Reykjavík, etc., Icelandic costumes, maps. Slides showing old architecture, drawings from the sagas and Old Norse myths, etc. Some are captioned on the image and others on labels pasted on the lanterns' frames.

All the slides are 9 x 11 cm. Dimensions are given in centimeters rounded off to the next whole centimeter up. Photographer, when known, identified following title.

1 *Reykjavík. Seen from Landakot.* K. K. Bergen. 1 lantern slide; image 5 x 8 cm.

2 *Scene on the road to Krísuvík.* Forbes. 1 lantern slide; image 5 x 8 cm.

3 *Gatklettur hjá Stapa.* Mackenzie. 1 lantern slide; image 5 x 8 cm.

4 *A seacave by Stapi. (Sævarhellir hjá Stapa).* R. Bright. 1 lantern slide; image 5 x 8 cm.

5 *Almannagjá.* Paijkull. 1 lantern slide; image 8 x 5 cm.

6 *Almannagjá.* Paijkull. 1 lantern slide; image 8 x 5 cm.

7 *Geysir.* Paijkull. 1 lantern slide; image 8 x 6 cm.

8 *Geysir.* Paijkull. 1 lantern slide; image 8 x 6 cm.

9 *The Great Geysir, when at rest.* 1 lantern slide; image 4 x 7 cm.

10 *Eruption of the Great Geysir.* Mackenzie. 1 lantern slide; image 8 x 5 cm.

11 *New Geysir.* Mackenzie. 1 lantern slide; image 8 x 5 cm.

12 *Strokkur with Geysir in the distance.* Metcalfe. 1 lantern slide; image 7 x 5 cm.

13 *Strokkur.* Paijkull. 1 lantern slide; image 6 x 7 cm.

14 *Hekla.* Pfeiffer. 1 lantern slide; image 4 x 7 cm.

15 *Mount Hekla from Oddi.* Mackenzie. 1 lantern slide; image 3 x 7 cm.

16 *Hekla from the banks of Rangá.* Forbes. 1 lantern slide; image 5 x 8 cm.

17 *Goðafoss.* Shepherd. 1 lantern slide; image 5 x 8 cm.

18 *Eldborg.* E. Henderson. 1 lantern slide; image 4 x 7 cm.

19 *Eldborg from the south.* Forbes. 1 lantern slide; image 4 x 7 cm.

20 *The Vestibute, Surtshellir.* Forbes. 1 lantern slide; image 8 x 5 cm.

21 *Reynisdrangar. (Needles of Portland Head).* Forbes. 1 lantern slide; image 5 x 6 cm.

22 *Reynisdrangar.* Paijkull. 1 lantern slide; image 6 x 7 cm.

23 *Dyrhólaey. (Portland).* Paijkull. 1 lantern slide; image 5 x 8 cm.

24 *Snæfellsjökull.* Forbes. 1 lantern slide; image 5 x 8 cm.

25 *Snæfellsjökull, as seen from the sea.* E. Henderson. 1 lantern slide; image 5 x 8 cm.

26 *Crossing the Brúará.* Forbes. 1 lantern slide; image 5 x 8 cm.

27 *Búlandshöfði. (The Búlandshöfði pass).* Forbes. 1 lantern slide; image 7 x 5 cm.

28 *A "Grettistak."* Metcalfe. 1 lantern slide; image 5 x 8 cm.

29 *Exhibition of Basalt near Höskuldsstaðr.* E. Henderson. 1 lantern slide; image 4 x 7 cm.

30 *Hólar í Hjaltadal.* E. Henderson. 1 lantern slide; image 5 x 7 cm.

31 *Ísafjörður - town.* Shepherd. 1 lantern slide; image 5 x 7 cm.

32 *The Icelandic Home.* Forbes. 1 lantern slide; image 5 x 8 cm.

33 *En isländsk præstgård.* Paijkull. 1 lantern slide; image 5 x 8 cm.

34 *En jomfru i bryllupsdragt.* Eggert Ólafsson. 1 lantern slide; image 8 x 4 cm.

35 *Icelandic national costumes.* 1 lantern slide; image 7 x 9 cm.

36 *Icelandic national costumes.* 1 lantern slide; image 9 x 6 cm.

37 *Isländska i hverdagsdragt.* Paijkull. 1 lantern slide; image 7 x 6 cm.

38 *Iceland. A map of Iceland.* 1 lantern slide; image 5 x 8 cm.

39 *A map of South-western Iceland.* 1 lantern slide; image 7 x 6 cm.

40 *Reykjavík.* Paijkull. 1 lantern slide; image 4 x 8 cm.

41 *Reykjavík. The Parliament House and the Cathedral.* 1 lantern slide; image 6 x 8 cm.

42 *Reykjavík from Tjarnargata.* 1 lantern slide; image 6 x 8 cm.

43 *Þingvellir. A map of Þingvellir.* 1 lantern slide; image 7 x 3 cm.

44 *Þingvellir. Plan and prospect of Öxará Alþing. (Alþingisstaðurinn forni).* Printed in Gutenberg, plate by Ólafur Hvanndal. 1 lantern slide; image 5 x 8 cm.

45 *Þingvellir. A map from 1922 of the place of the old Alþing. (Alþingisstaðurinn forni).* 1 lantern slide; image 5 x 8 cm.

46 *[Þingvellir. Almannagjá].* 1 lantern slide; image 6 x 8 cm.

47 *Þingvellir. Almannagjá.* 1 lantern slide; image 6 x 8 cm.

48 *Þingvellir. From Almannagjá.* 1 lantern slide; image 6 x 8 cm.

49 *[Þingvellir. Ösarárfoss].* 1 lantern slide; image 6 x 8 cm.

50 *Þingvellir 1930.* K. K. Bergen. 1 lantern slide; image 5 x 8 cm.

51 *Þingvellir 1930.* 1 lantern slide; image 5 x 8 cm.

52 *Þingvellir 1930.* K. K. Bergen. 1 lantern slide; image 5 x 8 cm. No. 2352.

53 *Þingvellir 1930. A religious ceremony.* K. K. Bergen. 1 lantern slide; image 5 x 8 cm.

54 *Þingvellir 1930. "Á þingi."* 1 lantern slide; image 5 x 8 cm.

55 *Þingvellir 1930. The crowd.* 1 lantern slide; image 5 x 8 cm.

56 *Þingvellir 1930. The crowd, the farm and the church in the distance.* 1 lantern slide; image 5 x 8 cm.

57 *Þingvellir 1930. The farm and the church.* 1 lantern slide; image 5 x 8 cm.

58 *Þingvellir 1930. The prime minister speaks.* K. K. Bergen. 1 lantern slide; image 5 x 8 cm.

59 *Þingvellir. Camping.* K. K. Bergen. 1 lantern slide; image 5 x 8 cm. No. 2345.

60 *Þingvellir Camping.* 1 lantern slide; image 5 x 8 cm.

61 *Þingvellir 1930. Booths and tents.* 1 lantern slide; image 5 x 8 cm.

62 *Þingvellir 1930. A group of students.* 1 lantern slide; image 5 x 8 cm.

63 *Þingvellir 1930. Sports (wrestling).* 1 lantern slide; image 5 x 8 cm.

64   *Þingvellir 1930. The King greets the wrestlers.* 1 lantern slide; image 5 x 8 cm.

65   *Þingvellir 1930. Horse-fight.* 1 lantern slide; image 5 x 8 cm.

66   *Þingvellir 1930. Historical costume, a man on a horse.* K. K. Bergen. 1 lantern slide; image 5 x 8 cm. No. 2349.

67   *Þingvellir 1930. Historical costumes.* 1 lantern slide; image 5 x 8 cm. No. 2351.

68   *Þingvellir 1930. Historical costumes.* K. K. Bergen. 1 lantern slide; image 5 x 8 cm. No. 2357.

69   *Þingvellir 1930. Historical costumes.* 1 lantern slide; image 5 x 8 cm.

70   *Landscape. A farm and a church in the distance.* 1 lantern slide; image 6 x 8 cm.

71   *Alþingisstaðurinn forni. Uppdráttur frá 1922.* 1 lantern slide; image 4 x 8 cm. A map.

72   *Sketch map showing the courses of the Wineland Voyages and identification of places mentioned in the sagas.* 1 lantern slide; image 7 x 6 cm.

73   *Öxarárfoss.* 1 lantern slide; image 6 x 8 cm.

74   *Landscape.* 1 lantern slide; image 6 x 8 cm.

75   *Landscape. A farm and a church in the distance.* 1 lantern slide; image 6 x 8 cm.

76   *Iceland. A map of Iceland.* 1 lantern slide; image 5 x 8 cm.

77   *Alþingi við Öxará. A map.* 1 lantern slide; image 4 x 7 cm.

78   *Alþingisstaðurinn forni. (Plan and prospect of Öxará Alþing).* 1 lantern slide; image 3 x 8 cm.

79   *Öxará á Þingvöllum.* 1 lantern slide; image 6 x 8 cm.

80   *Þingvellir. Almannagjá.* 1 lantern slide; image 6 x 8 cm.

81   *Þingvellir. A map of Alþing by Öxará.* 1 lantern slide; image 4 x 7 cm.

82   *Interior of Icelandic house.* 1 lantern slide; image 6 x 8 cm.

83   *Ground-plan of Icelandic house.* Dasent. 1 lantern slide; image 5 x 8 cm.

84   *A remake of "Hlaðbúð." A booth with walls of turf or stones.* 1 lantern slide; image 4 x 8 cm. No. 3.

85   *A remake of "Virkisbúð." A stronghold.* 1 lantern slide; image 6 x 8 cm. No. 4.

86   *Ireland during the Viking age. A map.* 1 lantern slide; image 7 x 5 cm.

87   *The ruins by Newport.* 1 lantern slide; image 7 x 6 cm.

88   *Grænlendinga þáttr. Beginning.* 1 lantern slide; image 6 x 5 cm.

89   *Ófeigr and Guðmundr ríki.* 1 lantern slide; image 8 x 5 cm.

90   *Gunnar meets Hallgerður.* 1 lantern slide; image 7 x 5 cm.

91   *Víglundur og Böðvildur.* Gehrts. 1 lantern slide; image 6 x 8 cm.

92   *Iðunn and the apples.* Penrose. 1 lantern slide; image 5 x 8 cm.

93   *Loki and Frigg.* Moe. 1 lantern slide; image 7 x 6 cm.

94   *Walhalls Wonnen.* Gehrts. 1 lantern slide; image 6 x 8 cm.
95   *Walkürien auf dem Schlachtfield.* 1 lantern slide; image 7 x 8 cm.
96   *Þrymskviða IV.* Frølich. 1 lantern slide; image 8 x 6 cm.
97   *Þrymskviða V.* Frølich. 1 lantern slide; image 6 x 9 cm.
98   *Þrymskviða VI.* Frølich. 1 lantern slide; image 6 x 8 cm.

15. Box 17

Lantern Slides from Iceland 2

A black box containing 50 lantern slides showing various maps of Iceland, the North Atlantic, etc., and a few slides showing Icelandic landscape and buildings. Identified on labels pasted on the lanterns' frames.

Slides are 9 x 11 cm, unless otherwise identified. Dimensions are given in centimeters rounded off to the next whole centimeter up.

1   *Sketch map showing the courses of the Wineland Voyages and identification of places mentioned in the sagas.* Published in *The Geogr. Review,* Jan. 1927. 1 lantern slide; image 7 x 6 cm.
2   *Garðakirkja. (Kakortok).* (Antiq. America). 1 lantern slide; image 7 x 5 cm.
3   *The North-Atlantic.* Hovgaard. 1 lantern slide; image 6 x 8 cm.
4   *A map of Vinland from accounts contained in Old Northern MSS.* Rafn. 1 lantern slide; image 8 x 6 cm.
5   *Families at Brattholt near Gullfoss.* 1 lantern slide; image 6 x 8 cm.
6   *Reconstruction of Kringla heimsins.* Björnbo. 1 lantern slide; image 8 x 7 cm.
7   *World-conception of Adam of Bremen.* Björnbo: Aarbøger. 1 lantern slide; image 6 x 8 cm.
8   *Reconstruction of Cl. Clavus's map.* Björnbo. 1 lantern slide; image 5 x 8 cm.
9   *The map of the North. The Nancy-map.* Clavus, Claudius. 1 lantern slide; image 6 x 8 cm.
10 *Martellus' copy of Claudius Clavus' map.* 1 lantern slide; image 5 x 8 cm.
11 *Nicolaus Germanus' copy of Claudius Clavus' map.* Germanus Nicolaus. 1 lantern slide; image 5 x 8 cm.
12 *Jacob Ziegler's map of the North, 1532.* 1 lantern slide; image 6 x 8 cm.

13   *Olavs Magnus' Carta Marina 1539.* 1 lantern slide; image 6 x 8 cm.

14   *The Zeni map — (Carta da navegar de Nicolo et Antonio Zeni Fvrono III Tramontana Lano .M.CCC.LXXX.)* 1 lantern slide; image 6 x 8 cm.

15   *The Atlantic as shown in the Globe of Martin Beheim, 1492.* 1 lantern slide; image 7 x 7 cm.

16   *The Atlantic Islands as shown in the Map of Andreas Bianca, 1436.* 1 lantern slide; image 7 x 6 cm.

17   *The Laurentian Portolano of 1351. (The Medicei Portolano).* 1 lantern slide; image 6 x 8 cm.

18   *Sketch-map of Fra Mauro's Mappe-monde.* 1 lantern slide; image 7 x 7 cm, on slide 7 x 11 cm.

19   *Waldseemüller, 1507.* 1 lantern slide; image 6 x 8 cm.

20   *The map of Salvat de Pilestrina or Kunstman No. III.* 1 lantern slide; image 7 x 5 cm.

21   *Catntio's map, 1502.* 1 lantern slide; image 7 x 7 cm.

22   *Tracing of the North Atlantic coastlines in La Cosa's map.* 1 lantern slide; image 7 x 8 cm.

23   *The map of Juan de la Cosa.* 1 lantern slide; image 5 x 8 cm.

24   *Map illustrating the geographical ideas of Columbus concerning the position of the eastern coast of Asia in relation to his fourth voyage.* 1 lantern slide; image 6 x 8 cm.

25   *Map showing the route of Columbus on his first voyage accross the Atlantic and return to illustrate his utilization of the winds and currents.* 1 lantern slide; image 5 x 8 cm.

26   *Garðar Church and Bishop's House. Ruins.* Hovgaard. 1 lantern slide; image 6 x 8 cm.

27   *Ruins of the Church at Kakortok (Sw).* 1 lantern slide; image 6 x 8 cm.

28   *Western settlement of the Norsemen in West Greenland.* 1 lantern slide; image 7 x 4 cm.

29   *Eastern settlement of the Norsemen in South-West Greenland.* 1 lantern slide; image 6 x 8 cm.

30   *A map of Greenland.* Hovgaard. 1 lantern slide; image 7 x 5 cm.

31   *A map of Iceland in Saga times. (Ísland á ofanverðri tíundu öld eptir Krists burð ok um aldamótin ár 1000).* 1 lantern slide; image 5 x 8 cm.

32   *The Northmen in Europe. A map.* Menke. 1 lantern slide; image 5 x 8 cm.

33   *Map illustrating Thorfinn Karlsefni's expedition about AD 1003 -1006, according to Babcock.* 1 lantern slide; image 7 x 4 cm.

34   *Thorfinn Karlsefni's voyage - Labrador, Newfoundland, and Nova Scotia.* Hovgaard. 1 lantern slide; image 8 x 5 cm.

35   *Various Hóp Formations - Iceland and Orkney Islands.* 1 lantern slide; image 6 x 8 cm.

36   *The Dighton Rock - View of the assonet inscription Rock.* (Antiq. America). 1 lantern slide; image 6 x 8 cm.

37   *The ruins at Newport, Rhode Island, America.* 1 lantern slide; image 8 x 5 cm.

38   *The runic stone at Kingiktórsuak.* 1 lantern slide; image 4 x 8 cm.

39   *Vinlandsreiserne. Storm.* 1 lantern slide; image 4 x 8 cm.

40   *Sandwich Bay on the Labrador Coast, just South of Hamilton Inlet. Straumfiord ? Hovgaard.* 1 lantern slide; image 8 x 5 cm.

41   *Seyðisfjörður (up) from Vestdalsfoss.* 1 lantern slide; image 6 x 8 cm.

42   *A map of Iceland.* Th. Thoroddsen. 1 lantern slide; image 6 x 8 cm.

43   *A map of the North by Sebastian Münster, 1540. The original is at the University library in Copenhagen.* 1 lantern slide; image 6 x 8 cm.

44   *Map by the Icelander Jón Guðmundsson, born 1574 [Torfæus, 1706].* 1 lantern slide; image 7 x 7 cm.

45   *Map of the North.* Sigurdi Stephanii. 1 lantern slide; image 7 x 6 cm.

46   *Dýpi Norðurhafa: Lýsing Íslands 1907.* Th. Thoroddsen. 1 lantern slide; image 7 x 7 cm.

47   *Grund í Skorradal.* 1 lantern slide; image 6 x 8 cm. A farmhouse in Western Iceland. See Howell, album v, 15.

48   *Þjórsá-ferry near Stóri Núpur.* 1 lantern slide; image 6 x 9 cm. See Howell, album ii, 50.

49   *The tract about St. Thomas and the ancient Hóp. Part of the British chart Nr. 318.* 1 lantern slide; image 7 x 5 cm.

50   *The ancient Straumfiord.* 1 lantern slide; image 8 x 4 cm.

16. Box 18

Lantern Slides from Iceland 3

Lantern slides of photographs by Frederick W. W. Howell and others, some made by J. P. Troy, Lantern Maker, Cornell University. The pictures are identified in ink on labels pasted on the lanterns' frames. The slides are in a cardboard box.

All the slides are 9 x 11 cm, unless otherwise identified. Dimensions are given in centimeters rounded off to the next whole centimeter up.

1   *Mayor's house, Reykjavík.* 1 lantern slide; image 7 x 9 cm. See Howell, album i, 11.

2   *Ponies crossing the pass to Krísuvík.* 1 lantern slide; image 6 x 8 cm. See Howell, album iii, 2.

3   *Reykjavík from the sea.* 1 lantern slide; image 6 x 8 cm. See Howell, album i, 5.

4   *Litli-Botn og Hvalfell, Hvalfjörður.* 1 lantern slide; image 6 x 8 cm. See Howell, album v, 8.

5   *Dyrhólar.* 1 lantern slide; image 4 x 7 cm. See Magnús Ólafsson, album vi, 75. Farmhouse.

6   *Reyðarvatn - farmhouse.* 1 lantern slide; image 6 x 9 cm. See Howell, album iii, 21.

7   *Family group at Grund in Skorradal.* 1 lantern slide; image 6 x 8 cm. See Howell, album v, 16.

8   *Ísafjörður from the hill.* 1 lantern slide; image 6 x 8 cm. See Howell, album v, 54.

9   *Kalmanstunga looking towards Geitlandsjökull.* 1 lantern slide; image 6 x 8 cm. See Perkins, album vi, 50.

10   *Icelandic Hayfield. S-coast, near Eyjafjallajökull.* 1 lantern slide; image 7 x 8 cm. See Howell, album iii, 52.

11   *Elliðaár (the Salmon river) near Reykjavík.* 1 lantern slide; image 6 x 8 cm. See Howell, album i, 36.

12   *An Icelandic Pack-train crossing bridge over Elliðaár, Reykjavík.* 1 lantern slide; image 6 x 9 cm. See Howell, album i, 13.

13   *Réttir* (J. Hermann: Island). 1 lantern slide; image 5 x 8 cm. Sheep-gathering in a pen.

14   *Icehole. Skeiðarársandur.* 1 lantern slide; image 6 x 8 cm. See Howell, album iii, 58.

15   *Icelandic festival and everyday dress.* (J. Hermann: Island). 1 lantern slide; image 7 x 6 cm. Three women.

16   *Stepping-stones. Brook near Brúará.* 1 lantern slide; image 6 x 9 cm. See Howell, album ii, 13.

17   *Gorge of Jökulsá (í Axarfirði) below Dettifoss.* 1 lantern slide; image 6 x 8 cm. See Howell, album iv, 40.

18   *An Icelander and his steed.* 1 lantern slide; image 6 x 8 cm. See Howell, album iv, 12.

19   *[Unidentified landscape].* 1 lantern slide; image 6 x 9 cm.

20   *Eyjafjörður from Akureyri. (Akureyri and Oddeyri).* 1 lantern slide; image 6 x 8 cm. See Howell, album iv, 49.

21   *Kláfur. Wirerope-bridge, Jökulsá á Brú.* 1 lantern slide; image 6 x 8 cm. See Howell, album iv, 30.

22   *Rjómabú hjá Seljalandi.* 1 lantern slide; image 6 x 8 cm. See Magnús Ólafsson, album vi, 74. Creamery.

23   *Fording Markarfljót.* 1 lantern slide; image 6 x 8 cm. See Howell, album iii, 35.

24   *Bridge over Þjórsá.* 1 lantern slide; image 6 x 8 cm. See Howell, album iii, 20.

25 *Atmospheric denudation, lower Markarfljót.* 1 lantern slide; image 7 x 8 cm. See Howell, album iii, 36.

26 *Woods by Rangá. Hekla.* 1 lantern slide; image 6 x 8 cm. See Howell, album iv, envelope inside back cover.

27 *Skriðufell under Langjökull. Photogr. July 5th 1900. 12 o'clock midnight.* 1 lantern slide; image 5 x 8 cm. See Howell, album vi, 18.

28 *Gullfoss (near Geysir).* 1 lantern slide; image 6 x 8 cm. See Howell, album ii, 38.

29 *Stórólfshvoll. The ponies' supper.* 1 lantern slide; image 6 x 8 cm. See Howell, album iii, 23.

30 *Arnarfellsjökull from the North (Hóp).* 1 lantern slide; image 6 x 8 cm. See Howell, album vi, 16.

31 *River above Eyjafjörður.* 1 lantern slide; image 6 x 8 cm. See Perkins, album vi, 51.

32 *Waters of part of Norðlingafljót coming form under lava stream into Hvítá.* 1 lantern slide; image 6 x 8 cm. See Howell, album v, 24

33 *Big sulphur-spring, Krísuvík.* 1 lantern slide; image 6 x 8 cm. See Howell, album iii, 4.

34 *Geysir and Haukadalur.* 1 lantern slide; image 6 x 8 cm. See Howell, album ii, 23. The glass is cracked.

35 *The fight of frost and fire, Kerlingarfjöll in the upper valley at Ásgarðsá.* 1 lantern slide; image 6 x 8 cm. See Howell, album vi, 26.

36 *Straumar í Norðurhöfum.* Thoroddsen: *Lýsing Íslands,* 1907. 1 lantern slide; image 5 x 8 cm.

37 *Thorvald's Expedition.* 1 lantern slide; image 7 x 7 cm. Sketch map.

38 *Suggested position of Straumfjord and Hóp.* 1 lantern slide; image 5 x 8 cm. Sketch map.

39 *Voyage of Bjarni Herjulfsson.* 1 lantern slide; image 7 x 7 cm. Sketch map.

40 *Map showing route of the Norsemen from Greenland to Wineland (Vínland).* 1 lantern slide; image 7 x 5 cm.

41 *Rafn: The North Atlantic. G.D.* 1 lantern slide; image 7 x 8 cm.

17. Folder 1

Collection of Photographs from Iceland

The photographs were apparently used in an exhibition about Iceland in New York. They are mounted on white boards with the name and address "C. T. Brady, Jr., Prince George Hotel, 14 E. 28th St., New York

16, N.Y." stamped on verso. Captioned on verso, besides on loose slips of paper enclosed with the photos.

1   *1 MAP OF ICELAND. From Ortelius, "Theatrum Orbis Terrarum," 1585.* A poster in colors; 29 x 40 cm, on board 50.6 x 40.5 cm.

2   *4 WAY TO CENTER OF THE EARTH. Jules Verne's "Voyage au Centre de la Terre," 1864, commences in the crater of extinct volcano Snæfellsnes. Above: view from Borgarnes towards the range which culminates in Snæfellsnes. Below: the volcano seen on the horizon, from over the harbor of Reykjavík.* 2 photoprints; 23 x 40.5 cm, and 22.6 x 40.5 cm, on a board 61 x 50.6 cm. The former picture has come loose from the mount.

3   *7 FIRST DAY OF SUMMER. Thursday, 23 April 1959. There are only two seasons, "Winter" and "Summer," and traditionally the Icelandic week begins on Thor's Day. Above: school children's parade, led by two men in Viking costume on Shetland ponies. Below, left: a national flag carried by the children. Below, right: booth in center of Reykjavík where children buy the flags, etc.* The first photoprint is 29.3 x 36.8 cm, the second is missing, the third, a colored photoprint, matted, visible image 11.4 x 16.5 cm, both mounted on board 61 x 50.6 cm.

4   *10 CHEERFULLY FACING THE FUTURE. A group of children at Borgarnes.* Photoprint, image 22.3 x 28.4 cm, mounted with red tape on a white board 50.7 x 40.5 cm.

5   *18 From Early Days. THEIR LITERARY HERITAGE. The National Library, Reykjavík, founded 1818. The inscriptions commemorate famous writers of the past: Ari Thorgilsson, 1067-1148; Snorri Sturluson, 1178-1241; Bishop Gudbrandur Thorlaksson, 1541-1627, etc.* Photoprint; 39 x 48.8 cm, on a white board 61 x 50.6 cm.

18. Folder 2

Photographs from the Exhibition in 1974

The photographs are all captioned on verso.

1   *Downtown Reykjavík.* Photoprint; 39.4 x 40 cm. Austurstræti 14; win-

dow signs: "Jóhannes Nordfjord úra- og skartgripaverzlun", and "Tóbaksverzlunin London."

2   *Residence of Einar Jónsson, sculptor (b. 1874) in Reykjavík. Open as a museum on Sundays.* Photoprint; 38.8 x 48.8 cm.

3   *Where the Althing meets, built in Reykjavík in 1881.* Photoprint; 28.5 x 38.7 cm. Lower right corner broken off.

4   *Hot water supply. Reykir, about 10 miles from Reykjavík, supplies heating and hot water to homes in the city.* Photoprint; 32.9 x 28.9 cm.

5   *Ornamental wooden brackets on a building with corrugated iron sheets.* Photoprint; 28.8 x 22.5 cm.

6   *Across the lake in Reykjavík as it appeared in 1959 on a day when clouds hid the far hills.* Photoprint; 17.3 x 28.7 cm. Lower right corner broken off.

7   *Children at play during recess at school in Reykjavík. In the background to the left, a modern apartment house.* Photoprint; 21.4 x 28.7 cm.

8   *Baby Geysir starting to erupt.* Photoprint; 18.9 x 23.9 cm.

9   *Pool of Great Geysir before eruption.* Photoprint; 11.2 x 16.4 cm.

10   *Older type farm building with turf walls.* Photoprint on glossy paper; 12.5 x 17.4 cm.

11   *Government building with sheet-iron walls.* Photoprint on glossy paper; 12.5 x 17.4 cm. The building is Fríkirkjuvegur 11.

Pictures of artifacts, etc.

12   *Later Times. Neoclassic Sculpture. "Zeus & Ganymede" by - or of the school of - Bertel Thorvaldsen (1770-1844), son of an Icelandic carver of ship figureheads. It is preserved by the American Scandinavian Foundation, New York.* Photoprint; 27.7 x 35.3 cm. On verso: "E 4159."

13   *Myths were still recalled. Inscribed planks, 12th century from house in*

Skagafjord, preserved in National Museum, Reykjavík. Photoprint; 36.3 x 29.2 cm. [Þjms. 8891]. Ref.: Kristján Eldjárn, *Hundrað ár í Þjóðminjasafni* (Reykjavík: Bókaútgáfa Menningarsjóðs, 3rd ed., 1969), p. 61.

14   *Decorative wood Carving. A church door, about A.D. 1200, now in National Museum, Reykjavík.* 2 photoprints; 26.8 x 39.7 cm, and 27.5 x 36 cm, the second is arched at top. Valþjófsstaðahurðin. [Þjms. 11009]. Ref.: Kristján Eldjárn, *Hundrað ár í Þjóðminjasafni* (Reykjavík: Bókaútgáfa Menningarsjóðs, 3rd ed., 1969), p. 68.

15   *Chalice - 5" high, probably of 13th century.* Photo by Victoria and Albert Museum, London. On verso: "56818."

16   *Women's wintertime work. Coverlet with biblical scenes, 17th century, by a woman named Thorbjorg.* Photo by Victoria and Albert Museum, London. Photoprint on glossy paper; 27.8 x 20.9 cm. On verso: "37087."

17   *Women's wintertime work. 18th-century textiles in National Museum, Reykjavík.* Photoprint; 17.9 x 28.7 cm.

18   *Silver paten, about 3 3/4" in diameter, from second half of 14th century.* Photo by Gunnar Rúnar. Photoprint on glossy paper; 17.2 x 22.5 cm.

19   *In "Alte Isländische Kunst" reads Filigram Schmuck aus vergoldetem Silber von einem Gürtel Wie er zur Nationaltracht der isländischen Frauen gehört."* Photo by Gunnar Rúnar. Photoprint on glossy paper; 14 x 24.1 cm.

20   *"Thorhammer," 2" long, silver amulet worn on necklace. Its resemblance to a cross was often noticed.* Photo by Gunnar Rúnar. Photoprint on glossy paper; 17 x 22.5 cm.

21   *Oak headpost found with ship timbers, in River Scheldt, near Termonde, Belgium about 3'8" high. ca. A.D. 900. diam of head about 10".* Photoprint on glossy paper; 22.4 x 16.5 cm.

22   *Image of a heathen god. From about A.D. 1000.* Postcard published by the National Museum of Iceland, Reykjavík.

23   *Rune stone with serpent, Upsala, Sweden.* Photoprint; 16.9 x 12.4 cm.

24   *Viking tombstone, about A.D. 1035, found in St. Paul's church yard, London.* Photoprint; 14.7 x 22.4 cm.

25   *Jellinge Stone, about A.D. 980, from replica in Garden of National Museum, Copenhagen.* Photoprint; 17.4 x 20.2 cm.

26   [*Unidentified*]. Photoprint; 21.2 x 20.1 cm. A rock, apparently with some runes or inscriptions.

27   *Chieftain's Hall, drawing by E. Rondahl, 1894.* 1 photoprint; 11.3 x 15.7 cm.

28   [*Statue of a Viking*]. Photoprint; 15.4 x 12.3 cm.

19. Folder 3

Miscellaneous Pictures: Posters, Prints, etc.

1   *ISLAND. Ó, Guð vors lands ...* The painting was made by Reinh. Christensen 1921. Printed at Chr. Cato, Copenhagen. Poster in colors, sheet 53.8 x 45 cm. On verso in pencil "Rec. 8/5 '23. Kr. 8^{50}." The first stanza of the Icelandic national anthem, a picture of the author, the Reverend Matthías Jochumsson above, with the Icelandic flag on both sides, a picture of the composer, Sveinbjörn Sveinbjörnsson, below and then the musical notes with a Viking boat to the left and a woman sitting by the shore to the right.

2   [*Hallgrímur Pétursson. Passíusálmar*]. Poster in colors, sheet 21 x 38.1 cm. Drawing by Sam[úel] Eggertsson, 1864-1949. Printed by Prentsmiðjan Gutenberg 1916. On verso in pencil "Rec. 16/10 '18. Kr. 1^{50}." The seventeenth-century clergyman and poet Hallgrímur Pétursson standing behind the pulpit. Quotations from his poetry.

3   *Kirkjuþing Vestur Islendinga, Winnipeg, 1898.* Poster in black and white; sheet 42.8 x 34.3 cm. Portraits of 44 "Western Icelanders", participants in a church conference held in Winnipeg in 1898. From top left: E. A. Melsted; Sigtr. Jónasson; E. Scheving; F. Björnsson; M. Pálsson; G. Gudvaldason; G. Jóhannsson; B. Marteinsson; F. S. Fridrikson [sic!]; O. G. Anderson; T. Ingjaldsson; Jón Björnsson; J. Þórdarson; Séra F. J. Bergmann; Jón A. Blöndal; S. Arason; Séra O. V. Gíslason; Séra J. Bjarnason; Séra N. S. Þorlaksson; A. Eggertson [sic!]; G. Eiriksson; B. B. Jonsson; Séra J. Clemens; J. Benediktsson; F. Fridrikson [sic!]; G. B. Olgeirsson; Séra J. A. Sigurdsson; J. K. Olafsson; O. Olafsson; S. Björnson [sic!]; R. Marteinson [sic!]; Þ.

Halldórsson; B. J. Brandsson; G. E. Gunnlaugsson; H. Pétrsson [sic!]; B. Jonson [sic!]; Gísli Egilsson; Stefán Gunnarson [sic!]; G. Ingimundsson [sic!]; A. Sigvaldason.

4   *Alþingismenn 1869.* Portrait photographs of the members of the Icelandic parliament in 1869. 28 photoprints: sepia toned; ca. 6 x 5 cm each, pasted on a stiff sheet 48.5 x 37.7 cm. The names are printed on slips of paper and pasted beneath the pictures. The title is also printed on a slip of paper and pasted on top. From top left: Eiríkur Kúld; Torfi Einarsson; Ráll J. Vídalín; Davíð Guðmundsson; Th. Jónassen; Guðmundur Einarsson; Daníel Thorlacius; Hjálmur Pétursson; Stefán Jónsson; Jón Pétursson; Jón Hjaltalín; Hilmar Finsen, konungsfulltrúi; Jón Sigurðsson forseti; Hallgrímur Jónsson; Tryggvi Gunnarsson; Bergur Thorberg; Pétur Pétursson; Halldór Kr. Friðriksson; Jón Sigurðsson; Ólafur Pálsson; Helgi Hálfdanarson; Benedikt Sveinsson; Þórarinn Böðvarsson; Halldór Jónsson; Grímur Thomsen; Páll Pálsson; Stefán Eiríksson; Sigurður Gunnarsson.

5   *Islands-Platten.* Printed by Pacht & Crone, Copenhagen. Poster in blue color; diam image 22.7 cm, on sheet 36 x 28 cm. Painting of a ship with the words "Drot og kaarne mænd mod Island stævner. 1907." bordered around it. The title is printed above the image.

6   *Öræfajökull.* Poster in colors of a painting by Ásgrímur Jónsson; sheet 24 x 38.3 cm; on verso: "Rec. 16/10 '18. Kr. 2^{oo}." Title written in pencil on verso in Halldór Hermannsson's hand.

7   *Höfn í Hornafirði.* Poster in colors of a painting by Ásgrímur Jónsson; sheet 32 x 44 cm. Printed by Andreasen & Lachmann Lit. On verso in pencil "Rec. 16/10 '18. Kr. 2^{oo}." Title written in pencil on verso in Halldór Hermannsson's hand.

8   *Kjötpottur landsins.* 2 prints in black and white; 19 x 26 cm.

9   *Rune-Døren fra Kirken i Valþjófstað i Island.* Drawing by Magnus Petersen. Print; image with text 29.5 x 12.6 cm. Valþjófsstaðahurðin, the original in the National Museum of Iceland.

10 *Til hins heimsfræga taflmanns í lotningar skyni frá Eugene Beauharnais Cook, samlanda hans.* Print: image black and white with red borders; sheet 17.7 x 52 cm. 6 specimens of chess-games. Beneath the pictures: "Í öllum dæmunum leikur hvítt fyrst og mátar í tveim leikum."

20. Framed Pictures

The pictures are arranged alphabetically according to subject. Dimensions are given in centimeters rounded off to the next whole centimeter up.

9 júní 1915. Poster commemorating the Icelandic flag; in a brown wooden frame, 81 x 62 cm. A stanza by Einar Benediktsson, "Skín þú, fáni, eynni yfir / eins og mjöll í fjallahlíð ...", printed on the picture. Made from a painting of Þingvellir and the Icelandic flag.

Fiske, D. W. Process print; oval image 22 x 14 cm, in a black wooden frame 36 x 30 cm. Made by Det Hoffensbergske Etabl., Copenhagen.

[*Halldór Hermannsson*]. Four Icelandic stamps with a picture of Halldór Hermannsson, matted and framed in a wooden frame 25 x 19 cm. The stamps were issued in 1978.

_____, Photoprint; visible area 17 x 12 cm, in a beige wooden frame 23 x 18 cm.

Islandia. Privilegio Imp. et Belgico decennati A. Ortel. excud. 1585. A map of Iceland published by Abraham Ortelius in 1590. Print: engraving; colored; 34 x 49 cm; black frame. Probably based on a map made originally by Bishop Guðbrandur Þorláksson. Ref.: Haraldur Sigurðsson *Kortasaga Íslands frá lokum 16. aldar til 1848* (Reykjavík: Bókaútgáfa Menningarsjóðs og Þjóðvinafélagsins, 1978), pp. 9-15. Halldór Hermannsson *Two Cartographers. Guðbrandur Thorláksson and Thórður Thorláksson.* Islandica XVII (Ithaca, 1926). A description of Iceland printed on the reverse of the map.

Jón Sigurðsson. Pr. sign. I. W. Tegner & Kittendorffs lith. Inst. Print: lithograph after a photograph; image ca. 21 x 16 cm, in a black wooden frame 46 x 35 cm.

Magnús Stephensen. Process print of a lithograph?; image ca. 10 x 9 cm, in a black wooden frame 36 x 32 cm.

Maurer, Konrad. Photoprint; image ca. 9 x 8 cm, in a black oval frame 21 x 12 cm.

_____, photoprint: sepia toned; visible image 33 x 28 cm, in a black wooden frame 55 x 50 cm; profile portrait.

[*Vilhjálmur Bjarnar*]. Photoprint; 26 x 21 cm, in a clip frame. Sitting with a manuscript in front of him.

Willard-foss. Jökulsá, Axarfjörður, Iceland. Between 1879 and 1904. Photoprint; image 17 x 23 cm, mounted on white sheet and framed in black wooden frame 28 x 35 cm. Made by Carl Olafsson, Reykjavík; framed by The Corner Bookstore, Ithaca. A waterfall named for Prof. Fiske in the summer of 1879, when he travelled in Iceland.

21. Photographs Inserted in Books

[*Guðmundur Magnússon*]. Photoprint: sepia toned; oval image on carte-de-visite; 10.3 x 6.3 cm; head and shoulders portrait. Inserted in his *Heima og erlendis. Nokkur ljóðmæli eftir Guðmund Magnússon* (Reykjavík: Ísafoldarprentsmiðja, 1899).

[*The Viking ship from Gokstad*]. Photoprint: sepia toned; 9.7 x 12.3 cm. Inserted in Nicolay Nicolaysen, *A Brief Description of the Ancient vessel found near Sandefjord in Norway. To accompany the model of the ship sent to the International ship-model Exhibition in London 1882* (Christiania, 1892).

INDEX

The index is divided into three parts. The first two are name and subject indexes of the manuscript material, and the third is an index of the graphic material. As the various correspondents in the correspondence section are arranged in alphabetical order, no index is needed for that part of the catalogue. The numbers in the first two indexes refer to entry numbers in the catalogue. The numbers in the third index refer to the boxes, folders or chapters as they are numbered in the catalogue, then to the album if relevant and, finally, to the entry number of each item.

Manuscript Material: Name Index

Manuscript Material: Subject Index

Graphic Material: Index

*Publications Relating to the Icelandic Collection
in the Cornell University Libraries*

ISLANDICA*

I. *Bibliography of the Icelandic Sagas and Minor Tales.* By Halldór Hermannsson. 1908.

II. *The Northmen in America (982–c. 1500).* By Halldór Hermannsson. 1909.

III. *Bibliography of the Sagas of the Kings of Norway and Related Sagas and Tales.* By Halldór Hermannsson. 1910.

IV. *The Ancient Laws of Norway and Iceland.* By Halldór Hermannsson. 1911.

V. *Bibliography of the Mythical-Heroic Sagas.* By Halldór Hermannsson. 1912.

VI. *Icelandic Authors of To-day* (with an appendix giving a list of works dealing with Modern Icelandic Literature). By Halldór Hermannsson. 1913.

VII. *The Story of Griselda in Iceland.* Ed. by Halldór Hermannsson. 1914.

VIII. *An Icelandic Satire* (Lof Lýginnar). By Þorleifur Halldórsson, ed. by Halldór Hermannsson. 1915.

IX. *Icelandic Books of the Sixteenth Century.* By Halldór Hermannsson. 1916.

X. *Annalium in Islandia farrago and De mirabilibus Islandiæ.* By Bishop Gísli Oddsson, ed. By Halldór Hermannsson. 1917.

XI. *The Periodical Literature of Iceland Down to the Year 1874: An Historical Sketch.* By Halldór Hermannsson. 1918.

XII. *Modern Icelandic: An Essay.* By Halldór Hermannsson. 1919.

XIII. *Bibliography of the Eddas.* By Halldór Hermannsson. 1920.

XIV. *Icelandic Books of the Seventeenth Century.* By Halldór Hermannsson. 1922.

XV. *Jón Guðmundsson and His Natural History of Iceland.* By Halldór Hermannsson. 1924.

XVI. *Eggert Ólafsson. A Biographical Sketch.* By Halldór Hermannsson. 1925.

XVII. *Two Cartographers: Guðbrandur Thorláksson and Thórður Thorláksson.* By Halldór Hermannson. 1926.

XVIII. *Sir Joseph Banks and Iceland.* By Halldór Hermannsson. 1928.

XIX. *Icelandic Manuscripts.* By Halldór Hermannsson. 1929.

XX. *The Book of the Icelanders (Íslendingabók).* By Ari Thorgilsson. Ed. and tr. with an introductory essay and notes by Halldór Hermannsson. 1930.

XXI. *The Cartography of Iceland.* By Halldór Hermannsson. 1931.

XXII. *Sæmund Sigfússon and the Oddaverjar.* By Halldór Hermannsson. 1932.

XXIII. *Old Icelandic Literature: A Bibliographical Essay.* By Halldór Hermannsson. 1933.

* Volumes I–XXII were first published by the Cornell University Library; later volumes were published by Cornell University Press. Volumes I–XXXVI have been reprinted by Kraus Reprint Co.

XXIV. *The Sagas of Icelanders (Íslendinga sögur): A Supplement to Bibliography of the Icelandic Sagas and Minor Tales.* By Halldór Hermannsson. 1935.

XXV. *The Problem of Wineland.* By Halldór Hermannsson. 1936.

XXVI. *The Sagas of the Kings and the Mythical-heroic Sagas: Two Bibliographical Supplements.* By Halldór Hermannsson. 1937.

XXVII. *The Icelandic Physiologus.* Facimile Edition with an introduction by Halldór Hermannsson. 1938.

XXVIII. *Illuminated Manuscripts of the Jónsbók.* By Halldór Hermannsson. 1940.

XXIX. *Bibliographical Notes.* By Halldór Hermannsson. 1942.

XXX. *The Vinland Sagas.* Ed. with an introduction, variants, and notes by Halldór Hermannson. 1944.

XXXI. *The Saga of Thorgils and Haflidi.* Ed. with an introduction and notes by Halldór Hermannsson. 1945.

XXXII and XXXIII. *History of Icelandic Prose Writers: 1800–1940.* By Stefán Einarsson. 1948.

XXXIV. *History of Icelandic Poets: 1800–1940.* By Richard Beck. 1950.

XXXV. *The Saga of Hrafn Sveinbjarnarson: The Life of an Icelandic Physician of the Thirteenth Century.* Tr. with an introduction and notes by Anne Tjomsland. 1951.

XXXVI. *The Age of the Sturlungs: Icelandic Civilization in the Thirteenth Century.* By Einar Ól. Sveinsson. Tr. by Jóhann S. Hannesson. 1953.

XXXVII. *Bibliography of the Eddas: A Supplement to ISLANDICA XIII.* By Jóhann S. Hannesson. 1955. (Out of print.)

XXXVIII. *The Sagas of Icelanders (Íslendinga Sögur): A Supplement to ISLANDICA I and XXIV.* By Jóhann S. Hannesson. 1957. (Out of print.)

XXXIX. *The Hólar Cato: An Icelandic Schoolbook of the Seventeenth Century.* Ed. with an introduction and two appendices by Halldór Hermannsson. 1958.

XL. *Bibliography of Modern Icelandic Literature in Translation, including Works Written by Icelanders in Other Languages.* Compiled by P.M. Mitchell and Kenneth H. Ober. 1975.

XLI. *Halldór Hermannsson.* By P.M. Mitchell. 1978.

XLII. *Old Norse Court Poetry: The Dróttkvætt Stanza.* By Roberta Frank. 1978.

XLIII. *The Legend of Brynhild.* By Theodore M. Andersson. 1980.

XLIV. *Bibliography of Old Norse-Icelandic Romances.* By Marianne E. Kalinke and P.M. Mitchell. 1985.

XLV. *Old Norse-Icelandic Literature: A Critical Guide.* Ed. by Carol J. Clover and John Lindow. 1985.

XLVI. *Bridal-Quest Romance in Medieval Iceland.* By Marianne E. Kalinke. 1990.

XLVII. *Bibliography of Modern Icelandic Literature in Translation (Supplement).* By Kenneth Ober. 1990.

XLVIII. *Manuscript Material, Correspondence, and Graphic Material in the Fiske Icelandic Collection: A Descriptive Catalogue.* Compiled by Þórunn Sigurðardóttir. 1994.

CATALOGUES

Catalogue of the Icelandic Collection Bequeathed by Willard Fiske. Compiled by
  Halldór Hermannsson. 1914.*
—: *Additions 1913–26.* 1927.
—: *Additions 1927–42.* 1943.
*Catalogue of Runic Literature forming a Part of the Icelandic Collection Be-
  queathed by Willard Fiske.* Compiled by Halldór Hermannsson. Oxford: Ox-
  ford University Press, 1917. (Out of print.)

*This volume and the additions were reprinted in 1960 by Cornell University Press.